ANGLO-OTTOMAN ENCOUNTERS
IN THE AGE OF REVOLUTION

By the same author:

The Early Correspondence of Richard Wood, 1831–1841
Eastern Questions in the Nineteenth Century

Anglo-Ottoman Encounters in the Age of Revolution

COLLECTED ESSAYS

VOLUME ONE

by
ALLAN CUNNINGHAM
Late Professor of History at Simon Fraser University
edited by
EDWARD INGRAM

Taylor & Francis Group

LONDON AND NEW YORK

First published 1993 by
FRANK CASS & CO. LTD.

Published 2013 by Routledge
2 Park Square, Milton Park, Abingdon, Oxfordshire OX14 4RN
711 Third Avenue, New York, NY 10017, USA

First issued in paperback 2016

Routledge is an imprint of the Taylor and Francis Group, an informa business

Copyright © 1993 Edward Ingram

British Library Cataloguing in Publication Data
Cunningham, Allan
  Anglo-Ottoman Encounters in the Age of
Revolution: Collected Essays
  I. Title II. Ingram, Edward
956

Library of Congress Cataloging-in-Publication Data
Cunningham, Allan, 1924–1988
  Anglo-Ottoman encounters in the age of revolution:
collected essays by Allan Cunningham;
edited by Edward Ingram.
    p. cm.
  Includes bibiographical references (p.) and index.
  1. Stratford de Redcliffe, Stratford Canning, Viscount,
1786–1880. 2. Great Britain–Foreign relations–19th
century. 3. Turkey–History–Ottoman Empire, 1288–
1918. 4. Great Britain–Foreign relations–Turkey.
I. Ingram, Edward. II. Title.
DA536.S89C86   1993
949.61'015–dc20   92–17165
                                                                      CIP

ISBN 13: 978-1-138-96355-9 (pbk)
ISBN 13: 978-0-7146-3494-4 (hbk)

*All rights reserved. No part of this publication may be
reproduced in any form or by any means, electronic, mechanical,
photocopying, recording or otherwise, without the prior
permission of the publisher.*

Typeset by Vitaset, Paddock Wood, Kent

To

Jean Douglas Cunningham

CONTENTS

Abbreviations		viii
Editor's Preface		xi
I	The Ochakov Debate	1
II	Robert Adair's Mission to St Petersburg	32
III	Robert Liston at Constantinople	51
IV	Robert Adair and the Treaty of the Dardanelles	103
V	Stratford Canning and the Treaty of Bucharest	144
VI	Lord Strangford and the Greek Revolt	188
VII	The Philhellenes, George Canning, and Greek Independence	233
VIII	Stratford Canning, Mahmud II, and Greece	276
Bibliography		324
Index		339

ABBREVIATIONS

Adm.	Public Record Office, Admiralty Records
Add. MSS	British Library, Additional Manuscripts
CO	Public Record Office, Colonial Office Records
Dropmore MSS	*The Manuscripts of J.B. Fortescue, Esq., Preserved at Dropmore*
FO	Public Record Office, Foreign Office Records
NLS	National Library of Scotland, Edinburgh
PRO	Public Record Office Manuscripts
SP	Public Record Office, State Papers, Foreign
SRO	Scottish Record Office, Edinburgh

He is an Anglo-Saxon messenger – and those are Anglo-Saxon attitudes.

Lewis Carroll, *Through the Looking Glass*,
Chapter 7

Preface

Allan Black Cunningham, who died suddenly and unexpectedly in the New Year of 1988 at the age of 63, was the first dean of arts and founding head of the department of history at Simon Fraser University. Educated at Durham University and Bedford College, London, where he was supervised by the redoubtable Dame Lillian Penson, in 1950 he joined the department of history in the University of the West Indies. He returned to England in 1955, to Royal Holloway College, London, moving in 1961 to St Antony's College, Oxford, as a senior research fellow. While there he edited the early correspondence of Richard Wood, in later life British consul-general at Damascus, for the Royal Historical Society. From Oxford he came to Canada. He belonged to the Royal Geographical Society as well as the Royal Historical Society and, during his twenties, led two expeditions to the Andes.

Professor Cunningham became better known in the United States than in Canada and was highly respected there. He spent 1971 at the Adlai Stevenson Institute at the University of Chicago, writing a book on higher education in North America and, in 1979, was awarded a Guggenheim Fellowship. His work was interrupted by sickness, partly the result of the tuberculosis he caught four years after moving to Canada. His enthusiasm for history never flagged, however. He was a magnificent lecturer to first-year classes, with an uncanny ability to arouse interest among his students. He is greatly missed.

Having had a lifelong interest in the Middle East, Cunningham, when he died, had been working for 25 years on a biography of Stratford Canning, surely one of the most famous diplomats of the nineteenth century – he has been accused of provoking the Crimean War – and on studies of the other British ambassadors at

Constantinople between the French Revolution and the First World War. His colleagues in the department, many of them hired by him in the university's early years, therefore decided that the most suitable memorial would be the publication of as much of this unfinished work as possible. I undertook to see what could be done and the president of the university, William Saywell, and the dean of arts, Robert C. Brown, generously offered to underwrite the cost.

Professor Cunningham's voluminous notes, written in ever tinier handwriting in ever tinier notebooks, include hundreds of unfinished drafts of chapters of books not written. These studies attest to Cunningham's frustration and disappointment. Biographers should admire or hate their subjects, but should beware of irritation and boredom. Cunningham clearly lost interest in Stratford Canning. He worked on him too long and found him wilting under the prolonged scrutiny. Nor could Cunningham finally decide how to handle him. He turned out not to be interesting enough for a biography; or not the sort of biography Cunningham had in mind. A psycho-historian might have done more with him. And his career, as a career, was not important enough. Cunningham was not interested in the United States and Switzerland, to which Stratford was posted in the years after the end of the Napoleonic Wars. The affairs of the Ottoman Empire, on the other hand, which did interest Cunningham passionately, could not be refracted through the prism of Stratford's five terms as British ambassador at Constantinople because, during many crucial developments, he was not there. Robert Adair negotiated the treaty of the Dardanelles in 1809; Viscount Strangford helped to prevent the Greek revolt from causing a Russo-Ottoman war; and Viscount Ponsonby handled the Muhammad Ali crises.

Stratford's moment came in the 1840s and early 1850s, the years of the *Tanzimat*, which he saw as a movement to reform the Ottoman Empire on European lines, and of the events leading to the outbreak of the Crimean War. But even here Cunningham was disappointed by Stratford. Cunningham instinctively, and correctly, played down the role of European diplomatists in the Ottoman Empire and played up the role of the Ottomans, giving them the responsibility for their own triumphs and disasters. He attributed neither the treaty of Bucharest, nor defeat at the hands of

Muhammad Ali, nor the outbreak of the Crimean War exclusively to European influence, whether beneficent or malign, and certainly not to British influence. Accordingly much of Cunningham's work was an attempt to pull Stratford off his pedestal as hero or ogre.

Cunningham's work on Stratford was incomplete (the chapter describing Stratford's activities during the Crimean War could not be found) and unresolved. The planned book was neither a biography nor the study of Stratford's career as British ambassador at Constantinople. Nor, in the end, did it seem feasible to publish extracts of the work as as group of separate studies. Two books did appear feasible, however. This is the first, a collection of essays on the British discovery of the Eastern Question and series of encounters with the Ottomans from the Ochakov crisis of 1791 to the battle of Navarino in 1827. The second book collects Cunningham's work on the Ottoman Empire from the first Muhammad Ali crisis of 1832 to the outbreak of the First World War.

Parts of Cunningham's work on Stratford Canning appear in both books. This book contains studies of Stratford's first mission to Constantinople, when he acted as a conduit for information between the Ottomans and the Russians during the negotiations leading to the treaty of Bucharest in 1812, and of his second, when he failed in 1826 to head off the need for the European intervention in the Greek war for independence that led to the destruction of the Turco-Egyptian fleet at the battle of Navarino. The other book contains a similar study of Stratford's third mission to Constantinople in 1831 and publishes the famous memorandum in which he tried to persuade the foreign secretary, Viscount Palmerston, to intervene in Ottoman affairs in support of Sultan Mahmud II against the viceroy of Egypt, Muhammad Ali. This is followed by a short study of Stratford's conception of the Ottoman programme of reform known as the *Tanzimat*, and a long study of his role in the preliminaries of the Crimean War, in particular his responsibility for persuading the Ottomans in 1853 to reject the Vienna Note.

In addition to two studies of Stratford, this book includes hitherto unpublished essays on three other ambassadors at Constantinople – Robert Liston during the French Revolution, Adair during the crisis following the treaty of Tilsit, and Strangford during the first phase of the Greek war for independence. And it contains two studies of the Ochakov crisis of 1791, when Pitt the

Younger was humiliated by Catherine II, on the one hand, and Charles James Fox, on the other, and a study of George Canning's relationship with the philhellenes and Greek nationalism. The last should be read in combination with the essays on Strangford and Stratford's second mission to Constantinople. All of Cunningham's work casts interesting light on the aims and style of both British and Ottoman diplomacy in the Middle East from the late eighteenth to the early twentieth centuries and on social and economic conditions in the region. Often when he seems to be writing about the British, his attention is focused on the Ottomans.

Although I have made as few changes as possible to Cunningham's text, I have cut out chunks of the colourful detail he found irresistible. Travel books were his favourite reading. I have also brushed up his notes, for he was careless of technical details, and have supplied citations where necessary. Otherwise, the text is as Cunningham wrote it. I have not brought it up to date. The bibliography lists the works he evidently had read.

Acknowledgements are due to the Controller of Her Majesty's Stationery Office for the use of Crown-copyright material in the Public Record Office; to the Right Honourable the Earl of Elgin and Kincardine and the Right Honourable the Earl of Harewood for the use of family papers; and to the Trustees of the British Library, the Scottish Record Office, and the National Library of Scotland for the use of material from their collections. Earlier versions of Chapters I and VI appeared in *Middle Eastern Studies* and of Chapter II in the *Bulletin of the Institute of Historical Research*. I am grateful to the editors and publishers for permission to publish a revised version.

I am also grateful to Dr T. R. Ravindranathan of Pittsburg State University for help with sorting Professor Cunningham's papers, to Kevin McQuinn, and to Jodi D. Shupe and Terence J. Ollerhead of *The International History Review*, for help with research and editing and for preparing an immaculate typescript. They are the most pleasant associates imaginable.

Edward Ingram
Simon Fraser University
All Saints' Day, 1991

CHAPTER I

The Ochakov Debate

'The Eastern Question', Lord Stratford de Redcliffe wrote to *The Times* in 1875, 'is a fact, a reality of indefinite duration.' A Russian might have penned the observation more fittingly than 'the voice of England in the East', for however one cares to define it, an Eastern Question has not always existed for Great Britain, even if one always existed for Stratford. The date of the beginning of this great problem varies with its definitions, but historians who have chosen to see it as the firm intrusion of the Ottoman Empire and its affairs into the diplomatic calculations of Great Britain also incline to date it from the late eighteenth century, and as often as not from 1791, a year in which the Tory ministry of the day proposed a naval augmentation to resist the aggression of Russia upon the Ottoman Empire. For instance, William Pitt the Younger's ablest biographer treated the debate in Parliament in 1791 as the prototype of all the great nineteenth-century disputations over the fate of the 'sick man of Europe', and he described the occasion as 'the first in which the Eastern Question in its new phase received adequate treatment'. What earlier phases were like is not specified, but Holland Rose clearly thought of them as relating to eastern Europe alone, and not to the Near East: this restrictive use of the term is well illustrated in Albert Sorel's *Eastern Question in the Eighteenth Century*, which deals with the partitions of Poland rather than with the Ottoman Empire. J.A.R. Marriott also saw the debate of 1791 as a new and significant enlargement of Great Britain's diplomatic horizons, and went so far as to call Pitt 'the first English statesman to appreciate the real and intimate concern of Great Britain in the affairs of the Near East'. It is a large claim, and one which Thomas Macaulay, in an encomium of Pitt which omitted very little that was in the subject's favour, never thought of making. The present purpose is to show that Pitt had no such special insight in 1791, and that while the Ottoman Empire was briefly on his lips, she had no real place in his calculations. W.E.H. Lecky's interpretation, that Pitt was goaded on by Prussia and irked into challenging Russia by Catherine II's proud resistance, is still the best one. Parenthetically, one may add that the Ottoman Empire *was* soon to enter Great Britain's diplomatic calculations, but with young General Bonaparte rather than Catherine II as her educator, and the man who foresaw the consequences for the future with the clearest insight was not Pitt but the earl of Elgin, whose brief embassy at Constantinople spanned the Egyptian expedition and the victory of the Nile.[1]

In 1787, Catherine II of Russia made her famous tour of the new Russian territory in the south taken and tamed by Prince Grigorii Potemkin. Joseph II of Austria accompanied her down the Dnieper, but behind his congratulations was a firm resolve not to be left behind in future. Consequently, when Catherine II returned to her capital, supposedly after predicting a great future for a Crimean village called Sebastopol, and sent an ultimatum for the surrender of Ottoman Georgia to the Porte, Joseph II joined her in the war which ensued upon Sultan Abdulhamid I's haughty refusal.[2] Yakov Bulgakov, Catherine II's emissary to the Ottomans, was thrown into a dungeon, and Potemkin and Count Peter Rumiantsev opened operations on the Moldavian front. In the spring of 1788, the Austrians struck towards Belgrade, the formality of a declaration of war following later. Catherine II's aims did not lack grandeur: a Greek principality for her grandson, a satellite state formed of Moldavia and east Wallachia, and her own frontier advanced to the Dniester. She encouraged Joseph II to believe he might recover lands Austria had held before the peace of Belgrade in 1739: northern Serbia, the *Banat*, and Wallachia as far east as the Oltet. Prince Anton von Kaunitz, the foremost of Austrian statesmen, was deeply concerned that Prussia would exploit Joseph II's involvement in the Balkans, but Joseph did not listen, nor worry about the initiative now handed to Prussia in Germany and the Low Countries. He was, as Frederick the Great described him, a man who invariably took the second step before the first. But Kaunitz was right: the war against the Ottoman Empire produced a chain reaction throughout Europe affecting nearly all capitals. Berlin reacted most strongly and instantly; French initiative would have been greater but for the congealing effect of approaching domestic upheaval; Great Britain came in last, yet with a deceptive appearance of vigour. Sweden and Denmark, Poland and the Stadtholderate felt the repercussions also.

In the ordinary way, diplomatic defence of Ottoman interests would have devolved on France, and this – and something more – was expected by cheering Ottomans who gathered outside the French embassy in Pera on the day war was announced.³ But the times were changing, and the count of Vergennes' death in 1787 was a major event in Franco-Ottoman relations. Vergennes recognized, as few contemporaries did, that the thrust of European ambitions and rivalries now reached as far east as the Ottoman Empire, which could experience the fate of Poland. One fact preserved the Ottomans: 'une partition de l'Empire Ottoman n'est pas difficile, mais je ne vois pas la compensation pour Constantinople.' The same difficulty was to confound and mutually alienate the conspirators at Tilsit 20 years later. With baleful insight, Vergennes predicted that the insolubility of the Ottoman question would ricochet fatally upon the remnant of independent Poland. Oddly, the most effective ally he could envisage to assist France in controlling the situation in the East was Great Britain, and at the height of the American War of Independence he warned that she must not be so enfeebled by her opponents as to be inadequate to this Continental role.⁴ So, with Vergennes' death, the French barrier round the Ottoman Empire fell, and it remained to be seen if Pitt would agree to take over the responsibility. It was proposed to him by his ally of the Triple Alliance of 1788, Prussia, rather than by France.

France retained her image in Great Britain as the nation's most formidable rival long after the recession of her challenge in India and North America, and Lecky outlines the steadiness of pro-Russian sentiment in Great Britain which helped Catherine II further. As Pitt's own father, the earl of Chatham, always endorsed pro-Russian and anti-French causes, he contributed substantially to his own son's difficulties in 1791. Chatham made a determined bid for a Russian alliance in 1766. In 1770, when a Russian fleet sailed to the Mediterranean from the Baltic to chastise the Ottomans, France and Spain were reminded that any interference with it would be treated as an attack on Great Britain. In 1773 came the celebrated confession to the earl of Shelburne that Chatham was 'quite a Russ', amplified with the hope that 'the Turk will pull down the house of Bourbon in his fall'.[5] The national enemy was France, the Ottoman Empire incidentally so, Russia not at all. A last attempt to win Russia to a British cause came in 1781 when Lord North asked for an alliance and offered Minorca, an arrangement Catherine II refused, to the anguish of Potemkin. Charles James Fox, taking over the Foreign Office in 1783, announced that alliances with northern powers like Russia and Prussia 'ever have been, and ever will be, the system of every enlightened Englishman', and reproached Shelburne for listening to Vergennes' fears of Russia. Distinguished support came from Sir James Harris, an equally opinionated oracle, who thought 'there is not the slightest doubt we should long ago have been allied with Russia'.[6] Neither evidently saw how much the northern allies were split over the Ottoman Empire, and Harris continued to hope for an arrangement with Russia long after the Triple Alliance with Prussia and the Stadtholderate in 1788 had disqualified Great Britain as a reliable partner in Russian eyes. There is evidence too of a countervailing irritation in Great Britain with some of Russia's recent actions – Catherine II's part in the creation of the Armed Neutrality of 1780, the raising of Russian import duties in 1783, a new navigation law in the same year, a Franco-Russian commercial treaty raised in 1786 on the ruins of the expiring Anglo-Russian one – yet Russia remained the lesser delinquent in any comparison with France, her actions in the East crowded out of view by the nearer web of western rivalries.

Thus when Pitt heard of the opening of the second Russo-Ottoman war, he told the Russian minister at London, Count Simon Vorontzov, that Great Britain could have no objection if Catherine II demanded territory from the Sultan. The prime minister was pacific, anxious to stabilize a weak budgetary position at home, and reluctant to obstruct so valuable a trading partner as Russia. Great Britain had no trade in the Black Sea to worry about, and the Turkey Merchants had actually refrained from seeking admittance to the Black Sea in case the French followed their example and beat them hands down in exploiting its commercial possibilities. In the Commons, therefore, Pitt had to encounter the arguments of a political caucus speaking for the Muscovy Company, but not any counter-pressure from the Levant Company. The latter was in the doldrums, impoverished and demoralized, kept alive by annual doles from Whitehall.[7]

In announcing Great Britain's 'perfect neutrality' to Vorontzov, Pitt added a characteristic qualification. If France took a hand in the eastern imbroglio, then so must Great Britain. To Lord Auckland, Great Britain's ambassador at the Hague, he explained, *'our general wish is to take no part*, but until we see more clearly what France means, we cannot authorise you before-hand to declare that we shall take no part if France does'.[8] The marquis of Carmarthen, the foreign secretary, and incidentally a governor of the Levant Company, agreed that Great Britain had no interest which could be 'materially affected' by the outcome of the struggle in the East so long as France remained 'perfectly indifferent'. The strange thing is that France played a negligible part in the diplomacy of the burgeoning war, yet Pitt, instead of acting on his avowed preference for neutrality, was by 1791 asking Parliament for supplies with which to fight Russia.

Robert Ainslie, the British ambassador to the Ottoman Empire from 1775 until 1793, was a bluff and capable Scot who liked Constantinople and had considerable contempt for the ignorance of his superiors in London. They, in their turn, left him to his own devices, to the extent that in only two years of his eastern residence, 1783 and 1788, did he receive as many as ten dispatches a year. The Levant Company, which paid his salary, was a fractionally more demanding employer, receiving fractionally more respect. The outbreak of the war in 1787 brought no increase in tempo to his existence, and in the next three years the only call for action, beyond an instruction to offer the Ottoman Empire his mediation in association with his Prussian colleague, was a directive of January 1790 telling him to warn the Ottomans that Catherine II was sending a body-snatching naval force to the Red Sea to carry off the revered bones of the Prophet himself.[9] The Ottomans liked Ainslie, none the less, and were fascinated by his craggy appearance and trombone voice. Alas, after Russia's rejection of the proffered mediation in 1788, he had nothing to offer except advice, his poor information from Europe comparing strikingly with the duke of Choiseul's steady supply of news which came to Smyrna from Marseilles by a special diplomatic postal service.[10] Ainslie's fellow

Scot at Vienna, Sir Robert Murray Keith, let in the occasional shaft of light. Sir Charles Whitworth, at St Petersburg, sent dramatic paragraphs in code from time to time: unfortunately, Ainslie's cypher key was a decade out of date.[11] It is no surprise that Ainslie had ample time for his extensive labours in the cause of Byzantine numismatism, for which alone he is still remembered.

The ambassador was, nevertheless, specifically blamed by Catherine II for the Ottoman declaration of war, and the French similarly claimed to have 'proofs too strong to admit of any doubts'.[12] Catherine II also demanded Ainslie's dismissal. There is no doubt that Ainslie was popular with Abdulhamid I, an unusually accessible sovereign, and was able to advance his ideas through the imperial physician, Dr Gobis: 'I have great influence with the doctor, and made him a present of a coach about six weeks ago.' He also spent money freely on shawls, blunderbusses, and beer, for which Ottoman officials had a decided weakness.[13] But, if anything, Ainslie was suspected of Russophilism by the Ottomans, and ridiculed 'the old story of my influence' over them. It is certainly ironic that at the time Catherine II was demanding his recall, he was striving to secure Bulgakov's release, paying the salaries of Catherine II's consuls who were cut off from home by the outbreak of war, and sheltering her chargé d'affaires under his own roof.[14] He refused to support the attempts of British merchants in Pera to obtain contracts to supply the Ottoman forces, and suspended an embassy dragoman who tried to oblige them secretly. The Sultan was cross enough in his turn to refuse a loan from the Levant Company, and Choiseul was not automatically disbelieved when he warned the Porte that the British might yet support Catherine II with an amphibious operation at the Dardanelles.

By way of contrast, Choiseul had no difficulty himself in obtaining permission from the Ottomans for a French frigate to take soundings along the Bosporus for his forthcoming book, *Voyage Pittoresque de la Grèce*, and up to the moment when the Paris revolution swept all his efforts away, he was the inspiration of the peace party in the Sultan's divan.[15] This party was led by Nasif Effendi, the husband of Abdulhamid I's adopted daughter, and included the aga of the janizaries himself. The *reis effendi*, a functionary resembling a western foreign minister, was likewise 'a thorough Frenchman', and through such associates Choiseul was able to cajole or harass the ageing Sultan, firing salutes to the birth of royal children one moment and threatening to withdraw the French artillerymen from the Ottoman army the next, unless hostilities stopped and France was entrusted with the task of peace-making. Ainslie, tethered by instructions enjoining 'the most perfect neutrality', could not compete, nor offer Abdulhamid I the sort of military aid the Sultan wanted.[16] His masters at home remained undisturbed by the Russian seizure of Jassy, 'which is, I believe, the capital of Moldavia', to use the foreign secretary's leisurely phrase, and the campaigns of 1788 along the Danube went entirely in favour of the Russians. No one in the Foreign Office noticed the siege of a town on the Bug estuary called Ochakov, or the complete slaughter of its Ottoman garrison when it fell in December. Yet Ochakov was soon to become a symbol.

The Prussian government was far more worried than the British by the progress of the war on the Danube, and doubly chagrined that Joseph II might obtain through partnership with Russia advantages he could not have obtained by his own unsupported efforts. Prussian jealousy was not mitigated by Austria's poor military performance or the successes over Austrian troops of the grand vizier, Yusuf Pasha, and throughout 1788 it was the aim of Prussia's chief minister, Count Ewald von Hertzberg, to turn the recent Triple Alliance signed with the British and the Dutch into an instrument of common action in eastern Europe. Pitt's chief purpose in signing the Triple Alliance was to share the burden of defending the *status quo* in the Low Countries and, as the alliance was couched in the phraseology of mutual defence, he acknowledged also the commitment to defend Prussia against attack from any quarter. But he was diffident in the extreme when it came to underwriting Prussian plans in eastern Europe. Hertzberg must have felt in his bones that the British government would not oblige him: the unreliability of the British was notorious to all patriotic readers of Frederick the Great's *Testament Politique*, and to middle-aged men who remembered the Seven Years War. But Hertzberg could not resist the prospect of a profitable diplomatic intervention in the Russo-Ottoman war, based on the legendary wealth and naval strength of Great Britain and the land power of Prussia, and he intended to gain in the Baltic compensation for the gains Catherine II and Joseph II presently sought in the Balkans.

Catherine II would have to purchase her free hand in Ottoman affairs by consenting to the Prussian acquisition of the city of Thorn and the port of Danzig. Poland would receive compensation for these losses in the form of the retrocession of Galicia, taken by Austria in the First Partition. And Austria? She might get western Wallachia, but best of all, nothing. Russia would obtain Bessarabia and, as a remote possibility, give the Crimea back to the Ottoman Empire. Hertzberg may seem to have been a hopeless visionary, but his plan was not unusual or rare by the standards of his times.

During the fighting of 1788, Hertzberg extolled his ideas with zeal rather than clarity to Joseph Ewart, the British ambassador at Berlin, a man whose influence over Pitt was great, and increasing all the time. Ewart was perhaps the best dispatch writer of the age, and he was captivated by the breadth and daring of Hertzberg's ideas, reporting them to London in persuasive language and professing himself unable to counter Hertzberg's logic. In one lucid moment, he confessed that the project for territorial exchanges was 'extravagant and absurd', but the prospect of a great alliance, built round Prussia and Great Britain and including also Denmark, Sweden, Poland, and the Ottoman Empire clearly excited him. A strong Poland, buttressed by new friendships against old fears, would be the means of holding Russia and Austria physically apart. Sweden was already in arms against Russia.[17] As to the Ottoman Empire,

> such an alliance with the Porte seems . . . to offer much advantage to England as well as Prussia, since the decided superiority of the former by sea would enable it to combine the interests of the Baltic with those of the Archipelago, while the advantageous situation of this country [i.e. Prussia] by land, especially through the means of Poland, would put it in its power to connect the north with the east by an uninterrupted chain of communication, supported by the most powerful military force.[18]

This was the state of Ewart's, and Hertzberg's, thinking by early 1789, and Ewart claimed to have seen some encouragement for the plan in more than one communication from Carmarthen during 1788. There was some justification behind the claim, too, that Carmarthen had hinted at a guarantee for the Ottoman Empire: during 1788, when Prussia and Great Britain offered their services as mediators to Russia and the Ottomans, Carmarthen had written that 'if a peace were to be made under their influence, a subsequent guarantee of the dominions of the Porte might make a part of the proposed system and the Porte itself be included in the general defensive alliance'.[19] Later on, Carmarthen acknowledged that Great Britain 'can never have the smallest objection' to the Prussian plan to conjoin Baltic and Ottoman affairs 'as objects of negotiation', a rather unwise concession from so reluctant a government.[20] The truth was that the Pitt ministry had no serious interest or wish to 'combine the interests of the Baltic with those of the Archipelago'; when this dawned on the Prussians, they relied on Ewart's personal influence over Pitt to bring the Tory administration round. Ewart almost did it. If, of course, Ainslie had been allowed to speak of guarantees for the Sultan's dominions, his position at the Porte would have been transformed, but however unguarded Carmarthen may have been in his dealings with Berlin, he was silent at Constantinople. Ewart, too, should have seen that there was a difference between mediating a settlement between the existing combatants on the one hand and, on the other, presenting the Hertzberg plan to Russia on the tip of a lance. More than once, Carmarthen pointed out that an offensive alliance 'is an object by no means in our view'.

Encouraged by Ewart, Hertzberg went into action on 26 May 1789, sending instructions to his minister to the Porte, Heinrich Dietz, and copies of them to London two days later. There was less candour in this than met the eye; Dietz, described by Ainslie as 'a young, aggressive person, of low education and inordinate pride', had been in action for 18 months already, promising the Ottomans Anglo-Prussian aid if they maintained the fight against Catherine II and Joseph II. When Ainslie challenged him for taking the name of Great Britain in vain, Dietz 'retorted with an elevated voice that he had always given me timely notice of his transaction, but could not charge his memory with the dates'. Dietz categorically and repeatedly promised the retrocession of the Crimea and when the Foreign Office passed on Ainslie's complaints to Berlin, the Prussian envoy was disavowed, but not recalled or silenced.[21] Dietz's achievement was, in some ways, a marvel of procrastination, a solitary diplomatic effort while his government was trying to enlist Great Britain. Yusuf Pasha, the redoubtable grand vizier, badly needed the Protestant embassies to slip him a few trumps under the table, but as Dietz's promises devalued with endless repetition and Ainslie held back, Choiseul more than held his own until, in September

1789, 'unexampled commotions in Paris' were heard of in Constantinople.[22] The kaptan pasha, commanding the Ottoman naval forces in the Black Sea, was regretfully sent away from an interview with Ainslie at which he pleaded for a British demonstration of support, and the ambassador as sadly watched him return to his squadron which was, symbolically, embedded in the thick ice of a wintry Bosporus.[23] The war party was only saved by the death of Abdulhamid I on 7 April 1789: the new and brilliant Sultan, Selim III, determined to fight on, move his capital forward to Edirne, and open new fronts in the Bukovina and Transcaucasia. Nasif, the leader of the peace party, was fatally compromised and was strangled in the outer court of Topkapi Saray. And in July, a treaty between the Ottoman Empire and Sweden, vigorously pushed by Dietz, came into being.[24] Gustavus III, with his voracious appetite for subsidies, met his match. Selim III paid a million piastres and agreed to pay another ten million 'later', that is, after some results.

Hertzberg's instructions of 26 May 1789 ordered Dietz to see Selim III, and no one of lesser degree, in order formally to offer a treaty of alliance in the name of Prussia. By it, Selim III would commit himself not to make peace except through the mediation of Poland, Prussia, and Sweden, while Prussia would agree to declare war in favour of the Ottoman Empire the moment Russian or Austrian troops crossed 'Mont Balcan'. In either event, Prussia would ensure that the Ottoman Empire obtained the Crimea and 'toute la sûreté imaginable' for Constantinople. Austria would not be accorded peace until she declared her readiness to surrender Galicia to Poland. With Russia and Austria submissive, 'les cours de Vienne, de Petersbourg et de Pologne s'arrangeraient en même termes avec le roi de Prusse sur leurs différences et intérêts respectifs': in short, Prussia would dictate the peace in accordance with her plans for Danzig and Thorn. With the treaty signed, Prussia's friends and allies – Great Britain, Holland, Sweden, and Poland – would guarantee the new frontiers of the Ottoman Empire.

There was a further task for Dietz, however, which was of so precarious a nature that his government only communicated it to him in a supplementary and confidential instruction. In this instruction, the Prussian government admitted its expectation that it would have to fight for the Ottoman Empire sooner or later to save her from defeat. Consequently, Dietz was gently to insinuate in his conversations with Selim III the price the Ottoman Empire must expect to pay for this aid, and to explain that western Wallachia might have to go to Austria and Bessarabia to Russia as the price for the return to the Ottoman Empire of the Crimea. The Prussian minister was to sweeten these bitter pills by the discretionary expenditure of 100,000 ducats, and to give 300,000 to any Ottoman minister brave enough to incorporate as a clause in the alliance an agreement that the Ottoman Empire would fight until Prussia got Thorn and Danzig.

Dietz's instructions were known in London at the end of May,[25] and Vorontzov, the Russian minister, and his Whig friends – Fox, the duke of Portland, and the duke of Devonshire – knew enough of what was at stake to fear that Great Britain was about to be enmeshed in the toils of Prussian ambition. The recovery of George III, and the end of the Regency crisis, intensified their gloom. In fact, Pitt had decided to clear the air, and did so in a dispatch to Ewart which is drafted in his own hand and dated 24 June.[26] Its purpose was to warn Ewart as well as Hertzberg, and it stressed once again that Great Britain was not 'in any degree bound to support a system of an offensive nature'. She would uphold Holland against French subversion, and Sweden against Russia, for these were matters of 'security', but the Ottoman Empire was not in this category and Great Britain would not involve herself further east 'on account of Turkey, either directly or indirectly'. The Hertzberg plan was one of 'aggrandizement rather than security', and its victim was, indeed, the Ottoman Empire herself, the state for whose welfare Prussia was claiming to be so concerned. Great Britain would do nothing to prolong the Russo-Ottoman war in order to make Russia more pliant to the will of Berlin. As to Hertzberg's instructions to Dietz, they had the weakness of resting on 'extreme cases, either of brilliant and repeated success [i.e., the Ottoman Empire winning without help] or a series of losses and defeats equally considerable' (from which Prussia would have to rescue the Ottoman Empire). If the Ottomans won by their own efforts, would they really exert themselves at the peace for allies who had not fired a shot? And in the event of a Prussian rescue operation, would they resist any passing attempt to come to terms with Russia or Austria? Furthermore, there had been some general notion abroad in Berlin that the Ottoman Empire would obtain a territorial guarantee after she had given up Bessarabia and Wallachia, but Pitt preferred to consider 'how far such a guarantee is either necessary or beneficial when the terms of peace come under discussion'. The British government was anxious to avoid any commitment to the Ottoman Empire which might preclude 'a future connection' with Russia. In a passage aimed more particularly at Ewart, Pitt reminded his impetuous subordinate that 'the real object of our interference [in Europe] was calculated for general views of public utility, and not founded upon motives of partiality for one power or resentment to another'. Here then, in brief but fairly unmistakable form, is the attitude of mind so admired and imitated by later men like Viscount Castlereagh: the unwillingness to change the existing Continental order for a hypothetically superior one, the consequent reluctance to accept obligations beyond the conservative and defensive category, the diffidence to guarantee an existing order unless national 'security' is involved, the refusal to guarantee anything at all prospectively.

The Prussian government was discouraged, and Ewart embarrassed, by the dispatch of 24 June, the ambassador making the most of the argument that Great Britain was renouncing a restraining influence over Berlin, a point which would have come better from someone less fond of Prussian military parades and manoeuvres in Silesia. The king of Prussia, Frederick William II, himself refused for some months to accept the dispatch as Great Britain's last word on the subject, arguing tirelessly that Great Britain *must* see that the conjunction of Baltic and Balkan affairs *was* a matter of Prussian security. With Russia and Austria marching to yet greater status in the Balkans – hardly an objective view of Austria's miserable military performance – Prussia, Poland, and Sweden were being left *'isolées dans un coin de l'Europe'*.[27] If Great Britain would not stand shoulder-to-shoulder in diplomacy, Prussia would have to fight alone. It was the language of a timorous burglar, for whatever his grievances to Ewart, Frederick William II wanted to coerce Austria and certainly not to fight Russia. Some of the outward signs looked dangerous, and the dying Joseph II was taken in by the threats of Prussian intervention in the Netherlands, in Hungary, in the war with the Ottoman Empire. In October, Dietz went into action again, hoping to follow up the Ottoman-

Swedish treaty with an Ottoman–Polish alliance, and in January 1790 actually produced a treaty, though not quite the one demanded, between Prussia and the Ottoman Empire. Frederick William II continued to speak of 'so powerful a demonstration as could not fail to overawe Russia and Austria and thereby prevent resistance'.[28] But Catherine II was too supple, and Pitt too stubborn, and when the Russians took Bender in October 1789, and Prince Repnin began to hammer at Ismail as a preliminary to crossing the Danube in force, the Prussian high command began to lower the strident, abrupt tones it had used that summer. Catherine II astutely chose her moment to inform Berlin that she could not object if Austria elected to give up Galicia, or Poland surrendered Thorn and Danzig to Prussia, provided her prospective gains in the Ottoman war did not come under discussion.

More cleverly still, Catherine II approached London, an unexpected and gratifying move which removed overnight the hurt caused in 1788 by her peremptory refusal of British mediation between herself and Abdulhamid I. Vorontzov explained in London that his empress had 'no intention of destroying the balance of Europe, and of annihilating the Ottoman monarchy', but simply wished to advance her frontier to the Dniester, obtain 'Akerman or Belgorod' on its right bank, and see Bessarabia and the Principalities unified in a single kingdom, 'governed by a sovereign of the Christian religion'. Carmarthen frigidly replied that Great Britain viewed Russia's plans 'with sincere regret' and refused to promote them at Constantinople. This was in January 1790,[29] and in February, when death removed Catherine II's collaborator, Joseph II, the latter's successor, Leopold II, sent for Lord Hervey the day after his accession and asked for Great Britain's mediation in his quarrels with Prussia.

In a flush of pacific and generous feeling, which he soon checked, Leopold II declared his readiness to give up Galicia, assist in the reconstruction of Poland, make peace with the Ottoman Empire, restore the abrogated rights of the Magyars, and make Great Britain and Prussia guarantors of a constitutional settlement for his Belgian subjects. This diversified and 'very interesting information' was sent home by Lord Hervey, its details being confirmed by Sir Robert Murray Keith.[30] In London there was relief, gratification, and a sense that the initiative had suddenly been transferred from impetuous Berlin, with all sides awaiting a British lead. The Tory ministry announced its determination to avoid war with Russia over the Ottoman Empire, or with Austria over the Netherlands. Keith was ordered to press for an immediate Austro-Ottoman armistice, and to suggest an international conference. By May 1790, Great Britain had offered her mediation to all the belligerents. Prussia and Austria, finding themselves without allies, grumbled a good deal, Prussia charging Great Britain with bad faith and Kaunitz in Vienna trying to stiffen Leopold II to hang on for western Wallachia and the old Passarowitz frontiers with the Ottoman Empire. But in late June, the conference of Reichenbach opened, and with it the rocky road to a reconciliation based on the *status quo*. With the storming of the Bastille almost a year in the past, and the Rhineland towns already full of *émigrés*, contemporary developments in Paris could be expected to provide a strong incentive to peace between the powers; in fact, their effect was still minimal and the diplomatic records indicate that none foresaw the hurricane.

Just before the conference of Reichenbach opened on 27 June, Pitt went out of his way to prove to the king of Prussia that Great Britain had not deserted him. Great Britain would not fight for the Hertzberg plan: on the other hand, she favoured common action in the East so long as 'that system of moderation to which he [George III] has uniformly endeavoured to adhere' was observed. Even if Prussia chose to fight, Great Britain would assist her in certain respects short of war, as a proof of her attachment to her ally. She had already guaranteed Sweden a subsidy for 1790 and that still stood; she would restrain France and Denmark in Prussia's rear, by force if necessary; Austrian troops would not be allowed in the Netherlands during the armistice now in force there. Indeed, if Pitt's real aim was to restrain Prussia in mid-1790, there was a danger that he was offering his chafing ally too much rather than too little. Having extricated himself from deep waters in 1789, Pitt, in 1790, now seemed to encourage Prussia into the same waves, albeit alone. However, he stressed his wish that Austro-Prussian difficulties should be disentangled amicably, and hoped that Russia, too, should come within the terms of settlement. Even so, it is intriguing to discover that Pitt was ready for something very like the Hertzberg plan if it could be negotiated amicably between the powers, on the basis of what he described as 'not sacrifices but exchanges of territory', a phrase to which we will return in a moment.

In a secret dispatch to Ewart of 23 May, Pitt revealed the influence of Vorontzov's ideas when he wrote of his own certainty that Catherine II would retain the Crimea, and likewise her conquests *as far as the Dniester and including Ochakov*.[31] Under these circumstances, he thought it was right that Sweden should recover the wider frontiers she enjoyed at the time of the peace of Nystadt. Austria could then obtain north Serbia and western Wallachia, and give up at least parts of Galicia, including Cracow, to Poland. This should secure at least Danzig to Prussia. A couple of days later, the Russian vice-chancellor, Count Ivan Ostermann, sent an affirmation to London that Russia was disposed to give up the idea of a Christian kingdom in the Principalities for the present, and content herself with a region containing 'nothing of any importance, except the single town of Ochakov'. In short, Russia had also given up hope of getting Bessarabia just yet. Pitt obviously found the Russian attitude acceptable, if Austria and Prussia would accept it too. There need be no 'sacrifices' for any great power. Only for the Ottoman Empire. So, only ten months before the Ochakov debate opened, Pitt is found recommending a partial dismemberment of the Ottoman Balkans if it can be amicably negotiated among the powers. The Prussians briefly hoped for a salvage operation along these lines, but Leopold II had lost his sweet reasonableness by now, and was gently putting out feelers to Russia. Briefly, he broke off relations with the Prussians at Reichenbach, and Hertzberg threatened to confirm his treaties with Poland and the Ottoman Empire. Eventually, both sides signed on the basis of the *status quo*, which meant the end of the Hertzberg plan. From that moment, any former tolerance of Russian ambition vanished, and the duke of Leeds (as Carmarthen had become) advised Catherine II to come to terms.

It was not, perhaps, unreasonable of Pitt to imagine that what had hitherto been an explosive Continental situation was stabilizing itself. Contemporaneously with the conference of Reichenbach, Gustavus III of Sweden made his peace with Russia at Verela.[32] Then negotiations between Austria and the Ottoman Empire opened at a congress at Sistovo, with both sides fairly clearly disposed to accept the *status quo ante*. So why should not Catherine II settle her differences with the Ottoman Empire on the same basis? The simple answer is that Catherine II did not need to do so, for Prussia as well as Austria was now trying to mend the bridges to St Petersburg.[33] Pitt only saw that Catherine II was without allies: but she was also without opponents. And when, in September 1790, Prussia and Great Britain offered their mediation between her and Selim III, she rebuffed them promptly. Whitworth said the mediation need not be formal, and promised that Great Britain would obtain an official renunciation of the Crimea by the Ottoman Empire, but Catherine II knew Great Britain did not enjoy that kind of influence at Constantinople. So she repudiated 'the unparalleled conduct' of the Triple Alliance in 'trying to dictate in so arbitrary a manner to a sovereign perfectly independent and in want of no assistance'. She would accept British intercession if it brought her Ochakov.[34] In December, the offer of mediation was replaced by a stiffer Anglo-Prussian demand for the restitution of all losses to the Ottoman Empire, but once more Catherine II discounted the official Prussian line, Hertzberg having confidentially told her minister at Berlin that he and his master were ready for a bilateral agreement in which Prussia would assent to the new Russian frontiers in the Balkans, if she was accorded a free hand over Danzig and Thorn.[35] Prussia was already trying to wriggle out of the self-denying ordinance signed at Reichenbach. Hertzberg's disloyalty, and Count Alexander Suvorov's capture of Ismail on 22 December, the suspension of the Austro-Ottoman negotiations at Sistovo for a period of weeks, and an underhand offer by Frederick William II to Leopold II to the effect that he would not insist on the *status quo* at Sistovo if Austria pressed Poland to give up Danzig and Thorn, all contributed to the isolation of Pitt in relation to Catherine II. Yet 'the success of Pitt playing the part of Petrucchio to Catherine II depended mainly on the steadiness of the Prussian and British Governments'.[36]

★ ★ ★

When Ostermann explained to Whitworth on 8 January 1791 that Russia must reject the demands of Prussia and Great Britain, the possibility of war loomed suddenly, with some men spotting the danger more quickly than others. Auckland, in particular, had been saying for months that the government was following an unreliable

The Ochakov Debate

ally into a cul-de-sac. Whitworth put Catherine II's resistance down to 'pride and obstinacy' and said both would evaporate. Ewart, coming home for the winter months, comforted Pitt that 'there can be little doubt of her accepting the terms offered before the spring since she can never venture to risk the consequences of a refusal'. But Auckland insisted that it would be Great Britain who gave way because of 'the state of our debt, of our revenue, of our trade, and the unsettled disposition of mankind in general'. Auckland at least sensed the stirring of the wind that was to sweep through Europe with a terrifying force. He was about the first to ask why Great Britain should oppose Russia 'for a desert tract of ground between two rivers'. Others soon asked the same thing. Meanwhile, Pitt came to the decision that Russia must be coerced by 35 British warships in the Baltic and a further handful in the Black Sea.[37]

Pitt had no excuse for mistaking the unreliability of the Prussian government. Ewart's deputy at Berlin, Francis Jackson, was a capable and watchful man who said Prussia was not to be relied on, as clearly as a subordinate dare. Daniel Hailes, at Warsaw, said the same more boldly, and Auckland loudest of all. Ewart contemplated the risk of hostilities with relish, led on by the grail of his 'grand federal chain which would assure a long time of peace to our hemisphere': *si vis pacem para bellum*. Leeds, who alone of the cabinet seemed to remember Harris's biting aphorism that Berlin contained neither an honest man nor a virtuous woman, was excluded from the discussions in which Pitt was 'daily closeted' during February, and the air was full of the 'great offers' to be made him if only he would resign. James Bland Burges, Leeds's loyal under-secretary, indignantly challenged Pitt's private secretary about the daily meetings between Pitt and such doubtful experts as Henry Dundas, Lord Grenville, and the duke of Richmond, to the exclusion of his own chief, to be told that 'there must be a mistake somewhere' in the procedure for calling meetings. Leeds himself kept his peace, not knowing 'whether I am to be dismissed, driven to resign, or [have] any arrangement proposed to me'. By 8 March, Ewart said the government 'have admitted my statement of facts to be just', and a number of men were shocked by his success: Auckland lamented that a man 'who would have forced the whole world into war' should have won over men 'so much wiser than himself'. After three years of caution, Pitt had moved to the side of

Prussia in as many weeks, ostensibly to preserve Ochakov for the Ottoman Empire. Interestingly, Pitt only investigated the importance of Ochakov *after* he had decided to fight for it.[38]

It was Auckland who found at the Hague one of the few Europeans able to discuss Ochakov with any authority. Convinced by Jackson that 'our friends in Berlin are in general at least as much afraid of a Russian war as I am', Auckland sought out the Dutch admiral, Jan Hendrick van Kingsbergen, who had served in the Russian navy and once prepared a plan of operations against Constantinople. He knew the Bug–Dnieper estuary well, and confirmed Auckland's impression that Ochakov had no great value. The ambassador immediately wrote to Pitt pressing him to consult the admiral, and in reply the prime minister admitted that Kingsbergen's views could be 'very material': he sent a list of questions.[39] If the Ottomans recovered Ochakov, could they control Russian shipping operating from Kerson and Sebastopol? If Russia kept it, would it confer on her control of the Dniester estuary? Kingsbergen's replies hardly offered ammunition for the debate to come. Ochakov, he said, was not a port at all; the navigable channel of the Bug–Dniester confluence being on the opposite, Kinburn side, beyond the reach of Ochakov's cannon. So Kerson shipping had nothing to fear. Sebastopol had even less to fear, being 200 miles away. Ochakov, he concluded, was small, well-defended, isolated, easily circumvented, unimportant. He could not say if Russian control over it could jeopardize Polish trade to the Black Sea. It may be added that contemporary maps of the region were good enough to have shown Pitt the truth of these observations, and why he fussed about Ochakov and stayed silent over Odessa is a mystery. For Odessa, too, lay within the Dniester frontier that Catherine II now claimed.

It is hard to ascertain who in the Cabinet was notified of Kingsbergen's opinions. They certainly demoralized Leeds, and despondency was affecting the lord chancellor, Lord Thurlow; the master-general of the Ordnance, the duke of Richmond; the marquis of Stafford; and Grenville, Leeds's designated successor. Leeds, when given a chance, argued that Catherine II could not be checked, and would take all 'from the Bug to the Dniester'. Then, on 21 March, the Prussian minister, Count Sigismund Redern, brought an autograph letter from his sovereign to the Foreign

Office. It disclosed that Austria had assured Prussia that Catherine II would stand alone if she refused the *status quo*, and invited Great Britain to join Prussia in a military operation, to coerce Russia. 'As the decisive moment is drawing near, I await a definite declaration on this subject.' The Cabinet discussed the matter for two days, Leeds's fears intensifying, Pitt's dissolving. The demand of the previous December for the restitution of the Ottoman Empire's losses was re-drafted by Pitt personally into an ultimatum, giving Catherine II ten days in which to surrender all except the Crimea. Pitt told his colleagues he was still sure the empress would give way. He asked the Dutch to provide a squadron in the Baltic, and was ready to pay £200,000 for the use of the Swedish ports.[40] And having won over a few men in his Cabinet, he set about obtaining a parliamentary majority. The debate opened on 28 March.

Writers who have insisted on Pitt's genius have also been far too reluctant to allow him any lapses from this high estate, and his failure over Ochakov has been attributed to party faction and the ignorance of his critics rather than to defects in his own case and his tactical handling of it. The most comprehensive exoneration of his performance[41] asserts that he did not know 'the extent of the Czarina's demands, which, at the request of Prussia, they were about to oppose'; that Leeds 'secretly doubted the wisdom of the policy'; that Pitt was not aware of the unimportance of Ochakov until too late; that the Dutch 'were most reluctant to take any part in the dispute'; and that Jackson in Berlin 'had not fathomed the depths of Hertzberg's duplicity'. Point by point, the exculpation can be queried, and on the sole basis of the information which made Pitt's more percipient colleagues afraid of the situation into which he was leading them. Catherine II's demands, for instance, *were* known to extend to the Dniester. Leeds openly doubted Pitt's wisdom and so was ignored and left out of the inner councils. The Kingsbergen replies arrived in time for the government to change its strategy, if not its mind. Auckland had been saying for months that the Dutch were not to be counted on. As for Jackson's insufficiency at Berlin, he had sent warning on 9 March that Hertzberg had spoken to him of the possible need to tone down their demands to Catherine II, and the very post which brought Frederick William II's personal appeal to Pitt also included a further warning from Jackson to the effect that the Prussian supreme commander, General Wichard von

Möllendorf, had confessed to him personally that war with Russia was impossible for Prussia. Corroboration came from the industrious Auckland who intercepted a letter in cypher from the king of Prussia to Redern, and decoded it successfully: 'His Prussian Majesty states in terms of strongest uneasiness that the Emperor's [Leopold II's] conduct becomes more suspicious and that he evidently intends to defeat the whole convention of Reichenbach.' Pitt received this information on the day he sent Russia his ultimatum, 27 March, a day which also brought from Count Bernstorff, Denmark's first minister, a peace proposal supposedly accepted by Catherine II as a basis for discussion.[42] One historian thought it too late in arriving for Pitt to respond to 'the reasonableness of the Tsarina', but when peace is at stake it is never too late to go back. A fast messenger could always be overtaken by a faster one. Auckland's explanation was that Ewart bamboozled Pitt utterly, thus bringing the ministry into 'a degree of ridicule, reproach and inconsistency'.[43]

And so to the debate.[44] On 28 March, Pitt invited the House of Commons to increase the naval strength of Great Britain to lend weight to official representations, hitherto unsuccessful, for the re-establishment of peace between Russia and the Ottoman Empire. The following day, Pitt said, had been reserved for the discussion of the motion, but Fox was on his feet at once, challenging 'this mode of plunging the nation into war and expense, without deigning to acquaint them with the cause, or even the pretext of such measures'. Fox, of course, knew far more than he said about the involutions of British diplomacy, thanks to Vorontzov's sources of information, but it is the case that most members of the House were caught unawares by the government's proposal. Leeds described the first skirmishes as 'very violent' and although the government was forced on the defensive at once, and into retreat within a very short time – by May a special envoy was off to Russia to make a humble accommodation, and by July it was conceded by both Great Britain and Prussia that Catherine II was free to annex everything as far as the Dniester – the debate went on intermittently, but in the same acrimonious tones, until Catherine II signed the treaty of Jassy in February 1792 and her demands were met. As early as 30 March, Fox told Vorontzov that Pitt was too experienced a tactician to persist with his proposal, and on the same day Richmond advised

Pitt to 'look out for some expedient to get out of the scrape'. This sort of defeatist whispering was disheartening for the prime minister, but much of it he brought on himself by his lack of candour with his followers, who were expected obediently to pull him through. Cabinet dissidents were expected to keep silent, and Thurlow spoke for several of them when he complained about 'being *gagged* in the debates'. William Wilberforce found it impossible to support his friend, and a string of others imitated his abstention.

Pitt's part in the debate on 29 March was perfunctory at the start, and non-existent long before its end. The parliamentary record will be searched in vain for signs of a higher wisdom, for evidence that he was 'the first Englishman to appreciate the real and intimate concern of Great Britain in the affairs of the Near East', and this is the more surprising since a ministry concealing the true mainsprings of its actions could be expected to scrape the barrel for arguments in favour of Ottoman integrity. This Pitt never really attempted, and while he explained that Ochakov was of value to the Ottoman Empire (which anyone could guess), he never explained in what ways the Ottoman Empire or the Near East mattered to Great Britain. The classic argument for preserving the land routes to India from Russian control was not yet generally accepted in Great Britain, but it was born, and Pitt's intimate friend, Henry Dundas, knew of it. It has been suggested with some justice that Pitt's concern was for Poland rather than the Ottoman Empire in 1791, that he wished to secure access to the Black Sea for Polish commerce, and this is certainly the purport of his speeches in the debate. Too detailed an exposé of his sense of obligation to Prussia spelled danger: he said so himself. If he had 'to state, as would then be indispensable, the precise ground on which [the need to fight Russia] arose', he could not have held his party together. His party stayed loyal once it knew he was only shadow-boxing, and the newspapers which ordinarily supported the government oscillated between hostility and fear until reassured that nothing serious was going to happen. 'The country throughout have told Mr. Pitt they will not got to war.'[45]

The idea of defending the Ottoman Empire was dismissed by the Whigs as eccentricity, the proposal to attack Russia as a financially ruinous course which would weaken the country and subvert the Muscovy Company. Fox, speaking on the 29th, hardly referred to the Ottoman Empire, except in flashes of contempt, and he insisted that the habit of alignment with Russia, which characterized Great Britain's recent history, would outlive temporary frictions. Great Britain had facilitated the entry of the Russian fleet into the Mediterranean to attack the Ottoman Empire a few years before. There had been no protest when Catherine II seized the Crimea in 1783. If the loss of Ochakov made a revision of foreign policy imperative, then why had this not been undertaken in 1788, when Ochakov fell? That event had not been noticed in the King's Speeches of 1789 or 1790, so why now? But in any case, and whether Russia kept Ochakov, gave it up, or blew it to pieces, why should Great Britain resent the growth of Russian power in the Black Sea, 'a sea in which, of all the seas of the globe, not a single British ship ever appears'? If the Russians were kept out, the Ottomans would soon let the French in. And as to Russia becoming a Mediterranean power, that would be a beneficial development enabling Great Britain to counter the rivalry of Spain and France. Fox concluded his peroration with an appeal to 'political arithmetic', to the hard facts that exports to Russia were worth £400,000 per annum, and imports £2,500,000, with British carriers almost monopolizing the two-way trade.

Edmund Burke wound up the first Whig assault on 29 March and, while ruminating for a bigger theme, allowed himself a few sonorous apostrophes at the expense of the 'Turkish savages', which fitted in with current prejudice and drew the expected applause. Primarily, he attacked the government for the many 'new' ideas it had brought forward. 'The confidence claimed by his Majesty's ministers was new. The considering the Turkish Empire any part of the balance of power was new.' The Ottoman Empire was actually of no consequence to Great Britain, and the government spoke of Ottoman integrity while seeking to restrict Russia's. As for Ochakov being critical to Ottoman security, 'we are in possession of Gibraltar and Spain is not dismembered', a truly Burkeian red herring. Pitt, in a brief reply, avoided a development of the case for defending the Ottoman Empire, and baldly said that Montesquieu, 'the leading authority', had shown the importance of the Ottoman Empire to Europe. The government came through by 228 votes to 135.[46]

Following Pitt's technique, Grenville moved in the House of

Lords on 29 March for the preparation of more ships 'for establishing and securing a solid pacific system over all Europe'. Even less was given away in the Lords than in the Commons, the foreign secretary remaining silent. The opposition attacked 'the conspiracy of silence' and Pitt's 'mad ambition'. The best speech came from Viscount Stormont, Russia's champion. Appraising the Ottoman Empire's place in international affairs, he said that 'every barber and newsmonger' knew that for years France had been inciting the Ottomans to resist Russia and to suspect Great Britain. Now that France was immobilized, Pitt was advancing this policy for her. In the Ottoman Empire, we were being invited to support 'a state with which we had the least to do of any on the face of the globe': Pitt's own father had always 'reprobated any connection with them'. If, despite all warnings, the country went to war, then there could be but one result, defeat. Subsequent speakers, anticipating the views current in 1815, called Russia an invincible colossus, and the marquis of Lansdowne reminded the government that, with Austria and Sweden going over to the other side in the event of a war, Great Britain would experience a new category of expense: Henry Pelham's 'piddling wars of four or five millions' were things of the past. Lord Loughborough indicated just how far the sinister chain reaction could extend; war meant increased taxation, the taxes would be levied mainly on malt, a malt tax would reduce the beer-drinking habit, and this, in its turn, would reduce the vigour of the proletariat. Replies came from Richmond, who would have served his cause better by imitating Leeds's silence, and Thurlow, clearly confused as to what was going on. The division in the Lords was 97 to 34 in the government's favour.

These opening exchanges in Parliament convinced Leeds that the government must retreat, and he told Richmond, another waverer, that he had expected failure from 'the beginning of the business'. Grenville was also worried, and has on occasion been blamed more than any other minister. At a cabinet meeting on 31 March, Stafford and Earl Camden made their unease clear, and Thurlow took sanctuary in feigned sleep. Evidence came in of rebellion on the back benches, the duke of Grafton withdrawing his own support and ordering his sons, whose seats he controlled, to do the same in the Lower House. Realizing he would have to modify existing plans, Pitt suggested sending a special messenger to Jackson to hold up the ultimatum to Russia until the Danish plan had been examined, but Leeds refused to sign any such document and pointedly offered to resign in favour of Grenville.[47]

Ewart was recalled from the country in early April, and he came to London hoping that Pitt would, somehow or other, press on. But all was over, and the prime minister confessed 'with tears in his eyes, that it was the greatest mortification he had ever experienced'. Pitt said, nevertheless, that it was not intended 'to knock under, but keep up a good countenance; that the armaments should therefore continue to be made with vigour, and the fleet ready for sailing, and that in the meantime he hoped means might be found to manage matters so as not to have the appearance of giving up the point'. He would not resign as that would be tantamount to 'abandoning the king'. It has been said that a good statesman co-operates with events rather than coerces them, and it remains a mystery why Pitt should tell Ewart that 'all my efforts to make the House of Commons understand the subject have been fruitless'.[48] Leeds gave up the seals of the Foreign Office in disgust on 21 April, refusing to be the agent through whom retreat was to be negotiated. There was a rash of mutual accusations, with the Pittites blaming Auckland for Leeds's defection, and Auckland blaming Ewart for everything.

The opposition naturally refused to let the matter drop once it discovered the ministers in flight, and the views of both sides were being put with greater precision and care in May, when it no longer mattered, than in March, when it did. Viscount Stanley was an improvement on Pitt, Grey on Fox, and R.B. Sheridan brisker than Burke. A speech by Sheridan on 12 April set the tone of these better performances, and in it he said it was time the government gave up the absurdity of discussing Ochakov as if it was the Worcester canal. Above all, Sheridan exposed the sense of obligation to Prussia as the real issue, and asked why Great Britain should care about the reactions of a state like Austria which had been ready enough to filch territory in the Principalities if the chance arose. Pitt was 'intriguing in all the courts of Europe . . . the great posture-master of the balance of power'. Perhaps the best contribution from either side was a speech on 25 May which gained in piquancy by being delivered by the foreign secretary's brother, Thomas Grenville.[49] Any treaty, Grenville said, must be open to some degree of interpretation, but a government must account publicly for an intention to act upon an interpretation other than the obvious one. In the present case, the government had spoken of the value of Ochakov to the Ottoman Empire – which was almost irrelevant to Great Britain – because it was even harder to speak of the value of Ochakov to Prussia. Yet it was Prussia who made Ochakov the *casus belli*. The treaty with Prussia, the Triple Alliance, was defensive, and Prussia had not been attacked. Ochakov had been in Russian hands before, in 1737, and again in the last two years, without much foreign comment. Would Pitt now seek to deny Russia a place which, under other circumstances and only a short time before, he had been content to leave in her hands? The importance of Ochakov was an improvisation, and it came hollowly from a government content to leave the Crimea, filched in time of peace, in Russian hands. Grenville added the inconvenient news that Danzig and Thorn, so gently concealed throughout the debate, far from being within the gift of the great powers, were explicitly guaranteed by several sovereigns, including Queen Anne and, as recently as 1767, Catherine II.

By the middle of 1791, Fox was able to say that the government's majority stabilized at around 100 every time Ochakov came up because the Tory members had been privately assured that hostilities were no longer to be feared. Grenville told a delegation of merchants it would be safe to trade to the Baltic for the moment, and the watchful Stormont noticed that the mercantile insurance brokers did not even bother to put up their premiums. In July, when Whitworth and Baron Bernard von der Goltz went cap-in-hand to Russia, Pitt stolidly refused to discuss Leeds's resignation, and suddenly Leeds broke silence and spoke for himself, saying the government would have done best to admit from the start that the sense of commitment to Prussia was behind its policy: 'a liberal construction of a friendly treaty' might have won the Commons over. When Ewart died in January 1792, there was a scuffle for his private papers, and his widow was offered a substantial sum if she would surrender them to the opposition Whigs.[50]

Enough has been said to show that Pitt's was not the voice of the future, and it might be claimed that the earl of Elgin's was. Elgin made his maiden speech in the Lords on 20 February in the last exchanges over the dead carcass of Ochakov. He was by no means the only speaker to express fear of Russia who, as Lord Mulgrave said, 'ever since she emerged from barbarism, about two hundred years ago, had been pursuing one regular scheme of ambition to extend her conquests far and wide',[51] and there was plenty of speculation in contemporary books and newspapers about the problems Russia might pose in the future for Great Britain.[52] But Elgin saw Ochakov as the symbol of an eternal struggle imposed on two neighbouring states by geographical propinquity and the discrepancy of strength between them. Great Britain, sooner or later, must be involved, for if ever the Ottoman inheritance was divided between Russia, France, and Austria, Russia and France would control the Mediterranean, while Russia and Austria would dominate central Europe and the Balkans. Poland and the Ottoman Empire, as states under peculiar pressure, could only look to Great Britain for survival and Great Britain needed to think now how she would answer their appeals.

The final charge against Pitt, then, is not that he was without a case in 1791, but that he failed to formulate it in a purposeful or convincing manner. This is not to suggest that the case would have had strong appeal at that date, but it is, nevertheless, possible that the loyal parliamentary following which saved him from rout in 1791 might have allowed itself to be talked into giving him a mandate for action, had he built his argument more candidly on the need to uphold Prussia in Europe. The snag here was that Pitt himself was only a reluctant supporter of Prussia, while his followers – like the parliamentary opposition and the country at large – were wholly opposed to the idea of bolstering the Ottoman Empire. Russophobia was certainly alive in 1791, but Turcophilism was not yet born.

Even so, the Ochakov debate was a valuable stimulant which produced a certain amount of ministerial thinking about the Levant, and the privy council for trade carried out some research for the Foreign Office by interviewing and questioning the London directors of the Levant Company about the trade of the Ottoman Empire and the Black Sea.[53] This was in October 1791, long after the retreat from Ochakov. The information supplied by the witnesses is striking on two accounts. First because it was all second-hand, drawn from French reports on the Black Sea trade. 'The best information that can be obtained concerning this commerce', the Privy Council for Trade informed Leeds, 'is in a book published by M. Peysonnel, entitled, *Traité sur le Commerce de la Mer Noire.*' Peysonnel had been French consul at Smyrna, and also consul to the khanates of the Crimea. The Levant Company, in fact, had no Black Sea trade of its own, and the directors timidly excused their notorious lack of enterprise by saying, 'It is reported that there is seldom a compass on board a Greek or Turkish ship, and that in most cases the master would not know how to make use of it if he had one'. They observed correctly that the Black Sea was dangerous, a place of storms, and unlit headlands, and shipwreck: they did not add that Austrian and Russian, as well as Greek and Ottoman vessels, survived somehow in its waters.

Yet Peysonnel's arguments for the Black Sea trade clearly intrigued the company's directors, particularly his views on the Crimea: 'he represents it as capable of being made a very important and advantageous branch of commerce.' This raises the second respect in which the directors' views are of special interest, namely, the hopes pinned on the Russian trade now that the commerce of the Ottoman Empire and Egypt were so run down. Far from being staunch protagonists of Ottoman integrity for economic reasons, the Turkey Merchants were beginning to look to southern Russia for the first rays of an economic renascence. They claimed that, with government backing, they could exploit all the provinces drained by the great rivers, the Danube, Dniester, Dnieper, and Don. There was no foreseeable limit to the sale of 'broad cloth, stuffs, muslins, callicoes, and every species of cotton manufactures, hardware, beer, pottery, hosiery of silk, cotton and worsted, tin, lead, tin plates, coffee, sugar, rum, copper in plates, and all implements for shipbuilding, and husbandry'. In return, the Levant Company could acquire for Great Britain, 'timber, hemp, hides, tallow, wax, potash, cordage, flax, iron, coarse linen, corn, isinglass, caviare, seed-oil, some furs, and some drugs'. In concluding their evidence, the directors agreed that Great Britain must maintain decent relations with the Sultan in order to obtain free use of the Straits, but the price for such relations need not be high. It would suffice if Great Britain promised the Ottoman Empire that she would not sell Russia ships for her Black Sea fleet.

The last word belongs to Pitt, who left in his private papers an undated, untidy, scribbled *post mortem* on the Ochakov debate.[54] Its internal evidence indicates that it was written at the very end of

1791, and that the Privy Council for Trade's report to Leeds was at Pitt's disposal when he composed it. In style, it reads like a speech, although there is no corresponding utterance in the *Parliamentary History*, and it may have been no more than an exculpatory memorandum, written to convince himself that he had been right all along.

Although it begins with the observation that 'it was the interest of Great Britain to prevent as far as circumstances permitted, the aggrandizement of the two Imperial courts at the expense of Turkey', its most notable disclosure – not made in Parliament – is that his chief motive for proposing a defence of the Ottoman Empire had been to gratify Prussia, *Great Britain's only possible great-power ally against France*. Prussia, he writes, fears encirclement, and her position in Europe is best maintained 'by preserving Turkey, Poland, and the Baltic powers, independent and friendly to us'. Only thus could Great Britain check Russia and Austria from indulging ambitions inimical to Prussian security. Prussia by land and Great Britain by sea could have curbed Russia in 1791. Great Britain was bound, Pitt claims (in fact she was not), by the Reichenbach agreement to stay in arms until Russia backed down.

The Ottoman Empire, Pitt concluded, would have fared far worse at Russian hands if Great Britain had not attempted an intervention at all. The case for Ottoman integrity was not perhaps strong, but it could be asserted that it was always a British interest 'to prevent any material change in the relative situation of other powers – particularly naval powers – and to diminish the temptation to wars of ambition'. Russia was not yet a naval power, but possession of the Black Sea would quickly make her so, and valuable opportunities of commercial exploitation went with such possession. The Ottoman Empire stood in the way of such a development, and so it was logical for Great Britain to obstruct Russian ambition by supporting the Sultan.

In this document, Pitt looks backwards and forwards, backwards to the existing obligations of a diplomatic alignment soon to be disarranged by a new European situation, forwards to ill-defined, half-discernible difficulties for British foreign policy in the Near East. He hints, in a brief phrase, at Russian 'rivalship with our interests in the East Indies', a premonition rather than a considered forecast of the shape of things to come. A more complete clarification of Russian intentions in the area was delayed and obscured by the coming of the war with Napoleonic France, a war which itself seemed to underline the continuance of French supremacy at Constantinople. Pitt was dead before the conspiracy was concluded in 1807 at Tilsit, and it was several years more before his countrymen came to understand that the Eastern Question, besides being a kind of back door into the affairs of eastern Europe, was a front door into the affairs of western Asia.

NOTES

1. J. Holland Rose, *William Pitt and the National Revival* (London, 1911), p. 613; A. Sorel, *The Eastern Question in the Eighteenth Century: The Partition of Poland and the Treaty of Kainardji* (London, 1898); J.A.R. Marriott, *The Eastern Question: An Historical Study in European Diplomacy* (Oxford, 4th ed., 1947), pp. 160–2; W.E.H. Lecky, *A History of England in the Eighteenth Century* (London, 1883–90), v. ch. xix.
2. Fitzherbert to Carmarthen, 3 May 1787, FO 65/15; G. Soloveytchik, *Potemkin: A Picture of Catherine's Russia* (London, 1949), pp. 175–90; Rose, *Pitt*, p. 487; *Annual Register* for 1788, pp. 2–26.
3. Royal Historical Society: *Despatches from Paris, 1784–1790*, ed. O. Browning (London, 1909–10), ii. 20.
4. A. de Circourt, *Histoire de l'Action commune de la France et de l'Amérique pour l'indépendance des États-Unis* (Paris, 1876), iii. 330.
5. Lecky, *History of England*, v. 210–14; *Diaries and Correspondence of James Harris, First Earl of Malmesbury*, ed. earl of Malmesbury (London, 1844), i. 256, 345, 364, 373; *Correspondence of William Pitt, Earl of Chatham*, ed. W.S. Taylor and J.H. Pringle (London, 1838–40), iii. 30–7, 79, 174, iv. 298.
6. Malmesbury, *Diaries*, ii. 50–4.
7. A.C. Wood, *A History of the Levant Company* (Oxford, 1935), pp. 161–4.
8. *The Journals and Correspondence of William, Lord Auckland*, ed. G. Hogge (London, 1860–62), i. 217, 291, 301–3.
9. Carmarthen to Ainslie, 8 Jan. 1790, most secret, FO 78/11.
10. Ainslie to Carmarthen, 22 July 1788, FO 78/9; Dorset to Carmarthen, 19 May, 20 Nov., 18 Dec. 1788, *Despatches from Paris*, ii. 53, 116, 127. That of 20 Nov. specifies six vessels as being employed on the bi-monthly Smyrna–Marseilles postal service.
11. Ainslie to Carmarthen, 7 April 1789, FO 78/10. Ainslie's situation was quite common and Sir Robert Murray Keith, ambassador at Vienna from 1772 until 1792, recollected (*Memoirs and Correspondence [Official and Familiar] of Sir Robert Murray Keith, K.B. Envoy Extraordinary and Minister Plenipotentiary at the Court of Dresden, Copenhagen and Vienna from 1769 to 1792*, ed. Amelia Gillespie Smith [London, 1849], ii. 219–24) that he had received a reply from London about once to every 40 of his own dispatches.
12. Fraser to Carmarthen, 5 Oct. 1787, FO 65/15; *Despatches from Paris*, ii. 6–8.
13. Ainslie to Carmarthen, 10 Jan., 22 June 1788, FO 78/9; 7 April, 8 May 1789, FO 78/10. In the last dispatch he wrote: 'All the world accuses us of being the

authors of the present war, on which account our situation is not at all agreeable, or even safe.'
14. Ainslie to Carmarthen, 22 Feb. 1788, Carmarthen to Ainslie, 11 April 1788, FO 78/9; Ainslie to Carmarthen, 22 April 1789, FO 78/10; *Despatches from Paris*, ii. 13.
15. Ainslie to Carmarthen, 1 March 1788, FO 78/9.
16. Ainslie to Carmarthen, 10 Jan., 16 May, Carmarthen to Ainslie, 1 Feb., 16 May 1788, FO 78/9.
17. Soloveytchik, *Potemkim*, p. 201; Rose, *Pitt*, p. 504, quoting Catherine II's reaction to the Swedish attack: 'Since Mr. Pitt has chosen to drive me from Petersburgh, he must forgive me if I take refuge at Constantinople.'
18. Ewart to Carmarthen, 28 Jan., 11 Feb., 14 March, 28 May, 12 July 1789, FO 64/15. Carmarthen succeeded his father as fifth duke of Leeds on 23 March 1789.
19. Leeds to Ewart, 14 May 1788, FO 64/13.
20. Leeds to Ewart, 14 Sept. 1789, FO 64/16.
21. Ainslie to Carmarthen, 1 July, 26 Aug., 9 Sept. 1788, FO 78/9; Ainslie to Leeds, 3 and 4 Jan., 8 Oct. 1789, FO 78/10. On 25 May 1789, Ainslie wrote a private complaint to Ewart, who wrote in a reply of 1 July that Dietz had 'repeated orders to act in perfect concert' with Ainslie. Foreign Office complaints against Dietz are in dispatches to Ewart of 17 Feb., 11 March, 7 April 1789, FO 64/15.
22. Ainslie to Leeds, 8 Sept. 1789, FO 78/10.
23. Ainslie to Leeds, 8 and 22 March 1789, FO 78/10. In a further dispatch of 8 June, Ainslie said the Ottoman Empire would make peace with Russia soon unless Great Britain acted: 'they have fought our battles without fear or reward. And independent of their apprehension of being left in the lurch, they claim a right of making the most of their situation.' When Selim III returned thanks to the embassies for their congratulations on his accession, he sent flowers to the Swedish and Prussian legations but not to the French or British.
24. Ainslie to Leeds, 14 July 1789, FO 78/10.
25. Ewart to Leeds, 28 May 1789, FO 64/15.
26. Leeds to Ewart, 24 June 1789, FO 64/15; Lecky, *History of England*, v. 239.
27. Encl. by king of Prussia in Ewart to Leeds, 12 July 1789, FO 64/16.
28. Ewart to Leeds, 17 and 20 Oct., 3 and 28 Nov., 7 Dec. 1789, FO 64/16.
29. Catherine II to Vorontzov, 19 Dec. 1789, Leeds to Vorontzov, 9 Feb. 1790, Leeds to Whitworth, 2 April 1790, FO 78/12B; *Annual Register* for 1788, pp. 2–26.
30. Rose, *Pitt*, pp. 519ff.; Leeds to Keith, 16 and 30 March 1790, Add. MSS 35542, fos. 74, 99; Leeds to Keith, 30 March, Keith to Leeds, 24 April, 1 and 15 May 1790, FO 7/19.
31. Pitt to Ewart, 23 May 1790, FO 64/17; Ostermann to Vorontzov, 26 May 1790, FO 78/12B; Leeds to Keith, secret, 23 May 1790, FO 7/20.
32. Rose, *Pitt*, p. 529.
33. Keith, *Memoirs*, ii. 365.
34. Leeds to Whitworth, 19 Oct., 14 and 18 Nov. 1790, Whitworth to Leeds, 18 Nov. 1790, FO 65/19; Whitworth to Leeds, 10 Jan. 1791, FO 65/20.
35. Rose, *Pitt*, p. 597.
36. Ibid., p. 608.
37. Whitworth to Leeds, 8 Jan. 1790, FO 65/18; Leeds to Whitworth, 28 Dec. 1790, FO 65/19; Ewart to Pitt, 16 Nov. 1790, PRO 30/8/332; Whitworth to Keith,

23 March 1790, Add. MSS 35542, fo. 93; Auckland to Huber, 2 Feb. 1791, Add. MSS 34435, fo. 792.
38. Royal Historical Society: *Political Memoranda of Francis, Fifth Duke of Leeds*, ed. O. Browning (London, 1884), p. 148; Auckland, *Journals*, ii. 392.
39. Auckland, *Journals*, ii. 381.
40. Leeds to Jackson, 8 Jan., 27 March 1791, FO 64/20; Paul C. Webb, 'Sea Power in the Ochakov Affair of 1791', *International History Review*, ii (1980), 13–33.
41. Rose, *Pitt*, pp. 608–13.
42. Drake to Leeds, 12 March 1791, FO 22/13.
43. Auckland, *Journals*, ii. 392.
44. *Parliamentary History of England*, ed. W. Cobbett (London, 1820), xxix, 31–79, 'Debate on the King's Message'.
45. Auckland, *Journals*, ii. 385. Storey wrote to Auckland, on 6 May 1791, 'I assure you in and out of Parliament (and this is not to be understood as the ignorant account of an interested party), there is not a word urged by way of argument for the Russian war . . . If keeping his word with Prussia would have drawn him into a scrape, opposition has relieved him [Pitt] from it.'
46. *Parliamentary History*, xxix. 52.
47. Leeds to Pitt, 9 April 1791, PRO 30/8/151.
48. Rose, *Pitt*, p. 617.
49. *Parliamentary History*, xxix, 'Grey's Motion respecting Preparations for a War with Russia', p. 164; 'Baker's Motion respecting the Armament against Russia', p. 218; 'Grenville's Motion against any Interference in the War between Russia and the Porte', p. 617; 'Fitzwilliam's Motion against War with Russia', p. 434.
50. Peace delegations came to Westminster from Manchester, Norwich, and the West Riding. Their general case was that imports from Russia averaged £1,500,000 per annum, and exports to Russia, £400,000 per annum. In spite of the adverse trade balance, Fitzwilliam moved in the House of Lords on 9 May 'to beseech His Majesty not to hazard the advantages of such friendly intercourse and the inestimable blessing of peace . . . for the purpose of effecting an arrangement respecting Oczakov, and the uncultivated districts adjacent'. This exposed the opposition to the Urquhartian retort, used by Lord Stanley, in the debate on Grey's motion, that Russia needed British gold to stabilize her note issue. Riga hemp, Great Britain's chief Baltic import, should be bought direct from Poland, and not through Russian agency.
51. *Parliamentary History*, xxix. 849.
52. M.S. Anderson, *Britain's Discovery of Russia, 1553–1815* (London, 1958), notably ch. 6.
53. Privy council for trade to FO, 19 Oct. 1791, FO 78/12A.
54. PRO 30/8/195, fos. 49–55.

CHAPTER II

Robert Adair's Mission to St Petersburg

No consistent editorial pressure was brought against nineteenth-century contributors to the *Dictionary of National Biography*, either to suppress important truths or provide statements merely cosmetic, but as there were other publications in which controversial careers could be discussed, contributors commonly stressed the established achievements of the distinguished departed and glossed a good deal of the rest. As a result, the *DNB* is useful, but often lacks savour. A case in point is the entry on Robert Adair, which is at its most reticent and tantalizing in a passage which says of this kinsman of Charles James Fox: 'When the French revolution broke out, he visited Berlin, Vienna, and St. Petersburg, to study its effects on foreign states . . . . Some of his political opponents believed that he had been despatched by Fox to Russia to thwart the policy of Mr. Pitt.' Indeed they did. In fact, Adair himself was more forthcoming than this, though always under pressure, and never forthcoming enough. Until his death in 1855 he remained scandalously famous for something he was widely believed to have done in 1791, and in the end the believers included many more people than just 'some of his political opponents'.[1]

Adair was the son of the sergeant-surgeon to George III and Lady Caroline Keppel. Had Fox been appointed foreign secretary in 1788, Adair, then only 25, would have become his under-secretary, and it would have been an unwise appointment. Not that Adair was a fool. On the contrary, the countess of Bessborough recalled that 'Bob Adair, tho' not a very pleasant, is certainly a well inform'd, and rather a clever man, a good deal above the common run'.[2] The trouble was that, at least since George Canning's rhyming flippancies over his love affairs at Göttingen University, Adair's personal life and opinions were forever becoming public. He got drunk easily and on the occasion of an alcoholic row with Richard Brinsley Sheridan, Lady Bessborough, whom he fascinated, pointedly said, 'Adair had truth and honour on his side, but alas! they were in bad hands.' Not that it mattered this time: Sheridan fell fast asleep.[3] But there were other occasions, like the one where we find Lady Bessborough (who else?) reading Adair's love letters to Lady Melbourne, amiably supplied by the latter.[4] Adair's wife, Angélique, was a subject of gossip too: daughter of a French marquis executed during the Revolution, she was thought, widely and accurately, to have curbed her husband's prospects as a career diplomat.[5] Above all else, however, it was Adair's exercise in unauthorized diplomacy at the court of Catherine II in 1791, conducted behind the backs of the Tory administration's accredited diplomats there, which made him ever after a marked man in British society. Edmund Burke went so far as to assert that, if Adair was not exactly guilty of high treason, his was at least 'a most unconstitutional act, and a high treasonable misdemeanour'.[6] The charge was never proven in Adair's lifetime. Was he as innocent as he always claimed, or as guilty as his critics said? It is intended here to describe first Adair's long rearguard action in obfuscation, then to disclose what he was actually hiding. Lady Bessborough, at least, would have liked to know.

In March 1793, Burke drafted his famous letter, signed also by almost a score of his associates, separating themselves from the Whig Club and the leadership of Charles James Fox.[7] They were unable any longer to support 'the tendency of the principal measures which Mr. Fox had proposed or supported at the present period', since they were 'detrimental to the interests of Great Britain' and increased 'the danger with which the independence of Europe, and the happiness of the whole civilized world are threatened'. Fox's tolerance of developments in France was positively unpatriotic. In these charges, Adair was not mentioned by name, but a radical journalist, William Augustus Miles, in a pamphlet supporting Burke, brought Adair's visit to Russia in 1791 into the open for the first time, making it out to be one of Fox's unpatriotic measures.[8] Actually, Miles had no authentic information: he was simply repeating rumour. In 1797, however, a long private letter from Burke addressed to the duke of Portland found its unauthorized way into the London dailies, and here the former ally of Fox said his confidence in the great Whig leader had been not merely damaged, but 'totally destroyed', as early as 1791 when Fox 'thought proper to send Mr. Adair, as his representative, and with his cypher, to St. Petersburg, there to frustrate the objects for which the minister from the crown [Sir Charles Whitworth] was authorized to treat'. Adair 'succeeded in this his design and did actually frustrate the king's minister.' It was this behaviour, Burke claimed, which would surely have been high treason if Great Britain and Russia had come to blows in 1791, and which remained 'a most unconstitutional act, and a high treasonable misdemeanour'.[9] By authorizing a secret mission behind his colleagues' backs, Fox had compromised the good names of the latter, beginning the rift which, by 1797, had become an unbridgeable gulf.

Adair came forward and defended himself, but not very well. 'Mr. Adair', the bedridden and dying Burke was told in February 1797, 'has written a foolish letter in some of the papers', in which 'the denial is very equivocal'.[10] It certainly was. Guessing that Burke's letter to Portland had been printed without the former's permission, Adair affected to believe Burke was not its author at all. The charge against him, he wrote, was not new, but had in the past come 'always from quarters beneath my notice'. He declared that 'if any better sentiment than curiosity can be gratified by my justification, I am ready to enter upon it'. But there Adair stopped, and many readers probably took his reticence as a sign of guilt. If he genuinely needed Burke to acknowledge the authenticity of the letter to Portland, then he had but a short time to wait, and even before that Miles, who quite properly saw himself as the quarter beneath Adair's notice, intervened once more. A friend told Burke that Adair had raised 'a sleeping hornet': however, the hornet in actuality only buzzed loudly, but lacked a fatal sting. Miles repeated what he had said four years before, with a little extra footnoting from Burke's recent letter to Portland. Adair was guilty, Miles wrote, of obstructing Pitt's foreign policy, having gone to Russia clandestinely for that purpose, and with Fox's permission.[11] The pressure on Adair to answer was intensified when Burke, or his executors, affirmed the ailing politician's authorship of the letter to Portland, as published in *The Times*, by issuing it in pamphlet form, amplified with 'fifty-four articles of impeachment against the Rt. Hon. C.J. Fox'.[12] In the very first article, Adair was indicted on the now familiar charges, but he continued to sit tight. There was no documentary evidence against him yet, and for 30 years his defence was that he had nothing material to answer. His verbal response to inquisitions was that he went to Russia of his own accord in 1791, was never Fox's agent while there, that he never behaved improperly while in St Petersburg, and that he never even discussed his visit with Fox on his return. But the mask began to slip a little in 1821 – 30 years after the visit to Russia – when George Tomline, bishop of Winchester and once Pitt's private tutor, repeated the hoary charges in his *Memoirs of the Life of William Pitt*, adding that the charges were 'attested by authentic documents among Mr. Pitt's papers'.[13]

Adair's generation-long complacency was jolted by this reference to surviving documents, for the passage of time had increasingly reassured him that nothing incriminating existed. Tomline's book had sold well, and a second edition was already in the press: might it be more explicit in its revelations than the first? Adair wrote to Tomline, privately and in haste,[14] with an outward defiance, accusing him of blaming the failure of Pitt's Russian diplomacy on Fox and Adair himself with no more evidence than 'a paper drawn up by Mr. Burke, addressed secretly by him to the heads of the Whig party in 1793, surreptitiously published by a bookseller in 1797, and declared afterwards by Mr. Burke himself to have been written in anger'.

This was a considerable corruption of the facts, and either Adair knew it was or his memory was beginning to desert him. But, clearly, he was worried, and instead of inducing a greater caution in him, the possibility that the 'authentic documents' in Tomline's custody might include some of his own letters to Fox led him to become vastly communicative, and to admit the earlier existence of at least one of these, for the first time. For 30 years previously he had never admitted to any correspondence with Fox from Russia. Also, instead of staying with his plain claim to have done no wrong in St Petersburg, he was tempted into an elaboration which hardly exculpated him. 'Your Lordship', he went on, 'will not expect me to reveal by what means I obtained, when I got there, a knowledge of events as they were passing, nor to name or designate the persons with whom I conversed.' It was true that he had 'expressed much exultation' at the diplomatic failures of Sir Charles Whitworth and the special envoy sent out by Pitt, Robert Fawkener, but the sentiment was communicated only in a private letter to Fox, and 'while I have been informed that this letter was opened and read previous to its delivery' to Fox, 'I will not believe it . . . I gave it [for posting in England] to an old schoolfellow whom I found at St. Petersburg.' Adair was obviously fishing to discover whether Tomline had this letter, hoping to hear in reply that he had not. But Tomline knew his man, and by maintaining a tantalizing silence, emboldened Adair to write yet again[15] after the lapse of six days: 'Am I to understand from your silence that you have no intention of noticing its [his first letter's] comments?' 'Dr. Parr', a more sympathetic and accurate author than Tomline, he claimed, had years ago confuted 'Mr. Burke's reasoning' in a way 'that admits of no answer'.

Adair's two letters are dated 23 and 29 May 1821, and Tomline suddenly descended on him with unexpected vigour in one of 2 June, going through his points in sequence.[16] Burke had indeed confessed to writing impetuously in 1797, but he never withdrew his charges against Adair or Fox, and he 'persevered in considering his statement true and accurate' to the end of his life. Responding to Adair's passing remarks that he had decided on the Russian visit independently without consulting Fox, Tomline declared that the material facts were that Adair *had* gone and *had* taken Fox's cypher. As for Adair's refusal to specify the people he consulted in Russia, 'they must have been the empress's ministers'. In fact, Tomline went on, Adair had now as good as admitted the charges against him. His letter to the *Morning Chronicle* in 1797 had promised a self-exoneration but did not constitute one: he 'never did reply'. As for the critical passage to which Adair had alluded in Parr's book, Tomline had taken the trouble to look it up and, far from confuting Burke, Parr had merely said: 'I am not enough acquainted with the circumstances of this transaction, either to justify or condemn the whole of it.' On the point that mattered most to Adair, Tomline refused to ease his anxiety: he would not say upon what documents in the Pitt papers the charges against Adair and his erstwhile chief rested. Nor would he hold up his second edition.

Adair could not resist replying.[17] Unhappy about Tomline's persistent reference to him as carrying Fox's cypher, he claimed a need to disguise the names of people who 'for even talking on political subjects with me, might be punished'. The cypher had never been used except upon 'a matter relating to the eventual conduct of another court', hardly an illuminating phrase, though it was clearly Adair's intention to deny that Catherine II's ministers had spoken to him with her knowledge. He had been but a fly on the wall, an interested listener, but not an accomplice in Whitworth's humiliation and defeat. Determined to end on a stirring note, Adair concluded with the impolite accusation that the distinguished prelate had chosen, after 'sitting snug on the old forsaken nest, to strut forth after an incubation period of fifteen years [since Pitt's death in 1806] at the head of your own sickly brood of constructive treasons, and vex, with your querulous cackle, the quiet of the dead and the patience of the living'.[18]

The final round of this particular correspondence came in 1822, when Tomline gratefully surrendered the task of answering the evasive and self-righteous Adair to a lawyer friend, who promptly published Adair's letters, and the responses to them – Tomline's and the lawyer's own – in yet another pamphlet, *A Reply to the Charges of Robert Adair Esq. against the Bishop of Winchester.*[19] The pamphlet began with an exquisite piece of cat-and-mouse torture by the lawyer himself. 'Do you [Adair] deny that his lordship has the documents to which he refers? No, Sir; in no one sentence . . . do you question the existence of such documents – you only dare his lordship to produce them. And why do you thus dare him?' Because, the lawyer says, Adair *knows* Tomline will not produce them. What has Tomline written in his book? 'I shall transcribe Mr. Burke's account . . . which I find attested by authentic documents among Mr. Pitt's papers.' That would be sufficient for the public. It must content Adair too. The rest of the attack was very sharp. Would Catherine II's ministers have taken the least notice of Adair had he not been Fox's agent? Had he not also said, in one sentence to Tomline, and *à propos* the Russian reply to Whitworth and Robert Fawkener, that he can 'by no means consider [that reply] blameable'? Then there had been the admission of 'exultation'. 'Exultation, Sir, arises from the attainment of an object after a contest.' The public would never need to see the data withheld in the Pitt papers: Adair had made that data superfluous by incriminating himself.

Adair never surrendered, and drew the usual advantages from

outliving his critics. We find him in 1842, 50 years after the disputed visit to Russia, telling a correspondent[20] why he had not answered the *Reply to the Charges* pamphlet, or Tomline's book, in 1822. 'I called upon him . . . in a language as strong as it was proper to address to his lordship, to produce his documents. That he never did.' To the same correspondent Adair wrote that he could still recall Fox's saying to him, 'Well, if you are determined to go, send us all the news'. Adair went on: 'I renew my most solemn declaration that I, and I alone, was the author, contriver – plotter, – call it what you will – of that journey.' He had gone to St Petersburg to discuss the Netherlands, the balance of power, and *a possible treaty with Russia*, and could not have subverted Pitt's anti-Russian stance as this had been given up before Adair even left Great Britain. Nor had he undermined the British ambassador, being quite unaware of the nature of the ambassador's instructions.

Nagging doubts remain.[21] Adair's parade of piety stirs the suspicions it attempted to allay. In another context, he says he went to Russia because there was a chance he would soon be in power at the Foreign Office. And if the visit to Russia was quite informal, why did he go, as we know he did, armed with letters of introduction from Count Vorontzov, the Russian ambassador at London, and stay at the Russian legation in Vienna, not the British embassy, on his journey out? Does a private citizen travel so far, to discuss matters so momentous as a possible treaty, behind the back of Catherine II (as he assured Tomline) who would eventually have to sign it, without consulting the government in power in London, and with no important personal contacts in prospect at his destination? Is it credible that Adair did not even talk to Fox on his return about the Russian visit, although we now know from other sources that Catherine II gave him specific messages for Fox? Above all, when the Whig leader gave him a cypher, as Burke originally charged and Adair admitted to Tomline only many years later – presumably to 'send all the news' – why did Adair not use it?[22] As we have seen, he admitted to one letter to Fox, which had, he knew, gone astray. 'I have searched in vain among my papers', he writes in 1842, 'for a copy of the letter, supposed to have been intercepted, which I wrote to Mr. Fox from Petersburg in 1791. I can find nothing on the subject.'[23] The man who can remember being asked by Fox to 'send all the news' seemingly could not remember what news he actually sent.

It is the present writer's suggestion that Adair recalled perfectly well what he wrote to Fox in 1791, and knew it incriminated both of them. Worst of all, he knew Fox never got the letter, heard that it had been intercepted, and so dared not fabricate its contents when Burke first accused him of a 'treasonable misdemeanour', or in the many following years of the controversy, in case the original were produced. In 1822, Adair was desperately anxious to know if the alleged 'authentic documents' included his letter, and challenged Tomline to produce it, no doubt hoping that it had been lost a second time, and permanently. The evidence against Adair was never produced, but we know it existed because it still does. Instead of the one letter, to which alone Adair admitted, he actually wrote four from St Petersburg.[24] Pitt indeed had them, locked in a drawer, and the under-secretary at the Foreign Office, James Bland Burges, took copies of them in 1791 and later showed them to Lord Grenville, when the latter replaced the duke of Leeds as foreign secretary. In 1822, Tomline still held the originals, found in Pitt's locked drawer, or at least Bland Burges's copies. They allow us to reconstruct Adair's behaviour while in Russia, which Tomline chose not to write about in detail in his *Memoirs*, and to judge the accuracy of Burke's original charge against 'Fox's Goose', as George Canning called Adair.

★ ★ ★

In the spring of 1788, Catherine II and Joseph II of Austria went to war with Sultan Abdulhamid I of the Ottoman Empire, the former to erect a Christian kingdom in the Danubian principalities, the latter to annex part of Wallachia. At first, the British government declared its 'perfect neutrality': 'our general wish is to take no part.' Had the Pitt government stayed with this decision, the prime minister would have avoided what he was soon to call 'the greatest mortification' of his career.[25] Unfortunately, Great Britain signed the defensive Triple Alliance with Holland and Prussia that same year, and the Prussian foreign minister, Count Hertzberg, chagrined that his country's associates in the first partition of Poland should have embarked on a new adventure without Prussia, decided that the Triple Alliance would be a suitable diplomatic instrument for forcing them to purchase Berlin's compliance. Pitt sensibly responded to the pleadings of his headstrong representative at Berlin, Joseph Ewart, that an offensive version of the Triple Alliance was 'an object by no means in our view', and in 1789 reiterated that Great Britain was not 'in any degree bound to support a system of an offensive nature'. Prussia would have to pull her *desiderata*, the Polish city of Thorn and the port of Danzig, out of the fire for herself. A turn in the Eastern situation favoured this cautious style. Early in 1790, Joseph II died, obliging Catherine II to drop her largest plans once it became obvious to her that Austria was backing out of the war. On the other hand, this very act of self-denial determined Catherine II to hold on at least to Bessarabia, which she had occupied for the previous two years. She therefore refused Anglo-Prussian offers of mediation made in September and December 1790 unless they brought her Bessarabia and its obscure citadel, the town of Ochakov.[26]

It was now, after two years of exemplary discretion, that Pitt foolishly listened to the belligerent Ewart, and the wiser heads of the diplomatic corps watched aghast as their chief, responding to Prussia's demand for a firmer line, personally drafted an ultimatum to Russia, demanding the restitution of all Ottoman losses over the previous three years. The foreign secretary, the duke of Leeds, was excluded from Pitt's private meetings with the returned Ewart and, unsure 'whether I am to be dismissed [or] driven to resign', chose the latter course. On 28 March 1791, the House of Commons was invited to increase the naval strength of Great Britain to lend weight to the ultimatum. By 30 March, Pitt recognized he had lost 'a very violent' debate. His cabinet was utterly demoralized, the back-benchers were in rebellion, and in early May a special envoy, Robert Fawkener, had to be sent in haste to Russia to withdraw the ultimatum sent so impetuously on 27 March.[27] Fox told Vorontzov that Pitt would soon cut his losses and desist from any claims whatever. This was quite true. Lord Grenville, succeeding Leeds at the Foreign Office, began his regime by assuring the Muscovy Company that it was safe for its summer convoy to sail for the Baltic.[28] The debate ran on a while longer, but Pitt dropped out of it after 30 March and it is hard to know what he meant in telling Ewart, 'all my efforts to make a majority of the House of Commons understand the subject have been fruitless'.[29] The seeming solicitude for the Ottomans was universally proclaimed absurd: Pitt, for his part, admitted he could never have held his party together by telling the simple truth, that he had supported Prussian claims in the Baltic in order to hold the Triple Alliance together.

In the parlance of today, the ambassador in Russia, Sir Charles Whitworth, was a hawk, like Ewart. He wanted more than an ultimatum; he wanted a war. Fawkener, sent to retrieve the ultimatum in May, was a dove. Adair followed Fawkener to Russia within a few days, claiming, as we have seen, that Pitt had been defeated already, and that he knew nothing of Fawkener's instructions. His departure from England caused great indignation at the Foreign Office. Grenville asked Lord Auckland, 'Is not the idea of ministers from Opposition to the different courts of Europe a new one in the country? I never heard it before.'[30] Nathaniel Wraxall, quite simply, thought it was Fox, not Adair, who should be impeached.[31] Disgraceful though Fox's behaviour was deemed to be, the blame for Adair's mission was sometimes placed on someone else. 'I am persuaded', Grenville wrote, that the Russian ambassador 'suggested the idea of employing Mr. Adair as an envoy from Mr. Fox to the empress.'[32] It does not follow from this that St Petersburg knew *exactly* why Adair was coming, and the British secretary of embassy there, William Lindsay, was asked by senior Russian statesmen about Adair before the latter's arrival, about 'his character, age, connections, etc.', and in particular 'if he was not nearly related to Mr. Fox'. Another opinion concerning Adair's political stature in England was probably supplied to the vice-chancellor, Count Ostermann, by Prince Galitzin, the Russian ambassador at Vienna, with whom Adair lodged on his eastward journey.[33] Whitworth and Fawkener were in consternation, unwilling to believe 'Englishmen so far capable of forgetting their duty', yet having no alternative explanation for Adair's impressive reception at Tsarskoe Selo than that he represented the Opposition's views and had come to press them.

Whitworth's annoyance and humiliation are understandable. Having pressed Pitt successfully to send Catherine II an ultimatum, he was never given a chance by the Russians to present it. He found himself required instead to join Pitt's special emissary, Fawkener, in negotiating a British retreat. In the light of Pitt's parliamentary defeat, any threat of force was now to be avoided. In his very first interview with Ostermann, Fawkener said that he came to make peace on terms acceptable to Catherine II and necessary to the peace of Europe. Small wonder that Prince Potemkin was genuinely delighted to meet Fawkener, saying Anglo-Russian misunderstandings could now be liquidated. In a cypher message to Grenville, written only two days after his arrival, Fawkener reported Potemkin's high fettle, his wish to hang the Ottoman grand vizier on the nearest tree, and his refusal to take to his royal mistress any proposal involving the surrender of Ochakov. When the Danube was the battle-line, why should Catherine II routinely surrender strong points over 100 miles behind it?

The region at issue between the British supplicants and the Russian court was a thinly populated strip of land, 100 miles wide, between the Bug (the existing frontier) and the Dniester further south. Ochakov was on the west (right) bank of the Bug estuary, Odessa on the east (left) bank of the Dniester. Both, therefore, lay in the debated region. Fawkener's proposals, in descending order of hopefulness,[34] were that Russia would make peace on the basis of the *status quo* which would enable the Ottoman Empire to keep both towns; that the Bug–Dniester region should become a demilitarized buffer zone between Russians and Ottomans; that Russia should have Ochakov and 'its district' but no more; that Russia should obtain the Bug–Dniester region in full sovereignty but not repair its defences (an obvious contradiction); that Russia should have the region and do what she liked with it but leave the Ottoman forts on the east (left) bank of the Dniester near Odessa in Ottoman hands; lastly and worst of all, that everything to the Dniester should be surrendered to Russia, the Sultan retaining only use of the Dniester itself for Ottoman and other shipping. This last arrangement was the only one that Catherine II ever intended to consider, and the two British delegates, after two months of ineffective pleading, were left empty-handed. Even in Russian circles, Lindsay said, Catherine II's ostentatious preference for her unofficial visitor over his official colleagues caused 'very general astonishment', the more so as Fawkener had once served in her army in a Danubian campaign.[35] Fairly naturally, the embassy people blamed Adair excessively for their own failures. And they revenged themselves on him in an interesting fashion.[36]

Adair was a great talker, and his reception at the court of Russia flattered him enormously. More dangerous still, he decided to write to England, entrusting his letters to the diplomatic bag of his own embassy. He ought to have known that, in that age, the British Post Office employed gentlemen known as 'official openers of the foreign correspondence', and that all private letters sent by diplomatic bag were liable to be examined and copied. In July, when his two-month stay at St Petersburg was half over, and one week after Fawkener's offer of good offices between Russia and the Ottoman Empire had been finally and brusquely brushed aside on the 20th, Adair posted four letters which never reached their destinations, one dated 27 July to a Mrs Mary Benwell,[37] one dated 28 July to his own bankers, Messrs Ransome, Moreland and Hammersley, and two to Charles James Fox, dated 21 and 28 July. Ironically, he wrote them in haste because Lindsay told him a post-bag was about to be dispatched to England, and Adair knew from Russian sources that the bag would contain Fawkener's final dispatches to London before that envoy set out for home himself. Adair was determined that Pitt should not be able to minimize Fawkener's defeat in Parliament: but his plan went astray. Once handed in at the embassy, his letters were opened and examined by Whitworth, Fawkener, and Lindsay, and declared by the last to be 'a tissue of ignorance, wickedness and indiscretion'. They also showed that Fox was 'laughed at and duped by Russia; fair words, civility and cajolery is all he ever got . . . and as they [the Russians] know he would make even the most important sacrifices to obtain these . . . they have of course not failed to lavish them on his friend and relation, Mr. Adair'. After weeks of mixing in Russian society, and dining with Catherine II, Potemkin, and other dignitaries of the court, Adair was coming home with a diamond ring for himself, praise for Burke's pamphlet on the French Revolution, and an assurance for Fox that Catherine II awaited his bust in order to set it in her gallery between Cicero and Demosthenes. Adair's intercepted letters were carried to Pitt, delivered personally by Lindsay.[38]

The letter to Mary Benwell reported accurately that Pitt's emissary had 'given way in all the material points, and the empress is now at liberty to make peace on the terms she has constantly offered the Turks'.[39] Pitt would not act against Russia 'unless Prussia forces him to it', but of this the chances were extremely small and Adair speculated that Lindsay – who 'may be safely entrusted [!]' – was coming home for orders from Pitt on how the final submission of Great Britain was to be conducted, by a document or a silence. The Ottomans, left to themselves, might capitulate or fight: it hardly mattered which. Pitt would need watching for a time. He would perhaps try to avoid standing down the fleet, as a means of keeping pressure on Catherine II. 'I know so thoroughly what sort of man Pitt is, that I am prepared for some trick of his.' Mrs Benwell was told to visit two banking houses, Beckford's and Cocker's, to assure them that there would be no war, and this passage of the letter was thought by Lindsay to show Adair was stock-jobbing.

The second letter, addressed to the banking house of Ransome's, was also intended to show that the war scare was effectively over. 'If you wish to have the terms, I can only refer you to the original demands of the empress, which have been in every respect acceded to as the *basis of a peace to be proposed to the Turks*.' The latter might not accept the terms, but that would not affect the British attitude:

> Our court has consented unequivocally that Russia shall keep the whole of the territory between the Bug and the Dniester and fortify Oczakov and any other part of it she likes – which is exactly what she demanded, and Russia consents to the free navigation of the Dniester, which she never thought of restraining . . . There will be no convention, the empress absolutely refusing to hear of Mr. Fawkener as a mediator, negotiator or in any other capacity than as a person sent to explain the amicable sentiments of Great Britain. In short, she has carried her point with a very high hand indeed.

This information was absolutely accurate and as Adair did not get it from his fellow countrymen at the British embassy, he can have got it only from his Russian hosts. His reference to the capitulation of 'our court' implies that the Russians also told or showed him details of Fawkener's final, unsuccessful, representations. Similarly, in the passage where he informs Ransome's that 'there will be no convention' because of Catherine II's 'absolutely refusing' to hear of Fawkener as 'a mediator, negotiator or in any other capacity', Adair seems, consciously or subconsciously, to be answering Fawkener's perplexed enquiry of Grenville, penned only a few days before Adair's own letter, asking if he was to conclude his special mission with any statement to the Russians, or simply with a silent withdrawal, his tail between his legs. Just in case Lindsay returned with some new diplomatic expedient of Pitt's, Adair also decided he would stay in Russia for as long as Fawkener did, another hint that he expected to be shown the written details of any further British approach.

Adair incriminated himself most of all in the two letters to Fox. Here, he leaves no doubt whatever but that he was privy to the details of Fawkener's negotiation in an entirely improper way. With regard to one of Fawkener's official papers sent in to Ostermann, he told Fox it was 'one of the most curious papers I ever saw'. He describes Fawkener as showing 'a determination to propose terms and modifications only for the purpose of conceding them'. He admits that he saw the final Russian reply to Fawkener before it was sent to the latter, and he describes Fawkener's response to it as a document of 'abject gratitude', in which Pitt's emissary declared his relief that Russia had consented to the free navigation of the Dniester as the British government had always attached much importance to this point. This statement mystified and amused the Russians who, according to Adair, had never intended to hinder navigation on the Dniester, but 'it will do well for the debates' in Parliament: Pitt would pretend he demanded and obtained this concession. Most valuable of all, perhaps, was Fawkener's assurance that the Ottomans were to be left either to accept Catherine II's terms or risk 'the events of war'.[40] This cleared Catherine II's – and Fox's – lingering doubts that Pitt might, at the last moment, produce a joint demand in collaboration with Prussia. And it allowed Adair to give first news of the fact to his bankers, and of Pitt's effective capitulation to Fox. To the very end, Catherine II had refused British mediation, or interference in any form.

There is surely little doubt that Adair, besides being shown Fawkener's communications to the Russian government, was consulted over the framing of the replies. Furthermore, he became involved in quite improper discussions about the course of British foreign policy whenever Fox should come to power. Catherine II was unhappy about Fox's republican predilections, which were in sharp contrast to her own readiness to give asylum to any members of the French nobility who could reach her territories, but she was unhappier still that Pitt might take advantage of the French Revolution to annex French colonies – 'West India Islands and God knows what' as Adair explained to Fox. Adair tried to soothe his hosts, he wrote, by saying the Opposition would resist Pitt in this matter, while Fox himself would have no such designs for Great Britain.

Whitworth and Fawkener were nettled by Adair's behaviour and letters, and chagrined by what they saw as his success.[41] That Adair was ready to undermine them to the end the letters make clear: his remark that he would not leave Russia until after Fawkener left surely bears no other construction. But it would be an exaggeration to imagine that Whitworth and Fawkener had any chance of success, whether Adair was at the Russian court or not. Catherine II was determined to have the Bug–Dniester confluence. Adair's intervention may have had one material effect, namely, in having the British special envoy sent away completely empty-handed. Had Baron von der Goltz, the Prussian envoy, and the British representatives stood firmly shoulder to shoulder, they just might have maintained an Ottoman presence on the east (left) bank of the Dniester. This is what Goltz was ordered to demand, at least initially. But the Prussians were themselves putting out feelers to St Petersburg, which confirmed Adair's belief that an Anglo-Prussian conjuction was not to be feared. The experience braced Catherine II with the confidence to reject Fawkener and plan the more complete liquidation of Poland, which soon followed on the heels of the Ochakov fiasco and Great Britain's involvement in war with revolutionary France.

It was in 1797, when Burke's *Observations* was published, and William Augustus Miles attacked Adair a second time, that the under-secretary at the Foreign Office, Bland Burges, remembered the intercepted letters from St Petersburg. Pitt kept the originals: 'he locked them up in one of his own boxes; since which time I have not seen them.'[42] But there was also an account by Lindsay based on the originals, drawn up in 1791 at Bland Burges's own request by the returned secretary of embassy, an account which quoted the incriminating letters in full. Burges thought Lord Grenville, on succeeding the duke of Leeds, would like to see this account: 'It has never been out of my hands or seen by anyone . . . and as it is undoubtedly authentic I think it right that your Lordship should have it.'

In sum, Adair's protestations of innocence concerning his Russian visit of 1791 are unacceptable. He declared he had gone to

Russia in a private capacity to discuss the Netherlands, the balance of power, and a possible treaty. The propriety of these confessed activities, whether they took place or not, can be left for the moment. Adair lies when he states that he did not know the British embassy's instructions and so could not have undermined them: his Russian hosts showed him official British communications which a man of more fastidious conduct would have refused to receive, or read, on the ground that a private citizen was not supposed to be privy to the king's business. Furthermore, the circumstantial evidence is strong that Adair helped shape the replies to these communications, unless we are to believe that the Russians showed him the record of these dealings with Fawkener and Whitworth without taking his opinion on them, an unlikely procedure. Whether or not Adair was Fox's chosen agent is unprovable: he says the visit to Russia was his own idea, but agrees that Fox asked for 'all the news'. He wrote more to Fox than he admits or remembers. That Adair was stock-jobbing is fairly certain from the letters to Mary Benwell and Messrs Ransome. By attempting to send letters to Fox by diplomatic bag, he was trying to provide inside information, to which he ought not to have been privy, to the leader of the parliamentary Opposition.

Was Adair also guilty in the way his critics believed, that is, of 'a most unconstitutional act' or a 'high treasonable misdemeanour'? It is necessary, in answering, to recall that he was a Member of Parliament, unable to divest himself of that status by the mere statement that he travelled as a private citizen. On the contrary, his Russian hosts attached special importance to his supposed relationship with Fox, and he accepted the honours bestowed on a semi-official guest. To an extent which would not have applied in the case of a truly private, apolitical visitor, there were also constitutional niceties to be observed by Adair. Even had he restricted himself, as he untruthfully said he did, to discussing the Netherlands, the balance of power, and a future treaty, it would have been constitutionally improper to make a commitment on behalf of a party not yet in power, and very close to impropriety even to have discussed such matters with Russian ministers acting in their official capacities. As it was, he definitely intervened in the diplomatic process between the British embassy at St Petersburg and the Russian government, avoiding the embassy officials and talking only with Russians. This was certainly unconstitutional. Was it a 'treasonable misdemeanour'? Treason means, among other things, violation by a subject of his allegiance to his country through some act of betrayal. Clearly, Adair's meddling was not 'high' treason and did not seriously endanger the national interest, but he did give active support to the interests of a foreign power. On the evidence, he could have been charged with a 'treasonable misdemeanour', as it is the duly appointed ministers of state alone who decide, in Cabinet, what the national interest is and how it shall be expressed through the channels of diplomacy.

NOTES

1. *Dictionary of National Biography*, 'Robert Adair'.
2. Lady Bessborough to Granville Leveson-Gower, Sept. 1798, in *Lord Granville Leveson-Gower: Private Correspondence, 1781 to 1821*, ed. Castalia, Countess Granville (London, 1916), i. 222.
3. Lady Bessborough to Leveson-Gower, 11 Sept. 1803, ibid., i. 432.
4. Ibid., i. 356.
5. Née Gabrielle, daughter of the Marquis d'Hazincourt. Lady Bessborough says obscurely that Adair went as ambassador to Austria in 1805 to be 'quitte de sa femme', but that he would soon be replaced as his wife had turned up unexpectedly at the Austrian capital, making his further stay at that post impossible (ibid., ii. 196, 288).
6. See Burke's 'Observations on the Conduct of the Minority', in *Works of the Right Hon. Edmund Burke* (London, 1854–89), iii. 469–510.
7. It appeared in, for instance, *The Morning Post*, 6 March 1793; it is reproduced in *Correspondence of Edmund Burke*, ed. T.W. Copeland *et al.* (Cambridge and Chicago, 1958–78), vii. 353.
8. W.A. Miles, *Conduct of France towards Great Britain Examined* (1793); idem, *Authentic Correspondence with M. Le Brun, the French Minister and Others, to Feb. 1793 Inclusive* (London, 1796).
9. 'Observations', in *Works of Burke*, iii. 472. *The Times*, 13 Feb. 1799, gave three full columns to publishing the 'Observations'. Next day, the 14th, *The Times* editorial observed that the Opposition papers were up in arms about the 'Observations', calling it 'a wilful misrepresentation of a common incident'. The editorial invited Fox, not Adair, to clarify the episode of 1791.
10. See *The Morning Chronicle*, 15 Feb. 1797, and *The Public Advertiser*, 16 Feb. 1797; French Laurence to Edmund Burke, 20 Feb. 1797, in Burke, *Correspondence*, xi. 248.
11. See *The Times*, 20 Feb. 1797.
12. E. Burke, *Letter . . . to his Grace the Duke of Portland on the Conduct of the Minority in Parliament; Containing 54 Articles of Impeachment against the Rt. Hon. C.J. Fox* (1779).
13. G. Tomline, *Memoirs of the Life of William Pitt* (London, 1821), ii. 445–7.
14. R. Adair, *Two Letters . . . to the Bishop of Winchester, in Answer to the Charge of a High Treasonable Misdemeanour* (1821), first letter, 23 May 1821.

15. Ibid., second letter, 29 May 1821.
16. Ibid., bishop of Winchester's reply, 2 June 1821.
17. Ibid., undated, pp. 37 ff.
18. Ibid., undated, p. 70.
19. [Anon.,] *A Reply to the Charges of Robert Adair Esq. against the Bishop of Winchester in Consequence of a Passage Contained in His Lordship's Memoirs of the Rt. Hon. W. Pitt* (1821), especially pp. 19, 23, 26, 29, 30, 36, 37, 39, 42, 45, 52. The pamphlet is written as from Lincoln's Inn Fields, 10 July 1821.
20. Adair to Allen, 2 Feb. 1842, in *Memorials and Correspondence of Charles James Fox*, ed. Lord John Russell (London, 1853–57), ii. Appendix.
21. The doubts were shared by the Canningite gang who were running the *Anti-Jacobin* at that time, Canning himself, and his friends Welbore Ellis, John Hookham Frere, and Colonel Walter Sneyd. Frere wrote to Sneyd, in an undated letter: 'We have got a bloody plot afoot which you must join in heart and hand . . . against that silly coxcomb Robert Adair', *Canning and His Friends*, ed. J. Bagot (London, 1909), i. 142. The result of the 'bloody plot' is a skit, entitled 'Translation of a Letter in Oriental Characters from Bawba-dara-adul-Phoola [Bob Adair, a dull fool] to Neek-awl-awretchied-Kooez [Nichol, a wretched quiz]', *Anti-Jacobin*, 28 June 1798. Nichol was a Whig member of the Commons much satirized in the cartoons of Canning's paid artist, the famous Gillray.
22. Rose, *Pitt*, pp. 622–5. Rose nevertheless exonerated Fox: 'We may accept his [Adair's] solemn declaration . . . that Fox had no hand in sending him.'
23. Adair to Allen, 2 Feb. 1842, in *Memorials of Fox*, ii. Appendix.
24. PRO 30/8/337, containing 'Some particulars regarding Mr. Adair's mission to Petersburgh', unsigned, but written by Lindsay, and enclosing the four intercepted letters of Adair, with an additional letter from a 'Mr. Browne' to Samuel Whitbread, dated 15 July 1791.
25. See ch. I, pp. 16–26 in this volume.
26. Whitworth to FO, 10 Jan. 1791, FO 65/20.
27. Fawkener to Grenville, 27 May 1791, FO 65/20; Whitworth to Grenville, 19, 24, and 27 May 1791, ibid.
28. E. Forster, secretary of Muscovy Company, to Grenville, [n.d.] 1791, FO 65/22.
29. Rose, *Pitt*, p. 617.
30. Grenville to Auckland, 29 July 1791, Add. MSS 34438, fo. 653.
31. *Historical Memoirs of Sir Nathaniel William Wraxall*, ed. H. B. Wheatley (London, 1884), i. 202; ii. 34.
32. Grenville to Auckland, 1 Aug. 1791, Add. MSS 34439, fo. 1.
33. PRO 30/8/337.
34. For these variations, and the early recognition that the harshest terms would probably have to be accepted, see Fawkener to Grenville, 2 and 7 June; Whitworth to Grenville, 7, 14, and 18 June, 1 July 1791, FO 65/20.
35. PRO 30/8/337.
36. Whitworth to Grenville, 5 Aug. 1791 (cypher), FO 65/20.
37. Mary Benwell could be a fictitious name but, as Adair addressed his letters to Fox openly, Mrs Benwell is assumed to be the real name of Adair's correspondent.
38. This paragraph was constructed entirely from PRO 30/8/337.
39. Fawkener to Grenville, 5 July 1791 (cypher), FO 65/20, says 'hopes of accommodation are at an end'. Whitworth to Grenville, 12 July 1791, FO 65/22, also admits that everything is lost, adding, 'I agree with your lordship that the

future security of the Turkish Empire will depend more on a powerful guarantee than any state of its frontier'. On 21 July, the day of Adair's first letter to Fox, Whitworth acknowledged to Grenville that Catherine II saw him and Fawkener the previous evening and refused any concession. It is almost certain that Adair knew of the interview as soon as it was over, and wrote to Fox next morning. Fawkener's dispatch of 21 July to Grenville says, 'I am much afraid we shall not be able to obtain from Her Imperial Majesty any more formal instrument' than her simple declaration of intent.

40. Fawkener lamely explained to Sir Robert Ainslie, the ambassador at Constantinople, on 28 July 1791, that the Ottomans might not like the terms, but they would have been worse without British intervention, FO 65/22.
41. Whitworth to Grenville, private, 21 July 1791, Add. MSS 34438, fo. 273, says 'he shows the most virulent opposition to His Majesty's measures and takes great pains to counteract the negotiation'.
42. Bland Burges to Grenville, 18 Feb. 1797, PRO 30/8/337.

CHAPTER III

Robert Liston at Constantinople

The assassination of Gustavus III of Sweden at the Stockholm Opera in March 1792 threw his domestic intimates and foreign supporters into such consternation and disarray that the British government of the day made an instant gesture of confidence in the new, fourth, Gustavus by recredentialling its representative in this anti-Russian capital. The gesture counted for little, however, and failed entirely to deflect the diplomat in question, Robert Liston, from a prior determination to leave Scandinavia at his earliest opportunity; after presenting his new credentials on 6 July, Liston left his post on 26 August, nominally to explain to his superiors why Great Britain's reputation would continue to slide at a much-neglected court but, much more, to forage in London for a more congenial appointment. Escaping a fourth Baltic winter added incentive to ambition for him and his Jamaican-born wife, Henrietta.

Liston was in luck. Wars accelerate the prospects of diplomats as auspiciously as those of military men, and hostilities between Great Britain and revolutionary France broke out while he was lingering on leave. Some resignations from the foreign service followed almost at once with the imminent severance of Great Britain from Europe, and in the resultant relocation of his men abroad, the foreign secretary raised plain Mr Liston, after some hesitation, from the second and ministerial level of dignity. He was appointed to Constantinople. There, Liston was to replace an old friend and fellow-Scot, Sir Robert Ainslie, on the point of final retirement after 18 years' unbroken exile as the representative of George III – the 'Messiah of Christendom', the Ottomans politely called the latter – to the court of the Ottoman Sultans.[1] Stockholm was meanwhile left in the custody of a restless 19-year-old Henry Wellesley, a young man with a name and a future, who soon gave himself leave to join his regiment at the siege of Dunkirk, an initiative which must have confirmed the Swedish impressions of British neglect which had so embarrassed Liston.

The Constantinople embassy would never have fallen to Liston had the foreign secretary, Lord Grenville, thought it an important, or even a lucrative, appointment. It was casually offered to a man of modest reputation because Grenville had no Ottoman policy yet, because the post was much the worst paid of the four full ambassadorships in the public service, and because the Levant Company rather than the British government paid, by ancient custom, the salary: the Foreign Office simply added an allowance of £3 a day.[2] There were other anomalies, which would gradually come to light. Liston himself had none of those helpful marriage connections possessed by such diplomatic grandees of the time as Lord Auckland or Lord Malmesbury, and his friendships, politically considered, were with all the wrong people; with the discredited Charles James Fox, Benjamin Franklin, and such sturdy Edinburgh liberals as Dugald Stewart, 'Principal' Robertson, David Hume, and 'the Man of Feeling', Henry Mackenzie. These he first met through his patrons, the Whig Elliots of Stobo. A connection of greater practical help might have been with his near neighbour in Midlothian, Henry Dundas, the prime minister's closest adviser and indestructible drinking companion; the homes of Dundas and Liston were only a few miles apart, respectively at Melville Castle and Millburn Tower.

Officially, however, Dundas's influence stopped at the doors of the Foreign Office, where he was much disliked, not least because of his extensive private correspondence with diplomats abroad, for it was ever difficult to draw frontiers round his pervasive authority. For the moment then, Liston's good fortune – for so, at first, the Constantinople posting seemed to be – must be due to the Elliots. In earlier times, Liston had acted as tutor to two of the young Elliots, Hugh and Gilbert, and he actually got his first taste of the diplomatic life as private secretary to Hugh, the younger.[3] By 1793 the other brother, now Sir Gilbert of Minto, a self-proclaimed and 'staunch whig', was prominent among those lapsed Foxites who followed Burke and the duke of Portland into the camp of William Pitt, leaving Fox with a following of about 50 on the Opposition benches. This loyal migration also occurred while Liston was in London, and five of its members were taken into a reconstructed cabinet while the others were provided with Tory sinecures. Having helped Burke prepare the prosecutions of Warren Hastings and Sir Elijah Impey, and having just recently lost the speakership of the Commons to Grenville in 1791, Sir Gilbert Elliot was clearly an important acquisition, and he presently embarked on a foreign career of his own which led from a brief viceroyalty in Corsica to something rather grander, the governor-generalship of India, Hastings' old position. Liston, too, had always been a zealous Whig, but the execution of Louis XVI, the coming of Anglo–French hostilities, and Fox's near treasonable parliamentary utterances changed all that. 'The conduct of the French Democrats has spoiled a noble Coup', he told a friend, 'and I am not half so great a Republican as I was.'[4] This change of heart was far more crucial to Liston's prospects than his decade of diplomatic experience, or his facility in ten languages. In the remote event that Grenville might have employed him so long as he kept his politics to himself, Dundas's massive veto power would have come into play at the expense of a politically unreformed Liston. As it was, Grenville was ready to oblige Gilbert Elliot. Liston served twice on the Bosporus, briefly now (1794–96) and for a decade later in his career (1812–21); only the first embassy is of concern here.

The duke of Portland liked to assert that Great Britain ought to be ruled by its 'natural aristocracy', without clarifying whether this was an aristocracy of birth or talent, probably because the two sufficiently coincided in his experience. This was not quite enough for Dundas, who ruled vigilantly over Scotland as if it were one vast rotten borough, and who often seems to overshadow Pitt himself in power and activity. Dundas was, in 1794, home secretary, treasurer to the navy, president of the Board of Control for India, groom of the stole, and signatory of the first war directives. He expected a strict political accountability and loyalty from all who sought his patronage from the time the earl of Shelburne had given him, in 1782, 'the recommendation of all offices which should fall vacant in Scotland', and he was eventually able to preen himself before Grenville, who could not stand him, as 'the cement of political strength to the present administration'.[5] Dundas used his remarkable control over Scotland's 45 parliamentary seats to nourish the 'natural aristocracy' of northern Britain – Jacobites included – so long as its members now deferred loyally to the Hanoverian dynasty. The losers, of course, were the leaderless Highland emigrants who were shipped off to Canada, victims of the notorious 'clearances' and eventual recipients of a belated, useless sentimentality. For the winners – an Ainslie returning to a seat in the Commons, an Abercromby, an Elphinstone, a Keith, a Murray Keith, an Elgin, a Liston – it was necessary to acquiesce in the encasement of Scotland's remarkable intellectual Enlightenment in a suffocating Toryism, vividly recoverable in Cockburn's *Memorials*, the annals of the disgusting Braxfield's Edinburgh court, or Buckle's withering thesis on the subservience of 'the Scottish Intellect' when confronted with religious, or merely English, authority.[6]

Besides carrying out the 'Scottishization' of India, as Lord Rosebery called it, Dundas then grafted a new Caledonian establishment on to the old one, pushed employment for its members in the foreign as well as the imperial service of Great Britain, and in general opened a wider world to a generation of ambitious public and professional men. Walter Scott described the reservoir of new opportunities as 'the corn chest', a place where 'we poor gentry must send our younger sons, as we sent our black cattle to the South'. It is from these beginnings that the empire would become sprinkled with the statues of Englishmen and the graves of Scotsmen. Throughout the war years, the Protestant Irish hierarchy benefited, relatively, as much as the Scots. Only gradually, after the death of George III in 1820, did the English begin to squeeze out these alien rivals from the 'plums' of the imperial and diplomatic careers, holding Paris, Vienna, the Hague, Madrid and the sunlit, lesser Italian courts largely to themselves. So Liston got Constantinople when it counted for little, and few would have taken it, endured Washington, and returned to the Bosporus when its importance had just been discovered; indeed, he helped to discover it, and raise it in the diplomatic ranking.

It would be an exaggeration to discourse on Liston's achievements in the East during the early years of the war with France. His first, brief embassy is interesting for its exposure of the cumbersome insufficiency of the mechanics of diplomacy for the approaching age of the 'Eastern Question', which first emerges as an enduring element in the complex of European international relations from the time the Continental balance of power began to embrace the Balkan lands, the waters of the Levant, and the peripheries of Ottoman Asia. The transfiguring event was the French invasion of Egypt in 1798, which affirmed the general suspicion that the Ottoman Empire, far from constituting a physical barrier separating Europe from further Asia, might be the facilitating conduit by which Asia was penetrated.

Of necessity, an examination of the stage on which so many characters of an international cast are to act out so many plots and scenes of high drama (not unmixed with considerable farce) leads one to ponder the maturation of the diplomatic life as a profession. Did it ever become one? The cronyism and favouritism which held the British establishment together had a high tolerance for mediocrity of performance, and it is safe to predict that a true professional of that time – a sailor-cartographer like James Cook or George Vancouver, an industrialist like Josiah Wedgwood, or a mathematician-astronomer like William Herschel – would have experienced difficulty in seeing the foreign functionaries of the 'natural aristocracy' as specialists, even as *savants*, most of all as *virtuosi*. Prince Metternich proclaimed that the East began beyond Vienna, but no European power trained its envoys, as distinct from a few bureaucrats, for that distant scene. The tapestry of great-power relations was woven, to a remarkable degree, by the great families of a European, including British, cosmopolitan order. Its defence was that diplomacy was an art and not a science, a vocation rather than a profession; to accuse it of amateurism is thus an irrelevance, experience providing the only valid training. It is an argument which overlooks the inconvenience that some men learn only slowly, if at all, from experience, and the important point here is to repudiate any inclination to suppose that, if European diplomacy was inexpert, professionalism elsewhere must always have been much worse. It is a wrong assumption. Far apart in technological expertise and intellectual achievement, British and Ottoman governments, for instance, perhaps stood nearest together in the *laissez-faire* of diplomatic practice; the difference lay in the circumstance that Great Britain, as the much greater power, could afford incompetence longer, and retrieve it faster. The picturesque chaos of the unawakened Foreign Office should proportion any contempt for Asiatic bureaucracies; it is natural, but unfortunate, to judge other societies by their performance, our own by its ideals.

Great Britain had 13 foreign ministers between 1782, when the Foreign Office was formed, and 1812; seven of them held the post for less than a year, and four for under three years. The duke of Leeds was foreign minister for seven and Lord Grenville for ten years. Had greater bureaucratic efficiency seemed important, Grenville had the greatest incentive and most time to bring it about, but the 'natural aristocracy' rarely felt the prickings of a sense of inadequacy, and the new office sagged under a growing burden of unsorted paper. The transference of the Foreign Office in 1793, while Liston was in London, from the Cockpit – part of the first lord of the Treasury's residence at 10 Downing Street – to three old adjoining houses in Cleveland Row, formerly but no longer deemed 'fit for persons of honour or quality', increased the chaos it was supposed to alleviate. Books from the old Northern and Southern departments were stacked three layers deep along the walls and corridors awaiting the organizing hand of Edward Hertslet, who from 1810 would turn them at last into a usable library. The map collection was rifled from travel books. Important treaties, like that of Utrecht, the foundation stone of the century, were nowhere to be found. Diplomatic archives, as one under-secretary told a disbelieving parliamentary committee, were in total disarray, piled unclassified in glass-fronted bookcases in the principal rooms. 'The immense number of despatches which come and go from foreign courts', he explained, 'are piled up but no note is taken of them . . . if anything is wanted the whole year's accumulation must be rummaged over.'[7] Retrieval of books and documents thus depended on the uncertain memories of ageing, underpaid clerks, one or two of whom in recent years had been foreigners. As for the incoming dispatches from Constantinople, most were with the Levant Company on the other side of London. Liston went there to consult them before setting forth. It would require 'a Herculean effort' to put things right, the investigating committee was told. In Grenville's time, they never were.

The department employed ten clerks under two under-secretaries, a far smaller secretariat than the East India Company required. One of them, known as the 'Turk', wrote the rare dispatch for the Bosporus embassy; his title did not imply proficiency in any oriental language, and when the first Ottoman envoy to London, Yusuf Aga Effendi, visited the Foreign Office in 1794 he brought his secretary – and a future *reis effendi* – with him to do the translating. There was, at that time, only one person teaching Turkish in London; interested persons, like the fabulous William Jones, taught themselves. It did not have to be this way. Grenville's standards would never have been tolerated in the head office of the East India Company where there was a marvellous library, and soon there was Charles Wilkins. Grenville's clerks were mere scriveners, drilled to write clearly but never asked to think; even the under-secretaries were treated as senior draftsmen of grammatical dispatches rather than consultants and, as they were eminently replaceable, we find one of the best of them, George Aust, whose duties included a routine scrutiny of the mail from the Bosporus before it went on to the Levant Company, being removed casually in 1795 to make room for a young flatterer of Pitt the Younger called George Canning, who had also abandoned Fox. The new boy had school French, a ready pen, no more. By comparison, Leadenhall Street trained true bureaucrats, such learned, aware, industrious assistants to the examiner of India correspondence as Edward Strachey, Thomas Love Peacock, Dr Johnson's friend 'Mr. Auditior Hoole', and the shoemaker's son, James Mill, historian of India. Thus, if diplomatic history ever was, as in G.M. Young's phrase, the record of what one clerk said to another, precious little of it was generated in Grenville's department. It has been said that in the later Foreign Office there were plenty of egos but only one opinion. Surfeited with egos in the Pitt Cabinet, Grenville wanted none in his department.

There was an interesting consequence; in the tentative structuring of a possible policy for the Ottoman Empire, the initiatives flowed in from the periphery to the centre rather than the other way about, and, for long, ambassadors were the people who speculated on the fears of their hosts and urged a more continuous appraisal of Ottoman requests for arms, money, instructors and, above all, alliances. Liston's energy, like Ainslie's before and the earl of Elgin's after him, obtained cursory approval, but the data from Constantinople were kept rather than read, as if the East need not exist until Grenville chose, reluctantly, to call it into being. William Huskisson, Dundas's ablest assistant, said Grenville's thinking never really crossed the Rhine,[8] to which possibility we must return later, and the best analogy for British policy-making during the war years is perhaps to be found in that passage in his *Commentaries* where Blackstone compares different branches of government with 'distinct powers of mechanics' which 'jointly impel the machine of government in a direction different from what either, acting by itself, would have done, but at the same time in a direction partaking of each and formed out of all'.[9]

★ ★ ★

Nominated for Constantinople in January 1794, illness prevented Liston setting out before April. Ainslie, chafing for release, filled up the interval with some enthusiastic letters about the glamour and profitability of his long years in the East.[10] These were not intended to mislead, for the old ambassador had genuinely been on the best of terms with Yusuf Pasha, an able grand vizier, and had enjoyed the personal esteem of the late Sultan, Abdulhamid I; he had collected Byzantine coins and classical statuary; in spite of a fixed salary, he had invested profitably in joint ventures with local British merchants; and at times had loaned his money to his employer, the Levant Company itself. The Bosporus life could hardly be bettered for a husband and wife who were enslaved by its beauty, had more Levantine than European friends, and took all cultural differences in their stride. But zeal caused Ainslie to gloss a good deal, and nothing much was disclosed about the recent collapse of British prestige at the Porte or the slow death of the Levant trade. After two years of inactivity, Liston was about to fall from the Swedish frying pan into the Ottoman fire.

As recently as 1791, Ainslie had been a considerable hero with his hosts, the consequence of Pitt's impulsive threat to fight Catherine II of Russia unless she abandoned her design to possess the mouldering Ottoman fortress of Ochakov. Fortunately for Pitt, though he did not think so at the time, Parliament refused to vote the essential supplies for so eccentric a purpose, and while he ever said Ochakov produced the biggest humiliation of his public career, the realization of his rash proposal would have produced one much bigger. Ainslie was advised, very tardily, that the Sultan must make the best of the changed situation.[11] For the disastrous treaty of Jassy (1792), the Ottoman ministers therefore blamed much on the inconstancy of Great Britain, a view Berlin encouraged, and Ainslie's friend, Yusuf Pasha, was disgraced. As Grenville abandoned Ainslie, writing to him no more than three times in 1793, Yusuf and Ainslie drowned their sorrows in reminiscence and raki, and a new vizier, Damat Mehmed, treated the old ambassador with a coolness quite outside his earlier experience.

When Grenville put out a peace feeler to St Petersburg, poor Ainslie was again told nothing about it and so 'did not hesitate in declaring [to the Ottomans] my total ignorance and disbelief of a measure which appeared to me altogether improbable and could be easily cleared up by his [the Sultan's] ambassador in London'.[12] Clarification came, but from a nearer source; from Count Kochubey, Ainslie's Russian colleague and friend, who told no less than the truth: Great Britain had indeed abandoned Selim III. Liston, it may be noticed here, was similarly destined, in 1795, to deny the existence of an Anglo–Russian agreement signed without his knowledge. Aimed at the French, the Ottomans naturally supposed they might be its victims too. In neither instance was Grenville being deliberately devious; Ottoman reactions were simply of no importance to him. Personal humiliation, then, had a good deal to do with a resignation Ainslie could not easily afford, and while a pension of £1,000 a year represented comfort, it could hardly sustain the brocaded luxury to which the East had accustomed him. With the Levant Company effectively bankrupt, and receiving annual doles from the British government, even his pension had to be fought for.

It was natural that Lord Grenville should still remember in 1794 that he had advanced to the foreign secretaryship three years before through the ruins of Leeds's anti-Russian policy. The bitterest critics of the pro-Ottoman intention, the very men who had made the Ochakov debate so 'very violent' and long, were to be encountered in Westminster every day. War with France may have divided them, but they were still of one mind concerning Ottomans. Grenville remembered Fox disposing of any economic justification for a war against Russia, and ridiculing the idea of supporting Ottoman sovereignty. He framed Liston's instructions as if the Levant had not changed in 20 years, and need not do so now. There was a new Ottoman embassy in London, but Grenville treated its incumbent 'with more than Coldness', and on the one occasion when he brought himself to feed Yusuf Effendi with 'lamb stuffed with Pistachio nuts', he had the earl of Mornington, destined for India, among the guests, but not Liston. The latter was in no way put out. His ideological hero, Burke, was quite right to say the Ottoman Empire lay 'outside the general system of political nations'; to reach it Liston would actually be 'taking leave of the diplomatic world'. In entrusting himself to 'the good faith of the barbarians of the Bosphorus' – the very phrase shows Liston read Constantin Volney's famous *Travels* before he set out – he considered his diplomatic life in abeyance while he undertook a money-making sabbatical.[13] If Grenville ignored Yusuf Effendi to please the Russian ambassador, Count Vorontzov, and placate Catherine II, he failed. She blamed Ainslie for proposing the Ottoman mission in London, and wanted him dismissed for suggesting so clever a move. She need not have worried. Grenville neither understood the fuss nor saw the opportunity, and in formulating Liston's orders acted in a significant way; he sent for Ainslie's old orders from 1774, and pencilled in the minimal changes necessary, a good example of the power of tradition and the tenacity of Great Britain's Russian connection.

Some remarks about the process of mutual discovery upon which the Ottomans and the British were about to embark are, however, apposite here. The Ottoman historian, Mustafa Nuri, comparing the loss of the Crimea in 1783 with that of Hungary 80 years earlier, stresses the greater significance of the former with the explanation that 'the Crimea was populated by two millions of True Believers', whereas Hungary, he implies, had merely Christian populations.[14] There followed an eminently practical, if insufficient, reaction. In that very same year, Sultan Abdulhamid I authorized, and his resolute grand vizier, Halil Hamid Pasha, initiated, an extensive programme of military expansion. Baron de Tott's famous artillery corps grew fivefold, and the necessary funding was squeezed out of the *sipahi* landowning class, in lieu of their lapsed, and now unwanted, feudal service as cavalrymen. A naval building programme, always less controversial because it was a smaller threat to vested Muslim interests, had already begun under the direction of the Algerian pirate-turned-patriot, Kaptan Pasha Jezairli Hasan. An early return on this investment in military improvement, perhaps more the result of a new mood than of the new technology, was the recovery of Mameluke Egypt in 1786.

Ottoman sources hardly anywhere suggest, as Western historians have since done, that refurbishing an Islamic imperium with borrowed, infidel technology presented serious moral dilemmas for those in authority, and Selim III, succeeding to the throne in 1789, did not have to choose between state power and religious purity because he could patronize both.

The attitudinal metamorphosis which really makes Selim III's reign so controversial was the acknowledgment by his followers that the Ottoman state could no longer hope to stand alone in a threatening world. Thomas Naff and J.C. Hurewitz separately show how, in Selim III's time, the Ottomans began to exchange a haughty, 'unilateral' style of announcing their intentions and displeasures to the foreign embassies on their doorstep for a more conciliatory and 'reciprocal' mode of international intercourse, opening permanent legations in the main capitals of the *Dahr ul-Harb*, first in London in 1793, in Paris only in 1797.[15] Hence, Yusuf Effendi's mission; and hence Grenville's incomprehension. The implicit recognition that association, if not exactly friendship, with one or more of the European powers would henceforth be a permanent necessity came none too soon; as a response to the Russian hammer-blows falling on the empire with the inexorable rhythm of a nine-year cycle – in 1774, 1783, 1792 – it was, however, much more controversial a step than mere military borrowing by its invocation of Christian might to secure Islamic survival, a far cry indeed from the great days of the 'daily increasing flame'.

The progress of decline was bitterly denied by many at the Porte, but the facts were visible enough. In 1774, the Black Sea, that 'virgin shut up in the harem' according to Ottoman imagery, had to be shared with Russia; in 1783, the Crimean loss was far more a resounding psychological than demographic blow; as for the 1792 peace settlement, Grenville's orders to Liston will show how seriously the Jassy and Sistovo negotiations embittered further the Porte's relations with St Petersburg and Vienna, frustrating in the process the too sanguine expectation of Ahmet Effendi, Selim III's private secretary, that the upheavals in Paris would tone down the victor's demands. It is, obviously, quite incorrect to suggest, as has been done, that the French Revolution was an internal affair of Christendom, with no relevance for Selim III. Ideologically, it made little impact; but otherwise, Ottomans were obsessed with its international effects, and its most humiliating lesson was that, except by the French, they were seen as liability rather than asset. To their chagrin and alarm, they were patronized in the very sphere of the military arts where they had given most cause for alarm in prior centuries. Not to be taken seriously was serious indeed; they were left at the mercy of Austria and Russia, which is why the diplomatic agents of the new France at the Porte, who were with one exception absurd incompetents, experienced little difficulty in sustaining the dominance inherited from Bourbon days.

Turning to Great Britain, one finds Edmund Burke proclaiming that 'any coffee house politician' knew William Pitt ran the war. William Windham, joining the Cabinet in 1794, said a 'duumvirate' of Pitt and Dundas did so. It is surely significant, though not necessarily inaccurate, that both views ignore Grenville, allegedly a cosmopolitan intellect; even, *mirabile dictu*, a student of geography; unquestionably a patriotic optimist and, most important, a diligent, directionless statesman who deployed so vast a private correspondence with agents abroad that he has yet to find a full-scale biographer. Grenville's temperamental defect was his inability to advance towards policy destinations except incrementally, a captain steering his vessel through the shoals by the light on the stern. Pitt was of no help to him, being at that point of his career where, as a concerned friend observed, he 'liked a glass of wine very well, and a bottle even better', a point dramatically upheld by his cellar bills. As resourceful as ever at raising money, the prime minister seemed ever less sure with the passage of time how it should be spent, a situation which allowed Henry Dundas to pursue his 'eccentric expeditions' to the Caribbean, the Cape of Good Hope, and Ceylon, at the cost of more serious losses than the duke of Wellington sustained in the entire Peninsular campaign a decade later. Grenville, *per contra*, was encouraged by three well-stocked minds, belonging to Malmesbury, his peripatetic brother, Tom, and Auckland at the Hague, to focus on the Low Countries as the area where the war would ultimately be won or lost, a military truth which, unfortunately, narrowed his diplomatic effort excessively, so that his thinking, which as we have seen worried Huskisson because it never crossed the Rhine, certainly did not reach Poland, descend the Danube, or easily envisage a Mediterranean world.

It is often hard to accept (or even follow) Grenville's occasional attempts to formulate diplomatic principles, such as when he claimed that the Low Countries form the chain which links England to the Continent, and the central knot to our relations with Austria and Russia. This was an extraordinarily inexact analysis. Austria was unwilling to fight France to keep her part of the Low Countries, if she could exchange them peaceably for Bavaria; the 'knot' to Russia had been untied in 1791 by Grenville himself; the Low Countries led most obviously to Berlin, the court he distrusted above all, so that while Liston was in the East, Grenville said he would resign rather than finance the Prussians again. This from a man who, nevertheless, was seeking, in the style of the earl of Chatham, some modern and agglomerated equivalent of Frederick the Great to call the French to a halt. It was all very well to deflate Pitt's Turcophilism and abandon the Prussians in 1791, but how, in 1794, did one deny Leeds's long-standing charge that this also meant, besides 'giving in to the Russian party in the House of Commons', ensuring the doom of Poland and merely deferring that of the Ottoman Empire? Joseph Ewart, at Berlin in 1791, had taught Grenville to distrust Hertzberg, the most powerful Prussian minister; Ewart's successor, Lord Elgin, taught Grenville to detest Hertzberg's successor, Haugwitz. Sir Charles Whitworth, however, was prevented by Vorontzov from teaching Grenville that Catherine II would be just as unlikely as anybody to put the imperatives of the anti-French crusade before her interests in that remote Europe which the foreign secretary knew not. Catherine II herself made her priorities plain enough: 'I am breaking my head to make the cabinets of Vienna and Berlin intervene in the affairs of France . . . in order to have my own hands free.' The revolution in France became the French Revolution thanks to thrice-partitioned Poland.

When Prussia went over to the side of France in 1795, Grenville 'gave up all idea of saving either Poland or Turkey'. Excellently briefed about the doom closing round the former in the shape of the Third Partition, he sent 'such assurance of His Majesty's goodwill as could be given without committing His Majesty to any particular line of Conduct', a remark which led Holland Rose to say it was Grenville who finally 'passed sentence of death on Poland'.[16] And the Ottomans? As soon as Poland was expunged from the map, Grenville proposed a Russian alliance, promising that Great Britain would never obstruct Russian campaigns against 'Asiatic powers' unless a third party – France – intervened. Russia was 'our old and natural ally', and the best power to coerce the Ottomans to fight the French. Catherine II's officers, many of them Scots, would surely be acceptable to a grateful Selim III? Dundas, who so often pulled in another direction from the foreign secretary, shared his indulgence for Russian ambitions, telling Pitt that 'every principle of policy, *present and future*, [emphasis added] point [*sic*] out that power as the natural ally of Great Britain and in all our transactions with her that principle ought never to be overlooked'. Dundas added: 'it is improper to disguise that the aversion of this country to renew any more subsidiary treaties' was due to the 'unfaithful execution' by Austria and Prussia of their obligations to the collapsed First Coalition, but 'the observation does not apply to Russia, of whose fidelity we entertain no doubts'.[17] The king was ready to give Catherine II Corsica; Dundas would have her take Malta, occupy Switzerland, or even 'open the markets of South America'. Even Pitt could see the error in all this; it remained, he said, 'the interest of Great Britain to prevent as far as circumstances permitted the aggrandisement of the two Imperial courts [Austria and Russia] at the expense of Turkey', if only to 'diminish the temptation to wars of ambition'.

Nothing was done, however, and no one could imagine anything that should be attempted to uphold the ramshackle archaism that was the Ottoman Empire, whose past was marked by 'unprovoked aggressions, breaches of oaths, treaties and capitulations, massacres and acts of cruelty and aggression', whereas 'the interests of Great Britain and Russia were inseparable and reciprocal', to the extent that 'the expulsion of the Ottomans from Europe would be more advantageous to Great Britain than even to Russia herself'.[18] Russia was not yet the huge, sinister figure she would become in British eyes. Nor could the Ottomans escape yet from the charge that they were incapable of joining a modern world; it was the immutability of their barbarism which allowed William Eton to condemn 'the elegant descriptions' and 'warm imagination' of one who had liked them, and to assure his readers that nothing had really changed between the ancient writings of 'Bushec, Leunclav, Montecuculli, Marsigli, Ricaut' and the 'modern' works of 'Boscovisch, Busimello . . . Sir James Porter,

Riedesel, Ludeke, Stoevers, Ferrières-Sauveboeuf, and Volney'.[19]

And so it was, read Liston in his instructions, 'most especially' for the 'good and benefit' of a moribund trading corporation, the Levant Company, that he was to go to Constantinople, where he would at once thank his exotic hosts for Great Britain's 'privileged participation in their trade and commerce, which is so beneficial . . . above that of any other nation'.[20] The foreign secretary cannot have believed this solemn nonsense since the British Turkey Merchants, as they were commonly called, had virtually no 'trade and commerce' left in the Mediterranean and were now scratching elsewhere to improvise a living. More of that later. The directors, of late upset by Ainslie's interest in diplomacy and neglect of their affairs, were displeased not to have been consulted over Liston's appointment, but were mollified by his lack of titles and dignities, which should make him easier to control. They assured him of 'the Gothic dinners' their factors in the Ottoman Empire would lay on and Liston, whose first concerns were mercenary, looked forward to 'the many presents which will pour in on me from all quarters of the Turkish Empire'.[21] He was warned by the directors to avoid costly interviews, to eschew diplomatic entanglements, to make no appointments without consulting London, but to revive the company's wilted prosperity. No one told him the company's factors in the Ottoman Empire nearly all now wore the Republican cockade and had, in most cases, taken out foreign citizenship as 'Venetians', or 'Sardinians', or 'Russians', to enable them to carry on trading as neutrals. No one in London even recognized the irony that the most patriotic 'Englishmen' in the Levant were the Ottomans inducted into embassy service. And as the ambassador was, by intention, custodian of a merchant community, he went forth unguided for a situation which Braxfield would have resolved by transporting the culprits to Australia.

Some afterthought led the foreign secretary to give his new ambassador some sketchy and supplementary diplomatic instructions after all; the urging may have come from his under-secretary, George Aust, or Count Vorontzov, a good friend of Grenville, or from that remarkable and secret source close to the decisions of the Committee of Public Safety in Paris. Vorontzov disclosed that the new Russian minister at Constantinople, Count V.P. Kochubey, would value Liston's aid in pressing the Porte not to raise its tariffs and in preventing an Ottoman attack on Russia at a critical moment in the history of the western part of the Continent. He was less forthcoming about Kochubey's other, larger duty, to push 'the unlimited right of appointing consuls and overseeing the rights and privileges of the protected [Christian] subjects of this empire', the earliest reference this writer has seen to a policy of internal colonization of the Ottoman Empire by Russia which eventually led to the Crimean War 60 years later. Grenville responded by advising Liston to work with Kochubey 'for the amiable adjustment of whatever differences *may arise* between the *tsarina* and the Porte'.[22] This bland remark conceals the angry altercation still going on between Russian and Ottoman over the fulfilment of the 1792 treaty and the failure of the special mission of General Kutusov to resolve it; Catherine II still had regiments in the Principalities, stripping their farms and food with the destructive efficiency of locusts, and the Austrians were reluctant to quit Serbian Chotzim until a Russo–Ottoman accommodation had been reached. How could the inexperienced Liston hope to make such situations palatable to his new hosts, the more so as 'Citizen' Descorches would be inflaming the Ottomans to resist them? Grenville's French informant protected himself from discovery with such care that his intelligence came to London by way of Genoa in the handwriting of a child, and from this critical source the foreign secretary heard that a few French warships and a great deal of French money, allegedly supplemented with some of Marie Antoinette's jewels, had been sent to Constantinople to obtain Ottoman recognition of the new Republic and to embroil Selim III's ministers in a new war with Russia.

In this connection, Liston was simply told to prevent recognition of 'the Executive government in France'. A little consideration will suggest that it was Selim III himself who needed Great Britain's good offices, without which the advocacy of Ottoman interests would remain, as in the past, with the French, while the current 'French Mania' reported by Ainslie was all the more likely to produce the formal recognition of the Republic which Liston was expected to obstruct. Once more, then, the past was being mistaken for a very different present; Liston was to protect a vanished commerce, simultaneously pushing Russian over French claims at the Porte. Until the very moment of hostilities in 1793, it is worth recalling, the French as much as the Russians were seeking money in London. Yusuf Aga Effendi's duty, 'to connect the interest of the Porte to those of Great Britain', offered an opportunity none in Cleveland Row or Downing Street even saw.[23] It is surely odd that the barbarous Ottomans, rather than the British, should have seen that the unconstrained mobility of great naval strength, by diminishing the ordinary effects of distance, allowed British guardianship to be brought to Ottoman needs, as the proverbial mountain to Muhammad, and British influence at the Porte to rise to unexampled heights.

With strictly mercenary intentions, and having no wish to be captured at sea by the French cruisers patrolling the waters of the Levant, Liston at last set out determined to 'struggle through the shocking road of Romania as best as I can'.[24] As the Foreign Office agreed to add £3 a day to his Levant Company salary, his intention was to serve five years at the Porte, add Turkish to his other languages, live on the office allowance and salt away his salary with Coutts, his banker, and eventually return home to enlarge Millburn Tower and improve his small Linlithgow estate.[25] Some stubborn facts, blurred by avarice, slowly emerged like uncharted rocks to sink these plans. His fixed salary of £2,000 was the same as Ainslie had received since 1776, with the difference that the commercial speculations once capable of more than doubling that sum had become much harder to find in an oriental capital experiencing steepening inflation, and in a trading area where, as his friend Sir Sidney Smith believed, British commercial operations were 'at their last effort'.[26] There was to be no Secret Service money: he had to pay out his own equipage expenses, reclaiming them afterwards, which took time. There were no travelling expenses. Even the traditional presents for the Sultan and his court – rich fabrics by the bale, chiming clocks, inlaid pistols, snuff-boxes, ordinarily paid for by the company though presented in the king's name – were for the first time withheld. Perhaps the biggest surprise of all was that, while the company would still pay the pittances to the *cancellier* (archivist), the 'druggermen' (interpreters), and the *giovani di lingua* (interpreter-trainees), there would be no diplomatic support staff; for instance, 'there is no secretary of embassy paid or appointed by the government' and Ainslie's resourceful helper, Alexander Straton, had been switched to Vienna. Liston would also pay, from his own pocket, the salaries of the Reverend Dallaway, the new embassy chaplain, and Dr

Sibthorp, the embassy physician. If he needed help with his paper work, he must find someone locally and pay for it.

Grenville certainly did not expect Liston to need such help; he need write home only twice a month, on the 10th and 26th, by any courier except a Frenchman. The office was not likely to bother him much, even with acknowledgements; Sir Robert Murray Keith in Vienna said he got one reply to every 40 dispatches he sent home; Ainslie had sometimes heard only twice a year from Whitehall. The Constantinople embassy thus appeared, in the great lottery of foreign appointments, to be a sinecure for anyone ready to concentrate on the Levant Company's negligible affairs, an anxious post for a man who liked the comfort of regular instructions, a snare for anyone who rather fancied himself as a big fish in a small pool, but unquestionably an excellent source of international intelligence, as it was one of the few courts left where most of the major powers, and several lesser ones, were still represented. A man who believed, as Liston did, that the safest way to send his wife money was to tear banknotes in half and post them separately is not, however, easily demoralized, and such was his optimism that he surrendered one of the greatest privileges of a gentleman: he paid off his debts. Difficulties awaited him, the first of them bearing the name of Ainslie, packed and waiting, ready to be off and beyond Bulgaria before the onset of the plague season. Little was discussed between the diplomats beyond the furnishings the old hand was ready to leave behind, at a price, for the new. Here, too, there was an excess of haste and years later an estranged Ainslie pursued his erstwhile friend through the Edinburgh courts for repayment of long-standing debts. The situation never really improved. Within two years, Liston was home again. Transferred to Washington in 1796, he could never have believed that the indifferent Lord Grenville would be guaranteeing the integrity of the Ottoman Empire a mere three years later. Nor, in his wildest dreams can he have supposed that one day, when he was in his seventies, he would accede when an abler, more attentive chief than Grenville offered him the post at Constantinople again.

* * *

The Ottoman chamberlain, sent to Sofia with a mounted escort in April 1794 to bring Liston through the dangerous Rumelian countryside, was accompanied by Bartholomew Pisani, the second in rank of Great Britain's four dragomans at Constantinople. Liston had heard 'very favourable accounts of [Pisani's] character, zeal, and ability',[27] and the dragoman was undoubtedly the ablest, most faithful, representative of a much-maligned profession. Beginning service 30 years before under Grenville's uncle, Pisani was still only half-way through his career, and served 11 ambassadors in unbroken succession. Sadly, his is the kind of fascinating story which, for lack of surviving private papers, seems beyond retrieval; Pisani on the Ottomans — as on his chiefs — would be well worth hearing. Totally at ease in Ottoman costume, language, diplomatic procedures, and high ceremonials, it would be as impossible to specify his first language as to doubt his first loyalty. He was a lively creature as well as an excellent official, who trained several of the ambassadors to understand their responsibilities fully; Disraeli, a later visitor, named his strangest novel after Pisani's daughter.

The rendezvous with Liston did not materialize as planned, for a reason which implanted itself deeply in the new ambassador's observation; Bulgarian bandits were ravaging the area round Adrianople, 'offering the inhabitants the hard alternatives of either contributing a most exorbitant sum of money or seeing a general waste laid to their country'. Clearly, these were far more than turbulent mobs on horseback and came closer in formation to a large army of irregulars, marching along 'with flying ensigns [and] a full complement of fire arms'. There were 'several French mixed with the insurgents', who turned out to be paid guerrillas of the rebel pasha of Widin, Pasvanoglu.[28] Liston's tortuous progress through the Balkans ended as an undignified flight. So it was with great relief that he and his unescorted party finally rode in through the Edirne Gate of Constantinople on 19 May 1794, six weeks after leaving Vienna, his anxieties briefly suspended by scenes 'the most entrancing that human eye ever beheld', and all cradled in 'the most beautiful of all positions on the globe'.[29] This was the usual first reaction of Europeans before closer examination brought on disillusionment. Like Scots before and after him, Liston was reminded of the winds of his native city as he ascended the steep, staircased lanes of the European quarter, Pera, much as the houses overleaning the same lanes recalled Holborn to English minds.

Ten European embassies stood along Pera's main street, and Ottomans respected 'a large household and a certain display of magnificence' more than reputations acquired far away. A modest establishment was an insult, Liston hinted meaningfully, and the Porte was 'extremely sensitive to any appearance of neglect and indifference'.[30] The usual trays of flowers and fruit were laid before the new envoy, but he waited four months for his official reception by the Sultan and, in point of protocol, was left in no doubt that he ranked behind the envoys of Spain and Venice. The French embassy staff was alleged to reach 300 persons by 1795; Kutusov, on special mission from Catherine II in 1794 had housed the overspill of his retinue of 600 in the Russian summer house at Buyukdere, on the Bosporus. By contrast with these probably exaggerated figures, the British 'Hotel' had a staff of ten, nine of them Levantines. It was Levant Company policy to pay only a small stipend, and employees were expected to earn the greater part of their salary through commerce. There were four dragomans. The first, Tomasso, was in England, and never returned. Pisani, nominally the second, was effectively the first; his salary in 1794 stood at £100 a year, about the income of an English rural clergyman. He was not the most senior at the embassy, an honour which belonged to Antonio Dané, a Venetian of great age and fading eyesight, who had joined the embassy 50 years earlier during the war of the Austrian Succession. The only Englishman on the staff was one Olifer, the *cancellier*, custodian of the chancery, provider of passports, guardian of all secret papers. Once unpaid consul in Salonika, Olifer had failed in business, now lived on a pittance, and was soon to die. Further down the scale was the embellisher, a Turk who wrote out all official communications to the Porte in the elegant script of the Ottoman court; he lived in a lane off the Grande Rue. Four locally recruited interpreters rounded out the staff. The embassy's shabby frugality extended to those janizary guards – the swineherds, as Ottomans called them – who protected its gates; at 8 piastres each per month (less than £1), they were the worst paid in Pera.

A deeply embarrassed Liston advised both the company and the Foreign Office that 'every officer in the service of the Right Worshipful Company is underpaid', including, as he quickly discovered, himself. He repudiated the familiar charges of Levantine corruption and unreliability, and thought his interpreters 'in general men of ability . . . entrusted with the management of delicate and difficult business'.[31] His most pressing need was, however, for a secretary of embassy, to which position he soon appointed the young Turkey Merchant, John Spencer Smith, once a page to Queen Charlotte in England and best remembered now because his wife, miscalled Constance, later became mistress to Lord Byron, allegedly with her husband's compliance. Smith was much attracted by Liston's 'polished manners, elegant hospitality, and friendly confidence', and naturally was of the view that ambassadors chiefly existed to promote the merchants' interests, an opinion destined to cause a furious row with Lord Elgin when he came out to Constantinople in 1799 to assume the position Smith had dared to hope would fall to him.[32]

While Liston was uncomfortable with his insufficient guidance on diplomatic matters, his private and public correspondence show how greatly merchants, capitalists, traders, and manufacturers at home pressed their interests upon him. The background has to be remembered. In its great days, the Levant Company had organized its own annual armada to the eastern seas, but that system of 'general shipping', as it was called, fell away after 1744, and the membership fee to join the company was lowered to £20 in 1753 because of a decline in the Levant trade. The downturn in prosperity has a radical, dual explanation; the delicately balanced exchange of British 'cloths' for Persian and Ottoman silks, a trade in which money hardly needed to change hands, was upset by falling demand on each side. Aleppo, bigger than any British city except London and the great silk market of the East, was undercut by Bengal and China, then stunned by the great plague of 1760 which cut its population by 80,000. On the other side, British 'cloths' lost ground to improved French fabrics, and a prohibition on the export of bullion denied the Levant Company the option of buying its way out of trouble. In spite of this, the old contradictory opinion concerning the company survived; its members, it was said, were incompetent, but also prosperous.

Liston's correspondents – most of them Glasgow industrialists and capitalists – wished at least to circumvent and, ideally, subvert such an anachronistic organization, and such sturdy apostles of Professor Adam Smith could point to the company's notorious failure to sustain the sale of British woollens in the East by undertaking what a later generation would entitle timely 'market research', and could footnote their charge with the example of

Halifax 'Shalloons', a fabric which had traditionally sold well but was now excluded from Ottoman markets by the brighter, lighter fabrics of Picardy and the Rhône valley. The company had similarly failed to inject Canadian furs into a market monopolized by the Russians. William Eton, Henry Dundas's oriental expert, was amazed and disgusted that Newfoundland fish was not sold in the Levant, except by Greeks and Portuguese, and the final chapter of the book he was currently writing on the Ottoman Empire bore the belligerent heading, 'The Necessity of Abolishing the Levant Company'.[33]

Glasgow and Manchester men in textiles were thus understandably determined to ensure that the immense promise of the cotton industry should not be squandered by these incompetent Turkey Merchants, whose pretension to understand the arcane mysteries of the commerce of the Levant stood exposed as an audacious sham. A major obstacle here was the company's residual power not only to charge an 11 per cent 'fine' on the goods of any 'interlopers' which bypassed its factors in the Levant, but also to impose a surcharge on raw cotton imported from the Levant into Great Britain even when the cotton had come indirectly through foreign middlemen in Venice and Ostend. The British Parliament admonished the company for this sort of parasitism in 1790, for its 'improvident acts' and 'injudicious by-laws', and free-traders were recurrently optimistic that the company must soon be allowed to flounder, but the ancient monopoly somehow survived.[34]

The coming of the war in 1793 had been expected to ruin the French Levant trade and lead to the resurgence of British trade; instead, something like the reverse happened, and the Turkey Merchants were blamed for it. The directors of the Levant Company were naturally very sensitive to criticisms to which they could not easily respond, but felt them doubly because their monopoly no longer guaranteed affluence, and even worked against them; for instance, the old prohibition on the export of bullion still stood, and ever since the American War for Independence the interrupted flow of 'colonial goods' (sugar, spirits, coffee, logwoods) had reduced proportionately the company's means for purchasing from the Ottomans the fine silks, brocades, dyes, skins, and great diversity of herbs for the European pharmacopeia, from all of which great profits had once been made.

With the abandonment of 'general shipping' and its replacement with the chartering of individual vessels, Barbary corsairs were bolder, Greek pirates had improved their skills, and after 1793 the Royal Navy offered no escort east of Cape Matapan. The Imposition Book of the Levant Company tells the sorry tale. Whereas the French navy ensured that the Marseilles convoy got clean through to the Levant in 1793 without sighting one British warship, the homeward-bound British convoy of 1794 lost 30 vessels to the enemy.[35] British merchantmen struggling eastwards fell steadily in numbers, 15 reaching Smyrna in 1792, ten in 1795, five in 1797, one in 1798, none at all in 1799. The death-blow was the total withdrawal of the Royal Navy from the Mediterranean between 1796 and 1798. So Liston arrived at Constantinople at a moment of deep depression for the Levant Company, while his Scottish correspondents, not knowing all the baneful circumstances, thought, wrongly, that their great day approached. They were unattracted by his dutiful invitation to them to join the trade by joining the company, paying the entrance fee of £20. They believed him obsequious; he thought them pernickety, and missing a great opportunity.

Paul Mantoux pointed out long ago that the lapse of Arkwright's patents for various textile-machines attracted a lot of men with money but no experience to the vast promise of the cotton industry. To this stimulus he could have added another at least as potent though slow to show itself, the rise in price of Indian finished cotton goods after the terrible Bengal famine of 1769–70, after which Indian fabrics were never again competitive in the European and Mediterranean markets. Malta died as Paisley flourished.[36] Most of Liston's correspondents actually knew what they were about, and David Dale, the Finlays, Kennedys, Hopkirks, and Gaults were more than mere capitalists; they were manufacturers and they were impatient to know what the sash-and-turban wearers thought of their new ginghams, calicoes, pulicats, chintzes, and muslins, the very names of which betray oriental origins. In the search for fast dyes, they explored the fugitive chemistry of cochineal, madder, indigo, and saffron.[37] Most of all, they had massive machine capacity; Paisley alone had 1,000 'mules', and William Kelly's water-powered version drove 400 spindles simultaneously, each spindle able to produce a mile of 'water twist' or thread from a pound of raw cotton. Supplies of the latter were already looking dangerously inadequate; put another way, if enough raw cotton could be found, then the inundation of the entire Asian market with fabrics of unprecedented quality and cheapness was a near and exciting possibility. The new United States, it must be recalled, would be Great Britain's sole supplier of the raw product by 1805, but in 1795 was a negligible source, the East Indies and the Levant being the critical suppliers of France as well as of Great Britain. Competition for the raw cotton was great. France took 30,000,000 pounds weight a year for all uses; British chandlers alone wanted 400,000 pounds a year for candlewick. All this put Liston in triple trouble; he was caught between the expectations of the Foreign Office and the Levant Company; he was caught between the demands of the company and the tribulations of the free-traders of New Lanark, Paisley, Oldham, Warrington, the Peak District, and Manchester, who would have taken the wheat of Thrace as well as its cotton; and, not least, he was caught between the directors in London and their own factors in the Ottoman Empire, so long left to fend for themselves, who greeted him with implausible protestations of loyalty and more believable testimony of near destitution. One sees why the new ambassador felt he had taken leave of the diplomatic world, and soon wanted reconnection with it.

Turning to the British community in Pera and the Ottoman outports, Liston found its size and importance absurdly exaggerated; the promised 'Gothic dinners' with merchant princes never transpired. It was hard to credit that so few complainants could be so noisily demanding. There were at that time not more than 50 British families anywhere in the Levant, a number to be halved in 1797 when a janizary was killed by a Venetian outside a Frank theatre in Smyrna, and the European quarter was reduced by a burning and killing mob to 'naked families and smoking ruins', with only 'one [British] house of trade and two private dwellings' surviving.[38] Twenty-six British families would lose everything. Even in 1795, only four Levant Company consulates remained open: at Smyrna (Anthony Hayes), Aleppo (Edward Abbott), Alexandria (George Baldwin), and Salonika (Peter Chassaud). Four prosperous Englishmen survived: Nicholas Strane in Patras, William Turner in Zante, and the Hayes, father and son, in Salonika. Levant Company operations suffered from under-capitalization, and these men only did well because they were long-term residents who raised money locally for their enterprises, and not from Englishmen alone; Strane exported sponges, olive oil, currants, fustic wood, and took in 'shalloons, cloths, velvets, muslins, fire arms, cutlery, watch work and lead shot'.[39] His endeavours were backed by Salonika Jews. Idle and anxious Levantine factors and vice-consuls, the local agents of British principals, were holding on here and there, hoping for better times: Frankuli in Uskudar, Foresti in Corfu, Vondiziano in Famagusta, Giudicci in Tenedos, and others in Limassol, Tino, Jaffa, Mikonos, and Ankara. The turning point would come in 1807, and no one in 1795 could have credited that the Levant Company would end its days in 1825 with 800 members. In 1797 the Aleppo factory closed for the first time since Shakespeare's time, and Latakhia, Alexandretta, and Syrian Tripoli soon followed suit. Absolutely no consulage fees were paid by Liston to the London head office, so dead was the trade everywhere. In the Ottoman capital, five merchants constituted a quorum for a meeting of the local factory or scale. The bottom had fallen out of their world, and 'only the worst manufactures in the world are to be found there. . . . Ask for a Turkey carpet . . . you must send for it to Smyrna, for Greek wines . . . to the Archipelago.' In addition to these, Liston found himself responsible for 39 *baratlis* and 80 *fermanlis*, Ottoman subjects living under British protection. Yet life was anything but peaceful, and Liston told George Aust his time was 'most unpleasantly and unprofitably spent trying to enforce the claims and avenge the wrongs of men with whom I should wish to have no connection'.[40] Humiliated, his mind was turning to more important matters.

His main objection to the members of the British community was that so few were remotely patriotic and most were traitorous Jacobins. Those compatriots who came to the 'Hotel' to pay their respects, however earnestly they called Great Britain 'Home', were Ottomans in dress and Frenchmen in their politics. Several were members of the local Republican Society of the Friends of Liberty and Equality. This seemed the more shocking as the names of nearly all were twisted into the very history of the Levant Company – Abbott, Barker, Blunt, Barbaud, Morier, Prior, Strane, Thornton, Tooke, Walrond, Thomas. Thornton, treasurer to the Constantinople scale, was an irascible man 'of insolent, bearish and intolerable behaviour', who recruited linguists to write and broadcast the French Republic's clandestine propaganda among the *ayan* and pashas of Bosnia and Rumelia. 'Citizen' Humphrys, once

American but now a rabble-rouser with a British passport, was notorious for his somewhat premature announcement that the revolution had erupted in the streets of London. Others helped organize the annual celebration of the execution of Louis XVI, an affair conducted 'with a Grand Civic Feast, and all their disgusting Songs, at a Public House in the principal Street'.[41] After calling on Liston to complain about the conditions of trade, and the absence of the Royal Navy, they in several cases wandered next to the French mission, there to read the *Gazette française*, or to drink and gossip with Fonton, the dragoman who had planned the ousting of Choiseul, that last and famous representative of the Bourbons. The evil genius of the French community, and popular with the English, was the minister, 'Proteus' Descorches, formerly the marquis de Sainte Croix, but now, Liston heard, 'active in disseminating the tempting doctrine of fraternity among the Turks', and circulating propagandist broadsheets to be read 'in the coffee houses of Constantinople'.[42] Descorches planted a Tree of Liberty outside Topkapi; later, Spencer Smith had the exquisite pleasure of cutting it down.[43]

Unlike his countryman, Henry Dundas, who saw Jacobin republicanism as an ideological distemper capable of driving orientals to political madness, Liston attached small importance to the bombast of the *Gazette française* or 'the propagation of democratic principles' by 'various classes of missionaries'. In any case, they had a printing press and money with which to buy popularity, and he had neither. On the other hand, there were large opportunities for diplomatic action here of which the British foreign secretary seemed wilfully ignorant. Liston told Aust about them. 'It has in general been thought that it was only at the moment of a threatened or existing rupture that this country deserved the interest of the rest of Europe', but it seemed to him that Grenville should be prepared 'to now and then read a few lines from hence without disgust', and look, not to the future, but to the needs of the present.[44] A Levant Company ambassador could imitate Spencer Smith's father-in-law, Baron d'Herbert who represented Austria, and settle into the life of a comfortable nonentity. He could resign all tasks to a subordinate, as was the case at the Swedish embassy, where the chargé d'affaires, though personally anti-French, left the duties of attendance at the Porte to his notorious Armenian dragoman, Mouradja d'Ohsson, who 'has rendered himself remarkable for his knowledge of this country, and his late predilection for the cause of the French Republic'. Liston suspected that d'Ohsson was in French pay: Grenville knew for sure. Certainly, the Armenian's political partialities were shared by others; by the Spanish representative, 'a most officious, intriguing partisan of the enemy', and even more by Count Medem, the Dutchman, 'a vile revolutionary character, and incorrigible apostate', as bad as the British merchants.[45]

Was it really enough, under such circumstances, for Liston to be no more than an occasional accessory to Russian interests, when Kochubey was well able to look after them alone? The French dominated in the Ottoman Empire, not for their bluster or for the ideas they preached, but for what they did, and the critical point was surely that they should be opposed, actively and ostentatiously. Liston's good friend, Sir Sidney Smith, brother to Spencer Smith, had served the Ottomans in the past and sensibly asserted that if Great Britain left the military regeneration of the Ottoman state in French hands, the latter would eventually turn the Ottomans against Great Britain as well as Russia. Selim III was hesitating to recognize the Republic in Paris and Liston's orders were to encourage him. Why, then, did not the British government win the Sultan's trust and confidence by proffering military and naval missions, thus squeezing the French out? A firm and open friendship would have the additional benefit of forcing the British 'Jacobins' to return to their senses or run the risk of excommunication, from Great Britain as much as from the Levant Company.

The ambassador's complaints were a storm in a teacup to Grenville, who sent no reply, and yet, under Pisani's guidance, Liston was touching the very heart of Ottoman concerns. Selim III, he heard, intended 'that the Sublime Porte during his reign [should] assume a rank among the nations proportionate to the extent and resources of his dominions', and that 'the superiority of the Christian nations in arts, in arms, in finance' should be overtaken. For any such plans, Selim III's resources were pathetically small, and presupposed a degree of centralized control not available to him; Pisani believed no more than £2,000,000 reached the Ottoman treasury each year, against which figure, for the purposes of scale, we may set the £2.4 million Pitt spent on the Royal Navy between

1786 and 1790. More than this, the Ottoman historian of the period, Cevdet, points out that too many of Selim III's itinerant analysts of European power were civilians who, ignorant of military matters, led their royal master into dangerous paths and optimistic assumptions. A first glance at the *sefaret name* of Ebubekir Effendi, a zealous reformer-activist sent to Vienna for eight months in 1791, seems to bear this out; in his report, Ebubekir asserted that military reform *in any country* was little other than a resourceful theft of the best ideas and men. 'Every nation, state and community', he writes, 'creates a *Nizam-i-Cedid* [new military order] by sending secret observers [abroad] and by means of generous financial offers attracts [foreign experts] skilled in the science of warfare.'[46] Historically, such a judgement drew heavily on fantasy, but Ebubekir dared not candidly admit that the French army or the British navy were technologically autonomous whereas the Ottoman state was in these areas a European dependency. He had to couch the case for importing infidel weaponry and training in terms palatable to that conservative majority in ruling circles which argued that realism as much as piety prescribed the rejuvenation of state power from inner rather than external sources. Thus Cevdet, instead of belittling Ebubekir's military inexperience, might more justly have approved his wariness and the astute fashion in which he daringly introduced even the case for foreign alliances, by using an orbital kind of logic reminiscent of the so-called 'Circle of Equity' so familiar to the intellect of the Ottoman bureaucracy. A disciplined army, it was argued in the *sefaret name*, was impossible without an honestly administered financial system; for this, loyal ministers and responsible civil servants were indispensable; such imperial servants could only raise large state revenues without injustice if the people at large were prosperous and content; *contentment rested on the security provided by foreign alliances*; alliances would not be available to the state unless it had a disciplined, respected army. And so the argument returned to its starting-point, military reform.

It has been claimed, without foundation, that Liston acquired his information by bribing his way into the inner councils of the Ottoman ministers. It is not so. Where Ainslie once paid out as much as £2,000 to one individual, and gave away coaches, Liston bought telescopes from London with his own money at £10 apiece, cut-price *douceurs* for a parsimonious period.[47] He made his acquaintances by a simpler method, by attending at the Porte on Tuesdays and Thursdays, the divan days for foreign envoys; he was soon recognized as an honest, sympathetic, powerless man, and we know exactly whom he knew. Above all, there was Charles Callimachi, the chief dragoman of the Porte, a Greek Fanariot aristocrat with whom Liston could converse directly as both had Hebrew as well as Greek. It was Callimachi who softened the British ambassador's cool reception by having the *Canada*, a small vessel bearing his worldly goods, escorted through the French blockade of the Dardanelles by an Ottoman frigate.[48] Pisani told Liston that Callimachi was under orders to establish whether the new ambassador brought any special powers or policy, particularly the power to promise subsidies.

Of other contacts, Liston had four among the 20 or so members of Selim III's 'kitchen cabinet' identified by modern research;[49] only six or seven of the twenty were fully ready for the risks of modernization. The grand admiral, Kucuk Huseyin, by experience a complete landlubber, was currently overhauling the Ottoman fleet with striking success; taking the Royal Navy as his model, Kucuk Huseyin remembered Sidney Smith, was very attentive to Liston, and should be seen as the founder of the Ottoman navy. His wife was Selim III's cousin. The *reis effendi*, Rashid, was a thorough Anglophile, courteous and accessible; his successor, however, was to be Ebubekir Effendi, a strong Francophile, who Liston also knew, but distrusted. Lastly, there was a doddering grand vizier reputedly 'between 80 and 90', Melek Mehmed Pasha, 'who feels no passion but that of avarice, and with a placid neutrality lends his name to every measure that is adopted by a majority of the council';[50] Liston lacked the status to meet Melek Pasha familiarly, but recognized his importance to the reformers. It must, nevertheless, be added that the most resolute reformer of all, the bold soldier Celebi Mustafa Reshid Pasha, founder in 1794 of the miniscule *Nizam-i-Cedid*, a Western-style unit of no more than 400 men, was quite unknown to Liston, who never once mentions him by name. Nor did Liston meet those other brave men who were to be swept away with their royal master in 1807, reformers like Yusuf Aga of the Royal Mint, Ismail Ferrukh of the Imperial Granaries, Said Ali Effendi of the Treasury, Ibrahim Effendi, the secretary to the grand vizier's deputy, the *kahya bey*. After their annihilation, much more than the modernization programme was at risk. The very dynasty of the Ottomans survived in the person of a solitary teenager hidden in a disused bath furnace while the avenging janizaries searched for him, the future Mahmud II.

The rejuvenation of state power in a conservative society where the powers of inertia and veto were by tradition deeply entrenched depended, to a degree only half-understood in Great Britain, upon the courage and persistence of the sovereign himself, and it is fitting that in Konstantin Kapidagli's famous portrait, Selim III's liquid black eyes gaze back calmly at the viewer, with only the slightest lift of the eyebrows and a downturn of his sardonic mouth, for the Ottoman ruler was, in truth, a brave and lonely man, inadequately supported, ignorant of his own resources, and unsure about Europeans. Selim III has not yet, and probably never can, surrender his secrets to the historian. But the heretical cast of his mind is established, if all too readily ascribed to a Circassian mother and his European doctors. He was very interested in the science of fortification as dispensed by Vauban, in military medicine, and in weaponry. He reintroduced the printing press, silent in Constantinople since 1742. He also, Liston noticed, 'showed greater partiality for the arts than is thought consistent with the system of a rigid Mussulman', employing Italian miniaturists, listening to European music, attending obscene parties with Europeans in the Belgrad Forest.

But what of reforms? To such men of that period as the baron de Tott, Sir James Porter, André Chenier, and d'Ohsson, it was already too late for anyone to overhaul the Ottoman state. To that zealot for military reform, Sir Sidney Smith, it was not too late, but Selim III was not the man for the task, as his chief characteristic, Smith believed, was 'timidity, and whose most energetic measures are dictated by his apprehensions . . . [he] has turned his thoughts seriously to the new modelling of his army and his navy; their arms and discipline are to be imported from Europe, but every step he takes in this reform shows he cannot proceed without European instructors'.[51] Smith's own evidence contradicts his suggestion that Selim III was immobilized by his fear, and as for European instructors, the tiny experiment with the *Nizam*, which consisted of a few hundred new recruits, wearing red cutaway tunics of

European pattern and carrying French and Brescian muskets, while receiving orders from French and Prussian instructors relayed to them through Armenian interpreters, was a beginning. Selim III's private memoranda to his ministers likewise testify to his resolution. 'It is for statesmen to advise,' he declares, 'and then for the Padishah to execute decisions.' He also knew time was not on his side. 'For the love of God tell us [your views] for the state is about to be lost. Later will do no good. We have revealed to you our views. You too share the government.'[52] Selim III was, in his daily life, obsessed with the need for an answer to a very simple question: how had 80,000 Russians defeated 120,000 Ottomans in the war which ended in the treaty of Jassy?

While admiring the Sultan, Liston nevertheless feared for him and his plans. In Great Britain, where George III reigned but did not rule, it was generally believed, or at least said, that oriental despots, like most European sovereigns, still did both, but ambassadors to Constantinople had long pondered this question and in several instances anticipated Liston by suspecting that sultans did neither. Only people looking at the Ottoman Empire from a great distance could allow themselves the facile belief that force of royal character is a sufficient basis for absolutism; the ambassadors saw that despots still need agents to carry out their will. Furthermore, Ottoman despots and their agents were reciprocally dependent, for the royal sanction, though greatly reduced by the turmoils of a state in which the Sultan was often no more than another active participant, remained indispensable to ministers who, in most cases, rose to the highest offices from near obscurity, and so lacked that public and natural eminence which primogeniture, inherited wealth, or historical visibility conferred on the great families – on the *ayan*, as we might reasonably describe them – of the British Establishment. Having long since hung up their own swords, the British *ayan* now controlled admission to the institutions of government, recruited aspirants to a bureaucracy increasingly separated from the mainstream of the nation's politics, and had legitimated the Hanoverian dynasty; these were experiences which prevented them understanding that Ottoman history was running in a reverse direction to their own, not towards centralized constitutionalism but towards the chaos of regional jurisdictions. Sir James Porter had spotted the resultant instability at the centre long before, and had commented that 'an Ottoman officer has Power, and no power, he receives an order one moment, the next it is contradicted. Things are done and undone in the same instant.' So precarious a situation, he went on, tempted office-holders 'to think how long they are to continue, how they can support themselves, and how to make what money they can, in the short space of a transitory power'.[53] Liston thought the position was now worse, under the increased pressures of neighbours with a vested interest in Ottoman collapse. The ship of state which might be repairable in the security of a dry-dock was barely salvageable on the high seas of international controversy. As he explained it: 'The unity of plan and energy of execution derived from the uncontrolled authority of one man have been lost and the heads of departments have assumed independence in their different spheres, and a great proportion of their time has been wasted in a constant struggle with their antagonists.'[54]

In sum, Liston believed the Ottoman Empire had great natural resources. Ottomans in general had impressive attributes as an imperial people. But if the empire's survival was of importance to Great Britain, she must find a policy aimed at assisting its besieged dynasty. The Russians obviously did not want the Sultan to find the answers to his problems, to which end Catherine II had haughtily forbidden Selim III, as if he were a provincial official rather than an independent sovereign, to raise his tariff on exports to Russia. There was, it is true, resistance to the Russians, but from the wrong quarter; 'it happens, unfortunately, that those who are most ready to give their assistance, in this as in every other article [sic], are the French. Their zeal and activity are beyond belief.'[55] Offended that London should find money for underachieving Continental allies, but nothing for Ottomans holding Russians, Austrians, and French at bay, Liston decided – in contradiction of an earlier promise to the Turkey Merchants to do his utmost 'for the security of your immunities and privileges' – to help his hosts in the one modest way available to him; the least he could do was probably also the most Grenville would permit. 'There is among the Turkish ministers', he had discovered, 'a zeal to prevent and reform all abuses on the part of the European nations,' whose commercial misdemeanours meant a steady fiscal haemorrhage for the Ottoman state. So Liston decided to discipline the Turkey Merchants on his doorstep.[56] Now even had the latter proceeded overnight to an immaculate observation of Ottoman regulations, a noticeable benefit to the Sultan's treasury was hardly to be expected, so Liston's plan may be seen as no more than an ingratiating gesture, as an example other embassies might feel constrained to follow, or as the necessary preliminary to an imminent boom for British free-trade in the Levant. Most probably all three were in his mind; thus the Levant Company's ambassador was early recognizing how much the company he served obstructed overdue diplomatic action.

★ ★ ★

Spotting the culprits among the British was no problem; they so often declared themselves in aggrieved tones, and included public servants as well as private traders. One of the worst was Samuel Manesty, the clever, avaricious East India Company agent at Basra, a young man permanently swollen with self-importance, whose removal was the very first favour asked of Liston by the Porte. Both Manesty and his assistant, Harford Jones, were in very bad odour with the pasha of Baghdad, the Sultan's viceroy for central and southern Mesopotamia, whose main complaint was less against their indiscriminate selling of 'protections' (*barats*) to Basra merchants than against their outrageous discourtesy to himself. Any pasha's duties naturally embraced the supervision of tax collection, whether the duties at ports like Basra or the equivalent of excise charges in the interior markets of his administrative domain. It was also very important that the chief Ottoman official in a pashalik with long traditions of tribal independence and turbulent urban affairs should seem to be in firm political control. The inflated references to 'British Subjects' who were actually nothing of the kind and to his own power to overrule a high Ottoman official on their behalf are sure signs of the East India mentality, and while Liston regretted to Callimachi that he was powerless to dismiss such a man summarily, he seems to have overlooked the fact that neither Manesty nor any other British functionary could perform duties within the Ottoman domains without an *exequatur* issued by the Constantinople embassy. Liston could not dismiss, but he could certainly suspend.

The issue which brought Manesty beneath Liston's unfavourable notice was a capital case, one in which Manesty boldly appeared in a Muslim court to defend one of his 'protected' community charged with the murder of a Basra Jew. Manesty tried to win over Muslim feeling by saying the Jewish community had frequently 'reviled the Christian religion', and he sent Harford Jones to the pasha in Baghdad to 'demand' that Suleiman fine the Jewish community and publicly bastinado its 14 leaders. The pasha notified the *reis effendi* that the British agent was 'a man of juvenile age, and deficient in sound judgement, accustomed to behave ill to all the inhabitants of Bussora', and he would not allow himself to be budged to intervene in the Basra *kadi*'s (judge's) court.[57] Liston fully supported this position: 'I cannot too strongly exhort you [Manesty] to observe that degree of moderation' towards Suleyman Pasha, whose 'character and influence are very high indeed';[58] and the ambassador advised London to dismiss both Englishmen, a recommendation accepted in principle but not in practice. However culpable they might be, replacing men in distant places was a costly matter. Manesty and Jones survived without mending their ways and Elgin, succeeding Liston, was to remind them – once more in vain – of 'the propriety and obligation of paying deference to the religious opinions and national habits of the Turks', and of respecting their administration. Jones eventually overleapt Manesty, to become British minister at Tehran, but Liston's general and judicious admonition of their conduct is worth remembering:

> Europeans who have resided for a length of time in Indostan are in danger of carrying into other situations the ideas imbibed in that country. Accustomed to consider the native inhabitants of the East as an inferior race of men they are apt to indulge the same feelings with respect to the uncivilised Turks, on their arrival in the dominions of the Grand Signior. But as Mahometans of these countries entertain similar sentiments of their own superiority over all Christians, it is easy to conceive the collision and discord that must be the consequence of this contrast. And it seems highly necessary that the gentlemen who are to succeed Mr. Manesty and Mr. Jones at Bussora should bring with them a conviction of the moderation and forbearance which is demanded by the change of scene.[59]

It was much easier, of course, for Liston to lecture Turkey Merchants than East India Company men. In Aleppo, acting consul Edward Abbott wanted the grand customer of that city, Ibrahim Aga, publicly disgraced by an Ottoman official specially sent down for the purpose from the Porte. Once more, the charge was improper Ottoman interference with the rights of foreign traders, but in this case, too, Liston dug in his toes, quite convinced that British officials were unlikely to be objective reporters of quarrels in which they had a personal financial stake. 'I cannot help observing', he replied to Abbott, 'that the duties paid in the Ottoman territories are so extremely low that any attempts to defraud the revenue strike me as being susceptible of no apology.'[60] If pashas occasionally exceeded their powers, foreigners must only complain if they themselves never overstepped their privileges. Consul Hayes at Smyrna, for example, had quite disqualified himself in this respect; first, he built a house which violated the Muslim building code, and when the *kadi* placed his seal on the door to forbid occupation until modifications were carried out, Hayes compounded his error by tearing off the seal.[61] Such slights by foreign nationals, particularly by officials, were indefensible.

Even in cases where the British seemed to be the aggrieved party, Liston was very wary. William Turner of Zante, a successful trader, had one of his chartered vessels fired upon as it passed outwards through the Dardanelles. The pasha of the Dardanelles, resident at Gelibolu, had strict orders to prohibit grain smuggling, and no doubt it was bad marksmanship rather than truly hostile intent which brought Turner's ship to a stop so that it could be boarded and searched. Turner demanded that the case be heard by the *reis effendi* himself, but Liston would not be trapped. The way in which the ship was detained 'was barbarous, savage, brutal, everything you please to call it', Liston agreed. 'But he [the pasha] was in the right as to the matter, though not as to the manner, of the difference between you.' The *reis effendi* had been informed, and had expressed disapproval; the case could be taken no further. 'Indeed, I doubt if all the power of the Crown in England could in a similar case punish the lowest customs house officer.'[62]

Most of all, it was what Liston called 'Baldwin's Balderdash' that convinced him that the remaining British in the Ottoman territories were far too independent – audacious policy-makers under a defective chain of command, flouting Ottoman sovereignty at every turn. George Baldwin, now very old and almost blind, had served in Egypt for 40 years as private trader, Levant Company agent, and, most recently, British consul-general, an appointment quashed by Grenville on economic grounds in the very month in which Anglo-French hostilities began in 1793. Grenville gave

Dundas an opportunity to take over the appointment, which the latter rather surprisingly refused. Knowing all this, Liston thought Baldwin should behave and go home. Over time, Baldwin had become a self-proclaimed opponent of the company he had once served, accusing its directors of perversely hanging on to a monopoly they were too timid and poor to exploit. He recalled with particular bitterness the occasion in 1791 when company representatives told a Privy Council committee on the eastern trade that, although the Nile delta lay indisputably in their monopoly area, they feared that opening the Red Sea route, as Baldwin wished, would serve chiefly to allow East India textiles coming by it to undersell those coming round the Cape of Good Hope. What this really meant was that their own dwindling trade in Indian goods, imported through Basra and Baghdad to the Anatolian seaports, would die completely in the face of such competition. One may add, parenthetically, that the same timidity was to manifest itself again in 1798 when Selim III, as a gesture of thanks for Nelson's victory at the Nile, offered the Turkey Merchants full access to the Black Sea trade. At first jubilant, the Levant Company quickly turned down the offer in the belief that if the gateway of the Bosporus were to be opened slightly to let them into the Black Sea trade, the French would soon force it open wider still and drive them out.

Attitudes like these were anathema to Baldwin, who had great faith in the potential of the Red Sea trade, and believed its development would give the semi-independent beys ruling Ottoman Egypt a vested interest in helping maintain the Suez route as a vital line of British communications with India, particularly if they were allowed to tax British goods in transit between the Red and Mediterranean seas. Necessarily, there had been high and low points in a career as long as Baldwin's; in his *Political Recollections*, he recalls that he 'had the satisfaction to convey the first advices of the war of 1778 [when France sided with the American colonists] to the East Indies, by means of which they were enabled, to the astonishment of all England . . . to expel the French from India [i.e., Pondicherry] before succours could reach them'.[63] Unfortunately, the same patriotic zeal led Baldwin, on another occasion, to charter a special vessel at a cost of £4,500 to carry dispatches to India, and this despite a specific order to return the dispatches to

London if they arrived too late at Suez to go by a regular East India Company packet. This ruinous sum he was expected to repay, but never did, and never could have done. Looking back through his archives, Liston was glad to find these singularly bold initiatives had never been approved by Ainslie, who had more than one 'violent personal difference' with the consul-general. On the other hand, Baldwin has to be recognized as the man with the acutest understanding of the true significance of Suez. Given Liston's own correspondence with the Glasgow textile people, he might have been expected at least to fall in with the idea of opening the Nile delta to the risk-taking, free-trade fraternity, but his official position under the Levant Company made this impossible, at least officially. Much more, it was the Porte's extremely hostile reaction to the idea of infidels opening up the Red Sea commercially that determined Liston's own.[64]

Ottoman governments, as so often in the past, created their own difficulties in the Red Sea argument by the carelessness with which they spelled out concessions to infidels. On the one hand, they said they were immovably opposed to any trading ventures by Europeans north of the port of Mocha because of the proximity to Mecca. On the other, they periodically overlooked the use of the Suez route for diplomatic communication with India. Sir Robert Ainslie's friends, the grand vizier, Yusuf Pasha, and grand admiral, Hasan Bey, both condoned this concession exceptionally, while saying it must not be construed as countenancing trading. Unfortunately, the British Capitulations were quite clear and unconditional in defining the right of the British to trade *anywhere* in the Ottoman Empire, and the result was an altercation – between infidels adhering to the letter of the Capitulations, and the Ottoman authorities who expected acquiescence in their varying interpretations of the spirit of them. Nor were the Ottomans ready to be outmanoeuvred by a Baldwin who contended that a formal agreement with the Mameluke beys of Egypt would actually obviate any need to get Ottoman permission to open the Red Sea to trade and imperial communications. Baldwin managed to obtain the signatures of Ibrahim and Murad, the chief beys, to an agreement, but an expedition to Egypt led by the Ottoman grand admiral in 1786 had temporarily extinguished their independence.

Unfortunately for the Ottomans, their local authority in Egypt crumbled away very quickly thereafter, and in 1794 Baldwin pressed Liston to have the divan ratify the original agreement with the beys, by which the beys would collect the usual three per cent import duty for the Ottoman government, plus six per cent for themselves. Baldwin admitted Ainslie had always resisted him, but claimed, truthfully, to have the support of Dundas. In 1795, he further admitted the insecurity of the Red Sea route; an emissary of his had died carrying proposals to India concerning the Suez trade, and another carrying the Indian packets from Suez to Cairo had been murdered in the desert, his dispatches scattered to the winds. In reply, Liston reminded Baldwin that the current ministers at the Porte 'have of late bent their best endeavours, if not to abolish, at least to curtail' all European attempts to mediate between themselves and provincial authorities. They were already worried enough about French interest in Egypt and the Republic's encouragement of the rebel *ayan* in the Balkans. Consequently, only 'fresh orders and powerful arguments' from Lord Grenville would persuade the ambassador to advance Baldwin's cause,[65] so Baldwin had better approach Grenville through Dundas. In fact, Liston privately concluded, the best way to undercut improper behaviour among the British in the Ottoman Empire was to diminish sharply the number of 'protected' Ottomans who were sheltering beneath that umbrella of extraterritorial privilege, the Capitulations, usually Ottomans, Jews, and Christians urging their British protectors to ever greater defiance of all meanings of Ottoman sovereignty.

By attacking abuses of the Capitulatory regime, Liston was incidentally chipping away at his ambassadorial salary.[66] From its earliest days, the Levant Company was intended to run its affairs and finance the embassy at Constantinople without resorting to the export of specie from England, and the envoys it sent out were permitted to compensate for fluctuations in their incomes by selling *barats* and *fermans* to Ottoman subjects at their discretion. Holders of these documents were, in effect, temporary British subjects by purchase, exempted from Muslim judicial process for as long as they remained in embassy or consular service. Ottoman authorities permitted the practice, thus making a foreign representative fully responsible for the good behaviour of his 'protected' servants as well as for his fellow-nationals. The intention was obviously an extension of the Ottoman state's own custom of providing justice to the non-Muslim subjects of the Sultan, by holding religious leaders responsible for the good behaviour of their denominational communities.

The privilege became abused as increasing numbers of Ottoman non-Muslims with no real connection with any embassy or consulate began to solicit, and embassies began to sell without limit or discretion, *barats* and *fermans*, thus permitting the holders to keep their testamentary affairs, commercial litigation, and, above all else, criminal suits in which they were involved with Muslims away from the uncertain outcome of a *kadi*'s court in which, it is important to notice, the uncorroborated testimony of a single Muslim witness could, and commonly did, outweigh the cumulative evidence of any number of Christians. Vanity came into the picture, too, though vanity with a practical dimension. A *baratli* or *fermanli* was not confined, as other non-Muslims were, to 'the graver and darker colours' of dress, and thus to pass unnoticed in a Muslim throng increased personal safety considerably. To one chief category of aspirants, the merchants, *barat* and *ferman* secured immunity from the Ottoman head tax imposed on all Christians, and, more valuable still, exempted them from the burdens of the Ottoman tariff, which touched Europeans hardly at all and bore heaviest on the Muslim mercantile community. Liston's experience tells us how these 'temporary naturalizations', as he rightly called them, benefited the rich Armenian broker, the Greek Orthodox sea-captain, the Basra Jew dealing in gold, the rising commercial genius of some sleepy port in the Archipelago, or the extortionist of any denomination ready to play the import-export agent for a select few, at the expense of neighbours and rivals in the ranks of the faithful. 'It was natural', Liston explains, 'that a patent which raised a tributary subject from a state of degradation, and procured respect for his person, security for his possessions, and the patronage of an ambassador at the seat of government, should soon become an object of ambition.' But the 'object of ambition' corrupted seller as well as purchaser, and ambassadors, consuls, and the pettiest levels of unpaid European officialdom dispensed protections until their numbers rose into the thousands. In the Syrian city of Aleppo, there were no fewer than 1,500 'protected' *baratlis* and *fermanlis* in Liston's time. 'People were seen strutting', he declared, 'in the habit of a diplomatick interpreter [presumably the black balloon hat and yellow slippers] who were unable to read the patent through which they held their privileges [and might well reside] a thousand miles distant from their master [i.e., ambassador].'[67]

The informal price list was everywhere an open secret, and a barometer of the local standing of the embassy concerned. Since about 1750, Liston discovered, Russian 'protections' cost about 10,000 piastres each, partly because they secured admission to the lucrative Black Sea wheat trade, partly because the Russian embassy was always the one Ottomans most feared to disoblige. French 'protections' were worth marginally less than the Russian; a British *barat* or *ferman* somewhere between 2,500 and 6,000 piastres. From the company books, Liston found that Ainslie had conventionally disposed of 39 *barats* for his personal advantage, natural attrition permitting him to resell three or four of them each year, thus bringing him about £1,500 a year. At lower prices, consuls and vice-consuls pocketed useful sums of money. Viewing the whole system with 'invincible repugnance', Liston notified both Foreign Office and company that here was a Rubicon he would never cross; the Ottomans really detested the system as much as he, 'and with the greatest possible appearance of reason'. Far from selling 'protections' for his own profit, he intended to call in as many as possible. He wanted a proper, consolidated salary for himself suitable to the times. There was an unexpected result; finding such honest intent inconvenient as well as eccentric, the company offered him unpaid leave in 1795, which he accepted; unwilling to pay for his return to the East, Grenville took advantage of Liston's presence in London to post him to the United States, and left the Ottoman Empire without an ambassador for four years.[68]

Without bothering to ask the company's permission, Liston cut back the luxuriant growth of the Capitulatory system on the principle that 'barats should be sought after, not offered', and, in the vast majority of cases, withdrawn completely.[9] The usual routine was for a new ambassador to renew all *barats* and *fermans* unquestioningly for a flat fee of 60 piastres as a friendly gesture, but knowing the Porte wished *barats* cut to 50 per embassy, Liston called in all documents held by 'British' families, examined them with care, and withheld a substantial number on the argument that their former holders had no official function to perform. He read all the consuls a lesson on the evils of corruption, and did not conceal his dislike for a system of employment which permitted many of them to trade; he wanted all consuls paid a proper salary, he wrote, and thought they should become political officers first, supervisors of expatriate trading communities only second. No consul, not even a consular dragoman, should have a stake in the commercial interests under his care.

Later history tells us that Liston was swimming against a quickening current. Also, the Foreign Office was unwilling to take over the consular establishment in the Levant so long as the Levant Company survived, and the company could not provide the salaries Liston wanted. The ambassador responded philosophically, 'I must look forward to the assistance of Government and wait for happier times', a very long wait.[70] It is unfortunate that his good intention was not supported more resolutely by the Porte, and there is evidence that Selim III, foolishly, was prepared to sell Capitulatory privileges himself as a source of income. In time, the European embassies became havens for Ottoman subjects seeking much more than commercial and personal privileges. As centres drawing on the religious loyalties which many Ottoman Christians were ready to accord them and, more ominously still, as focuses of encouragement and support for the rising political aspirations of Balkan subject peoples within the empire, they were destined to loosen the bonds of the Ottoman state and to sabotage it from within. In Liston's time, Russia alone had adopted this subversive role for her embassy.

★ ★ ★

Throughout this period, the French mocked Ottoman independence and neutrality, repairing their own ships in Ottoman ports, freely auctioning off their captures there, and never hesitating to seize neutral vessels in Ottoman waters or even harbours. The 'Conventional frigates', Liston grieved, dominated the waters of the Levant, and 'would not be bound by any article of the law of nations'.[71] At times, no less than 200 loaded merchantmen, most of them neutrals, lay in the Golden Horn, waiting for a strong northeast wind to propel them through the French blockade of the Dardanelles. Insurance rates were high; 'caravanning' from port to port in search of cargoes for Europe, once common practice, was given up. Sir Sidney Smith was disgusted that only four French frigates, regularly on station, kept the Levant seas safe for France and dangerous for everyone else, and complained to Grenville that 'our Turkey trade, already at its last effort, will be totally transferred' to enemy hands unless the Royal Navy intervened.[72] Liston agreed; his diplomatic efforts had 'no prospect of suppressing democratical insolence and securing our trade in the Levant Seas except by means of a formidable squadron of our own'.[73] When Liston finally went home, leaving Spencer Smith in charge of the embassy, the latter also argued with his superiors that 'the most urgent necessity exists for taking means to support the national interest and dignity in this part of the world', and that Liston had done everything humanly possible to diminish French influence, 'but every day offers fresh instances of the impossibility of effecting anything here without [naval] support'. Sir Sidney Smith returned to the same charge, claiming he had a secret correspondence with Selim III; that the latter would be delighted to flout the French if only a few British warships put in an appearance 'under the mouldering walls of the Seraglio'; and that Grenville himself must accept considerable personal responsibility for a sad situation so easily capable of repair. 'The French aimed at this influence, and we did not step forward in competition . . . . A very small force would convince him [Selim III] that France was not mistress of the Mediterranean.' Smith referred the foreign secretary to 'my good friend', Earl Spencer at the Admiralty, for enlightenment, but Grenville steadfastly refused to become educated about naval matters.[74]

Throughout these years, it is clear that the sailor Smith was more than willing to become the scourge of the French in the Levant, a role which finally fell to him in 1798 with the French invasion of Egypt. Meanwhile, the Ottomans behaved, in Liston's phrase, as if they had 'never spent a thought on the Law of Nations, and never heard of the existence of Vattel and Grotius', the great European theorists of international law.[75] How could it have been otherwise? Few European powers remembered Vattel and Grotius in their dealings with Ottomans, or each other. When Grenville did relent a little in 1795, it was to urge the Admiralty to respect Ottoman neutrality, and observe her international rights *as a token of friendship!*[76] This truth must have been driven home with Liston when Captain Samuel Hood turned up briefly in Levant waters in late 1794 with three warships under his command (*Aigle, Cyclops, Nemesis*), and a few support ships; if anything was more embarrassing than the navy's absence, it turned out to be its presence, and Hood squandered a marvellous opportunity to underpin the British embassy's diplomacy by behaving as the French had done.

The campaigns of the First Coalition had the usual devastating effects of war upon agriculture, and the mid-1790s was a period of widespread famine in Europe. It is the food shortages in France which underlie, and necessarily diminish, Lord Howe's celebrated sea victory off Ushant on 'the Glorious First of June' in 1794, an occasion on which Howe captured six French sail-of-the-line but missed entirely their convoy of 100 merchantmen, packed with American cereals. For years thereafter, French vessels of every size scoured the Mediterranean basin for grains: in Algiers, the south Ottoman ports, and, above all, Egypt. Ainslie believed the French employed 200 grain-carriers in the Black Sea alone.[77] Pisani once told Liston of a single convoy consisting of 33 *kirlangic*, each vessel carrying 5,000 *kilots*; some days out from Damietta, the convoy broke up and its members made for such points as Naples, Genoa, Leghorn, and Marseilles. All this time, the Ottoman cities stood in serious need themselves; summer weather in 1796 was so dry that mosques everywhere obeyed an imperial order to pray for rain; Pasvanoglu's disorders in Bulgaria interrupted grain supplies from Wallachia; and the Russians were still in Moldavia, where Ottoman speculators sold to them, in spite of official prohibitions on the export of foodstuffs from the empire. In Constantinople itself, Liston warned his government of 'the serious want of provisions' and 'the approach of famine'.[78] By a masterstroke, the French made a great show of seizing any Russian, Greek, Austrian, or Venetian carrier engaged in 'Black Sea speculations' trying to run their blockade of the Dardanelles, ostentatiously selling off some of the captured cereals in the bazaars of the Ottoman capital. In some instances, Descorches declared his readiness to adjudicate conjointly with the officials of an Ottoman prize-court, if only the kaptan pasha would agree: it was a neat way to keep the Ottoman Empire embroiled in argument with her other trading partners. Even Carolina rice had made a first appearance there, thanks to American ingenuity, so why should not Great Britain take control of this situation, regulate the flow of wheat, and earn Ottoman gratitude while exhibiting the might of her navy?

Hood quickly turned the situation round in Levant waters, scattering French grain-carriers in all directions as they dashed for sanctuary. In the process he seized a large French merchantman in the gulf of Smyrna, and this was the start of the long-lived 'Miconi affair', in which the Ottomans argued that the British capture was made within a mile of shore, and so in their territorial waters, while Hood grumbled that they had received no satisfaction from the French for similar offences. Hood's lesser captains were sometimes as lubberly as their chief; during one close-in interception, 'the guns of the *Romney* did damage to different churches, killed a number of cattle, so terrified the inhabitants as to occasion the miscarriage of several women, and . . . Captain Paget made a very disrespectful answer to the representations made to him by the chief men of the town'.[79] So disrespectful was it that no interpreter was required to explain, and Liston tartly reminded Hood, once more, that 'any capture made within cannon-shot of a neutral shore is illegal', not to be repeated.[80] Under pressure from the *reis effendi*, Rashid Effendi, Liston also asked Hood to release any intercepted grain ships which turned out to be destined for Constantinople. The city was in great need and the Sultan would appreciate the gesture. Hood refused. What, he asked, would prevent any intercepted Frenchman from saying he was carrying his cargo to Constantinople? Relations between the naval and diplomatic professions reached their lowest point when Liston requested the surrender of the controversial 'Miconi' capture to an Ottoman prize-court; Hood gave up the ship grudgingly, and it was promptly restored to its owners, as Liston had all along suspected might be the outcome.[81] A previous intervention by Lord Grenville may even have foreseen such an outcome, for in reply to his ambassador's account of Ottoman frustration, he had declared that neutrals must not expect immunity for their goods if they shipped them on belligerent carriers, and as for 'Miconi', the Ottomans must 'suffer that affair to rest in silence'[82] and remember that Portugal had been content with an apology when Admiral Boscawen smashed the French fleet in the territorial waters of the bay of Lagos. This was a shameful evasion, and no apology either.

Suddenly, however, it was Hood's turn to be the supplicant, and to show civility to an Ottoman prize-court. One of his ships, the *Nemesis*, ran aground in Smyrna harbour, whence the French captured it 'without, as it appears, any opposition on the part of the British frigate beyond a fierce remonstrance at the illegality of the measure'. Hood got the kaptan pasha himself to attend a shipboard carouse on his own flagship, and believed all would go in his favour. But it was not to be. In the autumn of 1795, Admiral Ganteaume escaped from Toulon with a squadron of six warships, 'captured a great many English, Russian and Neapolitan merchant-vessels' in the Levant, and removed the *Nemesis* to North Africa under escort.[83] Ganteaume then dashed for home at the news of a much bigger force coming after him under Captain Troubridge. The *Nemesis* thus became a prize of special importance to both British and French, and in early 1796 Sir John Jervis made a special point of taking her out of yet another neutral harbour, Tunis. His order said the vessel was to be seized 'by fair means or foul'. By then, however, Liston had gone home on leave, assuring Grenville that his secretary, Spencer Smith, could safely be left in charge, as he had 'a good knowledge of Turkish' and, more remarkably still, 'a perfect knowledge of the world'.[84] Actually, Smith had neither, but Liston had had enough of trying to make bricks without straw, and felt acutely his government's neglect and his own defeat by the local friends and allies of the French Republic.

★ ★ ★

In his sojourn in the East, Liston was unable to carry out his government's chief order, to prevent Ottoman recognition of the French Republic. Selim III withheld formal recognition for three years. When Descorches took forcible possession of the royalist French embassy in early 1795, Liston was told he must not interpret Selim III's acquiescence as 'an Acknowledgement of [Republican] sovereignty', but Selim III himself is supposed to have been incognito in the crowd which watched the tricolour run up the masthead. Later, when Ottoman envoys were sent to the different European courts, the kaptan pasha, Kucuk Huseyin, told Liston of 'his abhorrence of the ruling faction in France', but he too, as a typical anti-Russian official, would not recommend a formal break with Paris on ideological grounds – which, indeed, would have made no sense to him or any of his colleagues – if the only practical result was an intensification of Ottoman isolation and friendlessness in the eternal confrontation between the Ottoman and Russian Empires. When Suvorov, Catherine II's greatest general, announced after the final liquidation of Poland that he expected soon to be sent against the Ottomans, the latter had no difficulty in believing him. When Kochubey, the Russian ambassador, tried to damp down the effects of such talk, actually telling his hosts that Russia and France were 'no longer at peace', he was as readily disbelieved. It was the most obvious and routine response for Descorches to assure the Ottomans that only a Franco–Polish–Prussian coalition would serve for 'the future arrestation of Russian ambition'. Sensibly, the Ottomans began the repair of the Danubian fortresses in the spring of 1795. Then, in May, came Raymond Verninac to replace Descorches, swearing he would not even unpack until the Ottomans formally acknowledged the fact of French Republicanism. Within a week of the new envoy's arrival, Liston confirmed that some of Marie Antoinette's jewellery – the French 'Crown Jewels', he misleadingly called them – 'have been observed in circulation', while Mouradja d'Ohsson, now promoted from dragoman to chargé d'affaires at the Swedish embassy, was known to have demanded, and probably got, 50,000 French *livres* as his fee for winning the Ottoman ministers over.[85]

Now d'Ohsson was 'toujours ami de la Republique', but it would be too simplistic to think bribery alone produced the pro-French reconstruction of the Ottoman council on 7 May 1795. The Prussians, it should be noticed, had just recently made their notorious 'predatory alliance' with the Directory by the treaty of Basle, and the war in the west had gone so badly that Lord Auckland, the doyen of British diplomats, had suggested withdrawal from all continental exertions, and set a personal example by resigning the diplomatic career absolutely. When Izzet Mehmed Pasha replaced Melek Pasha as grand vizier, the 'Parisian' Ebubekir became *reis effendi* in place of the anglophile Rashid, and the eternal contest between the rival factions for the office of *Bas Tercuman* (interpreter to the Porte, effectively, under-secretary for foreign affairs) was temporarily resolved with the elevation of the Murusi over the Callimachi family, Liston was the first to see the changes in personnel as a natural consequence of the survival of Republican France and the collapse of the First Coalition. Callimachi's transfer to Moldavia as its *hospodar* could be seen as a promotion, but the British ambassador was distressed and regarded it as political rustication. Referring to the appearance of George Murusi in the garb of chief dragoman, he candidly agreed that 'the partiality of the family of Murusi [for the French] appears to be founded on a more solid basis than the temporary effect of corruption. They seem to have adopted a system which leads them to consider France as the natural ally and support of the country.'[86] Murusi actually asked Liston to provide 'passports' which would allow the French frigates under Ganteaume to sail home unmolested. The abiding Ottoman reliance on France is seen in one of Ebubekir's first acts as *reis effendi*; he sent Paris a list of instructors and technicians needed in the modernization programme. They went out with Albert du Bayet in 1796.

On 8 June, Verninac had his official audience with the grand vizier, the usual preliminary to presenting credentials to the Sultan in person. Verninac had already received visits, amounting to formal recognition, from his Venetian, Prussian, and Swedish colleagues. There was another influential factor; Liston knew Prussia had abandoned the First Coalition in April, the Dutch in May, the Spaniards in July, but was late in hearing of the Anglo-Russian defensive alliance also signed that spring. Catherine II agreed to supply 18 warships to fight the French, but Liston never received a copy of the treaty. Verninac naturally told the Ottomans the alliance might well be turned against them, while Kochubey denied this. With London silent on the matter, the new Ottoman ministry was inclined to believe Verninac. Presently, they recognized him, and the Directory he served.

'It was the misfortune of the Turkish reformists', Niyazi Berkes has written, 'that they were drawn to the point of striking up a friendship with France at a time when French public opinion and diplomacy were unfriendly to the Ottoman Empire.'[87] Liston, we may be sure, would not have characterized the Franco-Ottoman relationship as a 'friendship', but as a necessity forced on Selim III by his international isolation and his domestic weakness. The Ottomans had no friends, and in international relations such things are not to be expected, but their collaboration was available to any who approached them in a spirit of mutuality. For the time being, the French embassy was able to trade successfully on the marvellous assets inherited from a royalist past even though the undercurrent of French hostility towards the Ottoman Empire to which Berkes refers was also known in Constantinople where it divided officialdom, not between reformers and conservatives, but between those audaciously ready to ride the Republican tiger in the hope that it would really savage, and not just growl at, the Russian bear, and those others, more mindful of the scorn of Voltaire and Diderot, the pro-Russian preferences of Volney and d'Alembert, and the imperial recommendations at Ottoman expense of de Tott, Choiseul and Truguet, who believed that the empire should remain isolationist and external to all European affairs, able to hold the Russians at bay while rejuvenating itself from its own inner resources. In the year 1798, the lie was given to this residual hope. Liston himself adds a footnote to the Ottoman dilemma, many years later. In 1815, he was, once more, ambassador in the Ottoman Empire, where the news of the battle of Waterloo was received on 25 July. 'But it is impossible', Liston told Castlereagh, 'that the Sublime Porte in her present predicament can look forward without alarm to the complete success of the Grand Alliance [which would allow the Russians] to turn a part of their veteran and victorious troops against her Dominions.'[88]

NOTES

1. FO to Ainslie, 2 Aug. 1793, Ainslie to FO, 10 Sept. 1793, FO 78/14.
2. In 1791 the salaries for the various ambassadorial positions were as follows: France, Lord Gower, £8,320; Holland, Lord Auckland, £8,320; Spain, Lord St Helens, £8,320; Turkey, Sir Robert Ainslie, £1,095. After these four, there followed the major envoys extraordinaire and ministers plenipotentiary: Austria, Sir Robert Murray Keith, £4,405; Russia, Charles Whitworth, £3,520; Prussia, Joseph Ewart, £3,320. The other European courts with British representatives were Bavaria, Cologne, Denmark, Hesse-Cassel, Poland, Portugal, Sardinia, the Two Sicilies, South Netherlands [Belgium], Sweden, the Swiss Cantons, Tuscany, and Venice. As over one-half of the incumbents of these lesser courts had higher salaries than Liston, it is apparent that Constantinople did not figure as a major cost at all.
3. On the recommendation of Dugald Stewart, Sir Gilbert Elliot of Stobo gave Liston two years to prepare himself in law, languages, and dancing before taking the boys to Paris in 1764, where they were educated alongside Mirabeau, who became a close friend. Liston entered diplomatic life as the private secretary to Hugh Elliot – who incidentally fought in the Russian army against the Ottomans in 1772 – before entering the diplomatic service in 1773. Liston served with Elliot at Munich, Ratisbon, and Berlin. In 1783 he went with Lord Mountstewart (later marquis of Bute) to Spain as secretary of embassy, his first diplomatic appointment. After two months, Liston found himself as acting minister plenipotentiary, a post he was to hold for the next five years. He came home in August 1788 and was sent that same month as minister to Sweden. His official Foreign Office appointment to Constantinople falls between January 1794 and February 1796. After service in the United States as minister and in the

Batavian Republic, his second Constantinople embassy ran from 8 April 1812 to 18 October 1821. He was knighted in 1816, and died in 1836. The *Gentleman's Magazine*, ii (1836), 538, called him 'the father of the diplomatic corps throughout Europe'.
4. Liston to Aust, 11 Feb. 1794, NLS MS 5579.
5. Cyril Matheson, *The Life of Henry Dundas, First Viscount Melville, 1742–1811* (London, 1933), p. 84. Henry Cockburn wrote of Dundas that 'he who steered by him was safe; who disregarded his light was lost': *Life of Lord Jeffrey* (London, 1852), i. 77.
6. Henry Cockburn, *Memorials of His Time* (Edinburgh, 1856) – see especially pp. 104–8 for his attack on Braxfield; Henry Thomas Buckle, *The History of Civilization in England* (London, 1857), especially his chapters on Scotland in the seventeenth and eighteenth centuries.
7. *Selections from the Letters and Correspondence of J. Bland Burgess*, ed. J. Hutton (London, 1885), pp. 131–2. For accounts of the Foreign Office, a new department of state in 1782, see M.A. Thomas, *The Secretaries of State, 1681–1782* (Oxford, 1932); E. Jones-Parry, 'Under-Secretaries of State for Foreign Affairs, 1782–1855', *English Historical Review*, xlix (1934), 308–20; D.B. Horn, 'The Diplomatic Experience of the Secretaries of State, 1660–1852', *History*, xli (1956), 88–99.
8. Huskisson to Dundas, 4 Sept. 1798, SRO GD 51/1/768/80.
9. Sir William Blackstone, *Commentaries on the Laws of England* (London, 1783), i. 155.
10. Ainslie to Liston, 10 and 26 March, 30 April 1794, NLS MS 5579.
11. See chs. I and II in this volume.
12. Ainslie to FO, 25 April 1794, FO 78/15; FO to Ainslie, 28 April 1795, FO 78/16.
13. Liston to Aust, 11 Feb., 17 Nov. 1794, NLS MS 5579.
14. Mustafa Nuri, *Netaie ul-Vukuat* (Istanbul, 1877–79, 1909–18).
15. Thomas Naff, 'Ottoman Diplomatic Relations with Europe in the Eighteenth Century: Patterns and Trends', in *Studies in Eighteenth Century Islamic History*, ed. Thomas Naff and Roger Owen (Carbondale, 1977), pp. 88–107; see also Thomas Naff, 'Reform and the Conduct of Ottoman Diplomacy in the Reign of Selim III, 1789–1807', *Journal of the American Oriental Society*, lxxxiii (1963), 295–315; J.C. Hurewitz, 'Ottoman Diplomacy and the European State System', *Middle East Journal*, xv (1961), 141–52.
16. J. Holland Rose, *William Pitt and the National Revival* (London, 1911).
17. Dundas to Pitt, n.d. [Dec. 1794], *Dropmore MSS*, iv. 433.
18. Pitt, memo, 1791, PRO 30/8/195, fos. 49–55.
19. William E. Eton, *A Survey of the Turkish Empire* (London, 1799), p. 23.
20. FO to Liston, general instructions, n.d. [Feb. 1794], FO 78/15.
21. Liston to unidentified, 25 Nov. 1794, NLS MS 5580.
22. Grenville to Liston, 26 Feb. 1794, FO 78/15, no. 1.
23. Grenville was unaware that he had offended the Ottomans deeply by his discourteous treatment of Yusuf Aga, who was on his way to London before the guard at Dover Castle had turned out to welcome him. Moreover, Grenville refused to pay any of the costs of the Ottoman embassy; Christian envoys to London, on the other hand, received free passage when travelling through England. For Yusuf's embassy to England, see Ainslie to FO, 10 July, 10 Aug., 25 Oct., 21 Nov. 1793; FO to Ainslie, 4 Oct. 1793; Edward Smith, commander, Dover Castle, to FO, 21 Dec. 1793: FO 78/14. The dragoman of the Porte told Ainslie specifically that Liston was allowed to pay his own way through the

Balkans in 1794 because Grenville had done the same to Yusuf Aga. See Ainslie to Liston, 10 March; Murusi to Ainslie, 19 March; encl. in Ainslie to Grenville, 26 March 1794: NLS MS 5574.
24. Liston to Aust, 11 Feb. 1794, NL MS 5579.
25. See Liston to unidentified [Sir Sidney Smith?], 3 May 1794, NLS MS 5579.
26. Quoted in A. C. Wood, *A History of the Levant Company* (New York, 1964), p. 179.
27. Quoted in Liston to Pisani, 10 Jan. 1794, NLS MS 5579.
28. B. Pisani to Liston, 25 Feb. 1794, NLS MS 5581; same to same, 26 March, 5 and 6 May 1794, NLS MS 5575. In the first of these letters, Pisani estimated a rebel army threatening Smyrna at 10,000 men. Another was the one Liston encountered on his journey. Liston comments on 'the great joy and surprise of the peasants' when he paid for the victuals they supplied. For Liston's journey, see Liston to FO, 24 May 1794, FO 78/15.
29. Liston to J. Hopkirk, 28 June 1794; Liston to unidentified, 10 June 1794, NLS MS 5579.
30. For the British 'Hotel', see Messrs Hubah and Timoni (the owners) to Liston, 30 April 1794, NLS MS 5574; Liston to Levant Company, 10 July, NLS MS 5579, and 10 Dec. 1794, NLS MS 5580; B. Pisani to Liston, 24 Nov. 1794, NLS MS 5575, and same to same, 10 Feb. 1795, NLS MS 5581. Most of the embassies in Constantinople were rented from Christians in European service; thus, the Russian embassy was the property of Nicolo Pisani, the French legation belonged to Antoine Fonton, the Venetian to the family of Fornetti. The Hubah–Timoni partnership could have sold the British building before for £15,000, but agreed to keep renting it so long as the Levant Company rent was raised to offset inflation. The rent was £1,600 by 1768, £2,000 in 1774, £3,000 by 1794. In this last year the Company was offered the building for the sum of £9,000, but could not afford it.
31. Liston to Levant Company, 10 Dec. 1794, NLS MS 5580.
32. Spencer Smith to Grenville, private, 1 Feb. 1799, *Dropmore MSS*, iv. 463.
33. Eton to Levant Company, 23 Feb. 1799, SP 105/127.
34. In 1798, for example, when Bonaparte invaded Egypt, to be marooned by the battle of the Nile, Lord Loughborough wrote to Pitt describing how he had fallen in with a businessman who was a very good judge of the temper of the City 'who had said that money was so abundant and confidence so high' that opening the Levant trade 'will give a great spring to commerce'. Loughborough to Pitt, 5 Oct. 1798, *Dropmore MSS*, iv. 335.
35. *Spencer Papers*, ii. 9; SP 105/337, pp. 250–60. Imposition Books, 1731–1808, are in SP 105/169–72.
36. See A.T. Embree, *Charles Grant and British Rule in India* (New York, 1962), pp. 37–42.
37. David Dale, Robert Owen's father-in-law, introduced a very successful Turkey red dye at New Lanark with the help of a Frenchman appropriately called Papillon. See L. Conan, *From Granpa's Tea Chest* (London, 1951), pp. 291, 306, 335, 413.
38. Spencer Smith to FO, 16 April 1797, FO 78/18.
39. Coy to Straton, 28 Feb. 1805, SP 105/130; Edward D. Clarke, *Travels in Various Countries in Europe, Asia, and Africa* (London, 1810–23), i. 68–9.
40. Liston to the Levant Company, 25 July 1795, NLS MS 5581.
41. Ainslie to FO, 25 Jan. 1794, FO 78/15.
42. Quoted in N. Daniel, *Islam, Europe and Empire* (Edinburgh, 1966), p. 86.

43. For some consideration of the propaganda warfare in the Ottoman capital, and the impact of revolutionary ideology, see B. Lewis, 'The Impact of the French Revolution on Turkey', in *The New Asia: Readings in the History of Mankind*, ed. G.S. Métraux and F. Crouzet (London, 1965), pp. 81–9; also L. Lagarde, 'Note sur les journaux français de Constantinople à l'épogne révolutionnaire', *Journal Asiatique*, ccxxxvi (1948), 271ff. For Ottoman reservations about the aims of the Revolution, see Daniel, *Islam*, pp. 85 ff.
44. Liston to Ainslie, 17 Nov. 1794, NLS MS 5579.
45. Liston to FO, 10 Sept. 1794, FO 78/16 and Daniel, *Islam*, p. 86.
46. For a summary of Ebubekir Ratib Effendi's report, see Stanford J. Shaw, *Between Old and New: The Ottoman Empire under Sultan Selim III, 1789–1807* (Cambridge, Mass., 1971), pp. 95-8; Enver Ziaya Karal, 'Ebu Bekir Ratib Efendi'nin "Nizam-i Credit" Islahatinda Rolu', *Turk Tarih Kongresi, Ankara 12– 17 Nisan 1956: Kongreye sunulan tebligler* (Ankara, 1960), pp. 347–55.
47. Liston to Moore, 25 July 1794, NLS MS 5579; Ainslie to FO, 10 Jan. 1788, FO 78/9.
48. Liston to Hayes, 21 May 1794, NLS MS 5579.
49. Ainslie to FO, 26 March 1794, FO 78/15.
50. Daniel, *Islam*, p. 165.
51. Sidney Smith to Grenville, private and secret, 13 Jan. 1795, *Dropmore MSS*, iv. 2.
52. For a discussion of the Nizam-i Jedid army, see Shaw, *Between Old and New*, pp. 130–3.
53. Quoted in Daniel, *Islam*, p. 80.
54. Quoted in ibid., p. 163.
55. Liston to Aust, 17 Nov. 1794; to Whitworth, 16 June 1794: NLS MS 5579.
56. Liston to Aust, 17 Nov. 1794; to Abbott, 23 July 1794: NLS MS 5579.
57. Encl. by Suleiman Pasha, 23 May 1794, in Liston to Aust, 24 June 1794, NLS MS 5572. See also Daniel, *Islam*, pp. 155–6.
58. Liston to Manesty, 17 June, 9 Sept. 1794, NLS MS 5579.
59. Daniel, *Islam*, p. 149.
60. Liston to Abbott, 9 Sept. 1794, NLS MS 5579.
61. Liston to Levant Company, 10 Oct. 1794, NLS MS 5580.
62. Liston to Turner, 23 Dec. 1813, NLS MS 5658; Daniel, *Islam*, p. 148.
63. George Baldwin, *Political Recollections Relative to Egypt* (London, 1801), pp. 6–7.
64. Baldwin to Liston, 30 Oct. 1794, NLS MS 5580; Liston to Baldwin, 4 April 1795, NLS MS 5581.
65. Liston to Baldwin, 4 April 1795, NLS MS 5581; to FO, 16 June 1795, FO 78/16.
66. Liston to Levant Company, 10 Oct. 1794; to Wilkinson, 7 Oct. 1794, NLS MS 5580.
67. Liston to Levant Company, 25 Feb. 1795, NLS MS 5581.
68. Ibid.
69. Liston to Chassaud, 18 Oct. 1794, NLS MS 5580.
70. Liston to Levant Company, 25 July 1794, NLS MS 5581.
71. Liston to Hayes, 23 June 1794, NLS MS 5579; to FO, 10 Jan. 1795, FO 78/16.
72. Sir Sidney Smith to Grenville, private and secret, 13 Jan. 1795, *Dropmore MSS*, iv. 2.
73. Liston to Wilkinson, 27 Aug. 1794; to Captain Hood, 16 Aug. 1794: NLS MS 5579; to Levant Company, 10 Oct. 1794, NLS MS 5580.
74. Sir Sidney Smith to Grenville, private and secret, 13 Jan. 1795, *Dropmore MSS*, iv. 2.

75. Liston to FO, 25 Aug. 1795, FO 78/16.
76. Grenville to Liston, 12 May 1794, FO 78/16.
77. Ainslie to FO, 25 April, 12 May 1794, FO 78/16; B. Pisani to Liston, 18 Nov. 1794, NLS MS 5575.
78. Liston to Hood, 6 March, 9 May, 9 June 1795, NLS MS 5581.
79. Liston to Montgomery, 30 June 1794, NLS MS 5581.
80. Liston to Hood, 13 March 1795, NLS MS 5581; to FO, 24 March, 10 April 1795, FO 78/16.
81. Liston to FO, 26 May 1795, FO 78/16.
82. FO to Liston, 12 June 1795, FO 78/16.
83. Spencer Smith to FO, 25 Nov., 24 Dec. 1795, FO 78/16; Werry to Smith, 31 Dec. 1795, ibid.
84. Liston to FO, 25 June, 24 Oct., 4 Nov. 1795, FO 78/16; to Grenville, 9 May 1795, to Levant Company, 25 Sept. 1795: NLS MS 5581.
85. Liston to FO, 26 May, 10 June 1795, FO 78/16; to Whitworth, 12 May 1795, NLS MS 5581.
86. Daniel, *Islam*, pp. 85, 91; Liston to FO, 9 and 26 May, 25 June, 10 July, 12 Sept. 1795, FO 78/16.
87. Niyazi Berkes, *The Development of Secularism in Turkey* (Montreal, 1964), p. 64.
88. Liston to Castlereagh, 25 July 1815, NLS MS 5630.

CHAPTER IV

Robert Adair and the Treaty of the Dardanelles

The Ottoman Empire was, by the beginning of the nineteenth century, far past those great days when an Elizabethan ambassador declared it 'fearful and terrible to the whole world'. The failure to take Vienna in 1687 was perceived generally in Europe as a deliverance, the turning at last of a great tide, and the eighteenth century as an era of progressive Ottoman losses, in which the year 1774 stood out with particular significance as the Sultan, for the first time, lost Islamic populations (in the Crimea) to Catherine II. Formerly a cause of great European concern, the Ottomans were now the target of generalized scorn and contempt. The fate of Poland, swallowed up by her neighbours in three partitions, naturally led western diplomats – and some Ottomans – to ask what means the Ottoman Empire possessed for avoiding a similar fate. In short, the imagery of 'the sick man of Europe' had yet to be coined but the idea of it was abroad, mitigated by a widespread acknowledgement that, while Islam seemed mercifully to have lost its propulsive force, Ottoman resources in men and materials remained impressive, awaiting only the reordering genius of a mastermind to resist the acquisitive machinations of Russia, Austria, and Prussia. Unfortunately or, according to the point of view, fortunately, the Ottoman dynasty seemed unlikely to throw up such a man as the empire galloped to disintegration. With the coming of the Revolutionary and, even more, the Napoleonic ages, the fate of the Ottomans was deflected by their reconnection with the circulatory system of European diplomacy, and the principle of 'Ottoman integrity' received an unexpected, temporary, and precarious wartime validity.

France, rampaging through the successive coalitions raised against her, adopted the principle in order to embarrass Russia and to defer a political revision of the Muslim Eastern Mediterranean until such time as the European state system was brought to complete submission; Russia adopted the principle as an occasional necessary manoeuvre to disengage from the selected enemy barring her ingress on the Mediterranean and Mesopotamia in order to resist France and push her own territorial claims in eastern Europe; Austria, slain repeatedly by France between 1789 and 1813, and four times risen from the dead, adopted it because the problems of resurrection left little time to challenge Russian imperialism in the Balkans, a region towards which she was progressively reoriented, in the truest sense of that word, by the collapse of the Holy Roman Empire and the loss or diminution of her German, Polish, and Adriatic possessions.

The people who had the greatest difficulty in accepting a conservative commitment towards a decrepit empire in which they had no important economic or political interests, actual or prospective, were the British. Their unformulated wish was that everyone should pretend the Near East did not exist, but this anxiety to keep the region a power vacuum – a policy they repeatedly and mistakenly claimed as proof that they had no policy at all and were perfectly disinterested – drew them in, in order to keep others out. The other powers irritatingly misunderstood, and saw British activity, not as a response to their own, but as an initiative to be countered. The Napoleonic era, therefore, prevented the further decline of the Ottoman Empire in the European 'balance of power', until the final disintegration of that empire in the First World War.

In 1807, of course, the outlines of this portentous eastward extension of the game of nations were barely visible. The more particular point then was that French and British policies were beginning to move in contrary directions, with Napoleon putting aside his eastern aspirations, as he hoped, temporarily, while the British began to supplant him, permanently. The British were unprepared for this success, unsure how to utilize it, and reluctant, as Shelley put it, 'to brand their name with the indelible blot of an alliance with the enemies of domestic happiness, of Christianity, and civilisation'. Necessarily, they inherited the dilemma which was Napoleon's at Tilsit.

★ ★ ★

When Lord Salisbury, in 1896, revealed a growing indifference to the continuance of Ottoman authority in the Christian Balkans, he was making a return rather than a departure, as can be seen from the instructions George Canning gave first to Arthur Paget in 1807,[1] then to Robert Adair. A perusal of the very meagre archives dealing with Anglo-Ottoman affairs in his department could reveal only one 'policy' to the foreign minister: consistent neglect. In the traditional way, Paget was told to remember that 'your first Object is Peace, and the second, Peace with perfect satisfaction to Russia'. Had the Ottomans agreed to receive Paget in 1807, his prospects of a quick settlement had to be small for, even more unfeelingly, he was to tell them that, if they would not settle with him, Great Britain would feel free to recognize the independence of the Greeks and 'the Pashas of Janina and Syria'. The Ottomans must defer to the interests of Russia, even to the point of territorial concession, in order to resist the yet more drastic appetite of France. There was, at the time, a school of thought, stimulated by the influential William Eton, which proposed that if the Turks were driven out of Europe, and their force concentrated in Asia, they might possess the power to prevent any European power marching eastwards to India.[2] In 1798, Henry Dundas, president of the Board of Control for India, called Russia 'our natural ally', which his colleague Lord Grenville amplified to 'our old and natural ally'. In moments of believed extreme hazard, as when the French were in Egypt, Dundas was quite prepared to employ Russian troops in the defence of India. By 1807, his son, following him to power at the same board, likewise believed in the importance of keeping one's eyes on the main enemy, and urged Canning 'to exclude the French from all connection in any part of Africa and Asia, as might facilitate to them [sic] the means . . . of directing the efforts of any body of Troops against our Indian Territories'.[3]

Great Britain's deference to Russian interests fluctuated with the varying availability of the tsars in the anti-French crusade: Russia's prestige was low in Great Britain in 1793 when the second partition of Poland was begun, high in 1799 when she took up arms against France, fell in 1800 when she changed sides, rose again in 1805 when the Anglo-Russian alliance was made, fell once more after Tilsit, and began to edge up marginally when, by 1808, the two imperial conspirators were beginning to fall out. There was no comparable graph of Ottoman reputation to be plotted, though the Sultan was also allowed to be, in moments of indulgent phraseology, 'our ancient ally', which in truth he had in practice never been. The Anglo-Ottoman treaty of 1799, a response to the French invasion of Egypt, was the first between them. It broke down amid mutual recrimination, was soon replaced by open if undeclared war, and led in 1807 to Admiral Duckworth's violation of the Straits with the intention of bombarding Constantinople, not to mention General Fraser's invasion of Egypt, a failure as bad as Duckworth's. As Robert Adair, selected by Canning to repair this state of affairs, put it: 'Early in 1807 we find England at war with the Ottoman Empire: not for any wrongs of her own but for those of Russia; and later in the same year, at war with Russia herself. We had thus completely changed sides with regard to the Turks.'[4] Fearing France as they did, the Ottomans in 1809, and later, remained as unable as before to embrace the Russian bear as cordially as Great Britain intermittently argued they should.

The choice of Adair to repair Anglo-Ottoman relations in 1808 caused considerable comment in London society. A cousin to Lord Holland, Adair was an unrepentant Whig, christened 'Fox's Goose' by Canning himself, and once lampooned in the *Anti-Jacobin* by Canning as the farcical oriental potentate, *Bawb-adara-dul-phoola*. What was generally remembered against Adair was his notorious visit to St Petersburg in 1791 when he assured Catherine II that she could ignore Pitt's threat to fight Russia in defence of the Ottoman Empire: parliament would contain the Tory leader, as indeed it did. Would the Ottomans, with their long memories, receive such a man now?[5] Lord Malmesbury thought of a more human problem: Adair could never keep state secrets, least of all from pretty women.[6] Should he be in diplomacy at all? Canning thought so, and chose Adair because Adair knew Vienna – the great whispering gallery of international affairs – better than anyone else. He had been driven out by French pressure in 1808, but was very ready to return there and assist his old friend, Count Stadion, in keeping Austria in touch with Russia as well as Great Britain. Herein lay Adair's willingness to return to Vienna by way of Constantinople. 'European Turkey was', he recollected in his *Negotiations*, 'the only spot on the Continent from whence England can assist the House of Austria.' One might judge from this that Adair had drifted far beyond his one-time Russian sympathies, but this would be incorrect: 'Our peace with Turkey will be an easy matter. The great point will be to persuade them [the Ottomans] if possible to make peace with Russia, and this immediately, and almost at any price.'[7] Canning agreed thoroughly that a British settlement with the

Ottomans should be 'a work of little difficulty', as Great Britain had 'nothing to ask of the Porte' for herself. As to Ottoman concessions to Alexander I, these could be 'comparatively disadvantageous to us'. What Russia obtained territorially from the Ottoman Empire would be determined by what Austria, gathering her courage to resist France once more, would tolerate. Canning did not disclose on paper what the Ottoman Empire might in his view surrender, but we do know what territories Adair believed were in play: Moldavia and Wallachia. No wonder he was excited and grateful for his new appointment, or that he should assure Canning that his appointment 'of a person known to you by his connections with a party with which you are at variance is a proof of liberality on your part which does you the highest honour'.[8]

The instructions for the mission to Constantinople were jointly devised by Adair and Canning, Adair recalling later that the foreign secretary actually asked him if anything beyond Paget's orders was needed.[9] Both men belittled Duckworth's adventure as an indiscretion which should not obstruct a quick peace. A single-clause treaty would be enough to allow British merchants, currently chafing in Malta, to return to their Ottoman homes while Adair turned to the liquidation of the Russo-Ottoman war. Both also shared the facile opinion that self-interest must always bring the Ottoman Empire into the anti-French camp, as if she could not lose whichever side she chose.

The most interesting – and secret – passage in Adair's instructions rests on the speculation that, by the time he got to the East, he might just find that the French had been obliged to retain the collaboration of Alexander I by embarking on the partition of the Ottoman Empire which the Tilsit agreement promised. It might, for instance, be the price on which alone the tsar would agree to control Austria as France became enmeshed in Iberia, and was reason enough for Adair to avoid 'any precise and formal guarantee of the Dominions of the Porte'. Should the Ottomans be driven from the capital city they had held for three centuries, Great Britain would expect them to resist and would require the temporary surrender of the Ottoman fleet into British custody. Remembering the advice given by Sir Sidney Smith in 1800, Canning also mentioned Chios, Milos, and Crete as places Great Britain might have to occupy. 'So long as the Porte is willing and able to maintain an effective struggle for the Preservation of its European Dominions', Great Britain would fight alongside her, but *only until Constantinople was recovered*. On the ultimate fate of the Ottoman Balkans, Canning would not be drawn, but put some tentative ideas in the secret dispatch. If the Ottomans were driven into Asia, Great Britain would feed supplies and weaponry to Ali Pasha of Janina or any other leader ready to raise insurrections in the wake of French and Ottoman armies marching upon, and beyond, Constantinople. Necessarily, such leaders, and communities like the Greeks, might eventually qualify themselves for some degree of independence in return for services rendered. Adair would naturally conceal these long-term possibilities for as long as Ottoman resistance was a reality, and it would be enough, if an onslaught on the Ottoman Empire had not yet developed, to flatter Ali Pasha of Janina, for example, with nothing for the moment beyond inlaid pistols. Nothing, of course, was known in London about the new Sultan, Mustafa IV, to whom Adair was accredited. He might prove strong and resolute. If so, and Adair made peace, he would reside at Mustafa's court as ambassador,[10] challenge the authority of the French ambassador, General Horace Sébastiani, and reach out in conciliatory fashion to Austria and Russia.

★ ★ ★

On the afternoon of 28 June 1808, Adair arrived at Spithead to join the war frigate *Hyperion* – which had brought home his predecessor, Charles Arbuthnot – with a small suite consisting of John Bidwell and Stratford Canning – the foreign secretary's cousin – of the Foreign Office; his private secretary; and a Levant Company dragoman, conspicuous in his yellow shoes of office, called Berthold. The *Hyperion*'s captain, readying to return to the Mediterranean, had no orders to receive the ambassadorial party on board and Stratford Canning declared, on the first page of the journal Adair instructed him to write up each day, that the Admiralty had 'as usual, been very negligent'. Adair wrote a slashing attack about the matter,[11] but it should have warned him how little his way ahead had been planned by George Canning, and alerted him to the mutual ignorance of departments on whose collaboration his hopes of success depended.

Adair voiced a few doubts about what lay ahead. The earl of Elgin, going out in 1799, had taken a grand 'equipage' and rich presents for Ottoman ministers. In India, Marquis Wellesley had spent East India Company money like water. But Canning had been very firm, and forbade, even as an opening gesture of goodwill, any compensation for the losses Admiral Duckworth had inflicted. Nor were there to be any subsidies: Parliament would never finance the Ottomans. Watching muskets being handed over the ship's side to bobbing boatloads of Portuguese guerrillas, Stratford Canning offered his cousin his congratulations should 'the Power of Bonaparte be overthrown, and the Independence of Europe be re-established during your Administration'. He also allowed himself to grieve about 'the oppressive load of insignificance' now that he was sailing past the scene of momentous action, and would have gone home if he had had a chance.[12] He soon learned how laboriously political combinations are put together, how many details of planning are so often overlooked, and that making bricks without straw is the very shift of diplomatic enterprise. Adair, setting the example, was already writing, writing, writing, to friends and contacts in Europe, clandestinely disclosing his purpose, asking their aid.[13]

Like most travelling diplomats, Adair was a postman for numerous people along his route. He carried correspondence for naval officers, money for French *émigrés* at Palermo, blank receipts which illiterate guerrillas must sign to gratify audit office accountants, and an invitation to the Pope to take refuge in Constantinople, which no pope had done for a very long time. His own venture, however, seemed to command little interest in others. Admiral Cotton, presiding over landing operations at the Tagus, predicted that, with Joseph Bonaparte chased from a usurper's throne at Madrid, General Pierre Dupont surrendering an army of 18,000 Frenchmen at Bailen, and Sir Arthur Wellesley's main force coming ashore in two weeks' time at Mondego Bay, the navy would be stretched to capacity for the foreseeable future. Adair's proposal that Corfu be taken as a present for the Austrians was brushed aside. At Gibraltar, Admiral Collingwood, commanding in the Mediterranean, had obviously not been briefed to offer any contribution to the materialization of Canning's grand yet remote contingencies, and the old despot told Adair that Canning was being romantic. The islands he spoke of were barely usable; if an island had to be chosen, far better take Thasos, with its forests and water, than any other. But all this was academic: Canning must talk to the Admiralty, or even his Cabinet colleague Viscount Castlereagh, who had nominal direction of the war effort. Adair was so upset by his discouraging interviews that he thought at one moment of throwing up his mission and joining the revolutionary junta in Seville. But the naval men, convinced the Franco-Russian alignment was already breaking up, urged him on, assuring him the Ottomans would be waiting to give up a losing cause with their usual celerity.[14]

Other difficulties followed. At Palermo, the crew of the *Hyperion*, landlubbers provided by the crimps of Portsmouth, were in 'a disagreeable state', and quite unequal to the next stage of the voyage through the fickle channels of the Ionian Islands and the Cyclades. Another naval vessel had to be obtained from Malta. It was at Palermo, too, that Berthold, the interpreter, was sent back home, ostensibly for additional orders, in reality because the Foreign Office had discovered reasons to distrust him: once first dragoman of the British embassy at Constantinople, Berthold had been sacked by the Levant Company in 1800 for overstaying leave, and, as he was an Austrian by birth, Canning was not very happy about him now. Worst of all, Sir Charles Stuart, the army commander in Sicily, confirmed Collingwood's prediction that he would be unable to supply troops for any operations on the Anatolian coast: 'I have no difficulty in mentioning to yourself that I do not think any one unit of this Army could be spared for such garrisons at the present crisis, without paralysing the entire force.'[15] So Adair must not think of naval expeditions through the Straits, to protect the Ottomans or pressure the Russians. If Canning was seriously interested in the Levant, why had he abandoned so incomparable a base as Egypt to Muhammad Ali? Brightening up, Stuart advised Adair to do his best 'with an olive sprig in your hand', which, Adair said in reply, was hardly likely to 'get the mediation for the Russian peace with Turkey out of the hands of France'. Thus, for a time, Adair was quite becalmed, without a ship, a dragoman, or any show of naval support to encourage the Sultan to repudiate 'the artifices of Sébastiani'.

Adair was soon cursing about yet more frustrating news. There was a rumour of a further palace revolution at Constantinople, and a new ruler might annul the invitation given in February 'which constitutes the whole foundation of my mission'. Sailing to Malta, Adair received there a letter from Consul Francis Werry of Smyrna who had slipped quietly back to his post although Great Britain was still nominally at war with the Ottoman Empire. There had indeed, Werry reported, been a palace revolution, and there was for the moment no way of saying 'in what manner an intercourse can be opened with any of the leading persons, or who are the leading persons'.[16] It was rumoured, however, that Galib Effendi, the *reis effendi* who had belatedly invited Paget to return to Constantinople, was still in power. So, too, were a few other pro-British officials. Stratford Canning, meanwhile, was appalled at the lack of patriotism of the Levant Company merchants living in Malta as temporary refugees. He did not expect much from such 'mongrels' as Levantines, but it was upsetting to find English-born people 'detached from their country as much by interest as by distance', most of them jabbering behind Adair's back in the argot of the Orient, complaining about London's stupidity, and at least some of them making it clear that they did not now want a hasty restoration of peace, having discovered the profitability of smuggling goods back through the British blockade of the Dardanelles. 'Can anything like public spirit be reasonably expected from men whose only hope and pursuit is making money?' the young secretary asked himself, while vowing such people should never get any favours from him.

Presently, Adair's new ship was found: ironically, it was the *Sea Horse*, one of the blockaders, a vessel already infamous to the Ottomans for having seized several of their ships, including a frigate. The plan adopted was that Captain Stewart, the ship's commander, would keep Adair's party below decks, and on the pretext of exchanging prisoners at the outer strait, ask the pasha of the Dardanelles if a British emissary would still be received if one appeared. The *Sea Horse* only sailed for Tenedos on 10 September and, three months after leaving England, Adair's party lined the rail while the coast of Turkey came into view. Three months later again, George Canning heard they had arrived only to be turned away.[17] By then Adair had actually signed a peace treaty.

In his old age, Stratford Canning recollected that he was Adair's first intermediary in opening negotiations at the Dardanelles. This was not actually true. Having lost Berthold, Adair was compensated many times over by the acquisition in his place of David Morier, one of the four gifted sons of the British consul-general in the Ottoman Empire, Isaac Morier of Smyrna. Only slightly older than Stratford Canning, Morier was a tall, laughing cavalier; at home in Dutch, he also had a considerable command of Turkish, Italian, French, and Persian. Formerly secretary to Paget, he joined Adair from the court of Ali Pasha of Janina, and had written the outlines of a novel – *Photo the Suliot* – while in the Balkans. In time, he would be one of Castlereagh's most valuable aides at the congress of Vienna, but for the moment he was Adair's obvious and, indeed, only possible negotiator with the pasha of the Dardanelles. Going ahead of the *Sea Horse* in a small brig, in disguise and at night, Morier enquired if a negotiation was still feasible. The pasha told him Great Britain's great friend, the ex-grand vizier, Yusuf Pasha, had been sent to Arabia to fight the Wahabi but that the new *reis effendi*, Galib Effendi, who had tried to bring Paget back, had orders from the new Sultan, Mahmud II, to negotiate with Adair in utmost secrecy, without the French embassy hearing of it. The *Sea Horse* thereupon moved along the shore of Troy to the white-washed, windmill village known to sailors as 'Cape Janizary', there to wait a month for the arrival of an official negotiator from the Porte.[18]

Vahid Effendi, the same official who had been kept dangling by Armand de Caulaincourt at Warsaw in 1807 for a treaty with France which never materialized, and who uncovered 'the treachery of the French at Tilsit', arrived at the Dardanelles on 2 November 1808 as the Ottoman plenipotentiary sent to make peace with the British. His credentials were translated for Adair by Bartholomew Pisani, the senior dragoman of the British embassy, released from the prison at Konya to assist the negotiation. Stratford Canning smirked at the credentials, and found Pisani 'honest' but 'in his dotage'. The *Sea Horse* was invited through the Straits to the anchorage called Point Barbieri and fresh food at last came on board from Canakkale. A small farm was prepared for the conferences, and Adair looked forward to a brisk settlement.[19] Yet the treaty of the Dardanelles was not signed until almost two months later, on 5 January 1809.

Adair got off to a peevish start, finding himself treated as a supplicant by a French-speaking official who insisted on receiving the respect due to a seventeenth-generation descendant of the Prophet. Adair would have been wiser not to open the negotiation with a reference to Duckworth's 'forbearance', and to have avoided the threat that, unless a settlement was made quickly, Great Britain would simply sign a separate arrangement with Russia in which 'the interests of the Ottoman Empire at best will be forgotten'. This was play-acting, but it was indiscreet, since Ottomans did not need to be told that Europeans had small concern for their interests. Vahid, on his side, was in no hurry, had better information than Adair from Europe, and was determined to get far better terms than Canning's proposed single-clause settlement if his country was to risk a rupture of diplomatic relations with Latour-Maubourg, the deputy of the departed Sébastiani.

Stratford Canning thought Vahid merely frivolous considering the danger hanging over the Ottoman Empire, and wrote to his cousin that Vahid seemed 'anxious to amuse himself at the expense of Mr. Adair's patience by writing long accounts of nothing'. At one point Adair threatened to sail away, but Vahid responded that he was thinking of the same expedient himself. Adair stayed. Vahid Effendi was not really playing with Adair. He was playing with his own life, as presently Adair understood. A great glow in the night sky of 14 November, clearly visible from *Sea Horse*, testified to the destruction by fire of the Sublime Porte, the seat of Ottoman government, and to great upheavals in the capital city. Mustafa IV had gone. Had his young successor, Mahmud II, gone too? It was because Vahid needed to hear who his new masters were that further negotiation with Adair was suspended from 26 November until 12 December. In the interval, Adair had time to reflect on the quite unexpected counter-demands of his Ottoman opponent: the return of four naval ships taken by the British blockade;[20] compensation for Duckworth's devastations; a severe reduction in the number of Ottoman subjects enjoying extraterritorial rights as British-protected persons; and a clarification of the rules for the use by European powers of the Straits. Adair had difficulty in adjusting to the idea that, if British merchants were entitled to have their property back, the Ottomans should have theirs. One or two of the issues raised seemed to him to be best dealt with by the Levant Company. But Vahid, on his side, was endeavouring to strengthen the reality of Ottoman sovereignty, so constantly being shaken from without and now, once more, from within.

What a very few Europeans glimpsed indistinctly as a faction fight between rival heirs-apparent in Constantinople actually bore a sharp family resemblance to the crimes and struggles which had marked the progress of the English Reformation over two centuries before. In each situation, control of the throne was contested, and with a passionate brutality, between forces of conservatism and innovation; in each situation, the politics of religion were in fearsome play, the realm was devastated by overmighty subjects, and kingmakers rose and fell. The difference between the two was that in the English case the dynasty emerged stronger from the crucible, surviving further civil wars while integrating the national polity, whereas the Ottoman dynasty, though strengthened also, could never sufficiently exact the substance of power – in men, money, or supporters – to stabilize its position for long. While Adair's ship crossed the Mediterranean, Selim III was deposed, replaced by Mustafa IV, then murdered. This did not save Mustafa who was, in his turn, put aside by Selim III's great champion, the reformist pasha, Mustafa Alemdar of Ruscuk; replaced by Mahmud II; and strangled at his prayers. Afraid to let any opponents live, even in defeat, Mahmud II, or more probably his grim saviour, drowned the women of Mustafa's harem off the Prince's Islands. By this strategem, it was agreed, a chronic war of succession would become impossible.

The coup of 14 November merely announced the counter-coup of the janizaries, fearful for their own survival. They set fire to the Sublime Porte, reducing it to ashes along with thousands of nearby houses. The regiments of Selim III's 'new troops' were brutally suppressed or, as in the suburb of Levend, locked up in their barracks with their families and incinerated. Janizary control was established in the great Bosporus strong points: Rumeli-hisar, Tophane, Uskudar. The besieged Mustafa Alemdar died, it was said, by his own hand, in a flaming tower. Only young Mahmud II, the very last of the line of Othman, somehow survived, to wait and watch for revenge. When Stratford Canning first reached Constantinople the body of Mustafa Alemdar, salvaged from the ashes of his last citadel, was still on show, suspended by one leg, revolving, heedless of the insult heaped upon it. The sight taught the young secretary of embassy that he now inhabited an arena of peculiar precariousness and ferocity. From the distance of the Dardanelles, however, Adair stubbornly rejected Ottoman domestic politics as two-dimensional, even irrelevant, with no necessary place in his calculations; an important mistake, which Stratford Canning laboriously unlearned over time.[21]

When Vahid was authorized to resume negotiations with Adair in December, Adair once again proposed a restoration of peace, the return of British-sequestered property to its owners, and free use of the Straits again for commercial purposes, as the nucleus of a treaty. Vahid, however, wanted much more than this, and made it plain that a full treaty would be the *sine qua non* of Adair being allowed to travel further. In a startling *contre-projet*, Vahid asked for direct trade between the Ottoman Empire and the British colonies; a defensive alliance, as the Ottoman Empire was bound to be attacked by France for making peace with Great Britain; British mediation in the creation of peace between Russia and the Ottoman Empire; and a large cash subsidy. Adair was flabbergasted that anyone should lay impious hands on the Navigation Laws, and Stratford Canning added: 'Had I not been present at many of the conferences, I could hardly have given credit to many of the absurdities which he [Vahid] advanced.' But Vahid was adamant and reminded his guests that the Sultan did not forbid Europeans trading to *his* dominions! As for the subsidy, Vahid boldly claimed that George Canning had already promised one to the Ottoman envoy in London and that, furthermore, Paget had also been committed by his instructions to the principle of indemnification. Adair searched anxiously his copies of Paget's correspondence, then declared that Vahid was making 'the most unaccountable mistake' or risking 'the most audacious fraud'. He haughtily proclaimed that he would not 'buy peace', but the fact remains that it was Vahid who stood firm while Adair capitulated by degrees, Vahid tempting Adair onward by saying all awkward terms of their treaty could be buried in secret articles.[22]

On 12 December, with his staff fidgeting and a naval captain to placate, Adair made his first concessions by agreeing in principle that Great Britain certainly *ought* to assist the Sultan actively if the French attacked him, and help him make peace with Russia. This gesture, Vahid replied, gave him fresh life, and that he would now be able to proceed with alacrity and hope. By 20 December, Adair had gone as far as to agree, no longer in simple principle but to practical arrangements, to supply the Sultan with military stores, and to defend the Aegean Sea with British ships, should France attack. More generous still, he agreed that 'the departure of the French chargé d'affaires from Constantinople shall constitute a case in which the obligation of the above Article shall come into effect'. Thus Adair committed his country to supply ships and arms, which the naval and military chiefs had assured him were not available, and to supply them in a situation which the Ottomans could precipitate simply by expelling Latour-Maubourg, or the French by withdrawing him. When Vahid demanded a £1 million subsidy, 'to be absolute and not contingent upon a French attack', Adair struggled feebly, telling George Canning: 'I thought it fair to let him know that of all possible sorts of assistance that by subsidy would be most objectionable.' But when the alternative seemed to be an empty-handed departure, Adair made a compromise, promising £300,000 whether the French attacked or not within six months of the ratification of the treaty,[23] a treaty which by now was far more interesting for its secret than its public arrangements. Finally, as Stratford Canning wrote in the 'Precis of Despatches' which he compiled for Adair: 'W.E. [Vahid Effendi] refuses to agree to British Ships of War being allowed up to Constantinople. . . . Mr. A[dair] agrees to his arguments.' Beyond this, there was very little left for Adair to withhold or disagree about. All Canning's ideas were abandoned: the single-clause treaty 'of little difficulty', the refusal of subsidies, access to the Straits so that Great Britain could shield Constantinople or coerce Russia, and the limitation of Great Britain's defensive commitment to 'Turkey-in-Asia'.

This turn of events naturally heightened some of the earlier views taken of Vahid Effendi and his 'enormous demands'. Stratford Canning, who had originally spoken of Vahid's 'ignorance and childish petulance', now informed his cousin that 'he seems to have more reason and better understanding than what one is generally taught to expect from a Turk'. Vahid could not only read the European papers, but he affably supplied Stratford with copies of the *Frankfurt Journal* to bring him up to date. The Turk also had some surprising information, and told Stratford Canning complacently through Pisani that he had spies in Paris, that he knew all about the deterioration in Franco-Russian relations at Erfurt in October, and that he also knew the Foreign Office in London had received an agent from Ali Pasha of Janina. Stratford Canning opened his mouth to deny this when Vahid interrupted to say the emissary's name was Said Ahmet and that he had been presented to George III: Stratford Canning closed his mouth again.[24]

Vahid went one step further; having shown that he had intelligence and information, he revealed a sense of history:

> Indeed, if any credit is to be given to the word of a Turk, nothing can stand in the way of the Conclusion of Peace. . . . Mr. Adair had sent to ask the Effendi's permission for us to visit Troy; to which request he acceded with pleasure but added that if Mr. Adair would defer his visit till his answer should be received from Constantinople [authorizing signature of the treaty] he would himself accompany us, and if it pleased Mr. Adair, would sign the Treaty on that celebrated spot.

Nevertheless, there was no treaty of Troy in 1808, nor was it Vahid's fault. His government took a long look at a treaty Adair thought they could not seriously think of refusing.

To the end, the negotiation hung by a hair's breadth. 'On the 1st of January', Adair wrote in his later book, 'I actually hoisted sails to leave.' A grinning French consul sat in a row-boat, watching the Ottoman dragoman shaking Pisani's hand and going ashore while the British sailors were climbing the rigging to let out sail on the *Sea Horse*. Stratford Canning's thoughts were winging home in unpatriotic glee when news arrived at the last minute that Constantinople had ordered the treaty to be signed. 'Vahid fairly confessed that I could do no more than I had done to facilitate peace . . . if the peace should not be signed . . . he was a lost man, and that he must take refuge in England.'[25] Adair and Vahid put their signatures to the treaty of the Dardanelles on 5 January 1809. There is no evidence that Vahid had been hanging on in hopes of what an earlier British ambassador used to call 'the soothing palliative of a golden unction'. Quite simply, Vahid wanted Adair to sign his terms, and not vice versa.

The settlement which brought a century of peace between Great Britain and the Ottoman Empire was known in London in February, only days after the news that Adair had arrived in the East: it was ratified at Constantinople, after a fashion, on 27 July.[26] As Adair guessed, the treaty caused quite a stir at home. Sent to make a simple peace-settlement and defensive arrangements only if the Ottoman Empire were found to be *in extremis*, Adair with mixed feelings put his name to a document with 11 public and five secret clauses. In his haste, and in his anxiety to reach Constantinople to open communications with his friends in Vienna and urge the burning of Sebastopol as a means of hastening Russia's abandonment of France, he failed to draw up the treaty in English, signing versions in French and Turkish only. As Stratford Canning wryly informed his cousin, the treaty of the Dardanelles exhibited 'a perfect contempt for all diplomatick usages' but had 'the merit of being unique'.[27]

The public articles, with one exception, represented a liquidation of most Ottoman complaints against Great Britain, and a normalization of relations between the two sides. By them, the dispersed British merchants were allowed to return to their homes in the capital and Smyrna, and their sequestered property was restored to them, less the usual deduction for 'pilferage'. In spite of Vahid's earlier threats, the Black Sea remained open to the British merchants,[28] the tariff was unchanged, and no more was said about the heresy of Ottomans trading directly with British colonies. Compensation for Ottoman losses was also dropped by the Ottomans.

Pressure was successfully applied, on the other hand, to get the British to behave better in two related matters: the number of dragomans, or interpreters, was henceforth to correspond to the true needs of the British embassy; and the number of *baratlis* (licence-holders) – Ottoman citizens holding exemptions from Ottoman legal process which permitted them to live under the extraterritorial regime of one or other European power – was to be cut back sharply. The dragomans, often dressed as Europeans, engaged Ottoman dignitaries in negotiation with an audacious familiarity which outraged good Muslims and made the dragomans self-important heroes among the Christian millets; the Ottomans badly wanted to keep their numbers down. The *baratlis* were becoming a state within the state, their numbers running to thousands. For instance, there were thought to be 600 French *baratlis* in Smyrna at one time. British *baratlis* were less numerous, but the exemption from Ottoman laws – and taxes – was greatly cherished and British ambassadors had traditionally augmented their poor salaries by selling *barats* to eager Christian, and occasional

Muslim, merchants. Adair was content with four dragomans and also agreed to cut 126 existing 'publick instruments of protection' (*barats*) to 51.[29] It was Sébastiani who had first put it into Ottoman heads to abolish all Russian *barats* in 1806 as a means of preventing Greek traders from trading into the Black Sea under the Russian flag. Now it was Great Britain's turn to be disciplined, as part of the general Ottoman plan to prevent foreigners from flouting Islamic law, dressing in forbidden colours (green above all, the Prophet's colour), and in other ways setting a bad example to the empire's Christians.

Finally, of the public articles of the treaty of 1809, there is Article XI, the last. It is an instructive comment on the changing importance which different generations attach to treaties that Lord Palmerston was to dig out the treaty of the Dardanelles in 1833 to consider minutely this article to which George Canning appears not to have given a second thought. Article XI reads:

> As ships of war have ever been prohibited from entering the Canal of Constantinople, that is, through the Strait of the Dardanelles, or that of the Black Sea; and as this ancient rule of the Ottoman Empire ought equally to be observed for the future by every Power in time of peace, the Court of Great Britain promises to conform to this principle.[30]

Adair agreed to Article XI because, as he advised Canning, 'the Porte wishes to seize this opportunity of a war with Russia to put an end absolutely to the admission of ships of war of the Powers' through the Straits. This was, of course, quite true; since the alliance of 1799, Russian warships had made free use of the Straits in the process of supplying Russian admirals in the Adriatic. Furthermore, Greek subjects of the Sultan who were in the shipping trade had, in numerous cases, raised the Russian flag over their ships, and there was a thriving trade in Russian passports among them. So it was a great stroke to have Great Britain's formal act of self-denial in his pocket when the Sultan came to a peace negotiation with Russia. The Russians must not be allowed to imagine that the Straits were to become a waterway of permanent access to their warships, in peace as in war. But in addition, and as Adair evidently failed to understand, the Ottoman authorities drafted Article XI with the British in mind too. Admiral Duckworth had forced the

Dardanelles at a time when Great Britain and the Ottoman Empire were at *peace*; Sir John Louis was blockading the waters of a state which had still not declared war nor done Great Britain any harm. It followed that any power which made a commitment like Article XI and then, ever again, violated its promise to refrain from passing warships through the Straits in time of peace would be, in effect, committing an overt act of war. It followed also that only the Sublime Porte could decide who should use the Straits in wartime, and even the condition of alliance did not *routinely* provide access to foreign powers' ships, however friendly their governments might be.

The method chosen for reaffirming Ottoman sovereignty over the Straits was not, perhaps, very wise, and the British would not expect to have to assert their sovereignty over the Solent by a similar device.[31] The Law of Nations already committed foreign powers to respect the Ottoman Empire's sovereignty over the Straits, therefore Adair was simply acknowledging, in the form of a treaty, that Great Britain would refrain from acting contrarily to the Law of Nations. That the Ottomans felt they had to resort to such a method of preserving their right testifies to their own recognition of their insufficient status in international law or perhaps their ignorance of that subject. However, the 'ancient rule' had appeared for the first time in an international document, and was to be studied and interpreted afresh many times in the future. As it received general European acceptance only in 1841, Vahid Effendi did well to tie British hands so early in the century, and deserved well of his masters.

George Canning ratified the treaty of the Dardanelles in the form submitted to him by Adair, only admonishing his agent for neglecting to provide an English version. Those secret articles which would only become operative whenever France attacked the Ottoman Empire remained in suspense, as Napoleon never again reached out to the East. Adair's promise of £300,000 was treated in London in an interesting fashion; it was accepted along with the rest of the treaty but Adair, and later Stratford Canning, was told to hold it in reserve at the actual ratification ceremony, only exchanging it 'in the event of a war commenced against the Porte by France'. No merely technical state of hostilities, such as the withdrawal of the French mission, would produce the money.[32] The more rigorous criterion of hostility also headed off the other secret clauses, which promised arms, equipment, and a naval defence of the Aegean, until a critical situation genuinely arose. The promise to help the Sultan come to terms with the tsar was allowed to stand, complete with the words, 'with Independence to, and Complete Integrity of, the Ottoman Dominions'; it was not, after all, a binding obligation to secure 'Complete Integrity', simply a promise to aim at it.

★ ★ ★

'We are now waiting', wrote Stratford Canning to his cousin, the foreign secretary, on 7 January 1809, 'for Permission to go up to Constantinople with the first fair wind, and you will easily guess with what pleasure we look forward to the prospect of being at length released from the confinement of a Ship, in which we have been imprisoned for four months.'[33] Everyone on board was eager to see the legendary city of the Sultans, but, as Adair's vessel was a warship, the Ottoman authorities needed three weeks before agreeing to allow so early an infraction of the 'ancient rule' of the Straits, and the ship's company had to chafe a little longer at the Dardanelles. The complete and eternal closure of the Straits to all warships, in accordance with the recent treaty with Great Britain, was only announced at the Porte on 10 April 1809, *after* Adair was settled at the Porte. The wait at the outer Strait gave Adair an opportunity to appraise his instructions once more, to consider how far he had advanced them, and what he must now do. He decided he must disobey them completely.

When Adair left England, signs of a Franco-Russian split were promising but not conclusive, and Canning had wisely allowed for a situation in which the Tilsit conspirators might yet surmount their difficulties and jointly attack the Ottoman Empire. But it was largely Adair's achievement that Canning did not overlook in his instructions the possibility of another rupture, this time between France and Austria. This was well advised as, in the months after Adair left home, the deposition of the Braganzas taught the Habsburgs that no dynasty, however old, was secure, and exploratory contacts between Austria and Russia were initiated by Count Stadion, the Austrian war minister, in the middle of 1808. When Napoleon heard of them, he challenged Metternich in a famous scene on 15 August, and accused the Austrian government of plotting behind his back. One of his charges was that Austria and Russia were contemplating a partition of the Ottoman Empire, now that France was so involved in Spain. Metternich rejected this in his best icy fashion, 'with the Turkish ambassador at his elbow'.[34]

Adair was informed of this worsening of relations between Paris and Vienna by Stadion himself, in letters whose arrival at the Dardanelles, via a Constantinople merchant, astonished Vahid Effendi considerably. In the first of these Stadion told how his government had invited Alexander I to put the solution of his Ottoman difficulties in Adair's hands; in another that the news from Spain 'has raised public opinion [in Austria] to the highest pitch'. But then, Stadion's later letters reported, things had gone less well. In October 1808, Alexander I and Napoleon had met at Erfurt where Alexander consented to restrain Austria while Napoleon brought the Spanish situation under control. Stadion was in despair; Austrians were 'exasperated to the last degree' and ready to 'do anything to get rid of the French' but they dared not act alone.[35] An alliance with Great Britain was certainly needed. This information gave Adair his cue.

Having served at the court of Vienna, Adair was more conscious than the Foreign Office of the importance attached there to the Danubian Principalities, the two rich, agricultural provinces which also provided access to the Black Sea for their possessor.[36] But, even more, he had experienced the deep humiliation felt in Vienna as Napoleon reduced the once proud and powerful empire to vassalage. At Erfurt, yet greater dismemberment was threatened: the loss of Bavaria and the surrender of the part of Poland acquired in the partitions. Not the least part of Austria's grief was the prospect of Russia's prospering territorially as Napoleon's keeper of the peace in eastern Europe. Here, Adair recalled Napoleon's inability actually to see the Principalities pass into Russian possession; in 1806, Sébastiani had reduced Russia's privileges there by having the *hospodars* removed; in 1807, Tilsit seemed to put them back within Russian grasp; then Napoleon had hedged about letting them go; in 1808, the worsening Spanish position obliged him to tell Russia, at Erfurt, that the provinces were indeed hers to take. Adair hurried to assure Stadion that, in signing his treaty of the Dardanelles, Moldavia and Wallachia had been kept very much in sight: the peace he had signed, 'while not amounting to a Guarantee of the Ottoman states [sic] was yet sufficient to bind the good faith of the British Government to endeavour to procure a Peace for the Turks grounded on a restitution of their Provinces'. Napoleon had told the tsar he could make his peace with the Sultan directly and without Napoleon's mediation. Adair was sure that Sébastiani's successor at Constantinople, Latour-Maubourg, would have orders to obstruct such a peace, but believed that he could prevent it himself, so that Russia should be won over by Great Britain on terms which did not automatically alienate Vienna.

This was a big turn-around for a man who never hesitated to tell Vahid Effendi that Great Britain and Russia were 'natural friends', but for the present his determination was to prevent Russia from obtaining the spoils promised at Erfurt until she had come over resolutely to the 'allied' camp. To Canning, Adair announced that he would refrain for the moment from 'any step at Constantinople which may benefit Russia'; and to Stadion he explained: 'Afin d'encourager les Turcs à tenir ferme contre la cession des deux provinces, j'ai autorisé le négociateur Ottoman à Jassy à faire sentir aux Russes que l'Angleterre, ayant fait la paix avec la Porte, s'intéressait de la manière la plus vive a la conservation de l'indépendence et de l'integrité de son Empire.'[37] For the immediate future, then, Adair would support the Sultan against Russia; once Russia abandoned Napoleon, he would transfer himself to Vienna to lay the foundations of a new European coalition; indeed, it would be the final coalition. Canning agreed to all this, and was not so behind events as Adair, in his isolation, supposed.[38] The ill-fated Benjamin Bathurst had already undertaken the mission to Vienna from which he never returned, and the Russians reported to Napoleon the presence of Austrian diplomatic couriers in London. In March 1809, when Austria took the risk of declaring war on France, Great Britain followed with an immediate treaty of alliance with Vienna. What remained in abeyance was the final disposition of the Principalities, a question deferred but not answered. Would they be partitioned, like Poland, between Austria and Russia? Would the Sultan, upon any argument, surrender them?

The prospect of going on to Vienna from Constantinople excited Adair, but he had to find someone to hold the embassy on the Bosporus pending the arrival of a successor from London. It is odd that his choice did not fall on David Morier, but perhaps there was the old fear that a Levantine would put company before country; also, here was a chance to repay the foreign secretary for his extraordinary 'liberality' in retaining Adair in the service of the duke of Portland's administration. The *Sea Horse* was sailing up the Sea of Marmara beyond Gelibolu when Adair took Stratford Canning aside:

> Late one evening . . . as I was pacing the deck with Mr. Adair, he suddenly turned round to me and said that after the exchange of ratifications he was to be the King's ambassador at Constantinople, but that, instead of remaining there, he was to go to Vienna in the same character as soon as our relations with Vienna would admit of it. He then enquired whether I should like to have the appointment of secretary to the Turkish embassy, which, on his departure, might lead to my having for a time the direction of its affairs as minister-plenipotentiary. After thanking him for his kindness, I assured him that I had no wish but to resume my office in England.[39]

Stratford Canning hoped the subject ended there but it did not. Adair's faith in his ability was genuine, and Canning also believed he could manage the embassy until the foreign secretary's friend, John Hookham Frere, presently in Spain, could be sent out. At first, Stratford Canning was credentialled simply as secretary of embassy, but when Frere would not be moved eastwards, the credentials were upgraded to those of a minister-plenipotentiary, and for the good reason that Stratford Canning was to persist, like Adair before him, in the policy of reconciling Russia and the Ottoman Empire without the surrender of the Principalities.

As no one yet knew that Napoleon would give up hope of controlling the East after the withdrawal of Sébastiani from Constantinople in April 1808, some care was taken by the Ottomans not to offend the French embassy with an ostentatious reception of Adair. He was asked to go ashore at dead of night and to walk up (normally, there was a mounted procession for a diplomat's arrival) through the steep, staircased streets of Galata to the British embassy on the Grande Rue of Pera. Here a great shock awaited him. The British 'Palace', as it was misleadingly called, was a wooden ruin, although Charles Arbuthnot had been the first tenant of a new building. Empty for two winters, its roof had fallen in, and its garden had become 'a receptacle for everything offensive'.[40] At intervals, Ottoman custodians had visited the embassy 'pour faire l'inventoire des Meubles', but these raiding parties simplified the duty of cataloguing by making off with the curtains, plate and, as success went to their heads, furniture. Adair notified George Canning that repairs would cost about £7,000, and while construction was in hand he lived in a house on the Grande Rue rented from his first dragoman, Bartholomew Pisani. Most serious of all, the archives had been left in the care of Baron Hubsch, a 'most consummate rogue',[41] who represented Denmark at the Porte, and whose charitability with the material entrusted to his care explains the near complete run of Arbuthnot's papers to be found in the archives at Paris. Adair refused to be put out, and he had an amiable style which disarmed most of his fellow Europeans and drew unexpected smiles from otherwise inscrutable Ottoman officials. He took to his dragomans, trusted them, entertained them as equal members of his staff and not as untrustworthy subordinates, and paid out 11,000 piastres to save them from 'immediate indigence': they had not been paid since early 1807.[42] He thoroughly enjoyed presenting his credentials to the Sultan, which involved being fed a vast meal before being frog-marched with pinioned arms and flung on the ground in the imperial presence. In return, Adair handed out money to all sorts of functionaries with unpronounceable titles and rode back to Pera in high fettle.[43] Stratford Canning was offended by the indignities suffered, but his chief was relieved that the Ottoman government had braved the threats of the French embassy by receiving him. Adair proceeded to give a dinner in honour of his Austrian colleague, the Internuncio, Count Sturmer, at which Florimond de Latour-Maubourg, the French chargé d'affaires, severed relations with his Austrian colleague. Then came the news from Europe that Austria and France were, once again, at war.

Adair began his official duties by calling a meeting of the factory of the Levant Company at Constantinople. This was no longer the large gathering of the past. In 1809 the quorum for factory meetings was down to five; 15 would have been a capacity crowd. Business had, understandably, been bad for many years because of the long wars with France, and in 1799 had been declared at its last gasp. By 1806, a very promising revival was under way, with Lancashire cotton the great selling commodity, until Arbuthnot spoiled the bright prospect. There was anger and frustration that Adair was no longer a company servant; some dissatisfaction with the treaty of the Dardanelles, which had effectively prevented the Bosporus becoming an international waterway of free passage; and an accurate premonition that trade must henceforth accommodate itself to diplomacy.[44] Adair cut short any idea that the British government would compensate the British merchants for their recent trade losses. When he told them his instructions did not authorize him to drum the French mercantile community out of Pera, relations froze, and the invitations to dinner dwindled on both sides. Adair had much else to do.

As the Ottoman grand vizier was at the battle front from 1808 to 1812, Adair had to acquire the elements of oriental statecraft through dealings with lesser men. Vahid Effendi, the negotiator of the treaty of 1809, was the one man of real calibre set up against him. The first lesson to be learned was that in Constantinople, Europe was a long way off, whereas Russia was a presence in the very wind which blew down the Bosporus from the north. Mahmud II's new ministers, far from being bold innovators, lived miserably in the shadow of the janizary terror, and were more than ever disposed to keep Adair at arm's length when they heard that Russia had broken off the peace negotiations at Jassy in Moldavia because he had not been sent away.[45] In such a situation, Adair got a cool hearing when he suggested that the Ottoman fleet should destroy Sebastopol, and a cooler one still when he boldly offered to violate his own treaty and bring the British navy to the Black Sea to provide support.[46] Hastily, the Ottomans announced the closure of the Straits to all warships as from 10 April; the treaty of the Dardanelles was now in effect, and Adair was notified that the Ottoman fleet could effect its responsibilities unassisted. To silence Adair utterly he was asked, for the first but by no means the last time, for the £300,000 promised in his treaty.[47] Meanwhile, all commercial intercourse with Russia by sea was at an end for everyone. Russian wheat would have been of great value to the British fleet, and Latour-Maubourg, too, raged against the closure, but the Bosporus was shut to all merchantmen. Greeks, trading under Russia's flag, suffered most.

With the resumption of the Russo-Ottoman land war that spring, Adair and Stratford Canning also discovered that such encounters were fought in accordance with established tradition, not easily changed. Balkan fighting began in May, when the ruts and roads dried out, and terminated in time for the Russians to march home before the autumn rains. Between times, campaigns centred on the traditional crossings of the Danube – from west to east – for each one of which pitched battles were fought with pistol and scimitar, as well as artillery. Byron's description, as we find it in Canto II of *Childe Harold*, is reportage, not fiction. The Russians disliked fighting south of the Danube, as the Bulgarian summers were reputed to engender a particularly dangerous plague, so preferred to negotiate on the basis of victories won on the Danube. The Ottomans, on their side, tried to protract negotiations until the Russian armies had to turn about anyhow, so that the war had to be fought all over again next year. Any interference with the accustomed cycle, however well-intentioned, was disapproved of at the Porte. Reversing Clausewitz's famous dictum, Ottomans had a way of seeing diplomacy as a prolongation of war, as a way of winning at the conference table what they lost on the battlefield.

'I have pointed out to them', wrote Adair in an early mood of despair, 'that if they are seriously determined not to cede the territories in question [the Principalities], the war with Russia must begin afresh, and consequently that they will be looking for allies to support it.'[48] Or so he hoped. In fact, the Ottoman ministers proved unresponsive to the idea of joint Anglo-Ottoman naval action against Russia, and if anything appealed to them even less, it was Adair's suggestion that Austria should adhere to the treaty of the Dardanelles. The argument he adduced most often in pressing this advice was that the Ottoman Empire owed its survival to its association with European states, and not to its isolation from them. Along with Great Britain, Austria would be able to secure a 'fair and favourable' peace whenever Russia or France was brought to the conference table. The argument was plausible, no more; Galib, the *reis effendi*, on the few occasions he was home from the battlefront, usually replied that Austria was not to be trusted, while Great Britain herself could demonstrate her solicitude far more substantially than hitherto by supplying ships and war materials for the Ottoman fleet. All Ottoman ministers were absolutely obdurate about letting Royal Navy ships through the Straits for the purpose of chastising Russia.

It was this fatalistic reticence to give a hearing to reasonable advice, as the British embassy saw it, which led Stratford Canning to comment when he had come back from a visit to the Porte to examine 'a sample of 200 pickled heads and nine Prisoners' from the Danube front:

> destruction will not come upon this empire either *from the north or from the south*; it is rotten at the heart; the seat of corruption is in the government itself. Conscious of their weakness, and slaves to the Janissaries, of whom they have not discretion to make proper use, the ministers have lately introduced at home the same system of deceit that they have so long employed in their intercourse with foreign powers.[49]

Even with regard to the land war, Stratford Canning believed, the ministers were deceiving not merely the foreign embassies, not merely the Sultan, not merely the Ottoman people, but also themselves. They strutted proudly, in all their oriental finery, as though it was still the age of Suleiman the Magnificent, instead of the implacable age of Napoleonic war and diplomacy. In fairness to the Ottoman ministers, they had two difficulties which would have crippled the most resolute war policy by land; the first was the technical point that, in the disturbances of 1807 and 1808 which had seen the removal of two Sultans, the janizaries had destroyed nearly every tent the Ottoman army possessed; the second, which Stratford Canning discerned, that the janizaries were reluctant to let the new Sultan's ministers post them in too great numbers to the distant battle-fronts, away from the scene of their triumphs and their power. Stratford Canning was quite right when he said the ministers were slaves to the janizaries. The grand vizier had an army of 140,000 in the field in 1809, and it contained very few janizaries.[50]

Adair's naval and military proposals for aiding the Ottomans were brushed aside by Admiral Collingwood and Canning as well as by the Ottomans, and it is not difficult to see why. British troops and ships in 1809 were, as usual, heavily committed in other places, though not always for any clear reason. A force of nearly 15,000 men had been built up at Palermo for a futile dash on Naples in June. In the Peninsula, the new commander, Sir Arthur Wellesley, had just fought the battle of Talavera, claimed as a victory yet followed by a tactical withdrawal which bore a strong resemblance to a retreat. Above all, there was a force of 40,000 men and 35 ships assembling in the English Channel to sail to the Low Countries, the pet scheme of those in the cabinet who believed the importance of the Spanish theatre of war was being exaggerated. Against such men, Canning had to fight hard to maintain Wellesley in his high appointment, and his dissatisfaction was greatest with Lord Castlereagh, the secretary for war, whose duty it was to shape the Walcheren expedition. The Austrians asked for a British diversion in the Elbe region in April 1809, in the hope that Prussia might be tempted into the struggle. Instead, Austria was crushed at Wagram on 6 July, and three weeks later the British armada sailed for the Scheldt, where it squandered its strength for six months before returning home. The failure was due far less to Castlereagh than to the expedition's commander, universally known as 'the late Lord Chatham', but the fiasco of Walcheren in August and September 1809 intensified Canning's determination that Marquis Wellesley should come into the ministry in Castlereagh's place, and brought into the light of day his previous and devious attempts to procure that end. There followed the duel with Castlereagh in which Canning was wounded in the thigh, and this dramatic conclusion to the enmity of the two most unpopular men in the House of Commons broke up the government. Wellesley caused some surprise by taking Canning's office in the new Perceval ministry; Castlereagh received considerable sympathy for the way in which Canning, in spite of his explanations, was thought to have deceived him; while Canning's own poor reputation plunged further.

Private letters brought Adair glimpses of this discord in the British cabinet; his official dispatches simply ignored his request for naval operations against Russia in the Black Sea. It was all very frustrating for a man who had hopes of mediating between tsar and Sultan or, if Russia proved intractable, a triple alliance of Austria, Great Britain, and the Ottoman Empire. On the surface, nevertheless, there was an appearance of decent progress for his plans at Constantinople, with Anglo-Ottoman naval conversations, an Ottoman request for British-built ships for the Ottoman fleet in March 1809, the severance of relations between the Porte and the French embassy on 8 May, a refusal of passports to General Gardane to pass through Ottoman territories on his way home from Persia to France, the withdrawal of the Ottoman guard from the French embassy, the recognition by the Porte of a representative from the Spanish junta in June, and a refusal in July to accept Joseph

Bonaparte's chargé d'affaires, Duval, in place of the royalist, Rodrigo, who was permitted to keep up the Bourbon coat-of-arms on his residence.[51] But these were minor achievements, all capable of being reversed in a day, and Latour-Maubourg was treated noticeably more civilly when the news of Napoleon's great victory at Wagram reached the Ottoman Empire during the summer of 1809.

Latour-Maubourg's severance of relations with the Ottoman government, and theirs with him, was excellent news for Adair, but only half of what he wanted; his ambition was to provoke the Frenchman into leaving Constantinople entirely. One of the imaginative means he chose to achieve this end was to raise the question of the sovereignty of the Ionian Islands, which straggled round peninsular Greece from Corfu to Cythera. Once Ottoman, the islands had been occupied by Russia as a naval necessity after 1800, but surrendered to France in 1807; they had then been annexed progressively by Great Britain, with Corfu alone holding out until 1814. Adair, perhaps unwisely in the light of his desire to gratify the Ottomans, but hoping to stir a reaction at the French embassy, invited all Ionian traders to raise the Union Jack. When the man recognized in Constantinople as the unofficial spokesman for the Ionians, by name Dandrino, took this advice, and urged it on all Ionian craft in the harbour, Latour-Maubourg impetuously gaoled Dandrino in the French embassy, claiming he would only hand him over if the Ottomans promised not to release him to Adair. The latter threatened to withhold the ratification of the treaty of the Dardanelles if Dandrino was not freed at once, and even to quit his post. Pressed on all sides, the Ottomans did not know what to do, and on one occasion, the pro-British dragoman of the Porte, Prince Constantine Murusi, knelt before Adair and swore that it was more than his life was worth to rise until Adair promised to drop the whole business. From an opposite room, Stratford Canning watched Adair sink to *his* knee before Murusi, and heard him swear that he too would stay in that position until Murusi agreed to stand up. Adair won. The issue was resolved by the acting *reis effendi*, who astutely arranged that Dandrino should be recognized as an Ottoman subject, and so be freed. But the Ottomans were very indisposed to accept the loss to Great Britain of islands which had so recently been theirs, and listened with interest as well as politeness to Latour-Maubourg's violent harangues about the 'joug maritime de l'Angleterre'. There was obviously a good deal in what he said. Latour-Maubourg had the advantage over his British rival that he could speak Turkish, and his official severance of relations did not seriously interrupt his personal discourses at the offices of the Porte.[52]

In his main task before Wagram, the reinvigoration of the Ottoman war effort on the Danube and at sea, Adair thus had no luck at all, and the succession of squabbles with Latour-Maubourg, who maintained himself with magnificent insolence with even less guidance from home than Adair received, produced no enduring results either. The French embassy stayed open, the Russian embassy stayed shut. The French merchants, impoverished by the operation of the British Orders in Council, were in some cases loyal to the Bourbons and helpful to Adair, but in others were, in Stratford Canning's words, 'the vilest scum that ever fell from the overboilings of the pot of Imperial Jacobinism'.[53] There were scuffles between British and French patriots on the Grande Rue itself. To offset Latour-Maubourg's propaganda, which was disseminated in pamphlets locally printed in Arabic and Turkish, and the effects of the *Moniteur* and the *Bulletin de la Grande Armée*, a printing-press was set up in the grounds of the British 'Palace', with Stratford Canning appointed to supervise the material given to its local Jewish operator. The blue, British *Chiffons* were issued weekly in French and Levantine, and therefore catered to the local European community rather than to court circles and patriotic Ottoman opinion.[54]

If this was diplomacy, Stratford Canning did not much care for it, and he was anything but pleased when his credentials as minister-plenipotentiary arrived from England with the ratification of the treaty of the Dardanelles, in August 1809. In the covering letter, George Canning wrote: 'Mr. Adair's reports of you and yours of him lead me to wish that he will continue where he is, and you with him'; but the news of Wagram, and Adair's physical collapse at that news, seemed to ensure that Stratford Canning would not be abandoned just yet. Stratford Canning was, nevertheless, fully aware that if Adair found there was no hope of going on to Vienna, he would very soon find an excuse for going home, and he tried to head off this development by pleading for his own prior 'release', by advising his cousin 'you will perhaps be surprised to find that I am anxious to return immediately to England', there being 'so much to disgust me in this Country.... The climate I find very disagreeable. So I beg you to send me your permission to return home as soon as you can.'[55] It was to no avail.

After the Austrian defeat at Wagram, Stadion resigned, and there followed the sullen armistice of Znaim, converted in October into the drastic peace of Schönbrunn. The news was received at the Porte, Stratford Canning wrote, 'with all the Exaggerations of a French Report; nothing to soften or account for it, nothing to break the violence of the blow'. The Ottomans 'see the danger rolling nearer to themselves'. Latour-Maubourg was triumphant, while Sturmer, the Austrian minister, was helpless to defend the dignity of a state which the French had now conquered four times in under 20 years. Adair took to his bed for some days in a condition of 'terror and dejection', as David Morier described it, while Latour-Maubourg took the opportunity to remind the *reis effendi* that 'les Anglais n'ont que des Vaisseaux, lesquels ne peuvent rien contre la Terre-Ferme'.[56] As soon as he recovered, Adair warned the Ottoman ministers how France would strike through Greece and Russia through Serbia to the Bosporus. The dangers of 1807 had come again and, unless a total surrender was intended, the Porte must co-ordinate plans of naval defence with him.[57]

During the twilight period following the armistice of Znaim, Adair kept hoping for a Franco-Russian disagreement over the spoils of Wagram, and guessed correctly that the new Austrian ministers were hoping the same.[58] Alexander I wrote to Napoleon and Francis II, registering his opposition to the former's supposed intention to enlarge the grand duchy of Poland with Austrian Galicia, and Adair, like Stadion, half-hoped Napoleon would fall into the trap and take all Galicia for his Polish duchy, and so facilitate an Austrian *rapprochement* with the tsar. Napoleon was too astute, and while taking western Galicia for the duchy, gave eastern Galicia to Russia. It was a clever thrust. Prince Metternich, as Stadion's successor, bowed his head in submission: 'our system must be exclusively one of tacking, of obliterating ourselves, of accommodating ourselves to the victor. In this way alone shall we perhaps extend our existence until the day of general deliverance.' In other words, Austria was leaving the initiative to others for the future. She also began under Metternich to 'accommodate herself to the victor' with considerable enthusiasm. In mid-October, the

Schönbrunn arrangements deprived Austria of over three million subjects, 75 million francs, and extensive lands. After such an annihilation, Adair's dream of raising coalitions against France vanished, and he reverted to his original instructions to bring the Ottoman Empire and Russia to peace.

At home, there was a two-month interregnum at the Foreign Office between the fall of George Canning and the succession of Wellesley, during which Earl Bathurst was foreign secretary. In that brief spell, Bathurst told Adair that peace between Russia and the Ottoman Empire should again become Great Britain's first objective, and advised his minister to forget altogether any idea of Great Britain's wishing to coerce Russia by attacking her Black Sea coasts. Indeed, Bathurst told Adair to come home at once if the Ottomans refused to make peace with Russia on Alexander I's terms.[59] The new ministry headed by Spencer Perceval placed no reliance on the Ottomans' ability to hold the Straits against a Russian thrust by land, and so would not risk passing ships through them. Nor would it supply vessels for the Ottoman navy, for which the *reis effendi* had so often pleaded. Adair obtained a distinct impression that Bathurst had not read Article XI of the treaty of the Dardanelles.[60] Nevertheless, Bathurst gave Adair the courage to follow the path he had originally planned for himself, which was to open a tentative and secret line of communication with St Petersburg, and so keen was he to obtain some satisfactory conclusion to his embassy that he waived an opportunity to go home in September.[61]

Negotiations at Jassy between Ottomans and Russians, represented respectively by Galib, the *reis effendi*, and General A. A. Prosorowski, provided a more or less continuous diplomatic background to a foreground of less continuous military strife on the Danube and in Caucasia from 1806 to 1812. Ironically, the Russian military command gave as its reason for fighting on, year after year, the presence of Adair at the Porte. In late 1809, however, Stadion, who kept up his stream of letters to Adair after his loss of office, indicated that, just as there were patriotic Austrians like himself and the father of Austria's new minister, Prince Metternich, so in Russia there was a patriotic and anti-French school to whose opinions the tsar was increasingly sensitive. It was led by Count V. P. Kochubey, the chairman of the foreign affairs committee, whom Adair knew personally, and its members already looked beyond a peace with the

Ottoman Empire to the possibility of a new and victorious coalition against France. So Adair was to take heart, and not be too impressed with the anti-British sentiments of Russian military commanders in the Principalities, nor with the sensitivity of the Russian court where it was known (Latour-Maubourg saw to that) that Adair was pressing for the admission of British warships to the Black Sea for attacks on Russian ports.[62]

Adair went to work to provide material which could be fed to St Petersburg through two channels, the first being the count of St Julien, a minor Austrian diplomat at the Russian capital, whose main task had been to persuade the tsar to refuse the bribe of eastern Galicia, and the second, the duke of Richelieu, the French *emigré* governor of Odessa. The material Adair sent was, in effect, the information Russia would have acquired, in the ordinary way, from her Constantinople embassy had it been open, though naturally he gave it a slant appropriate to his purposes in his covering letters. The letters were not addressed or signed, and were carried to their destinations by Adair's own agents. In the main, they consisted of copies of Latour-Maubourg's anti-Russian letters and memoranda he sent in to the Porte, the copies themselves coming from Murusi, the dragoman of the Porte. Adair had the satisfaction of hearing that they began to reach the Russian court in February 1810, where they made a deep impression. Adair's main thesis was the duplicity of the French, in Persia as well as the Ottoman Empire.[63] If France was Russia's true friend, why had she left her mission open in the Ottoman Empire after the Chevalier d'Italinsky's departure in December 1806? And when Russia broke off battle-front negotiations with the Porte in 1809 for admitting Adair, why had not France done the same? Because, Adair suggested, Latour-Maubourg's duty was to prevent anything being surrendered to Russia. It was the same story in Persia. There, the British minister, Sir Harford Jones, had ample evidence that a new French agent, Joseph-Marie Jouannin, was trying to prolong the Russo-Persian war in Georgia, and Adair himself was responsible for detaining in Constantinople over several months 'a very dangerous Agent' of Persia named Husayn Khan who was proceeding to Paris to sign a formal treaty. Adair purchased copies of Husayn Khan's correspondence with Latour-Maubourg and sent these to Kochubey. In this correspondence Napoleon urged the shah to more vigorous effort against Russia in Azerbaijan. Adair did not mention that he and Harford Jones had themselves tried to arrange for the Ottoman Empire and Persia to synchronize their war efforts, and had he been taxed on the point, no doubt would have replied that whereas Latour-Maubourg was genuinely trying to prolong the Russo-Ottoman war as a means of weakening Russia, his own purpose was merely to bring the tsar to his senses by showing him how formidable these two Asiatic powers could make themselves.[64]

Adair would have preferred, of course, to be the promoter of Ottoman peace proposals rather than a mere supplier of information to the court of St Petersburg, and he offered to mediate any seriously resumed negotiation at Jassy by going there personally, but the Ottoman government paid less attention to him than did the Russian. The main reasons for his failure to establish enduring relations of confidence with the leading Ottoman ministers were twofold. First, no one at the Porte dared show any initiative in the absence at the front of the grand vizier, Yusuf Pasha, or of Galib Effendi during his visits to Jassy, a situation which led Adair to compare diplomacy in the East to cutting into dead flesh. His ideas were given a courteous hearing, but no one ever promised action, or even an answer. Second, Russia and Great Britain remained associated in the Ottoman mind as states that might as easily do a deal at Ottoman expense as any other pair of European powers, and it was not Latour-Maubourg alone who kept this fear alive. Adair himself had done a good deal of damage by his impetuous outbursts at Vahid Effendi, and these were not forgotten. He was just another European diplomat, adjusting his ideas to the see-saw of the Continental situation, while trying to pretend that he was moved most by Ottoman interests. He had no right to be astonished if Ottoman ministers somehow neglected to come running to him when, soon after the news of Wagram, the Ottoman armies on the Danube suffered a sequence of major defeats.[65]

Latour-Maubourg sustained himself through long months of neglect by reliance upon Napoleonic infallibility on the battlefield. In 1810, one might believe that Napoleon could be forced eventually into a compromise with the great states of Europe, but never that he would be beaten by them. Adair, cut off from any steady information from the Continent, and generally a minimum of six weeks behind the news, was frequently unaware of quite major developments, most notably, after Schönbrunn, of the rising conflict between French and Russian interests in Poland. 'The great wrong consummated not twenty years before [the last Polish Partition] had placed the courageous fervour of a patriotic people at the disposal of the highest bidder', and Metternich, for instance, was sure Napoleon would build a military bridge into Russia by offering the Poles independence and reunification. In Constantinople, however, it was freely assumed by Adair and his staff that Napoleon would always, as a last resort, buy his way out of any European deadlock by making huge concessions to Russia at Ottoman expense. Some greater access to Latour-Maubourg's papers would have rescued Adair from this fear by revealing to him Napoleon's temperamental, and eventually disastrous, inability to share. Denied this insight, Adair genuinely believed Napoleon might prevail absolutely, and become a world colossus through the misguided subservience of Russia. The evident flaccidity of the Ottoman state and the hopeless incompetence of its leadership intensified his fears. His duty was to fend off Russia and expose French machinations, but Adair's sense of approaching doom was so vivid that at one point he sent Stratford Canning on a tour of western Asia Minor to study the routes by which the populace of Constantinople might be evacuated. Stratford Canning could not take this duty very seriously: his confident patriotism forbade it and one almost hears him idly whistling in his letters back to his chief.[66]

Adair's meagre diplomatic system came to naught because his superiors at the Foreign Office were flagrantly guilty of the sin once attributed in a rhyming dispatch by George Canning to the Dutch, the sin of 'offering too little and asking too much'. Adair could get a hearing at St Petersburg in 1810 but not at the Porte, because he had nothing to offer. Latour-Maubourg was forever telling the Ottomans to stand firm and Napoleon would get them the Principalities back: Adair could not compete with this, or rather, dared not, for his government's views were not disclosed to him. It was by no means clear that Great Britain could, or would ever try to, outbid Latour-Maubourg for control of the Ottomans, and Adair grew very worried about it:

> If we mean to have any transactions with Mahomedan States we must content ourselves with very slender Security for the performance of their engagements. In the present state of the Politicks of Europe, and with a view to the Security of India . . . we must cultivate both Turkey and Persia, at the risk of being deceived by both, and . . . must gain these Powers at almost any price short of our honour.[67]

It was futile to imagine that self-interest would automatically align eastern powers with Great Britain. Unfortunately, Wellesley, the new foreign secretary and a former governor-general of India, was not in the habit of reading the dispatches from the Ottoman Empire and so showed no interest in such an idea. So, for as long as Napoleon appeared supreme in Europe, the Ottomans honoured his representative, maintained perfunctory hostilities with Russia, and were politely indifferent to Robert Adair.

Before coming home Adair made one singular effort to break out of this iron ring of circumstance. In the spring of 1810, the Russian government made a really serious offer to accelerate the peace negotiations with the Ottomans, before the opening of the campaigning season. The offer was made because France and Austria drew together after the latter's defeat at Wagram and, besides a royal Austrian bride for Napoleon in the person of Princess Marie-Louise, it became known in St Petersburg that Metternich was now as ready as the French to check Russian ambitions in the Balkans. Russia had to move quickly, and her offer to Mahmud II came through the notorious Baron Hubsch. As the Russian approach specified that the Ottoman Empire must give up the Principalities entirely – 'whose inhabitants were all Greek and consequently ought to belong to Russia rather than to the Porte' – the Ottoman government was on the point of sending an outright refusal to treat when Adair intervened, and got a civil reply sent back to St Petersburg expressing a readiness to negotiate provided the Russian government did not persist in the idea of acquiring Moldavia and Wallachia. Adair was desperately anxious to remove the negotiations from Hubsch's hands into his own, but felt sure that Latour-Maubourg would yet outmanoeuvre him, by obtaining from Paris a formal promise that France would not let Russia obtain the Principalities.[68]

It did not occur to Adair, although the facts were at his disposal, that Latour-Maubourg would have been greatly embarrassed if the

Ottomans had asked him for help, as his master in Paris had promised the Principalities to Russia at Tilsit and Erfurt, to the Ottoman Empire on all occasions, and to Metternich most recently of all. Nevertheless, on 23 March 1810, Adair suggested to the acting *reis effendi* that he should be allowed to propose to Russia that Moldavia and Wallachia stay in the Sultan's custody, and that in compensation for them, Great Britain would transfer to Russia 'a portion of that superflux of Colonial Establishments which the War has thrown into His Majesty's Hands'. Suddenly the British minister, agent of a hitherto suspect government, became the hero of the hour, and on this popular note he decided to quit the Ottoman Empire. To ward off the wrath of government, he wrote home that unless Great Britain was ready to give firm and unambiguous support to governments in the East, she would lose her only means of access to one, and possibly two, continents. 'Europe will be closed to Great Britain, perhaps forever' and will be controlled by a Franco-Russian 'Confederacy . . . acting through an embodied and disciplined Diplomacy'.[69] The Russians had already resumed hostilities on the Danube, and were demanding Bessarabia as well as the Principalities, and independence for Ottoman Serbia as well as an indemnity. Lectures on the European situation meant nothing to the Ottoman government, he wrote. Orientals understood only ships, guns, money, and with these alone could they be purchased.

Just two years after leaving England, Adair began his farewells at the various offices of senior Ottomans, taking coffee and sherbet, and leaving gifts behind him.[70] On 12 July, he sailed home, to receive a KCB but no more diplomatic appointments. Stratford Canning, homesick and lonely, returned to the embassy for which he was now responsible, locked himself in his room and, by his own confession, wept.

NOTES

1. Paget to Canning, 12 July, 14, 23, and 30 Aug. 1807; Canning to Paget, 14 Aug. 1807, FO 78/56.
2. William Eton, *A Survey of the Turkish Empire* (London, 1799).
3. Robert Dundas to Canning, 6 June 1807, Harewood MSS.
4. Robert Adair, *Negotiations for the Peace of the Dardanelles in 1808–09, with Despatches and Official Documents* (London, 1845), i. 'Introduction'.

5. In 1806, with Fox as foreign secretary, Adair had been sent to Vienna to apprise the Austrian court of the danger posed by the power of France. Upon his return he was dispatched by his old antagonist, George Canning, to Constantinople to open negotiations for peace with the Porte. Between 1831 and 1835 Adair undertook a special mission to the Netherlands. Also see above ch. II.
6. Adair responded very angrily to this imputation in the 'Introduction' to his *Negotiations*. He went on to charge Malmesbury with having tried to get him withdrawn from Vienna in 1807. See Canning to George III, minuted by the king, *The Later Correspondence of George III*, ed. A. Aspinall (Cambridge, 1963–70), iv. 562. Adair stayed at Vienna; Malmesbury's favourite and choice for the post, the earl of Pembroke, went out, proved to be useless, and was recalled.
7. Adair to Canning, 24 May 1808, *Negotiations*, i. 1.
8. Adair to Canning, 20 April 1808, Harewood MSS. Adair passed the news to Lady Holland, who relayed it to Lord Grey. 'I was told', Lady Holland wrote, 'that Mr. Canning was a man of very liberal mind, quite adverse to all party feelings and desirous of employing talents wherever he found them, and finding none to equal Adair's was willing to employ him.' She thought the foreign secretary might be trying to draw over Lord Morpeth to support the government. Lady Holland to Grey, 27 May 1808, Grey of Howick MSS.
9. Adair's full powers and instructions are contained in six dispatches of 26 June 1808, in FO 78/60. They are elaborated by Stratford Canning in FO 352/1/2.
10. The appointment of ambassador-extraordinary was sent out only after the treaty of the Dardanelles had been signed. See Canning to George III, 28 April 1809, *George III*, v. 264; Adair, *Negotiations*, i. 255.
11. Adair to Canning, 29 June 1808, Harewood MSS 52.
12. S. Canning to Canning, 5 July 1808, Harewood MSS 52; FO 352/1/2, journal, 25 June 1808.
13. Adair to Stadion, 26 June 1808, *Negotiations*, i. 7. Adair asked for assurances that Austria was not party to any Franco-Russian partition plans aimed at 'la chute de ce malheureux Empire' of the Ottomans. In *Negotiations*, ii. 121, Adair tells Canning that he is opening a correspondence with Razumovsky, the Austrian representative at St Petersburg.
14. FO 352/1/2, journal, 8, 9, 13, and 16 July 1808.
15. S. Canning to Canning, 6 Sept. 1808, Harewood MSS 52; FO 351/1/2, journal, 28 July, 3, 13, 20, 25, 30 Aug. 1808. Stuart, according to Stratford Canning's record, told Adair that Great Britain had abandoned the Egyptians as well as the Ottomans to Mehemet Ali's Albanian extortionists, and 'the talisman is now unfortunately broken, and we have fatally lost the tie which we held upon the mind and affections of the poor Egyptian'.
16. Adair to Canning, 17 Aug., 9 Sept. 1809, FO 78/60.
17. Adair to Canning, 17 and 30 Aug., 7 Sept. 1808, *Negotiations*, i. 13, 17, 19.
18. Stanley Lane-Poole, *The Life of the Right Honourable Stratford Canning, Viscount Stratford de Redcliffe* (London, 1888), i. 44. David Richard Morier, 1784–1877, has been appointed in 1804 secretary to the political mission sent to the court of Ali Pasha of Janina. In 1807 he had been transferred to Sir Arthur Paget's mission, then attempting to re-establish peace with the Porte. Soon afterwards he was sent to Egypt to negotiate for the release of British prisoners captured during General Fraser's abortive expedition against Rosetta in 1807. In the summer of 1808 he joined Adair, and from 1810 to 1812 was secretary of lega-

tion at Constantinople under Stratford Canning, returning with him to England in 1812. In 1813 he accompanied the earl of Aberdeen on his mission to Vienna, later joining Viscount Castlereagh. At the congress of Vienna he served as one of the secretaries of the British mission. In July 1815 he accompanied Castlereagh to Paris where he helped draft the treaties of 1815. He had been appointed consul-general for France in 1814, a post he held until its abolition in 1832, when he was made minister plenipotentiary to the Swiss Confederated States. He remained there until his retirement from the diplomatic service in 1847.

19. Adair to *reis effendi*, 11 Oct. 1808, *reis effendi* to Adair, n.d. [November], Adair to George Canning, 22 and 26 Nov. 1808: *Negotiations*, i. 36, 44, 48; FO 352/1/2, journal, memo C, covering all the negotiations at the Dardanelles.
20. Some of the captured Ottoman vessels were sold off, quite improperly, in Malta. See Collingwood to Hallowell, 28 Jan. 1809, *The Private Correspondence of Admiral Lord Collingwood*, ed. E. Hughes (London, 1957), p. 164, and *Correspondence, Despatches, and Other Papers of Viscount Castlereagh*, ed. marquis of Londonderry (London, 1848–53), viii. 192.
21. Adair to Canning, 22 and 26 Nov. 1808, FO 78/63. For an account of the 1808 disturbances in Constantinople, see A. de Juchereau de Saint Denys, *Revolutions de Constantinople en 1807 et 1808* (Paris, 1918); and Ottokar M. Von Schlechta-Wssehrd, *Die Revolutionen in Constantinopel in den Jahren 1807 und 1808* (Vienna, 1882). For the period of Mustafa Alemdar, see Ismail Hakki Uzunçarsili, *Meshur Rumeli Ayanindan Tirsinikli Ismail, Yilik Oglu Süleyman Agalar ve Alemdar Mustafa Pasa [The Famous Rumelia Notables; Tirsinikli Ismail and Yilik Oglu Süleyman Agas and Alemdar Mustafa Pasa]* (Istanbul, 1942).
22. S. Canning to Canning, 1 Dec. 1808, FO 352/1/3; Adair, *Negotiations*, i. 59–76. The Navigation Laws, Adair told Vahid, 'rendered it impossible to grant to Turkish vessels the liberty of going both to the British colonies, or carrying the produce of other countries to England'. On the demand for compensation, Adair noted, 'if he [Vahid] persisted, I should be under the necessity of declaring my mission at an end'. The technical reason for Adair's capitulation was the need to get settled before the weather broke.
23. Adair to Canning, 1 Jan. 1809, *Negotiations*, i. 110. Adair also thought that Canning might scratch together for Ottoman use some old, long-barrelled guns which had been lying at Woolwich for years, mostly taken from French prizes. Adair to Canning, 6 Jan. 1809, FO 78/63.
24. S. Canning to Canning, 1 and 7 Jan. 1809, Harewood MSS. Sidki had tackled Canning in London about receiving Ali Pasha's agent, and discussing the cession to him of the mainland fortress of Parga in Epirus, now cleared of the French. Canning, nevertheless, would not suspend a modest flow of arms to Janina. See Canning to Adair, 20 and 21 Aug. 1808, FO 78/60. The correspondence of Captain Leake, Great Britain's agent at Ali Pasha's court, is in FO 78/61.
25. Adair to Canning, 1 Jan. 1809, *Negotiations*, i. 112.
26. The original texts of the treaty, sent to London, are in FO 93/110/1A, 1B, 2. The first text is reproduced in *Diplomacy in the Near and Middle East: A Documentary Record*, ed. J.C. Hurewitz (Princeton, 1956), i. 81–4. Canning's criticism is in a dispatch to Adair dated 25 April 1809, FO 78/63. Adair's defence of his procedures is to be found in Adair to Canning, 6 July 1809, *Negotiations*, i. 229–30. He says an English version was out of the question because Vahid's dragoman had no English, only French. Adair reproduced the draft treaty in *Negotiations*, i. 116–23. The secret articles committed Britain: (i) to defend the

Ottoman Empire with 'a sufficient Fleet for that purpose' should France attack her, (ii) to provide 'warlike stores' for the defence of 'Bosnia and Dalmatzia', (iii) to evacuate Egypt, (iv) to help Turkey to obtain 'an advantageous and honourable peace' with Russia, and (v) to provide £300,000 in assistance to Turkey within six months.
27. S. Canning to Canning, 1 Dec. 1809, FO 352¹/3.
28. For the commercial privileges granted to British merchants in 1799, and renewed in 1802, see *Near and Middle East*, ed. Hurewitz, i. 67. Russia, by Article XI of her treaty of 1774, already enjoyed 'free and unimpeded' mercantile activity on the Black Sea, which the British had wanted to share. See *Recueil d'actes internationaux de l'empire Ottoman*, ed. Gabriel Noradounghian (Paris, 1897–1903), i. 351–3.
29. S. Canning to Canning, 1 Dec. 1809, Harewood MSS.
30. *Near and Middle East*, ed. Hurewitz, i. 83. The treaty was first translated into English at the Foreign Office in 1833, and examined with care. The first translation of Article XI says the admission of foreign warships through the Straits 'has at all times been prohibited', but this was pencilled over with 'was originally prohibited', presumably with the special exception of Russia in 1799.
31. A good discussion of the Straits' question is to be found in Coleman Phillipson and Noel Buxton, *The Question of the Bosphorus and Dardanelles* (London, 1917).
32. By an oversight, the offer of £300,000 was left in the first treaty, actually signed by George III, and the Great Seal placed on it. When the error was discovered, the king had to sign a second treaty with the offending clause struck out. The lord chancellor rescinded the first version. Canning to George III, 28 April 1809, *George III*, ed. Aspinall, v. 264.
33. S. Canning to Canning, 7 Jan. 1808, FO 352/1/3.
34. Andrei Lobanov Rostovsky, *Russia and Europe, 1789–1925* (Durham, NC, 1947), p. 178.
35. Stadion to Adair, 25 Sept., 8 Dec. 1808, Adair to Stadion 10 Feb. 1809, FO 352/1/5, copies; Lobanov Rostovsky, *Russia and Europe*, pp. 179–82; Vernon J. Puryear, *Napoleon and the Dardanelles* (Berkeley, 1951), pp. 340–3.
36. Lane-Poole, *Life*, i. 37.
37. Adair to Canning, 1 and 6 Jan. 1809, FO78/64; Stadion to Adair, 25 Sept., 8 Dec. 1808, Adair to Stadion, 10 Feb. 1809, FO 352/1/5, copies.
38. Canning probably recommended this course of action to Adair informally before the latter left England. When Consul Werry at Smyrna reported incorrectly that Adair had been sent away from the Dardanelles, the foreign secretary sent word to Malta for Adair to wait there until a way could be found for getting him to Vienna, to make peace and an alliance. Canning to Adair, 20 Dec. 1808, FO 78/60; Adair to Canning, 28 March 1809, FO 78/63.
39. S. Canning to Canning, 27 Sept. 1808, FO 352/1/5. Stratford wrote 'I can only thank you from the bottom of my heart [but] when the fight is over I am sure you will not hesitate to grant me my release. I only beg of you to send it to me by Mr. Adair's successor.'
40. Adair to Foreign Office, 15 Sept. 1809, FO 78/64. The degree of damage is indicated by the repairs now carried out: the roof and dome completely replaced, the upstairs walls braced, the kitchen rebuilt, all window grills replaced, rooms for embassy janizaries and porter replastered; inevitably, all locks had to be replaced. Adair to Bathurst, 5 Jan. 1810, FO 78/68; Adair, *Negotiations*, i. 263–5.

41. S. Canning to Canning, 26 May 1809, FO 352/1/3.
42. Bartholomew Pisani, Anthony Pisani, Francis Chabert, George Calavro. Besides Bidwell, Stratford Canning, David Morier, and the four dragomans, the staff included two dragoman-trainees, Frederick Pisani and Nicolo Navon, plus ten janizaries and two Turkish clerks. Adair to Foreign Office, 6 Jan., 24 Sept. 1809, FO 78/63. The total salary for interpreters at this time was 29,600 piastres, or just under £1,500. Adair to Bathurst, 5 Jan. 1810, FO 78/68.
43. Adair to Foreign Office, 10 Feb. 1809, FO 78/63. Adair mentions a dagger worth 100,000 piastres for Sultan Mahmud II.
44. Stephen Maltasa, the *cancellier*, was reminded by the merchants that 'the cancellarai is to be entirely and exclusively attached to our consulate-general, with all papers, documents, books and other effects appertaining to it, being a notarial office, solely intended for the affairs of this company, and its members, and the expense attending it being entirely borne by us'. Levant Company board to Maltasa, 10 Aug. 1804, in Adair to Canning, 19 April 1809, FO 78/63. The perverse intention here was to get Maltasa to withhold the embassy archives from Adair; however, Maltasa collaborated with Adair.
45. Stratford Canning misrecollected in his memoirs that 'a most friendly understanding' prevailed between the embassy and the Porte in 1809. Lane-Poole, *Life*, i. 129.
46. Adair to Canning, 12 and 18 April 1809, FO 78/63.
47. In 1809, the Ottoman fleet had 15 ships-of-the-line, seven frigates, and nine corvettes. Two more frigates were on the Alexandria station, and capital ships were being built at Rhodes, Mitylene, and Budrun. Adair to Canning, 25 March 1809, FO 78/63; Adair to Bathurst, 14 Feb. 1810, FO 78/68. Adair is found still asking for this money to be paid in his penultimate dispatch. Adair to Wellesley, 5 July 1810, FO 78/68.
48. Adair to Canning, 24 July, 29 Aug. 1809, FO 78/64.
49. S. Canning to Canning, 25 May 1809, FO 352/1/3.
50. Adair to Canning, 24 July 1809, FO 78/64; Puryear, *Napoleon and the Dardanelles*, p. 332. Relying on French sources, Puryear claims that 15,000 janizaries remained in Constantinople, 10,000 in Adrianople, and 7,000 in the Bosporus garrisons.
51. Adair to Canning, 10 and 19 March, 24 July 1809, FO 78/63. Kasim Pasha was the naval yard on the Golden Horn, headquarters of the kaptan pasha or naval commander-in-chief. The burning of Sebastopol was discussed over coffee, but not over maps, it seems. Naval conversations between Captain Stewart and Ottoman naval officers are in Adair to Canning, 25 March 1809, FO 78/63, with enclosures. The Ottoman break with the French embassy was a piece of ritual, and relations were restored within days. Stratford Canning told Canning, 'Were I Reis Efendi, I would not do it myself'. S. Canning to Canning, 27 April 1809, FO 352/1/3; Adair to Canning, 28 May, 3 June 1809, FO 78/63; 6 July 1809, FO 78/64.
52. Adair to Canning, 23 April 1809, FO 78/63; 13 July, 1 and 29 Nov., 26 Dec. 1809, FO 78/64; S. Canning to Canning, 14 Nov. 1809, FO 352/1/3.
53. S. Canning to Canning, 14 Nov. 1809, FO 352/1/3; Adair to Canning, 19 Feb. 1809, FO 78/63.
54. Canning to Adair, 29 July, 24 Sept. 1809, FO 78/64. Examples of the British news-sheets are to be found loose in FO 352/1/1. These are almost exclusively military in their contents, with such headings as, 'Alli 27 de Luglio 1809, L'Armata Inglese sotto'c Commando del Generale Sir Arthur Wellesley attacco

li Francesi Vicino Talavera, et li ha compuita mente disfatti'.
55. S. Canning to Canning, 8 Sept., 14 Nov. 1809, FO 352/1/3.
56. Lane-Poole, *Life*, i. 56; S. Canning to Canning, 8 Sept. 1809, FO 352/1/3.
57. It was in connection with the expected French descent on Greece from Italy, Corfu, and Croatia that Adair made the only appointment of his embassy, that of George Reggio as vice-consul in Crete, to report French penetration of the Morea. It was typical of the age that military intelligence was acquired not through direct espionage but by summarizing the information of traders and sailors. It was typical of the Levant Company that while it already had a vice-consul in Crete, it could not remember his name or if he were still alive. Adair to Canning, 15 June 1810, FO 78/68.
58. Adair to Canning, 24 July, 28 and 29 Aug. 1809, FO 78/64; Adair to Bathurst, 10 Feb. 1810, Adair to Wellesley, 22 Feb. 1810, FO 78/68.
59. Bathurst to Adair, 19 Oct., [n.d.] Nov. 1809, FO 78/64.
60. Adair to Bathurst, 26 Dec. 1809, FO 78/64.
61. Adair to Canning, 24 Sept. 1809, FO 78/64.
62. Adair to Bathurst, 10 Feb. 1810, FO 78/64; S. Canning to Canning, 27 Jan. 1810, Harewood MSS. These dispatches show how hard Adair had to struggle against the restraints of his own treaty. He asked for his dispatches to be allowed to come and go on 'a small vessel of war', and when he finally left the Porte he was able to do so on a frigate sent by Admiral Collingwood.
63. Adair to Bathurst, 26 Dec. 1809, FO 78/64; 10 Feb. 1810, FO 78/68.
64. Adair to Canning, 22 and 28 Aug., 12 Sept., 24 Dec. 1809, FO 78/64; Adair to Bathurst, 26 Dec. 1809, 10 Jan., 12 Feb. 1810, FO 78/68.
65. Vahid also fell from favour after Wagram, and even Stratford Canning is found lamenting his disappearance; 'not withstanding his obstinate temper, and all the trouble that he gave, [he] was sound at bottom, and never forgot the hostile demands which Bonaparte had upon his country', S. Canning to Canning, 14 Nov. 1809, FO 352/1/3.
66. S. Canning to Canning, 8 Sept. 1809, FO 352/1/3; Lane-Poole, *Life*, i. 60–6.
67. Adair to Canning, 24 Dec. 1809, FO 78/64.
68. Adair to Wellesley, 13 and 15 March 1810, FO 78/68.
69. Adair to Wellesley, 15 and 31 March, 24 April 1810, FO 78/65.
70. Adair to Wellesley, 5 July 1810, FO 78/68.

CHAPTER V

Stratford Canning and the Treaty of Bucharest

Stratford Canning fought long and hard to escape the greatness thrust upon him at Constantinople. He hoped at first that release would come with the ratification of the treaty of the Dardanelles, sent out in July 1809, but it did not. When he heard of his cousin George's duel with Viscount Castlereagh, he decided to follow him into retirement, but George Canning was too quick for him, sending 'the most positive injunctions' against any 'romantic' act and adding the warning: 'I may or may not have it in my power at some future time, to take you by the hand again. If not, you have a profession in which you may be useful to your country and do credit to your friends and yourself, and you must not lightly abandon it.'¹ Any letter of resignation would now be handled by a new foreign secretary, Marquis Wellesley, who just might listen to a plea of ill-health, but would quite properly regard a bald resignation of the embassy as a withdrawal from the diplomatic service itself. This was, of course, exactly Stratford's wish, to be out of diplomacy altogether, as should have been obvious from the private letters which terminated so often with variations on the same postscript: 'Pray have pity on me and give me leave to return home.' Some of the trouble was due to Joseph Planta, the friendly under-secretary at the Foreign Office who continued to write as if George Canning himself suspected that he was about to wander in the wilderness for some years.² Months after Canning had left office, Stratford was still preferring to argue that his cousin was unduly alarmist and, as a collector of illnesses, he thought one of these would be a good enough pretext for him to come home. This became his final resolution: he would wait until he got full charge of the embassy as a minister, which would bring him a good pension, following which he would resign on the grounds of ill-health. Not that he was ill or could prove that he would be again: he had been put to bed thrice by 'Egyptian plague' in 1809 but 'at present I have no reason to complain of it'. Stratford's clinching argument was financial: he would be ruined by the costs of running the embassy. But George Canning was no longer in office and Wellesley chose not to hear. From distant Tehran, Stratford's friend, David Morier, was amiably unsympathetic: 'my dear fellow: who the devil will consent to take your place so there you must stick till the Lord have mercy on you.'[3]

'How unfortunate it is,' he wrote to his sister, 'that our interests should sometimes be independent of our happiness! Yet this, I am told, is the case, though I am yet too young to comprehend the doctrine. However, there are duties the result of faith as well as conviction. In this world, we are often compelled to obey without knowing why.'[4] On the eve of actually taking over from Robert Adair, he wrote to his old school friend, Richard Wellesley, an illegitimate son of his new chief at the Foreign Office, and now on the point of entering parliament:

> I too, after four months of anxiety and putting off, am in the act of passing into a state of responsibility, which one can hardly do in times like these without certain feelings of apprehension. Mr Adair leaves the middle of next week, and then my diplomatic labours will begin in real earnest. How long they are to last, I know not: that depends on the noble marquis your father.[5]

Canning had not rescued Stratford, nor did Wellesley. The 'conqueror of India' gave everyone in the service of George III, and not Stratford alone, the impression that his victorious labours in the great subcontinent had exhausted him permanently, an impression which was heightened by his regular absence from cabinets, his gift for falling immediately asleep whenever he did put in an appearance, and his jocular reference to these little failings as the relics of 'Indian habits of business'. As Canning had fought his famous duel to get Wellesley into the ministry, most people thought Wellesley ought not to have accepted the Foreign Office on Canning's departure. Knowing this, Wellesley responded with 'supreme disdain' for his new colleagues, and sulked over the ministry's weakness as though he were not partly responsible. He had Canning's distressing habit of telling others how to run their departments instead of setting an example and, in 1812, after Spencer Perceval was assassinated, his colleagues retaliated by refusing to serve under him when he tried to form a government.

The main reason Wellesley forgot Stratford was his absorption with the Iberian war. Wellesley was absolutely right in urging unstinted support for his two brothers who were trying to co-ordinate the anarchic enthusiasm of the Portuguese and Spanish patriots into purposeful effort, and one can appreciate his feeling that Iberia was almost a family business which should come first, but there was little justification for his belief that British naval supremacy in the western basin of the Mediterranean automatically secured a quiet life for British trade in the Levant, and no excuse whatsoever for his complete failure to exploit Constantinople as the one formal point of diplomatic entry into Europe still at his disposal. In the spring of 1810, as Adair packed to come home, Wellesley was engrossed in peace proposals sent him by Napoleon's minister of police, Joseph Fouché, and was too busy estimating the feasibility of partitioning the United States with France to have much time for the question of a successor to Adair. He offered the embassy to the earl of Aberdeen, but when the latter refused unless Wellesley would 'do something' for the Greeks, no new arrangement was made for a year and Stratford was left as minister for two years.[6]

The evidence of Wellesley's neglect is dramatically simple. He received 33 dispatches from Constantinople over an eight-month period before acknowledging any, and sent nothing that could be called a directive at any time. In the course of the entire year of 1811, a critical year for the Ottoman Empire and for Stratford, only four dispatches were sent from the Foreign Office, the most anxious of which told Stratford to scour the bazaars for interesting manuscripts for Lord Sligo. 'In one instance,' Stratford recollected, 'no official communication reached me in the space of fifteen weeks.'[7] For all practical purposes, he was left to do his best, cut off from home, from other courts except for his clandestine correspondence, and from other embassies at Constantinople except the Austrian, the Swedish, and the Sicilian. The Russian embassy was shut for the whole of his mission, the Prussian guardedly neutral, the French hostile. Under such conditions, Stratford often repeated Adair's old pleas for guidance and, above all, for the exchange of the secret articles of the treaty of the Dardanelles, meaning the promised sum of £300,000. This had been the topic of Adair's last dispatch to the Foreign Office, as of many previous ones.[8] It was the main point of many of Stratford's pleadings too, but there was no response.

Besides sharing the view commonly held in Britain that the Ottoman Empire was near the end of its tether anyhow, the Foreign Office in 1811, as in 1916, mistakenly believed that in times of vast European conflict, the fate of the Ottoman Empire would be decided in European chancelleries, and that until that decision was taken the Ottomans themselves could neither influence their fate nor take any initiatives of their own.

The two years were fatiguing rather than eventful, and during them Stratford's diplomatic style took shape. Stanley Lane-Poole's account of him, hastening grim-faced and on foot through the lanes of Constantinople to confront the Ottoman ministers, is pure fantasy. Stratford certainly acquired his irascible mien at this time, partly as policy, partly because of his constant frustration. His letters home were sufficient to allow his mother to envisage him 'storming and raging' and she cautioned him against exploding 'among foreigners and strangers', adding that his temper was 'the only thing in your disposition that I have any fear of'. His secretary, David Morier, said much the same, referred to his 'lash', and said that 'were it not for that defect, for it is a great one, you would be the best fellow I know'. It was because he knew this fear about his temper was justified that Stratford cultivated a pose of lofty severity, which gave his face the look of a well-kept grave. But this was not done for the sake of the Ottomans for the simple reason that he hardly saw any – it was impossible, he decided, to have them to dinner or other social occasions. Like Adair, he worked through dragomans and, as the sociology of oriental diplomacy did not really interest him, he saw no purpose in standing at a dragoman's elbow while he jabbered in Ottoman Turkish. His private papers confirm this: they are full – were full – of the reports written by the dragomans on their return from Topkapi or the offices of the Porte. Why, then, the grim countenance, except as a measure of self-control? It was adopted for a wider, more important audience than Ottoman officials: it was to remind his own staff, his fellow-countrymen in the East, the whole European colony, that he was the British ambassador and, no small thing, a Canning.

His personal resources were narrow and, to judge from his

morale, insufficient. He was mildly bookish, had no ear for music nor eye for art, and soon lost any gift for natural conversation. He said he could barely recognize 'God Save the King' and he was unable to dance. As was said of Robert Peel, he had no small talk. As a result he did his work faithfully and well, but when the work ran out he was incapable of surveying it objectively or doing something else. His sense of duty – he was always talking about it – drove him to create work and, like Penelope, he would often take apart in the long night the work that had engrossed the day. Worst of all, he treated great and small matters as of equal importance, and really appears not to have known the difference. What was written in dispatches was written again twice and thrice in private letters, and thrice again in scattered 'notes' or 'memoranda' or 'digests'. This encyclopaedic habit remained with him. His diplomatic problems, his discontents, the myriad observations on Ottoman delinquency, written without humour or proportion, form a slag heap of despondency. And he kept it all.

Stratford endured this strangely isolated existence in the renovated embassy in Pera. After the repairs done by Adair, the structure looked much as it had when first opened, in the presence of the Sultan's master-builder, in 1805. A simple, two-storey structure, its bow-windows faced south-west to the Golden Horn. Framed between the trees of the garden, the skyline of Constantinople rose against the western sky, and during three separate missions, as bachelor, widower, and remarried man, this was Stratford's official residence. It was destroyed in the vast fire of July 1831 along with all the diplomatic archives. A home only latterly, in 1810 it was his workshop and his prison.

In an existence which was all correspondence, seven categories of paper can be discerned: the stream of dispatches to London; the directives for the dragomans who channelled Stratford's communications to the Porte; letters to and from the British naval captains who put in more frequent appearances in Levant waters now than in Adair's time; the correspondence with Sir Harford Jones, the British minister in Persia; a fitful correspondence with the British representative in Alexandria; and the sixth, correspondence with British representatives in the Adriatic zone such as Captain Leake in Albania or George Foresti in the Ionian Islands. To these we shall return.

If, however, Stratford's correspondence was arranged in descending order of volume, the seventh category would undoubtedly come first, and it is a token of his comprehensive zeal and his inability to delegate authority that he allowed it to take up so much of his time. This class of correspondence, which arose from the protection of British trade in the piratical seas of the Levant, would have been entrusted by a more experienced man to David Morier's father, Isaac, the consul-general, and in keeping it to himself Stratford obstructed the very purpose for which the British government had split the functions of ambassador and consul-general in 1804. Consequently, he got involved too often in rancorous quarrels at the Porte about ships and cargoes and privateers and convoys, and such disputes left a sediment of animosity and unpleasant recollection behind them, all too easily stirred when the time came to take up the far more important struggle for the soul of the Ottoman Empire. A characteristic entry in his private journal reads, with regard to a squabble with the Porte over unchastised piracy: 'Much anger on both sides, exposed on mine, concealed on theirs.' His harsh words, recorded on paper for Ottoman benefit, had the disadvantage that they could not be passed off as the anger of the moment. Stratford was not the sort of man to apologize for such an excess of diligence: 'I thought it the more incumbent on me to shun no responsibility which the exercise of an unshackled judgement might entail.' The trouble was that Stratford would never sacrifice small issues for the sake of big ones – he had to win every game.

One of the first independent judgements passed on Stratford as an envoy was by the eccentric Lady Hester Stanhope, who came to Constantinople and fraternized audaciously with Napoleon's chargé d'affaires, Florimond de Latour-Maubourg. Stratford had her shadowed as she promenaded with the Frenchman by the Bosporus, and finally remonstrated with her for such ostentatious disloyalty to her king. Lady Hester replied by sending Stratford a copy of a letter she had sent Wellesley, defending her own conduct and criticizing that of the youthful, impetuous, and ungallant minister – 'uneducated in your lordship's school of gallantry' – in her usual astringent terms. Her letter said that this 'religious and political methodist' was missing his true vocation: 'The best reward for his services would be to appoint him commander-in-chief at home and ambassador extraordinary abroad to the various societies for the suppression of vice and cultivation of patriotism. The latter consists in putting oneself into greater convulsions than the dervishes at the mention of Buonaparte's name.'[9]

★ ★ ★

Although the treaty of Bucharest has often been regarded as the triumphant conclusion of Stratford's first embassy at Constantinople (the treaty was signed in May 1812, and his successor, Robert Liston, arrived in June), his own contribution was useful rather than decisive, and certainly far less than is commonly supposed. As has been suggested above, normal diplomatic activity was largely excluded from his routine, the usual network of consultation between embassies having broken down with the closure of so many legations. This being so, Stratford could do little until either the Russians or the Ottomans called him to their service, and he was left to counter French influence as best as he could. As neither he nor Latour-Maubourg received any real guidance from home, their contest was a singularly personal one, in which means were confused with ends, and petty retaliations reported home as though they were important. Latour-Maubourg's self-appointed task was to keep the Russo-Ottoman war going by pretending that only the pressure of other commitments was preventing Napoleon lending his immense diplomatic influence to the Ottoman cause, while Stratford, carrying on where Adair left off, had to urge warlike measures against Russia on the Ottoman ministers simply as a means for bringing Russia to a peace negotiation on the basis of the *status quo*.

Thus the two ministers, though mutually hostile, were urging the same policy on the Ottomans, albeit for different reasons, and the Ottoman ministers refused to favour one at the expense of the other until they needed to. Stratford believed, like Adair before him, that only one or other of two possible developments could give him the upper hand as a real force in Ottoman statecraft, the first being a sharp decline in French fortunes in Europe, and the second a resolute and open adoption by Britain of Ottoman interests until the war was won. In fact, he was rescued from his position of impotence by a third development for which he did not sufficiently allow, namely, a direct Russo-Ottoman negotiation which would require some intermediary embassy to expedite the correspondence passing between the two capitals. Long before 1812, Latour-Maubourg had become ineligible for this role – in St Petersburg because relations with France deteriorated so swiftly after the end of 1810, and in Constantinople because it was sensed that Napoleon could, after all, be overthrown. The Ottomans beckoned for the assistance of Russia's likely friend, Britain, from the moment they ceased to believe in the invincibility of Russia's certain foe, France. Adair had already laid the groundwork.

Stratford's first essay in *haute diplomatie* was brief and disappointing, and was precipitated by the dramatic possibility that the Russo-Ottoman war, carried on fitfully since 1806, was actually coming to a conclusion, unfavourable to the Ottomans, in the summer of 1810. Just before Adair sailed for home, the Ottoman battle-line on the Danube was broken by Count Mikhail Kamenski, the conqueror of Finland, and Stratford had not been long in charge when worse news came from the front. The most important river crossings – Silistria, Sistova, and Ruscuk – all fell to the Russians, who were reported to have raised their tents at Shumla, well south of the Danube. From here, they proposed crushing terms to the Porte, demanding the Principalities, the Kuban, total independence for the Serbs and, as usual, the expulsion from Constantinople of the British mission.[10] A British commercial agent called Mair who came through the Russian and Ottoman lines told Stratford he had seen no defensive arrangements anywhere in Bulgaria capable of keeping the Russians out of Adrianople. However, Mair said, the Russian commanders all agreed that the poor state of relations with France might incline the tsar to favour a quick peace with the Ottoman Empire on the basis of limited gains.

Stratford soon found that the British government was expected to take up Adair's daring suggestion of buying off Russia with captured colonies in lieu of Ottoman provinces, and he further discovered that his audience with the Sultan was being delayed so that a favourable British response to Adair's proposal could turn the audience into a triumphant occasion. The idea only raised Wellesley's ire and he refused it out of hand; he further decided, as Canning had done before him, against providing the Ottomans with the £300,000 promised in the treaty of 1809 until the French and Ottoman armies were actually in conflict. Stratford filled in the period of waiting by sending to the Porte suggestions for amphibious operations against the Crimea and an assault upon Sebastopol. He also notified the Porte that whenever the Sultan took the field in person, he would accompany him, 'if it was thought I could be of any service'.[11] The Ottomans had no experience in the kind of warfare Stratford recommended and, if followed, his advice would have led to disaster. But if the worthless rulers of Sicily were worth £300,000 a year, honouring the secret subsidy clause of the treaty of the Dardanelles could have done no harm. On 28 August Stratford's long-delayed audience with the Sultan passed off quietly. He took the chance to express his 'impatience for the moment when your Imperial Majesty at their head will excite Ottoman troops to exertions which can terminate only in the entire destruction of the common foe', but as Mahmud II had heard all this before from Adair and, before him, General Sébastiani, he contented himself by replying through the dragoman that he would protect the British community. Stratford was obliged, for the moment, to turn to other duties.[12]

Paramount among these in 1810 was the constant search for ships' supplies – masts, timber, hemp, tallow – for the Royal Navy, and it has to be said at the outset that Stratford had little success because he persistently asked for help from the wrong people. The distracted navy commissioners in Malta who solicited his aid had the demanding duty of keeping in a state of high repair a fleet of sailing ships which always appeared to be hurrying wilfully into decline. The usual Baltic source of supply was uncertain and distant, and the oaks of Croatia and Serbia were inaccessible because of the interposition of the enemy's army of Illyria. Only pockets of potential supply were left – Albanian Durazzo, the Cyclades, and the island of Thasos. The anxiety of the Malta commissioners is visible in the prices they offered and the quantities they sought: the British embassy at Constantinople was advised that they would pay £58 a ton for copper, and would pay in full instantly for 6,000 tons of hemp if this were to be had.[13] In his ignorance, Stratford went to the Porte with his shopping-list, and then to the Levant Company factory, mistakes both. The Ottoman ministers knew neither how to collect the copper, the hemp, nor the lumber of Anatolia, although there were oak forests around Afyon extensive enough to support banditry as a local profession. But more important, there was a real anxiety at the Porte to obstruct anyone who could bring the desired commodities together, there being an irrational but genuine fear that an ulterior purpose of Europeans was to denude the Empire of strategic raw materials. The copper of Tokat was safe where it was; so, too, the hemp of Cyprus. Any request which enlarged the Europeans' pretext for using the Bosporus as a waterway was also treated warily. The Company merchants were no more helpful. A recent visitor, Edward Daniel Clarke, declared that it was an illusion to suppose Constantinople was a trading city at all: 'you are said to be in the centre of the commerce of the world' but, on closer examination, the Ottoman capital had 'miseries and deficiencies . . . so striking, that it must be considered the meanest and poorest metropolis in the world'.[14]

But Clarke, like Stratford, knew the wrong people. Instead of approaching ministers or merchants, Stratford should have sought out monopolists, men into whose hands – pockets? – were often funnelled the financial proceeds of a universally needed commodity, or the control of an entire branch of trade. Here, he was at the mercy of that common opinion which said that Muslims had no business sense, Greeks were rascals, and Balkan Slavs yokels: as the British merchants had no money (they could not raise £40,000 between them in 1810), no political power, and no knowledge of today as against yesterday, where else were entrepreneurs to be found? The Ottoman authorities obviously missed a great chance to increase British gratitude, but this is to ask men to have mental processes we know they did not possess. Stratford was loftily told that if the Sultan wanted cash (it was he, nevertheless, who asked the Levant Company for the £40,000), he could raise it in London against the collateral of his *vakf* income without having to stoop to trade. In his turn, the British minister left the navy people in Malta to scrape supplies where they could, because he lacked the imagination to make a more constructive effort on their behalf. And yet, what a marvellous report the under-employed David Morier could have produced, and what contracts he might have made in Thessaly and Epirus alone, where an expert Greek merchant marine, financed from Smyrna, was ever being tempted into the livelihood of piracy because, like Morier, it had too little that was legitimate to do. Stratford, we know from his own papers, was a convert to Pouqueville's view that the Ottoman Balkans were more or less a desert through progressive depopulation. But there was a consul in Salonika whose reports showed a city growing spectacularly, and a constant stream of information from Janina to Epirus to show that, in the phrase of Traian Stoianovich, 'Balkan merchants prospered, while the Balkan peasantry was subjected to new forms of oppression'.[15] Within the interstices of a stagnating Ottoman agricultural system, a new Christian commerce was extremely active and opportunistic. And Stratford could not yet see it.

At least as important as ships' supplies was grain, mainly for the growing armies in the Peninsula and the garrisons in the Ionian Islands. Here Stratford got virtually no co-operation from the Company merchants, as Bartholomew Pisani had cryptically forecast, because several of them – Sarell, Wilkinson, Green, and Willis – were in league with a network of merchants elsewhere, as well as with Ottoman officials, and were smuggling grain. The export of grain from the Sultan's territories was strictly forbidden, but occurred illegally on a grand scale. Thrace and Macedonia, for instance, exported almost half their grain, and the pasha of Salonika forbade the Sultan's firmans of prohibition to be read in his area of jurisdiction. In Smyrna, the English factory more than once petitioned the embassy to help retain the pliant governor in his office, for he condoned grain smuggling and invested in it himself, as Consul Francis Werry told Stratford.[16] The Constantinople merchants were instrumental in shipping grain at night down the Bosporus, it having come from the newly founded port of Odessa or the Bulgarian town of Varna. Consul Nicholas Strane at Patras advised the young minister against fighting all the sins of the world: better not to obstruct illegal supplies of a precious commodity until a legal supply could be negotiated. Most unwillingly, Stratford complied, but his eye turned more than ever to one place where the prohibition of grain sales 'was not intended to extend its operation', Egypt.[17] And here, for the first time, he became interested in a man who was unknown when he first landed in Egypt in 1800, yet who held the Sultan's firman as its *vali* by 1805.

There was nothing prescient in Stratford's opinion that Egypt would never again be ruled from Constantinople. Everyone said so. Few, on the other hand, predicted a long career for its new ruler, Muhammad Ali; both Comte Mathieu de Lesseps, the French agent in Egypt, and his British counterpart, Ernest Missett, had expected Muhammad Ali to fall as quickly as he had risen, and both put their money on his local rivals, the Mamelukes. By Stratford's time, Muhammad Ali had gone far to confound such predictions, on the Napoleonic principle of dividing enemies before defeating them in detail. The *vali* edged out the few Ottoman officials, set the Bardisi and Elfi factions of the Mamelukes against one another, and chased out the British themselves in 1807. In 1811, he set the seal on his supremacy by massacring 1,000 of the Mameluke leadership when they incautiously accepted his invitation to Cairo to witness the installation of his son as pasha of Jeddah and the inauguration of a major campaign against the heretical Wahabi people of the Hijaz. Thus it was the French in 1798 who first broke the Mameluke power, but it was Muhammad Ali who swept them off the stage of history. Stratford's school friend, Gally Knight, who was an eyewitness to the massacre, was the person who convinced Stratford most that the new dictator would not, after all, drop out of sight and that he was worth Britain's respectful consideration.[18] He ruled almost four million people, controlled a sea-route to India, and probably did not want the French back. He also personally monopolized the Egyptian grain trade. There were only three British families in Rosetta and perhaps the same in Cairo; no Levant Company vessel had been to the delta for 70 years. Stratford pressed for the immediate return of Missett (he had been chased out with the British expeditionary force in 1807) and in 1811 Missett duly returned as consul-general.[19]

Until Missett returned to his post Stratford worked in Egypt through the very talented archivist of the Levant Company, Stephen Maltass, who served Stratford and the British navy well. The south Russian grain supplies were officially cut off, the Ottoman bread-basket in the Principalities was temporarily a war zone, and the navy was unwilling to accept maize from Macedonia. Egypt, on the other hand, produced a succession of bumper crops of grain and Maltass had an exquisite sense of timing, knowing when to listen respectfully as Muhammad Ali explained that his loyalty to the Sultan would not allow him to trade in grain, and when to press a million piastres into his hand. The magnitude of Maltass's dealings can be seen in the instance of just one convoy sailing for the grinding mills of Malta in January 1811: there were 29 British vessels in it.[20]

In Egypt, more than wheat was at stake. It was commonly rumoured in Smyrna that there would be another French expedition to Egypt sometime, and the Ionians in Constantinople told Stratford's dragomans that the French purpose in hanging on so grimly in Corfu was to maintain the island as a stepping-stone to the East. The yards at Toulon were building transports, Marseilles was agitating for its Turkey trade to be re-opened, and Napoleon planned in 1812, if the circumstances were favourable, an expedition to Sicily or Egypt. This plan stood behind the amiability of Bernardin Drovetti, de Lesseps' successor as French consul, in his dealings with Muhammad Ali, and Latour-Maubourg did not hesitate to threaten the Ottomans with the loss of Egypt to his master. There was much, in Stratford's view, for the Sultan to learn from the example of his viceroy. If the Mamelukes could be overthrown, why not the janizaries? And if Mahmud II could not assert himself in his own capital, perhaps Britain should reach out to these men who had real claims, if not always impeccable title, to independence, such as Veli Pasha in the Morea, Ali Pasha in Janina, the independent pasha dynasty in Baghdad, the despots of Anatolia and, above all the others, the ruler of Egypt. In future years, Stratford would propose that Egypt should be augmented by the addition of Syria, an idea he reversed in 1832.

Britain should, he advised Wellesley, make a firm bid for the support of Muhammad Ali: 'it appears that he is of an enterprising character' and possessed, surprisingly, a pro-British bias. Was it not time for Britain to take advantage of his 'promising talents and friendly disposition', thus 'establishing our interests there [in Egypt] on some permanent basis'?[21] Wellesley, of course, did not answer this or any other proposal coming from the East, but to judge from Stratford's replies to Maltass's letters, the young British minister favoured treating Muhammad Ali as an independent ruler and offering him guarantees against French vengeance if he agreed to obstruct a further Napoleonic thrust towards India. This, it will be noticed, was a development of Canning's instruction to Adair that, if Mahmud II could not hold his lands in full sovereignty, Britain might have to deal with the successor-rulers in the Ottoman provinces.

Wellesley's silence, in comparison with Stratford's friendly solicitude, left Muhammad Ali in a quandary, to choose for himself between the French and British. The French bullied and flattered him without being able any longer to hurt or help him, whereas the British, with a far more tangible naval and mercantile presence in

Levant waters, handled him with an ineptness which puzzled him because he confused neglect for hostility. Napoleon's representatives, Drovetti in Cairo and Consul Saint Marcel in Alexandria, admonished Muhammad Ali for trading with Napoleon's enemies, violating the rules of the Continental System, and failing to provision Corfu. At least this vigorous concern was a form of recognition. The British on the other hand held Malta as determinedly as the French held Corfu, stood in dire need of his corn, paid for it readily and took it away expeditiously, yet beyond this kept aloof, to the extent that when an Egyptian frigate visited Britain *en route* for Suez via the Cape of Good Hope, her commander was warned that his projected journey would be a violation of the East India Company's monopoly in the Red Sea.[22] This galled Muhammad Ali enormously, and clouded his relationship with Stratford, to their mutual regret, for the young Englishman was quite ready for Egyptian independence. Twenty years were to pass before a British government actually solicited Stratford's opinions about the utility of supporting the ruler of Egypt at the expense of the Sultan in Constantinople. By then, it was still a straight choice between two ruling dynasties, one still sturdily upstart, the other still decrepit and old, and by then Stratford favoured the unregenerate Sultan over his great, reformist rival.

'Albania, indeed, I have seen more of than any Englishman (except a Mr Leake) for it is a country rarely visited.'[23] So wrote Byron to his mother in November 1809 having taken nine days to travel northward from Preveza on the coast of Epirus to the mountain court of Tepelene, to be received there by the most independent, opportunistic, and cruel potentate in all Ottoman Rumelia, the legendary Ali Pasha, the 'lion of Janina'. Byron had dressed himself up in 'a full suit of uniform with a very magnificent sabre' for the occasion and was enchanted with the barbaric splendours of Tepelene, of which his favourite recollection was that of the redoubtable old man telling him he was obviously aristocratic because he had small hands and ears. It is more than likely that Stratford heard all about Ali Pasha during Adair's illness, when the young minister-elect was obliged to escort Byron round the sights of Constantinople in the summer of 1810, and the poet may, therefore, be responsible for Stratford's habit of thinking and acting as if he were dealing with no more than a picturesque and bloodstained robber-baron. Ali Pasha certainly was as Byron described him, but he was a much larger political figure than the poet or the minister-elect ever quite understood.

Stratford showed greater reserve in his dealings with Ali Pasha than with most other self-constituted Ottoman authorities, remembering George Canning's instruction to Adair to do nothing to encourage Ali's claims to political independence in the west Balkans so long as the Sultans stood up to the Russians and the French. Captain Leake, sent to negotiate with him in 1807, found Ali Pasha to be a man of great ability but also great instability, on bad terms with his Sultan, and living in a dream world of his own importance. Adair had written to him to thank him for forwarding the Ottoman peace proposals of 1808 to the British naval authorities but, knowing how easily Ottoman suspicions were roused, had avoided any relationship which could be called confidential or cordial, and refused a direct correspondence. Ali Pasha was, indeed, a dangerous man to correspond with, so ready was he to misconstrue letters in his own favour.[24] He claimed to have letters from Admiral Collingwood and the Portland ministry, brought back to Janina by his personal agent in Britain, Said Ahmet, which promised him the island of Santa Maura and Parga, the mainland fortress, in outright possession, and he blamed Adair for thwarting this plan. In truth, Adair simply ignored it as preposterous.[25] Stratford, from the many letters he received from George Foresti, the British commercial agent in Janina in 1810, nevertheless found the pasha more anxious than ever to be adopted by Britain as an ally, claiming full responsibility for the overthrow of Mustafa, the pro-French bayrakdar at the Porte in 1808, and insisting that the British must withdraw all ships from the Baltic to protect him, their one true Balkan friend, from the importunities of the French in 1811![26]

Ali Pasha's exaggerations of his own importance and the dangers he was in were laughable, particularly when relayed to Stratford by Ali Pasha's agent in Constantinople, Suleyman Pasha, yet his position was far from easy and Stratford correctly discerned fear as well as avarice in the communications received from Janina. The French garrison in Corfu, swelling during 1810 from 9,000 to 15,000, was desperately short of food and its commander put great pressure on the Sultan and Ali Pasha to supply him. It was easy for the Sultan to say that, in answering in the negative, he was treating the French exactly as he treated the British whenever they made similar requests for their armies in Spain. Playing the dutiful subject, Ali Pasha followed suit, but he told Foresti to inform Stratford that the grand vizier was secretly pressing for the French to be supplied.[27] He was anxious about the 2,000 Albanian rebels, opponents of his rule, who had swollen the garrison of Corfu, and he was fully aware that French officers were supplying arms to other malcontents. Also, he disliked the ease with which the rather casual British blockade could be infiltrated from Italy and he sent Stratford details, which clearly shocked him, of an episode in February 1811 when four French frigates from Toulon reached Corfu with mortars, stores, 300 artillery pieces, and 'immense' quantities of provisions. As precautionary measures of his own, Ali Pasha advised the British embassy that he must look to his own interests and fortify his coastal positions against a possible French landing.

What he wanted, of course, was a British promise of eventual rewards, but the military in the Ionian Islands were warned in the strictest terms not to be drawn into discussions. Similarly, although Suleyman Pasha had orders from Ali Pasha to receive any communications from the French embassy courteously and instantly, and to show them all to Stratford before posting them off to Albania, Stratford was grateful but non-committal. To appease the old man's fears of the French, the blockade was tightened up considerably, so that by the summer of 1811 there were three ships-of-the-line, four frigates, and a sloop on the Adriatic station. They picked up many small ships converging on Corfu from the Italian ports, and Foresti had the satisfaction of notifying both Ali Pasha and Stratford of a haul of 20 small craft in three weeks, bringing the French prisoners taken to Zante in that same time to 'two colonels, many staff officers, 16 surgeons, and about 900 soldiers'.[28] Every French movement was now watched, with British agents examining each harbour and inlet, and scrutinizing every schooner and small boat. What Ali Pasha most wanted was, however, denied him. Stratford gave him no insight into the British role in bringing about Russo-Ottoman peace and this led Ali Pasha to believe the Russians might yet return to the Adriatic. The Ottomans and the Russians had taken over the Ionian Islands in 1800 and set up the Septinsular Republic. Would some such arrangement be part of the forthcoming peace between them? In his anxiety, Ali Pasha offered to be the peacemaker himself, and tried to play on Stratford's fears by warning him that the Sultan would always rather surrender much to France than even a little to Russia. Could the British not see that the real enemy, for them as well as Ali Pasha, was France in the Adriatic, not Russia on the Danube? In reality, a bigger responsibility than that of peacemaker was in store for Ali Pasha: suddenly, he was invited by his Sultan to be commander of the Ottoman forces on the Danube front for the 1811 campaign.

Ali Pasha refused the honour and one can see why. He dared not risk his head in Constantinople – he lost it the first time he went there – and he dared not leave Epirus. The Europeans who flattered him yesterday would not hesitate to raise his enemies against him today if it suited their purposes. The Russians had encouraged the Christian Montenegrins and the Bushatli family of north Albania to resist him. The French had armed his local opponents and warned Constantinople against his political infidelities as though they had had no part in them.[29] Now it was true the British had not encouraged his rivals that he knew of, but drawing him to Constantinople might be a trap. With him incarcerated, or worse, it would be the easier for the tsar and the Sultan to dispose of his patrimony. There is more than a likelihood that Ali Pasha also understood that, even if the invitation were genuine, the Ottoman land-forces would not easily be shaped into co-ordinated operations. His own career rather proved the point. He had been playing off Ottoman officials and commanders against one another for four decades. Stratford knew enough of Ottoman methods of summary dismissal to realize the old man's fears could not be discounted, and from the British point of view Ali Pasha was far better kept where he was.[30] Thus when the pasha's refusal of the military command reached the Porte, Stratford supported it ardently with the Ottoman ministries.

As has been explained, Stratford had no instructions of any value from the Foreign Office. Perhaps this is where his later impatience with unwelcome instructions was first encouraged into life. He dissuaded Ali Pasha from appointing a permanent delegate to London and in other ways decided that he should make it his duty to seduce the pasha's ambitions without antagonizing him.[31] The premonition that Britain probably had some ambitions of her own in the Adriatic was accurate, and based on the hints of the various sea-captains, naval and commercial, with whom he corresponded. He advised Suleyman Pasha to prepare his master for such an eventuality. He was, therefore, fairly non-committal, for the true usefulness of Ali Pasha to Britain really depended on what the French might attempt next. In fact, the French threat in the area was almost at an end, and the need to humour Ali Pasha dwindled accordingly. Gauging the reality of French activity was, nevertheless, a matter requiring constant vigilance, whether in the small violent world of Albania or the larger expanse of Qajar Persia.

Stratford's most wearying labours were on behalf of British shipping in the Levant seas. Each morning, after a cold bath and prayers in his bedroom, he would go to his office on the floor below and be writing by six, taking breakfast with Morier and Bidwell at nine. His work-room was cluttered with small tables, each with its burden of paper relating to one of the minister's current negotiations. Stratford's habit was to go from one table to the next, dragging his chair with him, reading and drafting replies to whatever was freshly in, from London, the Porte, Tehran, Bucharest, the Ionian Islands, Janina, Patras, Smyrna, Salonika; from the consul-general, sea-captains, naval officers, merchants, Christian subjects of the Porte; papers not always in English, but in French which he was getting to know well, Italian which he could manage, and Ottoman which he handed to a dragoman for a written translation. By far the largest volume of paper was on the table for correspondence with men of the sea. Idleness can make an envoy abroad feel neglected: Stratford's problem was the contrary one of convincing himself that he had achieved something useful after 10 or 12 hours with a quill in his hand. In fair weather he would take an afternoon ride on horseback, or sit in a caique while two embassy boatmen rowed him to Eyub, but after two hours of relaxation he found himself composing sentences again, and so turned back. He could depend upon it that during his absence his maritime correspondence, at least, had grown. Replies were drafted, and written in fine, usually under the pressure of a waiting king's messenger, or a ship waiting for the tide.

It would have helped very much had someone in the Foreign Office possessed the insight or time to assure Stratford he was a useful part of a bigger battle, and that on the widest scene the tide was turning perceptibly, perhaps permanently, in Britain's favour, as her control extended to Senegal, Martinique, Cayenne, Guadeloupe, Amboyna, Mauritius, and Java. At the very least, the Office could have supplied information from the Iberian Peninsula, as a means of impressing the Ottomans and neutralizing Latour-Maubourg. But because it did not, Stratford obtained this information piecemeal for himself, while his natural despondency led him to suppose that his own trials reflected a much wider situation than was actually the case. It was true, as one could read in Porter's *Progress of the Nation*, that naval supremacy did not appear to be sustaining the web of Britain's foreign trade: in 1810, her exports were worth £34,061,901, but in 1811 worth only £22,681,400.[32] It was also true that, in the eastern Mediterranean, Britain's attempts to inject her goods into Europe by circuitous routes and with great pertinacity, were being frustrated by swarms of privateers and an invertebrate Ottoman government. Britain's vaunted sea-power was hardly visible east of Sicily. What Stratford failed, nevertheless, to realize was that his very troubles over ships and pirates were the consequence of an upturn in Britain's Levant trade, itself a sign of reviving national prosperity.

What was visible, and daily so, was a chain reaction by which countless small merchant-ships were attracting the avarice of French privateers and Greek pirates, who in their turn drew the vengeance of the Royal Navy, which led to complaints from the Ottoman government, which then exposed Ottoman ministers to high-sounding justifications from a young minister who acidly enquired why a government incapable of policing its own territorial waters should object to naval captains who sometimes did. Stratford had a case. The Ottoman fleet in 1811 was believed to have ended its annual cruise at Mitylene because the kaptan pasha was afraid to tangle with the pirates, and it was simply vanity for the Sultan to demand that British frigates should desist from exacting the justice he could not provide.[33] As happened so often, it was not Stratford's case which was weak but his mode of prosecuting it. He frequently made it very difficult for his dragomans to soften his words.

Two years earlier and there would have been little British merchandise for privateers to feed on, but from 1809 there was a resurrection of the Levant trade, and such promise in it that 51 British merchants took out memberships in the Levant Company, the highest number in 50 years. Exports to the Ottoman Empire were officially valued at a mere £13,686 in 1808; they were up to £311,000 by 1812. The true value of the trade was much higher still, for there were many British interlopers in Levant waters, and Company merchants themselves encouraged the growth of an illicit free-trade by chartering Greek vessels for the redistribution of British goods round the Levant. There was, consequently, a great increase in the overall number of ships sailing directly from British ports to Smyrna, Zante, Patras, Alexandretta, and Constantinople. In 1812, the first British vessel to be seen in nine years dropped anchor at Salonika. The consulate at Aleppo, closed a dozen years, was re-opened. Dominant among British goods were the new, machine-produced, cotton textiles, which, by a most fortunate accident of timing, were for the first time able to undersell absolutely the best hand-crafted textiles of Bursa and Smyrna, and places beyond. As in Britain, so in the East, the craft-industries felt machine-competition first. In addition, colonial goods, so long in short supply, became more common, strengthening the case for better naval protection. Within a few years Mocha coffee became too expensive for pious Muslims, priced out by the infidel West Indian product. It would be the same story with sugar and much else. The resultant maritime situation was a confusing one: the British supplied most of the wholesalers in the Levant; Greek, Armenian, Vlach, and Levantine families financed the redistribution to retailers, by land as well as sea. Thus we find some Greeks bringing trade to life while others lived parasitically and piratically on it. Either way, Greeks were salting away profits which would, in a decade's time, allow islands like Hydra and Spezia to finance much of the war for Greek independence.

Bearing in mind how small merchant ships were then – most in the Levant trade were under 100 tons displacement and had less than 20 crew – the rise in the actual number of ships joining the Levant trade by 1811 was very steep, and as the Adriatic squadron was mainly concerned to stop the French provisioning Corfu, merchant-men were under-protected in their run beyond Cape Matapan through the Ionian, Cyclades, and Aegean islands. Piracy was the aptitude of the Greeks much as smuggling was a weakness of British mariners in the North Sea, and piracy grew apace in Cyprus, Corfu, Napoli di Romania, Navarino, and Agria Gramvousal. Corsairs from Barbary used Cerigo as a rendezvous. Navarino was a particular haunt of privateers carrying French letters-of-marque, and when its British vice-consul was beaten up, the town aga did nothing until the *kaymakam* of Tripolizza ordered him into action.³⁴ The privateers did very well, often seizing ships while they were tied up in the imagined safety of an Ottoman port, or running captives taken on the high seas into nearby Ottoman harbours to auction off the cargoes. Fresh outrages averaged two a week during Stratford's tenure at the embassy at Constantinople, sufficient to keep the fires of acrimony well-stoked and to justify his claim that Ottoman indifference was 'utterly incompatible with a state of neutrality'. He was urged on by irate captains of denuded ships, by outraged Turkey Merchants trying to trace stolen goods, by Ionian islanders with real and invented losses, and by naval captains fretting about dwindling wheat supplies. Such complaints brought Stratford very quickly to the boil. 'Everything I bring forward is received with distrust and ill-humour . . . the Capitulations are considered by the Porte as a mere dead letter. . . . The government which I serve will not suffer this, and even if it were weak enough to do so, I am not the man to be the instrument of its disgrace.'³⁵

There were three notorious cases, which Stratford remembered afterwards for the glaring injustice involved, and the absolute immovability of the Ottoman authorities.³⁶ In each instance, Stratford received a dossier of protests from the captain, the consignee of the cargo, injured crewmen, and the like, and in each instance the *reis effendi*, who knew nothing about prize-courts or the law of the sea, retreated through a series of prepared positions, telling the British dragomans that the vessels were taken outside territorial waters, or that the privateer involved was not an Ottoman subject, or that there would be a full investigation. The obvious answer, to set up a prize-court, was thought of at the Porte as likely to produce an early clash with Latour-Maubourg, a fair prediction, and Stratford was forced to watch helplessly as Frenchmen and Greeks sold their prizes 'under the very windows of my house, which is an insult to the King, my Master'.³⁷

On such occasions, his instructions to his dragomans were couched in the most intemperate and undiplomatic language, and when the *reis effendi* once retaliated with the threat that the Sultan might have to silence these gross insults by turning the British out of the Ottoman Empire altogether, the unabashed English kettle told the

Ottoman pot 'not to use such strong and improper language until it be first proved that the English are in the wrong'; Pisani was told, 'You will have the goodness to deliver this message *word for word*'. Then, a few days later, Stratford warned the *reis effendi* that he had had enough of Ottoman delay and injustice, and that henceforth British frigates would be called in to uphold the cause of right.

> I cannot conceal from the *reis effendi* my surprise at the tenor of the answer he has given to my note. . . . His refusal not only to redress the past, not only to provide against a recurrence of what I complain of, but even to enquire into the matter, is quite at variance with the assurances he pretends to give me from time to time of his readiness to do justice to H[is] M[ajesty's] subjects. Nor is the latter part of his answer less at variance with the rules of prudence, than the former part of it with those of justice. . . . Does he not see that . . . I shall be justified in authorizing H[is] M[ajesty's] cruisers no longer to respect the neutrality of the Porte, but to seize everything that has the least connection with our enemies even under the very cannon of the Turkish batteries? Nothing could be more advantageous for us; we should then be able to destroy in one moment those means of annoyance which the French still retain in the Archipelago under the shelter of our moderation and regard for the Porte. . . . For what purpose has the Porte declared itself in a state of neutrality if it is too weak to discharge the duties of that state?[38]

The charge was reasonable, as the threats accompanying it were unwise, but Stratford's patience was sorely tried and he imagined, with only limited justification, that Latour-Maubourg commanded a more respectful hearing at the Porte because he used stronger language. Both men were actually treated with substantial disregard by their hosts, but Latour-Maubourg, until the invasion of Russia began in June 1812, had the towering silhouette of his master behind him to secure him a hearing on the more important subjects. On the other hand, Latour-Maubourg had less and less to do, as time passed, and no French shipping to protect. And still no Ottoman prize-courts appeared.

British naval captains were meanwhile at their wits' end, so difficult was it to enforce the Orders in Council prohibiting neutrals from trading with the enemy, and protecting British vessels from pirates. In the former case, they were under the restraints of an order issued, at Adair's request, by Sir Dodmore Cotton, mitigating the full rigours of 'rights of search' where Ottoman ships were concerned, and, in the latter, the problem was to catch pirates who merged easily into the crowds of small vessels – brigs, polaccas, luggers – littering the eastern seas. What indeed, was 'an Ottoman ship'? Few local mariners knew any rules of the sea, their papers were often incomprehensible, their crews resisted investigation with spirit. An honest Greek or Muslim trader was ordinarily armed to the teeth to defend himself; he might fly the red-white-blue of an Ottoman infidel, the green-white-red of a good Muslim, a Union Jack if he came from the Ionian Islands, or a blue and white striped flag if he was in Greek waters. The only true test was to see his cargo and his ship's papers. So unless a pirate were actually caught at his trade, naval captains risked a diplomatic row every time they sent a boarding-party to search a suspect vessel.[39]

In 1811, it had become so impossible to get captured British ships released by Ottoman port authorities from the harbours into which pirates had brazenly run them for sale, that Stratford invited British naval captains to begin a period of self-help, and to take captured vessels out of Ottoman waters by force. A test case soon came when a Captain Hope followed the notorious pirate vessel, *Il Gallo*, into Napoli di Romania, and there demanded the garrison commander to release to him the pirate's two British captures, the *Active* and the *Alexandria*, taken by force out of another Ottoman harbour in Syria.[40]

Without denying these details, the Ottoman commander was afraid to take a decision; Captain Hope therefore sailed his ship, *Salsette*, into Napoli harbour in the face of heavy Ottoman gunfire, and destroyed the *Il Gallo*. He failed to bring out the prizes, however, and the *Active*'s cargo was later sold in Constantinople.[41] There were other incidents of this kind which made the Porte more intransigent than ever, and it is a statistical truth that in no single case was Stratford able to secure complete satisfaction for any plaintiff. Sometimes it was the cargo, sometimes the agreed compensation for the owners, sometimes the ships themselves, which were not handed over. Even in May 1812, when Stratford's assistance in the Russian negotiation was worth paying for, and when his relations with Ottoman ministers were at their best, he is found 'demanding a firman for the immediate restitution of the *Carniola* not only in right of my claim but in pursuance of the Porte's own engagements'. The fight, he said, had already gone on for ten months 'to no purpose': it outlasted his embassy. 'It is easy to see,' he concluded, 'that justice is not to be expected.'[42] No dispassionate reader of the shipping cases could say he exaggerated his grievances. British conduct on the high seas was not blameless, as Americans and Danes could attest, but it rested on some rules and had a purpose. Ottoman behaviour seemed to be beyond explanation. If it was difficult for the Sultan to protest against French misdemeanours or check piracy, Stratford thought he might at least overlook the occasional delinquencies of the British.

A complete understanding of Ottoman conduct escapes the historian, as it escaped Stratford and his contemporaries, and, as in so many problems to which the Ottomans were a party, an addition of all the possible explanations seems to leave the heart of the problem untouched. There was some inner reason, beyond Ottoman dislike of British claims to the Ionian Islands, beyond the prior importance attached to the war with Russia, beyond the muddy ignorance of international law and obligation, beyond the profits which some of the highest Ottoman officials drew from the chaos at sea, at the bottom of Stratford's difficulties in obtaining elementary justice. Why, he and others since have asked, was such scant appreciation shown in return for the special benevolence of the British embassy?

The answer becomes a good deal clearer if one takes a viewpoint contrary to Stratford's and allows that all the European powers looked alike to the Ottomans. Britain may not have played any part in eighteenth-century schemes to partition the Ottoman Empire, but she had not forbidden them either. And only four years earlier, in 1807, British ships had forced the Straits, sunk Ottoman ships, and, above all, threatened Constantinople with an immediacy not even Napoleon had managed. The Ottoman capital did not see another enemy until after the armistice of Mudros in 1918. It was no secret that, in the struggle still going on for the friendship of Russia, Britain was as ready as any other power to let the Ottoman Empire foot the bill. Would any European power take a friendly interest in the empire once the war with Napoleon was over? Mahmud II thought not, and did not rely too much on the fourth secret article of the treaty of the Dardanelles, by which Britain promised to obtain an 'advantageous and honourable' peace for the Ottomans, as she had already failed to honour the third. As a result, his ministers extracted any advantage they could from passing opportunity without gratitude, asserted his dignity when they dared, and remained silent, and sullen, in the face of superior power. In their impotence, they found offers of help and advice as galling as Latour-Maubourg's threats. There was, indeed, nothing especially Ottoman, and much that was merely human, in such reactions.

★ ★ ★

As has been mentioned, Stratford was given, but did not take, an opportunity to assert his superiority over Latour-Maubourg when the Ottoman government turned to him in fear and alarm after the evacuation of the Danube crossings at Ruscuk and Giurgevo, the withdrawal of the grand vizier's headquarters to Shumla, and the near collapse of the whole Danube front in the summer of 1810. The grand vizier opened negotiations with his opponents. How great this opportunity was, and how demoralized the Sultan felt, can be estimated from the extraordinary sequel to Adair's farewell interview (itself so extraordinary) when the dragoman of the Porte was sent aboard Adair's departing ship to assure the minister that Mahmud II now felt Britain 'to be the only one of the Great Powers that had nothing to covet which belonged to Turkey'. Turning to Adair's young successor, efforts were made through him to bring the British government into action, but Wellesley would not budge, and Stratford was left to bewail 'the lifeless languor' of Ottoman warfare, and 'the total want of information as well from England as from the Mediterranean'.[43]

A second approach to Stratford, destined to fail as the first had done, was made in October. It was preceded by a private visit from the *reis effendi*, Galib Effendi, and took the form of a direct appeal in a full divan to which the young minister was invited. The dragoman of the Porte asked him to press his government for the immediate exchange of the secret clauses of the treaty of 1809, requiring payment of £300,000, and an equally immediate naval diversion by Britain in the Baltic, thus 'forcing Russia into peace with the Porte by arms or negotiation'. Stratford examined the inscrutable faces around him but knew none except the dragoman, Murusi. Shortly afterwards, he was told a further Russian approach for peace had been received, made this time through the Prussian minister, Count Werther, as the last had been through Baron Hubsch. But the Sultan would still prefer to deal through the British minister. 'France is too much the friend of Russia, and Austria is too little her own mistress. . . .

Sweden, no more than Prussia, is in a situation to assume the impartial and imposing character of mediator.'[44]

Stratford was flattered and delighted. He was also naïve. He relayed the appeal to London the same day, with a reminder to Wellesley that 'a haughty government prefers hostility to neglect'. Wellesley replied eight months later. Not altogether wisely, Stratford also took the opportunity presented by his sudden eminence to demand a firm stand against piracy in the Aegean. Mahmud II, if he was provoked, did not show it, and sent in reply a letter in his own writing thanking Stratford for his solicitude.[45]

Mahmud II was no doubt worried for his throne, and perhaps his personal safety, as Stratford and David Morier both believed. There was great resentment and fear among new recruits brought up from the provinces for the Russian front and in Smyrna they fired the Burnabat district in true janizary fashion.[46] The war was very costly. Against this, the divan was carefully scrutinizing the European scene, measuring the growth of Franco-Russian hostilities against its own declining military position, hoping fervently that the first would outpace the second, and persuading itself that this was already happening. On 15 November, the former Russian minister to the Porte, the Chevalier d'Italinski, reached Bucharest, thus opening a second centre of negotiation in addition to Shumla to which the Ottomans might send representatives.[47] The divan noticed that this was a good deal more civil an approach than the strident demands made through Werther or by the Russian commanders at Shumla, and shrewdly guessed that the British might salvage more for them than the French by this date. Hence their pressure on Stratford.

In a précis Stratford compiled for himself as his New Year's Day relaxation in 1811, there is a statement on the current position in Europe which may be taken to represent Mahmud II's degree of information as much as Stratford's, since the British legation made a point of feeding political and military intelligence to the Porte:

> The Hanseatic towns Lubeck, Hamburg, Bremen, *annexed to the French Empire – duchy of Oldenbourg comprised* – insult to Russia – Prussia suspected of favouring English trade – necessary, therefore, for France to shut up the Belts, or to seize the whole coast up to Memel – Denmark will probably soon be seized – and Norway and some islands ceded to Sweden – Russia ought to be alarmed at this –

> Bonaparte's plan without doubt to extend his empire to the Black Sea – *Conscription of 120m men decreed* – *Austria not indifferent to the progress of France* – *preparations announced by Bonaparte for an attack on our possessions in India* – It is said that General Lauriston, late governor of Dalmatia is to go to the congress of Bucharest to delay the negotiations.[48]

The association of Russia and France was, as the Ottomans guessed and Stratford's analysis of news indicated, sharply on the wane. Throughout the previous year Alexander I had been angered by Napoleon's refusal publicly to declare that he had no intention of resurrecting the kingdom of Poland, and the French emperor in his turn had been deeply concerned by Russian evasions of the Continental System. Russia was admitting British colonial produce, and Napoleon complained that of 2,000 ships entering the Baltic in 1810 with prohibited goods, flying neutral flags but in reality all British carriers, most had found their way ultimately to Russian ports, and he pleaded with Alexander I to put a stop to the nefarious trade. But Napoleon threatened as well as pleaded, in this instance by annexing the North Sea coast of Germany as far as Holstein, and adding to his empire, among other principalities, the duchy of Oldenburg. This was, as Stratford noted, an 'insult to Russia' because the Oldenburg heir had married the tsar's sister, and at the very time Stratford drew up his report on the Continental situation, the tsar was refusing to exclude colonial goods from his domains and actually putting the first taxes on overland imports, which were largely French. By April 1811 Napoleon was predicting war, and by August explaining by what strategy he would win it.

The year 1811 was one of great mobilizations on both sides, with Napoleon's confidence in himself undiminished. He saw no need to contract his manifold plans, to the execution of which he would now proceed alone since the tsar would not join him. The great harbour works at Cherbourg and Antwerp, springboards for the invasion of Britain, were pushed forward; he spoke of recovering the French West Indies and being in a position to withdraw men from Spain at need. The plan against Russia grew and ramified, with fresh conscriptions, bigger arms contracts, the establishment of depots along his proposed route, and a rattle of his sabre at all the courts of Europe.

At the centre of everything, the intention to return to the East is plain, and perhaps seemed nearer to him now than at any time since 1803, when he had spoken of an early campaign on the Ganges. In 1811, he expected 100 ships-of-the-line to be at his early disposal to cover the transports which would carry the *Grande Armée* to Britain, Sicily, and Egypt. Toulon was a bustling, noisy, expectant place, as the elements of a new expedition for the East were put together, and at the time Stratford was urging the Ottomans to make peace with Russia, Napoleon was examining the first models of shallow-draught gunboats with which to navigate the Nile. Fascinated, the divan watched Napoleon mobilize Europe against Russia, amazed as he extracted huge armies from the lands he had humbled. If Poles, Spaniards, Dutch, Danes, Swiss, Prussians, Austrians, Italians, and every description of German could consent to march beneath his banners in this way, could the tsar resist for a moment? It seemed that Russia must make peace with the Ottomans for the reason she tried, and failed, to raise alliances with Prussia and Austria, to shield herself against the coming onslaught from Napoleon. And, however much Stratford might rage at Ottoman folly, the Sultan's ministers were merely following the example of European powers in putting their own interests above anti-French solidarity. In fact, the Ottoman Empire pursued a more modest ideal than states which had previously felt the weight of French supremacy: she dreamed of a peace with Russia by which she would recover all the lands so recently lost, while they, even in their darkest moments, hoped for some opportunity to enlarge their frontiers whenever the French god of war was toppled in final defeat.

Throughout 1811, Stratford largely ignored Vienna and allowed his earlier friendly relations with Count Barthelemy Sturmer, the Internuncio, to lapse. Where formerly they had met often in the garden of the Swedish embassy at night to exchange news and information, and Sturmer had been entrusted with the dispatch of Stratford's confidential letters to Count Stadion, this trust was withdrawn when Stratford heard that Prince Metternich was reading his letters, Metternich whom he disliked and distrusted, now and always. Count Hardenberg, the Hanoverian minister at Vienna, took over where Stadion left off, but his letters were few and not very enlightening, and Stratford accepted the offer of a local merchant, Giuseppe Molo, when the latter offered 'to fill up in a satisfactory manner that chasm in your correspondence with this part of the continent'. Molo rarely had anything dramatic to retail from his business contacts in Austria and Russia, but he did discover, in October 1811, that d'Italinski at Bucharest had secret orders from the tsar to make peace with the Ottomans 'on such terms as can be obtained'.[49] Stratford, in his turn, passed a great deal of information to Russia through the Sicilian minister at Constantinople, Count Ludolf, who sent it via Vienna to his colleague at St Petersburg, the duke of Serra Capriola, Stratford himself having no British diplomatic colleague at the Russian court.[50]

Having once, in May 1810, actually proclaimed the annexation to Russia of the Principalities, the tsar had no intention of terminating a costly war with nothing to show for his efforts, and Stratford guessed perfectly accurately, and as early as February 1811, that the ultimate adjustment would bring Bessarabia into the Romanov empire, even though the Ottomans were 'hardly yet prepared for ceding to the Pruth'. It was his self-appointed task to condition the Sultan to precisely this frontier, an arrangement which he believed would be far more spectacular for what the Russians gave back than for what the Ottomans gave up. 'I urged them [the Ottomans],' he wrote in his memoirs, 'to reinforce their armies, and to redouble their exertions, not in the idle hope of recovering their old frontier, in its whole extent, but with the sober calculation of discouraging their enemy, and disposing him to peace on grounds of mutual concession.'[51] For many months, Russian reactions to the Pruth as a frontier were distinctly hostile, and Serra Capriola's letters showed that the Russian peace party, and not just intransigent men like the chancellor, Count Rumiantsev, and Count Aleksei Arakcheiev, hoped the Ottomans would give up the Principalities as well as Bessarabia, while Britain compensated the Sultan in the Caribbean, a bold reversal of Adair's suggestion.[52]

Wellesley was in no hurry to help Russia through her difficulties, arguing that Continental states rushed too precipitately into disastrous conflicts with Napoleon. What most of them needed in 1811, he said was 'a curb and not a spur'. Wellesley was also furious at the idea of giving up hard-won colonies, and on the offending dispatch in which Stratford asked for an answer to the Russian proposal about Caribbean compensations for the Ottomans, the foreign secretary pencilled, 'to be sure. England must always pay for everybody.'[53] Consistent to the last, however, he omitted to communicate his indignation to the East, and Stratford was left in considerable embarrassment, as both Russians and Ottomans expected him to make a decisive move in their favour. The grand vizier, Yusuf Ziya Pasha, sent a cordial private letter to Stratford from Shumla, and the Russian commander sent his best wishes.

By the late spring of 1811, the British minister to the Porte was a recluse, avoiding the *reis effendi*, rarely visiting the Porte, and asking the Foreign Office repeatedly for 'prompt and decisive support' which never came. He was positively relieved, therefore, when Pisani one day brought him an announcement that 'there is no intention to invite you to interfere in the negotiation in the event of one being set on foot, unless Russia was to support or desire it'.[54] Even so, the *reis effendi* tried to panic Stratford by telling him that the Sultan was thinking of ordering Ali Pasha to provision Corfu, and he followed up with a very real concession to Latour-Maubourg by permitting the Frenchman to move into the Spanish embassy from which he had been so firmly excluded in the past. Stratford broke off relations with the *reis effendi*, a mistake he put right by saying he had only severed *private* relations. In July, once more, he pressed Wellesley without success. 'It is really necessary that some mark of the interest which Britain is declared to take in the welfare of the Porte, or at least some expression of regard and attention to its concerns, should come immediately from His Majesty's government.'[55] None did.

Fortunately for Stratford, the Austrian government was making it plain at this very time that the annexation of the Principalities would be fatal to any chances of Austro-Russian collaboration against France, and it was also known to Wellesley's successor, Castlereagh, that Austria opposed strongly Russia's patronage of the Serbian uprising against the Ottomans. When a Russian force strayed near the banat of Temesvar in the process of moving up artillery to bombard the Ottoman garrison of Orsova, the Austrians told the Russians that Orsova was neutral territory which they would defend if the Russians did not withdraw. Austria's attitude, and Russia's growing need of her aid, lowered Russian pretensions far more than anything Stratford achieved.[56] In June the Russians evacuated Silistria, Nicopolis, and other Balkan forts, mining them before they left. The Ottomans promptly re-entered and repaired them, and the *reis effendi*, in re-establishing friendly relations with Stratford after their June estrangement, said Mahmud II was now ready for peace with Alexander I.

Stratford's temper, never good, grew considerably worse under the strain of so many simultaneous and exhausting negotiations, to which the Russo-Ottoman reconciliation was now added. For instance, in the month of May he severed private relations with the *reis effendi*; worried over the fall of the Mamelukes and the rise of Muhammad Ali in case French interest in Egypt was rising again; threatened to break off public relations with the Porte if Corfu was provisioned; advised the naval chiefs at Malta not to surrender French ships captured in Ottoman waters; became suspicious that the *reis effendi* was taking advantage of their estrangement to cultivate Latour-Maubourg; impetuously put the guards of the British palace in front of the Spanish legation to stop Latour-Maubourg moving into residence (the effect was somewhat lost as he was already installed and it looked as if the British were paying him the courtesy of a guard of honour); and wound himself up into a paroxysm of fury over the seizure of a British merchant ship. He was brusque in his dispatches home, described the *reis effendi* as 'obstinate and ignorant', lost his temper with the faithful dragoman Pisani and called him an 'ass', and wrote off all Ottomans as 'stupidly indifferent to the consequences of their misconduct'. Only Count Pozzo di Borgo, passing through Constantinople on his way to Britain, pleased Stratford, who recommended him to Wellesley as 'among innumerable false [people, he is] unmoved, unshaken, unseduced, unterrifyed'.[57] Pozzo liked Stratford as well.

Serious Ottoman peace negotiations with Russia were preceded by major changes in the personnel of the Ottoman government, the most important being the dismissal of the faithful but militarily unfortunate grand vizier, Yusef Ziya Pasha, on 10 April 1811, in favour of a 'strong man', Laz Ahmet Pasha, who set off for Shumla with great panache, where he quickly proved to be not strong enough. Galib, the *reis effendi* since 1808, lost office in July, and was replaced by Kucuk Arif, but was retained for the negotiations presently opening at Bucharest with d'Italinski.[58] The appointment of the new grand vizier was mere window-dressing, but of the sort Stratford approved. He believed the Ottomans would get the best terms by appearing ready to fight on against Marshal Kutusov, the new Russian commander in the south.

Galib Effendi, taking over from Hamit Effendi at Bucharest behind the Russian lines, was in charge of one negotiation, with d'Italinski. A second, complicating the first, was forced on the new grand vizier in October 1811 when Kutusov, acting under orders to snatch a decisive victory before it became necessary to start withdrawing further troops for the defence of Russia, opened a swift campaign and cut off the grand vizier himself, with a force of only 5,000 men, at Giurgevo. It cannot be said that Kutusov succeeded militarily where his predecessors had failed. Undoubtedly, he broke up the main Ottoman camp, and virtually captured the Ottoman commander-in-chief, but Russian military successes, now as ever, somehow vanished in the sand. The southern Russian military effort in 1811 was extremely impressive on the map – the front ran westward along the Danube from the Dobruja in the east as far west as Orsova, only 100 miles from Belgrade, and worried Austria greatly – but it could not be held long and the Sultan knew it. When the grand vizier impulsively offered to make peace with the river Sireth as the new Russo-Ottoman frontier, an arrangement which would have handed over all of Moldavia to the tsar, the Porte simply repudiated him and sent full powers to the delegates at Bucharest.[59]

On the outskirts of the negotiations, Stratford yet saw himself as their centre, and importantly claimed, 'I had to dispose the Turkish ministers to a peace with Russia on the basis of territorial concession, to nourish in their minds a perpetual mistrust of France, and, without committing my government, to make them look solely to England for counsel and support'.[60] His contribution to the settlement was not, in the estimate of the Porte, important enough to be mentioned in the court chronicle, and appears in no Ottoman history. Occasionally, he was made to look very foolish, as on the occasion when the divan silenced his pomposity by asking what Britain's intentions were regarding the Ionian Islands. Stratford simply did not know.

That Stratford exerted himself greatly on behalf of the cause of peace is easily shown, from the mass of information he passed to the Ottomans on the growing French threat to Russia, and to the Russian government on the shifting attitudes of the divan. How much either side took notice of him cannot be ascertained, and each had other sources of information to draw on. As late as 18 November, Stratford could still admit that, in spite of all his efforts, 'the Turkish government had hitherto given no opening to any step on my part'.[61] It recognized that he was playing a lone hand, and was not altogether happy about his correspondence with Serra Capriola at St Petersburg.

The Ottomans had reason to be suspicious, for about this time Stratford probably offered his services in a formal capacity as an intermediary with d'Italinski at Bucharest. Certainly, he had great misgivings when he heard that the divan had sent full powers to its negotiators at Bucharest. He was also, like the divan, taken aback by the Russian government's tough line about Poti, having persuaded himself that Russian arrogance was bound to deflate as time passed.[62] Unfortunately, and with that inability to sacrifice small for the sake of great causes which was one of his greatest temperamental flaws, Stratford accompanied the tender of his services with a request that British stations in the Mediterranean should be permitted to ship wheat directly from south Russia as soon as peace was made. This immediately raised Ottoman fears. Nor would the Ottomans take a hint and break off relations with Latour-Maubourg, and the dragoman Francis Chabert, reporting back to Stratford after having carried that suggestion to the Porte, wrote, 'Je me suis levé pour partir, mais je l'interrogeais encore une fois s'il ne voulait pas accéder à votre dernière demande, exprimée dans la Note Officielle que je venais de lui présenter. Il répondit, Non, absolument.' Stratford was also refused a conference on the piracy question at this juncture, which he pressed with undue severity, bringing on himself a reply from the *reis effendi* which said, 'It must not be supposed that a conference is *refused* him at the present time; it is only avoided that he may not, by acting as before, create new difficulties; it is avoided with a view to preserve the respectability of his rank.' The wonder is that he was let into the Bucharest negotiation at all.[63]

Yet within a short time of these disagreements, Stratford was being used to plead the Ottoman case with d'Italinski, and being allowed to write letters to Galib, the ex-*reis effendi*, who went to Bucharest via the demoralized camp of the grand vizier. From the Ottoman standpoint, Stratford's main function now was to persuade the Russian government to drop two additional demands it was trying to tack on to Kutusov's claim for the Sireth line; these were, first, independence for the Serbs, and second, the hinterland of Poti. The latter issue interested Stratford most as such a loss, he said, would be 'considered unfriendly to England because directly prejudicial to her ally, Persia'.[64]

The weekly letters to St Petersburg through Count Ludolf were maintained, and when the Ottomans seemed unduly concerned by them, Stratford began sending copies to the divan. His relations with the members of the divan were at moments so cool that only the Sultan's personal intervention seems to have allowed the pleadings with St Petersburg to continue, and Mahmud II sent his encouragements and thanks in a private message:

> I have seen the translation of the papers written by the English minister, and I feel much gratified at the interest he has thus taken in favour of my royal affairs. Whatever may be the effect of these papers in the quarter they are designed for, the purport of them clearly shows the perfect friendship which England professes for my Sublime Porte. Let the originals be sent to their destination.[65]

These particular letters to Serra Capriola were posted on 21 February 1812 and, on the 24th, Latour-Maubourg received instructions from Paris ordering him to make a last mighty effort to persuade Mahmud II to break off the negotiation. Latour-Maubourg was to announce the imminent arrival of a new ambassador in the person of General Andréossy, and to say that, as France was about to attack Russia, the Ottomans could only benefit by delay. An Austrian officer would be offered to command the Ottoman armies in the Principalities, and in the Austro-French treaty of alliance, presently to be signed in Paris, an express guarantee of Ottoman integrity was to be included. All the Ottomans had to do was keep the Balkan war in being, and heighten their efforts. Latour-Maubourg had to fight hard even to get an audience in which to present his terms of friendship and alliance, and Stratford urged the *reis effendi* not to receive him, but the delayed interview finally occurred on 29 March. With such terms to offer, Latour-Maubourg did not expect much difficulty in obtaining the acquiescence of the Ottoman government in a triple alliance with France and Austria which would leave Russia exposed to assault along an immense southern front, and Stratford certainly thought the game was finally up. Interestingly, he identified Mahmud II himself as head of a tiny peace party, with a formidable array of divan members anxious to fight on. 'I have long struggled. ... But ... I am a simple individual without any reputation or other pretensions on which to establish a personal influence over Turkish ministers.' In fact, Stratford was within sight of the end of his thankless labours, and it was Latour-Maubourg who stood on the rim of failure.[66]

Not at Constantinople alone, but throughout Europe generally, the kaleidoscope of international alignment was dissolving into a new pattern, and Russia's abrupt accommodation with the Ottomans in May 1812, along lines of self-denial exceeding even Stratford's hopes, resulted from a situation in which Napoleon commanded an impressive array of allies while Russia had to look across the seas for the two powers which stood by her, Sweden and Britain. In the race for allies, Alexander I had alarmingly poor luck. The attempt made through Count Nesselrode in Paris, to reach beyond Napoleon to the France of Talleyrand and Fouché, was perhaps destined not to get very far, but great hopes were pinned on the success of appeals to Prussia and Austria. If Austria had stood firmly with Russia, Prussia would have followed suit, according to Scharnhorst who was sent to interview Metternich. The latter, for reasons von Srbik finds defensible, urged Frederick William III to stand by Alexander I, but himself provided Napoleon with 30,000 men to protect his Volhynian flank in the drive to Smolensk. For this service, Napoleon was prepared to pay highly, offering Austria Serbia and the Principalities, and the possibility of recovering the Illyrian provinces if, after the war with Russia, Austria would give up her part of Galicia to the Polish kingdom. To clinch the deal, Napoleon even offered Silesia, a good reason for Metternich to urge Prussia to another experience of national ruin. Prussia, providentially for herself, made no difficulties for France, provided a contribution of 20,000 troops and access through her territories for the *Grande Armée*, and so deflected on to Russia the undivided wrath of Napoleon.

The tsar stood isolated, and the news of the Austrian treaty, far more than that of the Prussian deal, forced him to modify his earlier plans. Although, by the Austrian treaty, Metternich refused the territories Napoleon professed himself ready to give, and stipulated instead a guarantee of Ottoman integrity as a condition of the alliance, the tsar gave up his intention to make a stand at the Vistula, and fell back on the retreating, defensive policy by which the French were finally drawn on as far as Moscow. Getting wind of the Austrian treaty in April, the Russians decided they must come to terms with Persia and the Ottoman Empire: the former did not respond quickly enough but the settlement with the Ottomans was made in May. Metternich quickly followed up the disclosure to Russia of his secret treaty with France with an assurance that Austria would distress Russia as little as possible, and to keep her in this mood, Alexander I dared not hold out in his final dealings with the Ottomans for the very provinces which Metternich had so ostentatiously abjured. There was an even more compelling reason for Russia not wanting them at this juncture. The Principalities were a crude crescent-moon of land, as big as peninsular Italy, presenting its concave side to the frontiers of Austrian Hungary. They could also present Napoleon with an obvious line of attack, and the Sultan would find the offer of their retrocession irresistible. Russia wisely abandoned them for the time being. They would not run away.

The Ottomans were more disposed to make peace with Russia than war on the side of France. The balance of power in the divan was fine and even the *reis effendi* told Chabert how splendid it would be if Russia were annihilated. Latour-Maubourg's sweeping promises, supported by a rather miserable Sturmer, who as a result found it very embarrassing to meet Stratford socially, were communicated to Stratford by the Ottomans in detail, usually on the following day. He responded to the *reis effendi*'s wish to discuss the likely attitude of Austria by sending him a copy of a detailed Austrian plan for an attack on the Ottoman Empire. Adair had procured it three years before, and now it was used with great effect.[67] As for the negotiations at Bucharest and with Kutusov on the Danube, the Ottomans clearly preferred to deal with the milder d'Italinski, and Stratford was able to accelerate the signature of peace by sending a personal emissary to plead with the Russians for moderation as well as haste.[68] The emissary crossed the Danube at Sistovo on 5 May, and after long talks with d'Italinski, was sent on to Kutusov, who asked him one question: were the Ottomans pro-French, or would they sign a treaty now? Kutusov himself had his mind on bigger responsibilities further north. Returning to d'Italinski, whom he saw each day for a week despite the French consul in Bucharest, Stratford's emissary was told that Russian policy towards the Ottoman Empire was undergoing serious reassessment: 'The Russians, so far from having the design of destroying the Ottoman Empire, were rather anxious for its preservation.' All they asked for in Asia was 'the Nations of Mount Caucasus', while in the Balkans they would like the Sireth frontier but would settle for the Pruth.[69]

Any idea that Russia was being greatly inconvenienced by the number of troops she had deployed against the Ottomans was put within perspective by the disclosure that all but 22,000 had been drawn off already for use in Poland. If d'Italinski was belittling the Ottoman war, his terms nevertheless met the needs of Galib, who signed a treaty on 28 May, and the grand vizier, Laz Ahmet Pasha, and Kutusov, who signed a slightly different version a day or so later at Giurgievo. So while it could be said that Stratford's patient provision of information contributed something, and possibly a great deal, to the final settlement, it cannot be said that he shaped the final terms. On 28 June, Robert Liston arrived, unannounced, as Stratford's successor at Constantinople: Napoleon had just fought his first encounter with the Russians at Memel. It was said that his baggage contained the coronation robes he intended to wear on his installation as emperor of the new Byzantium.[70]

As no more than a pause in an historic conflict, the treaty of Bucharest decided little except the transfer of Bessarabia to Russia, a trivial sacrifice in Stratford's judgement, but an event of sufficient importance to make him the object of great Ottoman ill-humour. 'I met with nothing but jealousies, suspicions and insults,' he recalled.[71] The city populace reacted to the proclamation of peace in the mosques by starting several large fires, a conventional method at that time for expressing disapproval of the government. Murusi, the wretched intermediary between Stratford and the Porte, was used as a scapegoat by the Sultan's ministers and strangled at Topkapi. Stratford came away from Constantinople in 1812 a marked man, and allegedly a fairly supple Russian agent.[72] The charge was patently exaggerated, to the point of absurdity, but Stratford was only paying the price of involvement with officials now desperately anxious to put the responsibility for their own concessions on to someone else. It is quite true that the modified Danube frontier was offered 'on condition that no territorial concession should be required in Asia', but Stratford was not responsible for the Ottoman's sacrifices on either front. He had only kept realities before the divan, and it was forgotten at the Porte that even Latour-Maubourg offered little beyond what was actually recovered.

Had the treaty's clumsiness of phrase not been due to haste as much as ignorance, the temptation to see its ambiguities as a form of diplomatic Machiavellianism would be tempting. Even Article 4, which advanced the Russian frontier to the river Pruth, bristled with problems for the future. Below Renai, where the Pruth flowed into the Danube, the new frontier followed the northernmost, Kilia branch of the river, and the Kilia followed a seasonally fluctuating course through marshes and lakes. Could a political frontier be allowed to fluctuate with the rhythms of nature? Article 5 specified the withdrawal of Russian troops from the Principalities within a year, but a foot was kept in that door too by the confirmation of Russia's ancient privileges there, as secured by the treaty of Jassy. By Article 8, the Serbs seemed to have been abandoned by Russia – certainly the Serbs thought so, and by 1815 they turned to the policy of self-help – but while the Sultan still fixed the annual tribute and even increased his garrisons, the Serbs were promised control over their *'affaires intérieures'*, a phrase which would require later clarification. The claim to the hinterland around Poti was given up for the moment, but a Separate Article to the treaty maintained Russia's right of access to Georgia by way of it in the most imprecise way. This last article so worried the Ottomans, and Mahmud II particularly, that they took the remarkable step of supplying Galib with two sets of ratifications, one leaving the concession out altogether. He was to persuade d'Italinski to accept this version if he could. According to Liston, Galib was successful, and the clause was reserved in a 'separate and secret article' for 'future discussion'. The Ottomans regarded this as a triumph.[73] Probably the Russians did also. The treaty of Bucharest was ratified in that city on 13 July 1812.

Russia was glad to be rid of the Ottoman war, although d'Italinski claimed that it was almost too insignificant to notice, and

Stratford was sent rather perfunctory thanks for his aid by the tsar. In Britain, both the press and the government took the same view of war and peace in far away, little-known places. The *Annual Register* for 1812 reported: 'Thus was terminated a destructive and protracted war, with an acquisition to Russia of an unhealthy strip of country to her already unwieldy mass of territory.' Drafting Liston's instructions as Stratford's successor, Castlereagh added only a few political remarks to the ancient Levant Company instructions which were otherwise in a standardized format. It did not matter to Britain, the foreign secretary wrote, upon what terms Russia and the Ottoman Empire made peace, so long as Britain did not have to provide colonial compensation for either party. So Adair's suggestion of 1810 was still offending official sensibilities! Liston, taking over at the Porte, was more impressed with Stratford's paperwork than his diplomacy, and reported to London: 'The papers and official correspondence have been placed in my hands in a state of order and correctness which I have hardly ever witnessed.' When it came to recommending men for further employment, however, Liston's eyes fell on someone else – David Morier:[74] it would not have been tactful perhaps to recommend a Canning to Castlereagh. As a beginning to his official duties, Liston addressed himself to the complete opening of the Black Sea to British traders, and to persuading the Ottoman government to accept the British presence in the Ionian Islands as a likely permanency. High diplomacy was over for the moment.

Far and away the most handsome tribute for arranging the treaty of Bucharest, came, however, from the duke of Wellington, who somehow imagined that his brother, Wellesley, Castlereagh's predecessor at the Foreign Office, had guided the Russians and the Ottomans towards it. 'If the great statesman,' the duke wrote,

> who at that period conducted the foreign affairs of Great Britain, had never rendered to his country or the world any other service . . . his name would have gone down to posterity as the man who had foreseen and had afterwards seized the opportunity of rendering to the world the most important service that ever fell to the lot of an individual to perform.

Such a verdict deserves to go down to posterity also as the most wildly extravagant and misdirected praise ever heaped by one individual upon another, wild even for one Wellesley talking about another. The duke's acclaim was due to his opinion that, without the release of Russian troops from the Danube front secured by the treaty, Napoleon would not have met with Tchichagov's fierce resistance at the crossing of the Beresina during the retreat from Moscow. This surmise in itself may be true, but the duke was in a position to find out, even if he did not know, that the *Grande Armée* of over 600,000 men which invaded Russia was reduced to less than 50,000 before the time it stumbled homeward over the rickety bridges of Studianka on 27 November 1812. The fight at the Beresina simply ensured that a further 12,000 of that tragic remnant should lie forever in Russia. If, as is surely so, the Russian campaign broke Napoleon's fortune, then it was already broken before the Beresina. What British contribution there was to the treaty of Bucharest was purely Stratford's work. All the evidence suggests that there would have been a treaty without him, at about the time and on precisely the terms agreed.[75]

NOTES

1. Canning to Stratford, 9 Oct. 1809, Lane-Poole, *Life*, i. 79; Stratford to Canning, 14 Nov. 1809, FO 352/1/3.
2. Planta to Stratford, 2–4 Oct. 1809, ibid., i. 72–6.
3. Morier to Stratford, 5 Dec. 1809, Stratford to Canning, 8 Jan. 1810, ibid., i. 73, 77–9. Stratford's salary as secretary to Adair was £300 'equipage' money: about £200 went in Foreign Office fees. Adair was paid about twice as much.
4. Stratford to his sister, 12 Jan. 1810, Lane-Poole, *Life*, i. 80–1.
5. Stratford to R. Wellesley, 7 July 1810, ibid., i. 87.
6. *The Wellesley Papers*, ed. L.S. Benjamin (London, 1914), i. 290; Aberdeen to Wellesley, 19 Feb. 1810, Add. MSS 37309. Stratford's successor, Robert Liston, was gazetted in the spring of 1811 as ambassador.
7. Wellesley sent Adair only four dispatches in 1810 before the latter left Constantinople on 12 July, the last of which was dated 17 Nov. and congratulated Adair on his arrival back home! (Wellesley to Adair, 5 March, 14 and 26 April, 17 Nov. 1810, FO 78/68.) The four dispatches to Stratford in 1811 were dated 10 Jan., 1 April, 4 June, 14 Dec., FO 78/73. Complaints from Stratford and the Ottoman ministers are collected in Lane-Poole, *Life*, i. 129–30, 167.
8. Adair to Wellesley, 5 July 1810, FO 78/68.
9. Lane-Poole, *Life*, i. 115–17; Stratford to Canning, 25 Aug. 1811, Harewood MSS.
10. Adair to Wellesley, 5 July 1810, FO 78/68.
11. Stratford to *reis effendi*, 31 July 1810, FO 352/2A/1; Stratford to Wellesley, 3 Sept. 1810, FO 78/70, and 28 Feb. 1811, FO 78/73.

12. 'Audience and Speech at the Seraqilio', 28 Aug. 1810, FO 352/1/7.
13. Strane to Stratford, 23 Oct. 1810, FO 352/1/9; Cotton to Stratford, 25 Nov. 1810, FO 352/1/8; Stratford to Pisani, 24 Dec. 1810, FO 352/1/7; Stratford to Wellesley, 21 Dec. 1810, FO 78/70; Fraser to Adair, 10 Nov. 1809, and to Stratford, 4 Sept., 3 Nov. 1810, 5 July 1811, FO 352/2B/5.
14. Edward D. Clarke, *Travels in Various Countries in Europe, Asia, and Africa* (London, 1810–16), pt. 1, section 1, 450–1.
15. Traian Stoianovich, 'The Conquering Balkan Orthodox Merchant', *Journal of Economic History*, xx (1960), 263.
16. Werry to Stratford, 2, 12, and 17 Oct. 1810, FO 352/1/9.
17. Pisani to Stratford, 21 July, 14 Aug. 1810, FO 352/1/7, and 22 Oct., 19 Nov. 1811, FO 352/2A/1; Charnaud to Stratford, 14 Nov. 1810, FO 352/1/9; Stratford to Pisani, 24 Dec. 1810, FO 352/1/7; Strane to Stratford, 23 Oct. 1810, FO 352/1/9; Stratford to Wellesley, 31 July, 17 Sept., 21 Dec. 1810, FO 78/70. Most of the smuggled grain passing through Constantinople came from southern Russia, on neutral ships. Stratford took it upon himself to keep the Americans out of the wheat trade, however disadvantageous to Wellington in Spain and to the British garrisons in Zante, Cerigo, Cephalonia (taken in 1809), and Santa Maura (1810). A Russian invitation to American shippers to enter the Black Sea trade was sent to the Russian consul-general in Washington, but Stratford intercepted the letter, taking it from an American ship's captain.
18. Knight to Stratford, 18 March 1811, Lane-Poole, *Life*, i. 107–9.
19. Missett to Stratford, 11 Aug., 2 and 11 Sept., 28 Oct. 1811, FO 352/2A/3.
20. Maltass to Stratford, 7 Jan., 19 June, 2 and 14 July 1811, FO 352/2B/5; Stratford to Wellesley, 15 March 1811, FO 78/73; V.J. Puryear, *Napoleon and the Dardanelles* (Berkeley, 1951), pp. 382–6.
21. Stratford to Wellesley, 15 March 1811, FO 78/73.
22. Missett to Stratford, 6 Nov. 1811, FO 352/2A/3.
23. Byron to Lady Byron, 12 Nov. 1809, *Lord Byron: Selected Letters and Journals*, ed. Leslie A. Marchand (Cambridge, Mass., 1982), pp. 29–34.
24. Foresti to Adair, 20 June, 8 July 1810, to Stratford, 20 Oct., 6 and 17 Nov., 18 Dec. 1810, FO 352/1/9.
25. 'Précis of correspondence of Ali Pasha and Captain Stewart', 6 Aug. 1811; Wood to Stratford, 26 Oct. 1811, FO 352/1/9.
26. Pisani to Stratford, 10 July 1811, FO 352/2A/1.
27. Foresti to Stratford, 8 Dec. 1810, 16 and 18 Jan., 2 Feb. 1811, FO 352/1/9; Stratford to Wellesley, 9 March 1811, FO 78/73.
28. Foresti to Stratford, 10 March 1811, FO 352/1/9.
29. Foresti describes the encouragement given by the French to Ibrahim Pasha, Ottoman governor of Avlona, to seize Ali Pasha's northernmost strongpoint in Albania, at Barat. The attempt was made while Ali Pasha was visiting Larissa; he doubled back, and won a pitched battle involving 300 casualties, an event which was 'not remembered to have taken place in Albania before where it is not uncommon for parties to contend for months without losing any men'. Foresti to Stratford, 29 Sept. 1810, FO 352/1/9.
30. It is difficult to know what to make of Lane-Poole's observation (*Life*, i. 105), that 'so long as [Stratford] Canning remained at the Porte the "Old Lion of Janina" was safe from the Sultan's caprice: it was in his absence that Ali was killed'. The impression given is that Stratford had only turned his back for a moment, whereas Ali was betrayed and executed in 1820, eight years after Stratford left Constantinople, as he thought, for ever.

31. Foresti to Adair, 30 June 1810, FO 352/1/9; Stratford to Wellesley, 20 July 1810, FO 78/70.
32. George Richard Porter, *Progress of a Nation in its Various and Economic Relations from the Beginning of the Nineteenth Century* (London, 1912), p. 477.
33. Cotton to Stratford, 25 Aug. 1810, FO 352/1/8.
34. Strane to Stratford, 2 and 4 Feb., 20 March 1811, FO 352/2A/3.
35. 'Memo read at the *Reis Effendi*'s House', 17 Dec. 1810, FO 352/1/7.
36. Pisani to Stratford, 22 April 1811, FO 352/2A/1; Stratford to Wellesley, 24 May, 13 June 1811, FO 78/73, and 8 Nov. 1811, with enclosures, FO 78/74; Lane-Poole, *Life*, i. 77–9, 101–3.
37. Stratford to Pisani, 30 March 1812, FO 352/3/1.
38. Stratford to Pisani, 26 Oct., 13 Nov. 1810, FO 352/1/7; other examples are to be found in Lane-Poole, *Life*, i. 96–7. On p. 98, Lane-Poole adds that Stratford always retrieved the situation 'with some conciliatory act or word' and that it was 'the shifting policy of the Turks' which 'perpetually interrupted' good relations with the British embassy. The archives contain no example of Stratford's 'conciliatory act or word', but an abundance of aggressive communications. That he was immensely provoked is also clear.
39. Cotton to Stratford, 25 Nov. 1810, FO 352/1/8.
40. Stratford to Wellesley, 28 Nov. 1811, FO 78/74; Stratford to Pisani, 24 March, 2, 12, and 23 May 1812, FO 352/2A/1.
41. Strane to Stratford, 12 Dec. 1811, FO 352/2A/3; Hope to Stratford, 19 Oct., 1 Dec. 1811, FO 352/2B/6; Lane-Poole, *Life*, i. 100, 102.
42. Stratford to Pisani, 29 May 1812, FO 352/2A/1.
43. Stratford to Wellesley, 3 Sept., 30 Oct. 1810, FO 78/70; Wellesley to Stratford, 11 Dec. 1810, FO 352/1/4.
44. Stratford to Wellesley, secret, 14 and 18 Oct. 1810, FO 78/70.
45. Stratford to Wellesley, 14 Oct. 1810, FO 78/70. Wellesley replied eight months later, see Wellesley to Stratford, 21 March 1811, FO 78/73.
46. Werry to Stratford, 5 July 1810, FO 352/1/9.
47. Stratford to Wellesley, 26 Nov. 1810, FO 78/70; 1 Jan. 1811, FO 78/73.
48. 'Précis of information', 1 Jan. 1811, FO 352/1/2.
49. Molo to Stratford, 2 and 17 Sept., 17 Oct. 1811, FO 352/2B/7. Molo provided Stratford, and Stratford provided the *reis effendi*, with the first information of the Russian troop withdrawal from the Balkan fronts.
50. Subsequently, the British government paid Ludolf £500 for his services; see Castlereagh to Liston, secret, March 1812, FO 78/79. Napoleon officially cut this Constantinople – Vienna – St Petersburg line in late 1810, but a voluminous, confidential correspondence was kept up; see Adair to FO, 10 Feb., 13 March, 19 May 1810, FO 78/68; Stratford to Wellesley, secret, 7 Aug. 1810, FO 78/70.
51. 'Diary of his mission to Constantinople', 1 Feb. 1811, FO 352/1/2; memoirs, in Lane-Poole, *Life*, i. 139; see also Stratford to Wellesley, 4 Aug. 1810, FO 78/70.
52. Stratford to Wellesley, 1 and 2 Jan., 3 and 28 Feb., 15 March, 8 May 1811, FO 78/73.
53. Comments on Stratford to Wellesley, secret, 2 Jan. 1811, FO 78/73; see also Wellesley's 'Notes on the general state of Europe', 15 May 1811, *Wellesley Papers*, ii. 33, where he deals with every country down to Denmark and Sicily, but has no thoughts on the Ottoman Empire.
54. Stratford to Wellesley, private, 13 April 1811, FO 78/73; Pisani to Stratford,

12 March 1811, Stratford to Pisani, 22 and 29 Jan., 10 Feb. 1811, FO 352/2A/1.
55. Stratford to Wellesley, 8 and 15 May, FO 78/73; 22 June, 13 July 1811, FO 78/74.
56. Stratford to Wellesley, 3 and 28 Feb. 1811, FO 78/73.
57. Stratford to Wellesley, 13 April 1811, FO 78/73; Lane-Poole, *Life*, i. 122–3.
58. Stratford to Wellesley, 13 July, 1 Sept. 1811, FO 78/74. Hamid Bey became the Ottoman minister at London.
59. See Stratford to Wellesley, 13 July, 1 Sept., 29 Oct., 18 Nov., 15 Dec. 1811, FO 78/74.
60. Stratford to Wellesley, 29 June 1811, Lane-Poole, *Life*, i. 153.
61. Stratford to Wellesley, 6, 21, and 28 Feb. 1812, FO 78/77.
62. Stratford to Wellesley, 17 Jan., 6 and 28 Feb. 1812, FO 78/77.
63. Chabert to Stratford, 27 Nov. 1811, FO 352/3/1; *reis effendi* to Stratford, 'Reply to Note of 27 November' (undated), FO 352/3/1.
64. Memos of 3 June, 18 and 22 July 1812, FO 352/3/4; see also Stratford to Wellesley, 6 and 21 Feb. 1812, Lane-Poole, *Life*, i. 161–2.
65. Memoirs, in Lane-Poole, *Life*, i. 163; in Stratford to Wellesley, 21 Feb. 1812, FO 78/77. A week before the treaty of Bucharest was signed, Stratford briefed Pisani for an interview at the Porte as follows: 'I have nothing to add about the Russian business. The conduct of the Porte has made me indifferent to it. . . . We have sacrificed too much to our regard for this Empire. It is time to provide for our own interests elsewhere,' Stratford to Pisani, 20 May 1812, Lane-Poole, *Life*, i. 173. There is no evidence, incidentally, for Lane-Poole's claim (*Life*, i. 157) that Stratford had a secret correspondence with the Sultan.
66. Stratford to Wellesley, 28 Feb., 17 March, 12 and 26 April 1812, FO 78/77.
67. This 'alarming and unprincipled paper' began with a candid discussion of Ottoman partition.
   I conveyed [it] in the most impressive manner to the *reis effendi*, and the effect it produced on that minister was fully equal to my expectations. . . . He said he had embarrassed the Internuncio, by asking how Austria was to be indemnified for the part of Galicia which in virtue of her new connections [with France] she would have to make over to the kingdom of Poland.
   Memoirs, in Lane-Poole, *Life*, i. 166; see also Stratford to Wellesley, 12 and 26 April 1812, FO 78/77.
68. Lane-Poole, *Life*, i. 169.
69. Stratford to Castlereagh, secret, 12 June 1812, FO 78/77; Gordon to Stratford, 13 June 1812, FO 352/3/4.
70. FO to Liston, secret, 15 May 1812; Liston to Castlereagh, 18 July 1812, FO 78/79.
71. Stratford to Wellesley, 10 June 1812, FO 78/77.
72. Liston to Castlereagh, 12 Nov., 9 Dec. 1812, FO 78/79.
73. Stratford to Wellesley, 12 June 1812, Liston to FO, 29 June 1812, FO 78/77; Stratford to Pisani, 13 June 1812, FO 352/2A/1.
74. *Annual Register*, 1812, p. 183; Castlereagh to Liston, 27 and 28 March 1812, FO 78/79; Lane-Poole, *Life*, i. 175–6. Liston to Castlereagh, 11 July 1812, FO 78/79, says of Morier:
   This gentleman's extensive acquaintance with the modern languages, his practical knowledge of business, the mildness of his manners, the prudence, propriety and address with which he conducts every matter point him out as a person who might be employed with some advantage in His Majesty's Service.

Morier became one of Castlereagh's aides at the congress of Vienna.
75. The reader should be made aware, however, of Lane-Poole's extravagant conclusion concerning Stratford's part in the making of the treaty. Lane-Poole says,
> Adair gave up the task in despair; and his secretary was left to carry it out alone. . . . To bend Napoleon in his dreams of universal empire was a task most men would think twice about. To withstand him alone, without a single advisor, and on one's own responsibility, must appear downright madness. . . . Yet this is precisely what he did.

Lane-Poole, *Life*, i. 126–8. Harold Temperley states that 'Stratford always claimed that this success, with which he began his diplomatic career, was the greatest of his life'. H.W.V. Temperley, *England and the Near East: the Crimea* (London, 1936), p. 50. Stratford never said this, nor ever thought it, and, as his memoirs show, had only a hazy recollection of these years by the end of his career.

CHAPTER VI

Lord Strangford and the Greek Revolt

Percy Clinton Smythe, sixth Viscount Strangford, stepped ashore in Constantinople in February 1821 to succeed Sir Robert Liston as British ambassador to the Ottoman Empire. He therefore arrived only two weeks before the event which, by conventional chronology, is regarded as the curtain-raiser to the Greek war for independence. On 5 March, Prince Alexander Ipsilantis crossed the river Pruth near Skouleni with a small army, an act intended to inflame the spirit of revolution throughout the Ottoman Balkans.

Aged 41, Strangford was handsome, able, experienced, and autocratic. He had served his government in places as distant as South America and Sweden. Already he had something of a reputation, and officials in London knew him as a man sensitive to criticism, who had a way of defending his diplomacy most strenuously at exactly those moments when everyone else thought him most obviously in the wrong. Perhaps this does not make Strangford so unusual, but it lost him friends in high places, and sometimes made him seem a born loser. Only the indulgent biographer of the Strangford family has been able to discern that Strangford's proclivity for getting into scrapes was extenuated by 'a marvellous grace for getting out of them again',[1] and the truth is that Strangford's numerous quarrels, whether with critics like Byron of his verse translations, or with men like Charles James Napier who exposed his habit of portraying himself in gaudy colours as a man of action, rarely ended on a note of reconciliation.

Strangford's friends at home in England were, nevertheless, powerful people, and his European friends more powerful still. They were conservative, except where they were downright reactionaries. They included the duke of Cumberland; John Wilson Croker, who had been at Trinity College, Dublin, with him; and

Lord Eldon, with whom he would presently agree that railways were a bad thing as they would help to spread the radical spirit in Europe. In 1821, the main objects of Strangford's detestation were the Whig Lords Brougham and Holland, parliamentary reform, and Catholic emancipation, probably in that order. His persistent habit of calling the Whigs 'the party of reform' shows how much he could ignore the more recent facts of political life. Abroad, Strangford maintained a correspondence with Friedrich von Gentz and another with Prince Metternich, whom he thought was the greatest man living, an opinion the Austrian chancellor shared. As ambassador at Constantinople, Strangford was destined to lose his zeal for congress diplomacy once he saw how strongly the Sultan, whom he was supposed to manage, disliked these international gatherings of European autocrats. But until the day he died, the ambassador retained his faith in the regulation of international crises by men of aristocratic birth and ultra-conservative outlook, by men who, as Metternich used to say, were 'comme il faut'. Strangford had, as Acton later said of Burke, no conception of the evils of class government.

In books which refer to his Constantinople embassy at all, Strangford usually gets a dishonourable mention-in-dispatches.[2] A rabid pro-Ottoman from the very first stages of the Greek uprising, he is supposed to have been a bitter anti-Hellenist who approved of the execution of the Greek patriarch of Constantinople, and who reported home with much complacency the arrival from the scenes of strife of basketloads of human ears, cropped from the bodies of slain Greeks. There is, allegedly, no dispute about the ambassador's wrong-headedness, as he convicted himself and his diplomacy with the boast, 'I, the Turk *par excellence*'.[3] Once that other reactionary, the British foreign secretary, Viscount Castlereagh, committed suicide, the story goes, Strangford's days were numbered. His new chief, the liberal George Canning, would not condone the policy of the *status quo* when it was clear that the Ottomans were incapable of actually suppressing the Greeks, and the rising tide of philhellenism which swept the Greeks forward to independence swept Strangford out of his embassy.

This usual view of the decline and fall of Lord Strangford raises a problem: partly with Canning's support, Strangford (whose title was Irish) was given the English title of Baron Penshurst on his return from Constantinople in 1825. Soon afterwards, Canning appointed him to St Petersburg, the most important post in the diplomatic service and the capital city of the Sultan's most implacable foe.[4] As Canning had won his personal battle with his own sovereign by 1825, he no longer needed to offer appointments to George IV's cronies. Did he promote Strangford as a means of disposing of a difficult and influential subordinate? Hardly. Canning's evolving ideas on the Greek question did not permit him to squander on an unreliable ambassador the embassy of the country with which he most wanted to work. In any case, Canning was not afraid to demote, as he had already shown by withdrawing his close friend, Sir Charles Bagot, from that same, St Petersburg, embassy.

Even a cursory look through Strangford's Constantinople correspondence casts immediate doubt on any theory of his uncompromising Turcophilism. An examination of his dispatches, set alongside a perusal of his personal letters, reveals a man who thought, quite imaginatively, that the complex of international treaties which regulated the relations of the powers, if examined honestly, revealed the inconvenient but undoubted fact that even Ottomans had rights, and not obligations only. The indiscreet boast 'I, the Turk *par excellence*', loses its customary interpretation when given the benefit of its proper context, for it was penned in a spirit of incredulity, not vain self-satisfaction. Strangford was not, nor did he ever become, an expert on Eastern affairs. Nor can we fit him tidily into any of those familiar and over-simplified categories, Turcophile, anti-Hellenist, Russophobe. Strangford regarded himself as a diplomatic broker, appointed to resolve a conflict of interests by peaceful means in order to avert a one-sided Russian solution imposed by military means. He was often a Turcophile, yet one who claimed, honestly, to give the Ottomans 'harder knocks than anybody else'; a Russophobe who felt that a tsar had treaty rights which Ottomans must honour as well as claims which Ottomans must resist; and an anti-Hellenist who kept Greek refugees in his embassy garden at his own expense and would not give them up, and who complained loudly of Ottoman barbarism in the Morea. After 1822, there were times when the Ottoman ministers complained that the British ambassador, and not the Russians only, was a 'Greek'.

Lord Strangford and the Greek Revolt

In other words, Strangford had a mind of his own. He had to have one as, like most of his predecessors at Constantinople, he suffered under a Foreign Office tradition of neglecting the Eastern ambassador while berating him for not guessing in advance what London wanted. Castlereagh, burdened with the paper work of congress diplomacy, sent Strangford no useful dispatches before September 1821, and only seven in 1822 before his suicide in August. Canning sent more dispatches, one of them admonitory, most of them very approving. The recognition of the Greeks as entitled to the rights of belligerents – Canning's one positive decision while Strangford was in the East – does not seem to have been communicated to Strangford officially, nor to have particularly upset him when he did hear of it. It was what might come next that worried Strangford. Historians like to see Canning's recognition as the thin edge of the wedge, his first, cautious measure on behalf of a people he already intended to see liberated from Ottoman control. In fact, there were moments when Strangford was ahead of Canning in wishing to negotiate with the Greeks, and it was Canning who held him back. Far from seizing upon his shortage of instructions as an opportunity to push his own conservative preferences, Strangford was in agonies of doubt for months at a time, and complained frequently about his position.

The ambassador was not much helped by a beautiful, eccentric wife, who raised her talented children to dance on pictures of the Pope, and who was in other ways one of the marvels of the Constantinople scene. He was distracted, too, when a much-beloved son contracted tuberculosis in the East, and almost died of it. He was harassed, as every ambassador before 1825 was harassed, by the Turkey Merchants of the Levant Company, who complained that the Greek uprising was bad for business and that British philhellenism jeopardized their own safety. It is hardly surprising that Strangford found his embassy an exhausting experience.[5]

Yet, while there, and while his superiors in London groped their way towards a solution of the dilemmas in which the Greek uprising placed them, an ambassador whose blind spot was emergent Greek nationalism was an appropriate representative for Castlereagh, and a good enough one for Canning, too, when we consider that Strangford left the East in 1824 and that Canning only began to find the first elements of a constructive policy towards

Greece in 1825. The instructions supplied to Strangford by the Foreign Office in 1820 promised little in the way of challenge or excitement in his new post. The very least that can be asked of an ambassador is that he shall maintain decent relations with the government to which he is accredited.[6] This was not only Strangford's minimal duty; it was his only one. It had also been the main task of almost all his predecessors over the two and a half centuries during which Great Britain had maintained an embassy on the Bosporus, and during the greater part of which time the said ambassadors had been the humble servants of the Levant Company. Even so, it may occasion the reader some surprise – it did not bother Strangford, who thought the East itself would be trial enough – that the Napoleonic epoch had not sharpened British vigilance in the Levant in ways which post-Napoleonic arrangements and diplomatic instructions would reflect.

To feel this would, none the less, overlook Castlereagh's sanguine hope that congress diplomacy would solve all problems. As a supporter in international relations of the Metternichian principle of 'conservation', and as the architect of the system of periodic congresses between government leaders, he hoped to lance all crises which might otherwise poison the relations between great powers. Doubtful that the congress method should be allowed to degenerate, as Alexander I of Russia once hoped, into a mere club of crowned heads, loyal to each other and submissive before God under the title of the Holy Alliance, Castlereagh believed the diplomatic expertise of Europe should be wasted no longer in adversary relationships and the pursuit of unilateral advantages, but should instead serve the collective interests of the Continent, or at least the collective interests of its major powers. Consequently, congress diplomacy was intended by him to maintain the map of Europe as laid down in 1815, and by peaceful means. Any adjustments would be the result of consultations within Europe.[7] This made it the easier, in Castlereagh's view, to draft Strangford's instructions by rummaging first through those provided for Strangford's predecessors, John Hookham Frere and Sir Robert Liston, and, on the basis of what he found there, writing a dreadful rigmarole of advice.[8]

Only Castlereagh, of all British foreign secretaries, could take so great a number of pages to say that there were no outstanding issues between Great Britain and the Ottoman Empire, thus making it possible for Strangford to restrict his activities to preserving 'the Relations of amity and commerce which at present so happily subsist' between the two empires.[9] Strangford would show a proper civility to his European colleagues at Constantinople, neither supporting nor hindering them in any way. He would find the French had given up the imperialistic visions and bombastic diplomacy of 20 years before. As for Russian ambitions in the East, Castlereagh enjoined the same 'complying policy' – and largely in the same language – that had been recommended to Liston a decade earlier. Strangford would find his Russian colleague, Count Grigory Stroganov, enmeshed in those more or less perennial quarrels between tsar and Sultan, which ordinarily centred on the latter's recurrent failure to honour his treaties with the former. But Strangford would not take sides in them. Castlereagh could not easily forget that, in 1815, when he tried to bring the Ottoman Empire within the framework of the general peace, and to provide her with a territorial guarantee, it was her rulers who had been 'absurd' enough to let the priceless chance go by.[10] So for now, Strangford would remain aloof. Any larger excitements, any Russian pretensions which smelled of danger, would be, of course, reported by Strangford, and taken up with the tsar directly by the British government.

Controlling the tsar of Russia after 1815 resembled in its danger and delicacy the art of leading a bear by a chain which the creature can break whenever it loses its temper. It was all very well for Metternich to suppose that 'it is only necessary to place four energetic men, who know what they want and are agreed on the manner of carrying out their wishes, in the four corners of Europe'. Exercising almost complete personal control over Austria's foreign policy, he could the more easily believe that the energetic men, inspired by the same 'moral principles', could construct a 'system'. Castlereagh himself would have liked such a 'system', and was at one time in some danger of mistaking the rough compatibility of great power interests for one. He even tried, behind the back of Parliament, to promote this 'system', but ran into difficulties with cabinet colleagues who had a greater respect for parliamentary and public opinion, and felt secret diplomacy was risky. More to the point, however, was the rising distrust of Russia in Great Britain after 1815 which began to produce, in Sir Charles Webster's words, 'a kind of diplomatic duel between the two countries which extended over a large area', and was more or less visible at Paris, Madrid, Naples, the picturesque capitals of the South German states, and, much further east, at Constantinople and Tehran.[11]

The 'duel' was, fundamentally, a running disagreement over the purposes of the 'moral union' of the great powers, and the degree to which a congress system originally intended to keep the peace of Europe should be used for any other purpose, such as intervention in the internal affairs of lesser states whenever thrones were rocked by popular revolutions. By 1820, Alexander I was anxious to intervene in a revolutionary situation in Spain with an allied army, and to suppress the popular constitution forced on an unwilling king. Castlereagh, as convinced a conservative as Strangford, nevertheless felt compelled to respond to such a proposal with a famous declaration, written only a few months before Strangford was sent East. In this declaration, often called the foundation of Great Britain's subsequent foreign policy, Castlereagh insisted that the congress system was an outgrowth of the 'Union for the reconquest and liberation of a great proportion of the continent of Europe from the military dominion of France', but that Great Britain must go her own way if it was now to become an instrument for 'the Government of the World' and 'the Superintendence of the Internal Affairs of Other States'. If great upheavals ever endangered Europe again, Great Britain would be found in her place, but 'this country cannot, and will not, act upon abstract and speculative principles of precaution'. Great Britain, her own dynasty and constitution the results of domestic upheaval, could not deny to other states the chance to change their forms of government. The resurgence of 'Revolutionary Power, more particularly in its military character', was a threat always to be resisted, but Great Britain had no place in an alliance dedicated to the suppression of 'democratic principles'.[12]

While Strangford was on the high seas for Constantinople in late 1820, a European congress without British representation met at Troppau. The three rulers of Eastern Europe there signed a circular, drafted by the Russian delegation, asserting their readiness to make war on revolution wherever it raised its head. Castlereagh told the House of Commons such a declaration was 'destitute of common sense',[13] but the Austrians took it seriously enough and, in the spring of 1821, Austrian armies marched into Italy, destroyed revolutionary movements in Naples and Piedmont, abolished the popular constitutions so recently adopted, and restored the kings to their former positions. Metternich seemingly led the Russian bear by the chain. In March 1821, however, a different kind of revolution broke out, a revolution neither democratic nor constitutional in its purposes, to which the tsar responded in very different fashion. This was the Greek revolution, which began two weeks after Strangford landed at Constantinople. Metternich believed there was no difference between a revolution against the Ottoman Sultan and a revolution against Ferdinand of Naples: in each case, monarchy was endangered. Alexander I thought differently, and presently he snapped his chain, transforming in the process Strangford's prospects of a quiet sojourn on the Bosporus.

Strangford's arrival went almost unnoticed by the Ottomans. After a 15-week journey from England, half of it spent battling fickle winds and heavy seas, he and his family were exhausted and quite appalled by the stark amenities and rickety decay of the British 'palace'. They were unhappy, too, at its proximity to one of the noisiest and most disreputable sections of the so-called Grande Rue of Pera. Soon after settling in, Lady Strangford was beaten up by a street mob on her way to church. Presently, the new ambassador fell out with his secretary, Terrick Hamilton, and he could not bury himself in work because there hardly seemed to be any. Even had there been something to write about, there was nothing to write on; there was no stationery in the embassy and he had to borrow some from the nearest British legation, at Vienna. What came back was appropriate to his mood: he was sent a small mountain of 'black-edged', the stationery embassies used whenever they were ordered into mourning on the death of royalty. Strangford could only wait for the day when the Ottomans would allow him to present his credentials to the Sultan, and as this ceremony could only take place on a janizary pay-day, of which there were but three a year, some weeks of inactivity still lay ahead.[14] Or so it seemed.

In the meantime, Strangford heard that Sultan Mahmud II was not very fond of the British. To begin with, they sometimes chose their friends from among the Sultan's enemies, such as Ali Pasha of Janina and the shah of Persia. Then there was a British community on the Sultan's doorstep whose behaviour was not to his liking. There were two main complaints against the Turkey Merchants of Pera, the first, that they speculated heavily in Russian corn whenever Ottoman harvests were poor, the second, that they evaded Ottoman monetary laws, by hoarding old coinage for its precious-metal content. The charges were quite true. A further complaint against the British government itself concerned the legal status of the Ionians who were always in great numbers in the taverns and on the wharves of Galata. Great Britain had taken over the Ionian Islands in 1815, but while Castlereagh denied that Ionians were British subjects, he never got round to saying whose subjects they actually were.[15] Meanwhile, the Ionians at Constantinople enjoyed their exquisitely anomalous position to the full, slipping with ease through the net of Ottoman justice by explaining in court that they came from a British-protected republic in the Adriatic. Many were induced by the more permanent Greek residents of the *Fener* district, to join the local branch of the *Filiki Eteria*, the Greek patriotic secret society.[16] George Canning remembered Strangford's complaints against the local British merchants when, in 1825, he decided to abolish the Levant Company. As for the Ionians, they were to make a vital contribution to the revolution which broke out on 5 March. The same event produced a sharp increase of official Ottoman interest in Strangford, as the man most likely to assist in the steeply escalating quarrel with the Russian ambassador. Suddenly, Strangford, to his surprise, was visited by messengers from the Sublime Porte, who encouraged him to seek to present his credentials ahead of the duly-appointed date. And so he went into action.

Stroganov, the Russian ambassador, was a man of energy and ability, as he had already proved in a five-year altercation with the Ottoman authorities over three questions: the Danube frontier, the Transcaucasian frontier, and the Serbs. Coming to Constantinople soon after the congress of Vienna, Stroganov brought the impressive reputation of an envoy whose family had been on intimate terms with Alexander I for over 20 years, who sat on the Eastern Affairs Committee under Count Ioannis Kapodistrias' chairmanship whenever he returned to visit Russia, and who was, at various times, familiar with nearly all the prominent Russians whose names the Ottomans had ever heard – Novosiltsev, Kochubey, Czartoryski,

Orlov, Galitzin, Suvorov, Kutuzov. More impressive than his connections was his refusal ever to give up. From 1816 to 1821, Stroganov persisted, in the face of every artifice and delay known to Ottoman negotiators, until he got what he wanted without conceding to his hosts what they wanted in return. The background to much of his embassy was the unrest, and occasional hostilities, of the Serbs against their Ottoman rulers. This unrest had begun in 1807.

In the foreground, Stroganov's most important duty was to obtain a revision of the Danube frontier as laid down in the treaty of Bucharest of 1812. That treaty, concluded in haste so that Russia could turn all her energies against the French invaders of her soil, terminated protracted hostilities with the Ottoman surrender of Bessarabia to the tsar, thus advancing Russia's coastal position on the Black Sea from the estuary of the Pruth to the complex deltaic area of the lower Danube. In 1812, the young Stratford Canning had been a go-between for both Ottomans and Russians in the negotiations for the treaty, and was not remembered now by the Ottomans with much affection. The frontier he helped to draw followed the river Pruth down to its entry into the northernmost branch of the Danube – the Kilia – which wanders through marshes and lakes, and in flood seasons changes its course, before reaching the sea. The Russians wanted the frontier rationalized at Ottoman expense by moving it south from the meandering Kilia to the main and unvarying Sulina estuary of the great river.

In Great Britain, officials were quite ready to acknowledge that the treaty of Bucharest, in its existing form, did less than justice to Russia's real preponderance in the Black Sea area; even George Canning, presently to become Strangford's chief, thought so. As for the ambassador's present superior, Castlereagh thought the Ottomans were mad not to have settled the Sulina question years before. In fact, their general tendency to evade their treaty obligations, of whatever sort and wherever possible, exposed them more than ever to the insistence of Russian demands. In 1821, Strangford, called by the Ottomans to their aid, soon decided that Castlereagh was absolutely right. If only the Ottoman ministers would stand very firmly on the text of existing treaties, it would be much harder for Russia to fault them and much easier for others to help them. As things stood, Great Britain could not 'arrest him [the tsar of Russia] in his efforts against the Turks', and Stroganov had been, at least on paper, very successful.

Stroganov toiled alone in his diplomatic conflict with the Ottoman government. He said openly that, with the exception of the new Austrian minister in 1818, Count Lutzov, none of his other European colleagues was worth bothering with. The French embassy could do little until Paris was rid of the allied army of occupation and France had resumed her place in the comity of nations. Liston, Strangford's predecessor, had orders to mind his own business, and Strangford's orders were no different. The Ottomans, nevertheless, saw Stroganov as the hostile knight-errant of Europe, a mistaken idea which, however, was useful to Stroganov in pressing his case. The Ottoman ministers had heard about the plan for periodic, international congresses in Europe; they noted that the despoilers of Poland were of the company; and they deduced reasonably enough that the Ottoman Empire itself must sooner or later appear on the agenda – or was it the menu? – of one of these congresses. Sensing all this, Stroganov urged his hosts to deflect the wrath of Europe by a punctilious observation of the obligations of existing treaties.

His hosts were not, any longer, as naïve and ignorant about Europe as they had been before the French Revolution, when leading Ottoman ministers were asking if Spain was in Africa and Gibraltar a town in England, and the Napoleonic era taught them a lot about the futility of diplomatic punctilio. They had seen treaties signed and broken in short order, and no state, great or small, had been saved simply by honouring its contracts. There was the further point that, besides repudiating treaty obligations, Europeans had a flair for elasticating treaty privileges. Stroganov, for instance, wished to 'rationalize' the debated treaty of Bucharest by claiming yet more territory for Russia in the Danube delta. But when asked in his turn to 'rationalize' the situation in Transcaucasia by having Russian troops withdrawn from the hinterland of the port of Poti, which gave access to Tiflis, this seemed less understood, and in spite of the retrocession of territory promised by Alexander I himself in 1815, the military percolation into Transcaucasia which had begun in 1801 went forward without interruption. Some people – the British, for instance – did not seem to mind the cynical contradictions in Russia's demands, and

Castlereagh offered Stroganov the quite misguided opinion that if the Ottomans would only oblige the Russians over Serbia, 'the Emperor, I have no doubt, will be proportionately liberal on the side of Asia'.[17]

Stroganov eventually won. Russia obtained the Sulina line; the Ottomans never held Poti again. In 1817, Milosh Obrenovic was elected hereditary prince of Serbia, thus reducing the substance of Ottoman power to a shadow in a province the Ottomans had held long before seizing Constantinople itself. They held the garrison fortresses, but nothing else. The Greek revolt, therefore, coming hard on the heels of these concessions, and beginning with a foray from Russian soil, seemed one more proof that the unbelievers, and most particularly the Russians, could never be permanently bought off. More sombrely still, the Sultan's means of resistance to foreign pressure were clearly insufficient. It is no wonder that the Sultans, in their frustration, had a habit of disgracing or executing the Ottoman delegates who signed away lands and privileges to foreign powers.

Russo-Ottoman relations could only worsen when in 1821 a Russian general, born in Constantinople of a wealthy Greek family which stood high in the Ottoman bureaucratic hierarchy, led a small army from a base in Russia into Ottoman Moldavia, announcing as he did so that he had the support of a great power. The general was Alexander Ipsilantis; his family had ruled in Wallachia as hospodars; his army of 4,500 volunteers had four cannons and a few horsemen; and the great power was surely Russia. Ipsilantis' proclamations called the Orthodox peoples of the Balkans to arms. Alexander I denounced the adventure and deprived Ipsilantis of his rank in the Russian army,[18] and the Orthodox patriarch of Constantinople prudently excommunicated him. The 'invasion' of the Ottoman Empire fell apart in skirmishes and small actions, and Ipsilantis, who should have known better, accepted a safe-conduct from Metternich and crossed the Austrian frontier. He was incarcerated, and died in prison seven years later. Meanwhile, the Ottoman army which had defeated Ipsilantis showed no signs of quitting the Principalities, although in the ordinary way the Sultan was committed by existing agreements with Russia to maintain no standing forces, and only a handful of Russian-approved administrators, in Moldavia and Wallachia. The

Ottomans naturally took the view that their sovereignty in the Principalities was endangered by Ipsilantis, and when, only a month after Ipsilantis' invasion, the Greek population in the Morea flew to arms, the Sultan felt he was now dealing with a co-ordinated Russian-inspired military uprising. The Ottoman army in the Principalities was told to stay where it was for the time being.

The Greek war for independence, traditionally portrayed in European historiography as an example of spontaneous ignition, was seen differently by the Ottomans at the time of its outbreak. To them, it was part of a wider complex of plans to destroy their power in the Balkans, and while they never had all the pieces of the jigsaw in their hands, they had enough of the picture to think they could safely guess the rest. Their informants included some of the conspirators themselves. The Ottoman authorities were wrong, therefore, in thinking there was a co-ordinated, master plan to drive them out of the Balkans to which all revolutionary leaders subscribed, but they were right in thinking that these leaders had, with varying success, reached out to one another through a form of subterranean diplomacy in order to explore the possibilities of collaboration. The Ottomans also seem to have been right in suspecting Stroganov of using his embassy as a clearing house of information and intelligence. Then, as today, there were no durable secrets, and the Greek secret revolutionary society, the *Filiki Eteria*, was both a formidable, revolutionary's postal service and a gratifying source of leaks to the Ottomans. Before 1821, numerous messengers were caught carrying secret documents from which the Ottoman divan constructed the details of a great, conspiratorial network. At different times, usually when plans went wrong, or disagreements arose, Teodoro Vladimirescu, the Romanian peasant leader; the *Eterist*, Nikolas Galatis, who pretended he was related to the tsar's adviser, Kapodistrias; and Obrenovic, the new prince of the Serbs who sent the head of his predecessor, the patriot Karageorge, to the Sultan: all these provided details of what they knew of their rivals' plans to the Porte. Now and then, an embassy made its contribution; for instance, the British embassy informed the Ottomans of a Greek plan to seize the Ottoman fleet.

It was easier for the Sultan and his ministers to feel threatened when they knew that much of this plotting was going on under their noses, around dinner tables in the Greek quarter of Constantinople, and even in government departments where, again, infidels were commonly employed. The *Filiki Eteria* began life in the Russian grain port of Odessa in 1812; in 1818, the headquarters moved to Constantinople itself. The membership did not exceed 30 for a year or so, but by 1821, it ran into the thousands. Prosperous Greeks, Russian consuls (who were often Greeks), Ottoman officials, merchants, sea-captains, Orthodox clergy, the leaders of clans, families, and districts in Greece, occasionally Serbs, Romanians, and Bulgars, and everywhere the secretaries and physicians who stood at the elbows of dangerously independent, unsophisticated Balkan despots, were among the *Eterists*. Karageorge himself had been one; Gabrial Katakazis, one of Stroganov's secretaries, was one; and from time to time, Ali Pasha of Janina, the most colourful rebel of the day, pretended he was one. Quite minor public figures, like the dragoman to the Russian consul at Patras, were members. Russo-Ottoman relations were severed when the Sultan struck at the nearest and most prestigious of all suspects, the Orthodox patriarch, Grigorios.[19]

Grigorios was already a marked man. As bishop of Smyrna, he had in earlier times been deposed twice for intriguing with the Sultan's enemies, respectively the French and the British. When Ipsilantis appealed to all Orthodox peoples to rise, he convinced the Ottomans that the widely conceived movement was indeed about to erupt. It was easy to see that Ipsilantis had timed his invasion to embarrass the Ottoman attempt, then actively in hand, to suppress the final and most ambitious bid of Ali of Janina to establish an independent territory in Albania and Epirus. Ipsilantis' further plans, to seize the Ottoman fleet and the Ottoman capital itself through an uprising of the city's Orthodox population, were also known at the Porte, and the patriarch's doom was sealed by them. The seizure of the city was expected at Easter, and the preparations for celebrating that religious festival seemed to the watchful Ottomans to be unusually ostentatious and industrious. On Easter Sunday, 22 April 1821, they moved swiftly, and hanged Grigorios outside his metropolitan church. Then came the news of the rising in the Morea, which began with the slaughter of Ottoman villagers and townsmen who lived in Greece. The British embassy chaplain watched the rise in temperature in the streets of Constantinople, his nerves already frayed after having seen the body of the patriarch dragged through the mud of the Jewish quarter and thrown into the Bosporus. Stroganov fished the corpse up and sent it to Odessa for decent burial.[20] It was an inauspicious time for him to open any further negotiations with the Ottoman government.

The Ottomans called Strangford to their assistance early in May after Stroganov presented them with an official protest against the execution of the patriarch; complaints against the damage to Orthodox foundations in Constantinople; one demand that the beaten Ipsilantis should be allowed to withdraw unmolested from the Principalities, and another that the Ottoman army which had broken Ipsilantis' fragile dream should now be withdrawn from the Principalities.[21]

Strangford would not, at first, listen to the Ottomans' argument that the Russian government was party to the expedition of Ipsilantis, and advised them to trust in Alexander I's horror of revolution. He joined Stroganov in protesting against the way in which the patriarch had been murdered and, as the Russian Synod, urged on by the hysterical Archimandrite Photis, was likely to bring great pressure on the tsar as soon as he arrived back at St Petersburg from the congress of Laibach, Strangford thought the tsar would need a 'full and fair disclosure of the evidence on which he [the patriarch] was condemned'.[22] This disconcerted the Ottoman ministers a good deal, and when they asked Strangford if Great Britain would, as Stroganov threatened, join a coalition of European states to make war on the Ottoman Empire, he 'thought it only fair and manly' to acknowledge that Great Britain would stand by Russia in any 'just cause'.[23] This did not mean that Great Britain would attack the Sultan; it simply meant that a 'just cause' would make it impossible for Great Britain to help him. Castlereagh made it absolutely clear that Great Britain had no partiality for 'the fanatick and insubordinate Population' in Greece, but that the ambassador's task was to assuage 'the fury of resentment on either side'.[24] This was not, of course, much help to the Ottomans, nor was it enough for Stroganov either, who was in a towering passion and impatient to sever diplomatic relations and go home. He agitated the Ottoman ministers very much when he said Europe only tolerated the Ottoman Empire on condition that it treated its Christian subjects well, that Russia was the sole judge of that treatment, and that she could call the congress powers to a crusade any time she chose. Complaints were made in London against Strangford, and Castlereagh took the trouble to go through Strangford's dispatches with the Russian minister, Baron Nicolai, in order to prove that Strangford, far from being disloyal to Stroganov, supported his Russian colleague where he thought he conscientiously could. Castlereagh absolutely refused to censure Strangford.[25]

Stroganov may not have expected Ipsilantis to have great military success, but he certainly seems to have been disappointed that the invasion of the Principalities failed to set off a general rising in the Balkans. In this regard, then, he belongs to those men in the Russian bureaucracy, like Kapodistrias, who were sobered by Alexander I's reiterated refusal to sponsor revolutions, or encourage the plans of the *Eterists*. Kapodistrias twice refused the presidency of the *Filiki Eteria* out of deference to his royal master's will, and advised Ipsilantis, to whom the leadership passed, not to accept it without Alexander I's express consent. The tsar did not withhold his assent, but both Kapodistrias and Ipsilantis felt their function was to restrain the Greek revolutionary movement until some occasion when Russo-Ottoman relations collapsed, and war was precipitated.[26] At one stage, it was hoped Stroganov would fail to get the treaty of Bucharest modified in the way Russia wanted, but the Ottomans eventually acceded to his pressure. In 1821, Stroganov's extraordinarily provoking behaviour was that of a man who wanted to disrupt diplomatic relations, not sustain them. In this sense, then, Alexander I was considerably behind some of his own advisers, and it was this very important fact that Strangford hoped the Ottomans would understand. He advised them not to put themselves in the wrong, to observe the strict letter of existing treaties by withdrawing their armies from the Principalities, and to reach past the hot-headed Stroganov to Count Carl Nesselrode, Kapodistrias' coadjutor in the direction of Russian foreign affairs.[27]

Strangford was not the first of Stroganov's European colleagues to draw off from him: Count Lutzov, the Austrian, was. Lutzov worked honestly and patiently with Stroganov through April and May, but by June 1821, the diplomatic corps deserted Stroganov completely, so violent was his language. He provoked the Ottoman ministers by peremptorily ordering a Russian packet bringing him important dispatches to sail into the Bosporus without the customary permission from the Customs House. He then demanded a special *firman* to permit the packet to sail away again with his own dispatches. In short, he wanted the Ottomans to confess their inability to impose their own rulings on him. Under the persuasion of Strangford, who was horrified at a half-hint that they were thinking of having Stroganov 'restrained', meaning murdered, the ministers at the Porte eventually refused either to be provoked or to comply with Stroganov's demand.[28] In the *firman* issued for the Russian packet's return voyage, they described it as a merchant ship which happened to have brought down Russian embassy mail. They also gave it 48 hours to be out of the Bosporus. Stroganov suspended all communications with the Porte, transferred himself, his staff, and his archives to another Russian vessel, but did not sail away for a further month. Through his dragomans, the Franchini brothers, he let it be known that he actually had discretion to sail away whenever he chose. Strangford, who was being supplied by the British consul at Odessa with copies of Stroganov's intercepted dispatches home, was able to steady the Ottoman ministers with the news that this was not true, and that Alexander I genuinely wished to avoid war.[29] Consequently, letters from the grand vizier to Nesselrode played many variations on the theme of the 'mal revolutionnaire' which Alexander I had so recently denounced at the congress of Laibach.[30] Strangford was wrong, of course, to think Alexander I would consult the letter of treaties only and his Christian conscience never. The Ottomans were more misguided still in thinking they would be allowed to suppress the Greeks, ignore the demand that they should withdraw from the Principalities, and have Europe tie the tsar's hands for them. Hamid Bey, the *reis effendi*, was even disposed to see Stroganov's departure as a kind of triumph, as if Russian pressure could be repudiated altogether. Nesselrode's reply to the Ottoman ministers, presented on 18 July, clarified the position simply and swiftly: unless the Ottomans agreed to a prompt withdrawal from the Principalities, Stroganov would indeed be called home.[31]

The embassy of Stroganov ended on a note of absurdity. When the Russian ultimatum expired on 26 July, the Franchinis were sent to the Porte for the official Ottoman reply, to be told that the reply was still being drafted. The dragomans withdrew in lofty silence. Three hours later, word was sent from the Porte that the reply could be collected. But by now one Franchini was ill, and the other was on his way up the Bosporus to the bay of Buyukdere, where Stroganov's ship lay anchored opposite the garden of his summer residence. The following day, the Franchinis came to the Porte for Stroganov's passports, and Strangford followed them to prevent diplomatic relations breaking down on such absurd technicalities. He was unsuccessful. Stroganov circulated to the embassies his complaint that the Ottoman reply was unsatisfactory (he had not even seen it!) and too late anyhow. He was going home,[32] and on 10 August, his small convoy sailed north out of the Bosporus. Ottoman patriots, lazing under the Judas trees, felt free to take pot-shots with their muskets at the departing infidel. Prayers offered up in the churches of the *Fener* for Stroganov's prosperous voyage were successful. He landed safely at Odessa, to be hailed, somewhat prematurely, as the liberator of Greece. Before travelling on to St Petersburg, he took the opportunity of a social function to be rude to Strangford's informant, the British consul, James Yeames. Whether the Ottomans actually gave way to Stroganov's demands in the document the Franchinis refused to collect is not known. But Stroganov's departure indisposed any Ottoman minister to suggest evacuation of the Principalities to his royal master. It became Strangford's job to talk the Ottomans out of the Principalities, and to prevent Russia using the fact of severed relations with the Porte as an excuse for listening to the appeals of the Greek revolutionaries.

In August 1821, Joseph Planta, permanent under-secretary for foreign affairs, explained in a private letter to his friend Stratford Canning, now British minister to the United States, that the departure of Stroganov from Constantinople had suddenly raised the prospect of a serious international situation. 'Abroad, we have no subject of interest but the Greeks, the Turks, and the Russians; and the war which everybody fears between Russia and the Porte.' Though the details surrounding Stroganov's departure had not yet reached England, Planta was inclined to blame Strangford for the rupture, who should have done more to restrain his Russian colleague and coax the Ottomans to a more conciliatory attitude: 'we have not a very cautious tool in him, *as we had in 1812*' (when Stratford Canning was British minister at Constantinople).[33] Planta did not mean Strangford was pro-Ottoman; merely that he had probably reacted very sharply to Stroganov's pro-Greek sympathies, and advised the

Ottomans not to countenance them. It was an accurate estimate, based on Planta's reading of Strangford's dispatches. We may also add that Strangford had acted in accordance with his instructions.

Planta had no objections to the possibility of a Greek state. In the same letter to Stratford Canning, he wrote that Great Britain should give the Ionian Islands to any Greece that came into existence. His fundamental complaint against Strangford's behaviour was that everything should have been done to prevent the severance of Russo-Ottoman relations, as the new situation only gave greater freedom to Russian ambitions in the East. Planta believed that the main function of the British embassy at Constantinople was to maintain for as long as possible the exhausting, age-long quarrel between the tsar and the Sultan, ideally for another 50 years: 'This will give us capital breathing time to refit.' In 1821, however, Russia could do as she pleased in the East, and Great Britain could not prevail against her by force; 'we are determined to keep out of whatever happens and not to allow ourselves to be drawn into war in any manner'. In short, Planta agreed with Castlereagh that the only available line for Great Britain was the 'complying policy', that is, the compliancy towards Russian interests which, through diplomacy, might be slowed but could hardly be checked. A region like Greece, Planta hoped, could be the incidental beneficiary of this restraining policy. As for the Ottomans, they must see that, however great Russian provocation might occasionally be, the Sultan, like Great Britain, must face the facts of life and recognize those moments when discretion was the better part of valour or, more precisely, when concession was safer than resistance. Planta was really saying the Ottomans had no redoubtable friends, but that the Ottoman Empire had its uses.

Planta's chief, Castlereagh, was also in the process of thinking out the consequences of the 'complying policy', which had been an albatross round the neck of every British ambassador at Constantinople for 20 years and more. Castlereagh committed his cabinet colleagues, if not his countrymen, to a major role in the reconstruction of Europe after 1815. His Quadruple Alliance, originally a military league levelled at Napoleon, became the shaping force of the peace settlement. To play her due part, Great Britain had to give up that earlier outlook, in which her European interests were more particularized, centred on such strategic points as the Scheldt, or upon such countries as Spain. Instead, Great Britain was now tentatively committed to the preservation of Continental stability. The congress system, growing out of the Quadruple Alliance, alarmed liberal opinion in Great Britain, yet what seemed a new national policy was actually but a new technique for sustaining a very old British belief in the balance of power. After the very first congress in 1818, Castlereagh began to have his doubts, and stood aside from the next two, but by 1821, the unfolding Greek crisis was leading him back towards further experimentation with the congress method. In this, his wish to work with Russia stood far above any partiality for Greeks. Until 1821, the foreign secretary worked hard to ensure that Russia and Great Britain – who he believed capable between them of coercing the other powers – put the common interests of the Continent before the particular interests of any single state. He reminded his colleagues that 'with none of the Allied Courts [did] we draw better at Paris [in 1814] than with Russia', and he instructed the diplomatic corps to work openly and earnestly with Russian colleagues. To Sir William A'Court, his minister at Naples who found great Russian activity in south Italy, he explained patiently that 'we ought not to be too susceptible to her minor relations'.[34] To Sir George Rose, at Berlin, he wrote that Great Britain was 'equally the ally of all'.[35] To Liston's occasional deputy at Constantinople, John Hookham Frere, he had urged the avoidance of any close association with the Austrian embassy at the expense of the Russians.[36] Of the Russian government itself, Castlereagh asked that all Russian diplomats should be likewise circularized to be above the temptations of intrigue, and to devote themselves to the creation of a true, international collaboration at every court.[37]

This greatly helps to explain, at least in part, the impulse which drove Castlereagh back towards congress diplomacy in 1821. But what of that other idea, also held by him from the earliest years of the peace, that the Grand Alliance of the victorious powers was for the defence of small states and not only the propagation of the interests of the big ones? As he was about to discover – more accurately, rediscover – there was a lot of truth in Count Pozzo di Borgo's remark that 'the secondary Courts, if I may thus express it, rarely help those of the first rank in great difficulties, but they are very active and dextrous in tiring them out and raising small difficulties for them'.[38] Rather unfairly, there was a growing opinion in the Foreign Office, touched on in Planta's letter to Stratford Canning, that Strangford had allowed a 'secondary Court' (the Ottoman) to raise a 'small difficulty' (over Greece) which was quickly becoming a large difficulty.

It is true that Strangford, knowing that Alexander I had denounced Ipsilantis' rising, discounted Stroganov's threats as unauthorized, and advised the Ottomans to stand firmly by the scrupulous observation of existing treaties.[39] Like Metternich and, he hoped, like Alexander I also, Strangford believed the great powers could somehow congeal the political evolution of the Continent, an attitude which was most available to ministers with no public opinion to consult and an exaggerated view of their own powers. It was Castlereagh, and presently the tsar, too, who began to feel, for quite different reasons, the impossibility of abandoning the Greek revolt to the tender mercies of the Sultan's armies, now that it had reached a certain point of visibility.[40] One does not, therefore, need to await the advent of George Canning to the Foreign Office, upon the suicide of Castlereagh, to sense something of the actual shape of things to come and, in particular, to anticipate from the known attitudes of Russia and Great Britain towards the Ottoman Empire, the likelihood of a collaboration between Great Britain and the European state she feared and respected most in order to deal with the Greek affair.

Castlereagh and Metternich met for the last time in October 1821, in Hanover, taking advantage of an official visit by George IV to his Continental kingdom. Metternich could only observe with complacency that the prodigal son was ready to return to the fold of the congress system; he did not see that the purpose was strictly limited.[41] The meeting in Hanover proved to Metternich that he had been right all along about Castlereagh: 'He is like a great lover of music who is at Church; he wishes to applaud but dare not.'[42] Whether Castlereagh really wished to applaud the music heard at the recent congress of Laibach is debatable, and the fact that when the Hanover meetings were over, Metternich could still assert 'Mon entente avec Lord Londonderry est complète', is an indication that Castlereagh was misunderstood as much by the reactionaries as by the liberals of Europe in this last year of his life.[43] Perhaps the fault is Castlereagh's. He was always bad at expressing himself verbally. Perhaps the fault is Metternich's, who was a bad listener. Castlereagh was certainly disquieted by all the talk which blossomed with the revolt in the Morea of partitioning the Ottoman Empire. He knew the Greeks were inviting the French to extend a protectorate over the Morea, much as the Serbs had, in earlier years, sought a formal protectorate from Russia, then France, then Austria. He also recalled that Austria and Russia had a long tradition of devising plans for dividing the Ottoman inheritance. So he would not agree to a mere conference of the great power ambassadors at Vienna under the chairmanship of the Austrian chancellor, and wished to establish personally that Metternich's resolution would not wobble by making parallel appeals to the tsar. This it did.[44]

Castlereagh was anxious to head off a Russian action against the Ottoman Empire, much as France wished to keep Russia out of Spanish affairs and Metternich wished to keep her out of Italy. His plan was to rechain the bear before it ran wild, and he felt a glimmer of hope had been revealed to him by his ambassador at St Petersburg, Sir Charles Bagot. 'The language of the Emperor to Sir Charles Bagot, and especially His Imperial Majesty's reference to our having the winter before us for pacific discussions, seem to throw the notion of war to a considerable distance.'[45] Strangford was right. The tsar was not as impetuous as his emissary, Stroganov, had led everyone to believe. Even so, Castlereagh, meeting Metternich at Hanover, was cautious. He avoided a joint representation to the tsar, and in a dispatch of 28 October he led by himself, leaving Metternich to follow in communications of lesser force. The communications of both, however, opposed any idea of a Greek state, but made it clear that they also opposed a savage repression of the Greeks, thus leaving Alexander I in no possible doubt that if he disregarded their advice he would be alone in Europe or, even worse, aligned only with the revolutionaries.

Because Castlereagh was in no position to 'make the British lion roar' over the Eastern Question, as Viscount Palmerston was to do within another dozen years or so, he had to be content with a loud meow. In the dispatch of 28 October 1821, he wrote for the eyes of a tsar whose patience, he well knew, had to be close to breaking-point. He wisely refrained from specifying the British reaction if the tsar went to war with the Ottoman Empire: 'No Great Power could forecast what its position would be during so portentous a contest.'

But he did say the difficulties of establishing a Greek state 'originating in a system of revolt which has been reproved by the Emperor' would be insuperable. If any Russian minister believed the plan feasible (a hint at Kapodistrias), he must not expect sympathetic advice from within the alliance. For his own part, Castlereagh wrote, he discerned tangible responses to the appeals already made to the Sultan to suppress the revolt firmly yet humanely.

Castlereagh's peroration on the right of the Ottoman Empire to exist is of particular interest:

> It will naturally occur to every virtuous and generous mind, and to none more probably than to the Emperor of Russia's own, – indeed it is the first impression which presents itself to every reflecting observer when he contemplates the internal state of European Turkey – viz: Is it fit that such a state of things should continue to exist? Ought the Turkish yoke to be forever rivetted upon the necks of their suffering and Christian subjects. . . . It is impossible not to feel the appeal; and if a statesman were permitted to regulate his conduct by the counsels of his heart instead of the dictates of his understanding, I really see no limits to the impulse, which might be given to his conduct, upon a case so stated. But we must always recollect that his is the grave task of providing for the peace and security of those interests immediately committed to his care. . . . I cannot, therefore, reconcile it to my sense of duty to embark in a scheme for new modelling the position of the Greek population at the hazard of all the destructive confusion and disunion which such an attempt may lead to, not only within Turkey, but in Europe.[46]

So, after several years during which he had made no effort to aid the Ottomans in quarrels with Russia over Serbia, Transcaucasia, and the Danube frontier, years in which he had advised that 'the preservation of peace to the Porte is of infinitely greater consequence than any or even the whole of the points on which it is at issue' with Russia, we find Castlereagh in 1821 resisting any degree of recognition for the Greeks. His stance has been seen, admittedly only rarely, as the dim outline of Great Britain's coming advocacy of Ottoman integrity. It has been treated, more commonly, as one more proof of his indifference to the passionate cause of struggling nationality, the characteristic emanation of a cold, legalistic mind. Is either view sustainable? On the first point, Castlereagh thought the Ottoman Empire a necessary evil, a guarantee against the onset of an even greater confusion and evil than she herself represented. As he put it, 'barbarous as it is, Turkey forms in the system of Europe a necessary part', and the 'European system would gain nothing by substituting for the embarrassments of a Turkish system those of a Greek'. It is hardly a warm or classic case for Ottoman integrity, and the foreign secretary always shunned the idea of fighting for the Sultan. Notice his stress on the prior importance of the 'European system'.

As for Greek nationalism, that subject had come before Castlereagh in several forms. He is unlikely to have been ignorant of the rising of 1770, which foundered for lack of Russian support. He was in the government which authorized the raising of the Duke of York's Greek Light Infantry, which assisted Great Britain's own annexation of the Ionian Islands, in which islands both France and Russia had at various times inflamed national feelings. In his own departmental archives lay the first Greek petition for British aid and protection, submitted to his predecessor by the first British philhellene activist, Richard Church.[47] At the congress of Vienna, both Castlereagh and his colleague, Earl Cathcart, had asked for, and received, further information from Church on the islands. Finally, of course, Great Britain took the islands herself, calling them the Septinsular Republic, though ruling them like a Crown colony. Church, Kapodistrias, Sir Thomas Maitland, and others all stressed the fact that, to mainland Greeks, the Ionian Islands were a beacon, a fragment of a Greek state, an example to be followed, more independent in theory and in practice than any Balkan region, such as the Principalities, for which the Russians had extorted privileges from the Porte. Trusted by a cabinet which included two ex-foreign secretaries (the earl of Liverpool and Earl Bathurst), and diffident about doing anything which could be construed as a violation of his own firm principle of non-intervention in the internal affairs of other states, Castlereagh thought the Ionian Islands were, indeed, a sufficient first step, and that the Greeks could, as he said 'await the hand of Time and Fortune'.

Many who called themselves liberals were angry with Castlereagh, thinking the Greeks would be slaughtered while waiting. In fact, the foreign secretary was in some interesting, pro-Greek, company. When Kapodistrias refused the presidency of the *Filiki Eteria*, he implored its leadership not to be too precipitate. The tsar also told Ipsilantis, who thought peninsular Greece would not be ready to fight realistically until 1825, to restrain the movement. Byron, who detested Castlereagh by name and in verse, nevertheless shared one of his victim's opinions quite openly, and expresses it in the *Age of Bronze*, where he points to the futility of any rising which merely turns the Greeks into another Balkan protectorate of the great slave-state, Russia.[48] In 1821, then, Castlereagh felt Greeks lacked the means to secure their own independence, that the Balkans contained enough quasi-autonomous regions as it was, and that, up to that time, Russia had spoken out for the protection of her co-religionists but not for their political independence. If Castlereagh was in any sense original in 1821, it was not for any prescience about Ottoman integrity, but for discerning that the Balkans could yet destroy the working partnership of the great powers. So he denied the Russian view that, somehow, the Ottoman Empire stood beyond Europe. The rest of the century amply sustains his opinion.

Once Prussia and France were persuaded to join the British and Austrian representation at St Petersburg, Alexander I gave in to the pressure put upon him. As he told Bagot, the British ambassador, 'he had already endured the present state of things for more than six months, and that he continued patiently, though with anxiety, to await the effects which the combined influence of other Powers might yet produce upon the Turkish Councils'. Bagot himself added that, unless the powers really did help out, the tsar would have to fight in the 1822 campaigning season 'for decency's sake'.[49] Much depended on Bagot himself, 'the great Pacificator' as Planta called him.[50] Much depended, too, on the Ottomans coming to some sort of terms with the tsar. But what sort of terms, and would they include concessions to Greece? When the tsar finally acceded to the pressure of the other four great powers in the spring of 1822, Russia's demands crystallized in the so-called Four Points, which called for the evacuation of Ottoman forces from the Principalities and the return of these provinces to the accepted method of governing them; restoration of the Greek churches destroyed in Constantinople and elsewhere; protection of the Greek religion; and immunity from indiscriminate vengeance for the civil populace of Greece. The Four Points therefore embrace the issues on which Stroganov severed relations with the Ottomans in 1821, and they were to be re-submitted to the Porte by the diplomatic representatives of Austria, Great Britain, France, and Prussia. Castlereagh agreed that the Austrian Internuncio, Lutzov, should open the attack.[51]

This looked ominous for Strangford. His sin, in the view of the Foreign Office, was not his lack of sympathy for the Greeks, which was acceptable enough, but his firmness towards the Russians. Castlereagh refused to blame his ambassador for Stroganov's departure from the Bosporus, but allowed himself to be persuaded by Metternich, and perhaps Planta also, that Strangford was not now the best man to have a leading role in rebuilding the bridge between Russia and the Ottoman Empire. The argument allowed Metternich to resume, for a little longer, control of Europe's diplomacy at Constantinople, yet Castlereagh was hardly consistent in accepting it. If Strangford was straying from the letter or spirit of his instructions, this was not made clear to him. In fact, very little about anything was made clear as Castlereagh rarely wrote to the East, leaving Strangford to suppose that he understood the general outlook of his superiors, and that of the other courts, towards revolution. Strangford made great efforts to control the Ottomans, and spent £7,217 in extraordinary expenses in the process, a sum almost as big as his salary. He was also an honest dispatch writer, who felt he had no need to misrepresent his performance to a chief whose views he understood and shared.

Strangford's behaviour, as the Foreign Office saw it, had credit and debit columns. The ambassador was to be commended for having advanced the presentation of his credentials only after notifying Stroganov that he had been invited to do so. He was right to advise the Ottomans to trust Alexander I even if they could not trust Stroganov. When Stroganov first required the evacuation of the Principalities, Strangford had told the Ottomans they had 'no just plea for resisting his Demands'. When they countered that the withdrawal of the Ottoman forces which had chastised Ipsilantis' followers would lead Russia to march in, Strangford had replied that such a risk had to be taken: the Ottoman Empire was committed by existing treaties to maintain minimal garrisons in Moldavia and Wallachia, and an army of 30,000 men was not a minimal force. When Stroganov became inflamed over the damage to Orthodox churches in the Ottoman capital, and the Ottomans pleaded innocence, Strangford had reminded them that while it was true only one out of 76 had been destroyed, 13 had been plundered. He had also confirmed that the Russians had a right to complain under Articles 7 and 14 of the Russo-Ottoman treaty of 1774.[52] Beyond responding to Ottoman pleas and complaints, Strangford had made important recommendations of his own, and had been successful in all, though they lost him some of his popularity. He had pressed the Sultan to send orders to his commanders in Greece to pursue the war rigorously against the Morean rebels but to be meticulous in sparing peaceful populations. That the *Hatti-Sharif*, ordaining clemency and consideration for the civil population, had had little noticeable effect was as much due to Greeks as to Ottomans: after 1822, the war was one of 'barbarian against barbarian', as the philhellene volunteers often found out to their distress and embarrassment. Strangford's last services to Stroganov were materially the most important. He had persuaded the Ottomans it would be madness either to imprison or otherwise do violence to the tsar's representative.[53]

On the other side of the ledger are to be found those other acts and decisions which have been interpreted with hindsight as blindly anti-Greek, but which concerned Strangford's superiors most because they seemed provocations to the tsar. It is, of course, true that a diplomat is not supposed to rock any boats, and Strangford's retort would be – indeed, was – that it was Stroganov who did that.[54] He himself had to restrain Ottomans as well as Russians. In judging him, it is worth recalling his situation. He was enjoined by his general instructions to maintain good relations with the Porte and to hold himself aloof from the business of the other embassies, only to be presented with a serious situation almost as soon as he stepped ashore. Constantinople was in a mood of tremendous excitement at the news that the Greeks, whom the Ottomans regarded as the most favoured of the Christian millets, were in revolt, and had slaughtered thousands of Ottomans. The natural instinct was for the Sultan to wave publicly the Flag of the Prophet, and call for a jihad, a holy war of revenge. The Greeks of the capital lived in terrible jeopardy, suspected of complicity and ingratitude, the vulnerable prey of a boiling and fanatical public opinion, constantly stoked by the religious leaders of the Muslim community. The trade of the Europeans, including the merchants Strangford was supposed to protect, was at a standstill. The men who had penned his instructions in Whitehall had no inkling of the explosive situation in which he passed his days. One of his near predecessors, Charles Arbuthnot, and his immediate successor, Stratford Canning, both ran away from their posts, completely unauthorized, when the fierce mood of Constantinople broke their nerve. Strangford stayed, but deemed it wise to be sensitive to Ottoman feelings where he could. Hence the concessions he made to them.

Embarrassed by the behaviour of the Ionians, who were prominent in the underground movement which spirited hundreds of Greek refugees out of Constantinople, Strangford agreed that British ships should undergo search.[55] Arms and ammunition, as well as refugees, were occasionally uncovered. When Stroganov's banker, Dainese, was apprehended by the Ottomans, organizing and financing the escape of Greeks to Odessa, Strangford refused to protest against the arrest. When his diplomatic colleagues sent in a joint note to the Porte, protesting against the poor security under which Europeans were compelled to live, he stood aside on the ground that this was one of the risks of troubled times.[56] When the Ottomans asked him why they should not demand the extradition from Odessa of the broken remnants of Ipsilantis' defeated army, he agreed that this seemed valid under the terms of the treaty of 1774, that foundation stone of Russo-Ottoman relations. Nesselrode rebuffed this idea, saying Russia was not obliged by any '*droit positif*' to extradite Ottoman subjects.[57]

Above all, two matters damaged Strangford most. One was his refusal to join Lutzov and the Prussian minister, Count Miltitz, in an official note urging the Ottomans to humour Stroganov in order to prevent his departure. Strangford said he would agree to a joint offer of good offices to be made to the Russians and the Porte, but no more. The other matter was, of course, his inclination to justify the execution of the Patriarch Grigorios. Strangford had joined Stroganov in protesting against the form taken by the Sultan's vengeance, but his dispatches home reported details of the patriarch's past, as well as his incredibly unwise efforts to smuggle out of Constantinople the family of the late and disgraced Greek dragoman of the Porte, Demetrius Murusi, who along with his brother, Panagios, had been executed in 1812 for surrendering too much to Russia by the treaty of Bucharest. Strangford never lived down his palliation of Ottoman vengeance. Forever after, he was the man who excused the brutal murder of a major ecclesiastical leader.[58]

By contrast, Strangford's views on the Greeks gave no offence to Castlereagh, who called Greece 'the head of the revolutionary torrent'. In an official dispatch, Strangford asked: 'Surely the Emperor [of Russia] cannot think that the principles and conduct of these ragamuffins are worthy of *his* Protection?' Gradually, however, by the spring of 1822, Strangford was less impressed with the ostentation of Ottoman military parades, and the noisy clack of hammers in the naval shipyards of Kasim Pasha beneath his embassy windows. Quite suddenly, he began to sense that the Ottomans are 'too feeble to suppress the Insurgents'.[59] The Greeks were in high fettle, sweeping the seas with innumerable small ships adapted for warfare, and fighting resolutely by land. If only the tsar would publicly renounce the Greek cause, it might yet fall flat; at least, the Ottomans would then be free to give it their undivided attention. They had already broken the power of their most formidable Balkan opponent, Ali Pasha of Janina. In February 1822, the old pasha's head was on show at the Porte, and an Englishman was anxiously trying to purchase the grisly but historic souvenir.[60]

Someone else besides Strangford was beginning to fear that the Greek revolution might yet prosper. This was Metternich, who ordered Lutzov into action immediately after the Hanover meetings. Like Castlereagh, Metternich felt that the tsar would never send an ambassador to Constantinople again until the Four Points were conceded, and that until diplomatic relations were restored between Russia and the Ottoman Empire there was always a chance that he would be pushed to help the Greeks.[61] As for Strangford, Metternich quite admired him, but felt he was a marked man in St Petersburg. Stroganov would see to that. Unfortunately, Castlereagh felt the same thing, and so left his ambassador without instructions for five months after his return from Hanover. One can sympathize with Strangford. His European colleagues at Constantinople asked for his aid in pushing the Four Points, knowing his popularity with the Ottoman ministers, and when he said he had no instructions, he was disbelieved.[62] He was aware of his growing reputation as a fierce anti-Greek. Yet when he tried to prod London for instructions, nothing happened. Asking Castlereagh for guidance, he grumbled, was like asking for the governor-generalship of India. To confound him further, the perfunctory dispatches which did come his way had a habit of seeming to approve him. Castlereagh, for instance, advised Strangford not to irritate the Ottomans to the extent of making them feel he was pro-Russian! Then he perplexed his ambassador further by writing that his behaviour had been 'equally beneficial to the interests of the Alliance, and honourable to the Councils of your own State'.[63] Castlereagh was, in fact, staking everything on a new congress somewhere in Italy (it eventually met in Verona), at which he and Metternich would persuade the tsar to stand firm against the appeals of the Greeks. He was worried, on the other hand, by the rising tide of pro-Greek sentiment in Parliament, and even more by the candour of anti-Russian feeling. Whenever he laid any of Strangford's dispatches before George IV, the king scribbled his approval all over them. This made it difficult to censure the ambassador, so Castlereagh simply neglected him.

The Ottomans, on the other hand, did not abandon Strangford. Pressed by the Austrian and Prussian envoys to come to a 'categorical decision' about the Four Points, the divan was furious to learn that Europe was simultaneously preparing to hold an international congress on Greece in the autumn of 1822. The divan was also deeply divided into moderate and extreme groupings, with the moderates appealing to Strangford and the extreme patriots seeming to refuse Lutzov and Miltitz. Why, the extremists asked, should the Four Points be accepted unless Russia gave in return some categorical promise not to try to change the status of the Greeks? When Nesselrode declared that no '*droit positif*' required Russia to surrender the remnants of Ipsilantis' shattered force, the moderates were thrown out of office, and Hamid Bey, the *reis effendi*, was banished to Sivas. The extremists decided that Ottoman forces would stay in the Principalities until the Russians expelled Ipsilantis' confederates and the Greek crisis was over.[64] Strangford was able to maintain some contact with the militants of the divan through Ismail Bey, a former Ottoman minister at London, now retired, and Strangford associated himself with Lutzov's warnings although without instructions from London. Ismail Bey carried his messages faithfully, 'on the Honour of a man', as he put it, 'who once possessed the Friendship of Mr. Pitt'.[65] Strangford personally met the new strong man of the divan, Galib Effendi, with whom he argued that 'peace with Russia could not be considered dearly bought by the sacrifice of every unfriendly feeling . . . and by the abandonment of those measures which had, perhaps justly, excited similar feelings on the part of H[is] I[mperial] Majesty'. The *reis effendi* replied that 'God and Great Britain' would save the Sultan's dignity, but Strangford urged him not to rely on the lesser end of such a partnership.[66] Slowly and gradually, the divan recovered from this fit of militant defiance, and by the summer of 1822, actually began to evacuate the Principalities and to concentrate on suppressing the Greeks.[67] The prospects of a war with Russia, and of Europe holding a congress on Greece, seemed to be receding.

Unfortunately, one event undid the improving situation, in the process making it almost impossible for the Sultan's friends to help him any more: the good effect of accepting the Four Points on paper was ruined by the massacre of the Greek population of Chios in 1822. Europe, in its selective compassion, hardly noticed the slaughter by the Greeks of the entire population, garrison and refugees alike, of Tripolizza, the largest Ottoman town in the Morea in 1821: 8,000 people were slain in 24 hours. Consul Samuel Werry of Smyrna reported how the Greeks 'insulted and polluted the Mosques by every filthy contrivance . . . and had committed the most dreadful enormities on prisoners, women and children'.[68] But Europe noticed only the massacre of 100,000 Greeks on Chios. The event, Castlereagh informed Strangford, 'inflicted a sensible wound on the King's mind and filled the British Nation with horror and disgust', and the great powers might now withdraw their missions as a reproach to 'the most ferocious and hateful Barbarism'.[69] Even Metternich threatened to bring Lutzov away. The tsar, depending on his allies, refused to be provoked and told Kapodistrias: 'If we reply to the Turks with war the Paris directing committee will triumph and no government will be left standing. I do not intend to leave a free field to the enemies of order. At all costs means must be found of avoiding war with Turkey.'[70] Kapodistrias resigned the Russian service and retired to Switzerland. In that same month, August 1822, Castlereagh committed suicide.

At the time of Castlereagh's death, no one any longer thought the Greek revolution would end soon. But no one knew how it would conclude, which partly explains why Strangford felt the Foreign Office's neglect of him was quite scandalous. He himself was all for pushing the Ottomans into negotiations with the Greeks but this he hardly dared suggest without authorization from London. The military situation in Greece remained obscure, with each side publicizing its successes and hiding its failures. But certain facts did stand out. The Greeks held the Morea and the Acropolis fell to them in July 1822. Also, though the Ottoman government did its best to conceal the details, it was generally known, at least at Constantinople, that the highly successful thrust of the Ottoman army of Eastern Greece into the Morea began to flounder in the late summer. The army commander, Dramali Pasha, failed to secure his long land lines of communication (which would not have been needed at all if the Ottoman fleet had been even slightly competent), found himself critically short of rations and reinforcements, and paid the ultimate penalty. His diseased, starved forces dwindled from 23,000 to 6,000, and he lost his own life. The Ottomans never landed so large a force again in Greece, the Sultan presently calling on the formidable help of Egypt.[71]

Politically, some sense of unified purpose was emerging among the Greeks, and a provisional constitution was declared at Epidavros in January 1822. This was in large measure window-dressing to gratify liberal opinion in Europe, urged upon the Greeks by people like Kapodistrias, for beneath the orderly language of democracy lay a seething political situation in which each of the three regional assemblies – none of them democratically composed – tried to subvert or win over the membership of the others.[72] As Douglas Dakin astutely observes, the aim of most of the revolutionary leaders was to create in a liberated Greece an 'Ottoman society without the Turks', in which the traditional, feudal prerogatives of primates (clan and village leaders) and *kapetani* (feudal military retainers employed by the primates) would be enhanced.[73] Beginning as a struggle organized along class lines, the war for independence was in real danger by 1823 of foundering in a civil war fought on the basis of regional loyalties. Power passed briefly through many hands – Alexandros Mavrocordates, Dimitrios Ipsilantis, Theodoros Kolokotronis, 'Petrobey' (Petros Mavromichalis), Georgios Konduriotis, Ioannis Kolettis – and in all the quarrelling the prestige of Russia plunged, first, because no material help came in the critical early stages of the struggle; then, in 1822, because Alexander I agreed to a congress to be held in September;

and, most of all, in 1824, when he came up with the suggestion that the Sultan might create three Greek principalities, with the same administrative structure as Moldavia and Wallachia. By then, the Greeks were in a far better position to settle for nothing short of independence.[74]

At the time of his death, Castlereagh was preparing to attend the congress of Verona, where Strangford was to join him. In fact, Strangford got news of the foreign secretary's death only the day before he set out from Constantinople on the long journey to Vienna, where there was to be preliminary discussion about Greece before the parties interested in that subject moved to Verona. It was only when he reached Vienna, therefore, that Strangford found out that George Canning had sent the duke of Wellington as first British delegate, bearing for his guidance the instructions which Castlereagh had drawn up for his own use. Canning had no reason to alter any of Castlereagh's tentative thinking about Greece, his own being no more developed.[75] Canning also approved of Strangford's presence, as the ambassador's dispatches after the Chios massacre were marked by an asperity towards the Ottomans which inspired, as Strangford claimed himself, 'just that degree of alarm which [is] necessary and proper'.[76] Canning thought this could do no harm. From the dispatches of his friend Bagot, the ambassador at St Petersburg, it was also fairly clear that the tsar had not run wild after breaking his chain. It was, for the moment, better to listen to the tsar than lecture him, a course of policy the Greeks would not have approved had they known of it.

When Strangford set off for Vienna on 6 September, he declared that his relations with the Ottomans had never been worse. The Ottomans refused to send delegates to the congress. The Greeks, on the other hand, did so. They were not given a hearing. The Ottomans were careful, however, not to throw away all support, and made some effort to substantiate their assertion that the Principalities were almost evacuated, that new hospodars were appointed to rule them, and that the Sultan's Greek subjects who were not actively in arms had little to complain about.

Strangford set off in good spirits. His embassy in the East was now half over, and he observed, 'I have always adhered to the view that, what the Porte had admitted in principle, she would *sooner or later* practically execute'.[77] His secretary of embassy, Terrick

Hamilton, who was given permission to return to England because Strangford gave him nothing to do, was amazed at his chief's resilience: 'He is always so brimful of hope and confidence that he is daily tormented with disappointment', yet somehow Strangford always seemed to bounce back. He was quite convinced that 'it is to England, and to England alone, that these people [the Ottomans] look, with anything like respect or confidence'.[78] Strangford personally deserved that confidence. His government did not.

During his four months away from 'the ancient Pandemonium', as he called Constantinople, Strangford experienced all those mercurial changes of morale which characterized his temperament. Things went badly at first. In Vienna, he was much hurt by Nesselrode's tactless behaviour, and the circulation of a confidential memorandum which blamed him for doing less than his best for Russian interests.[79] Not having received any instructions from Canning, he naturally approached Wellington, whom he found remote and not very interested in Greece anyhow. He was suspicious of Canning, having noticed more than a 'tinge of Grecism' in his recent speeches in Parliament, and he was inclined to idealize, quite inaccurately, his relationship with Castlereagh, as when he is found writing, 'I comprehended all that Lord Londonderry wished, and understood his system perfectly'. This is certainly not the impression Strangford had given his chief correspondents, whether Metternich or Robert Gordon, the chargé d'affaires in Vienna, who were always being told, 'I am fairly at my wits' end' [for instructions] or asked to *take care of me* with the Foreign Office'.[80] With Metternich and Gentz, however, he resumed an easy and candid relationship, which allowed the three to share their regrets at Castlereagh's death, their reservations about Canning and Greece, and their conviction that the tsar must get an ambassador back to Constantinople very soon. Metternich also provided the information Wellington was inclined to withhold or did not possess. Canning's supplementary instructions to the duke were somewhat disturbing, but not seriously so. If the Ottomans could suppress the Greeks, so be it; if they could not, the day might come when Great Britain, and not Great Britain alone, would at least have to acknowledge the existence of the Greeks. 'Belligerency', said Canning in a well-known phrase, 'was not so much a principle but a fact.'[81]

The agenda of the congress of Verona was dominated by other, more pressing matters. Even the tsar thought these came first, or said that they did, and his preoccupation with events in Spain and Italy, and even Pacific America, gave Metternich and Strangford their opportunity. Metternich worked on the tsar, too, and persuaded him to soothe Strangford's ruffled feathers. By the time he went back to Constantinople, with the tsar's personal request that he should handle his interests, and Nesselrode's assurance that Russia was ready to re-establish relations with the Ottomans, Strangford's spirits were up again.[82] He had never wanted a congress to discuss Greece, and the rumour of one had weakened his influence at the Porte. He had always avowed 'the hopeless and visionary nature of the Greek Enterprize' unless the Ottomans were silly enough to provoke Russia too far. And now the game was back in his hands, placed there by no less a person than Alexander I himself. The Sultan must settle the affair of the Principalities once and for all, abandon his harassing restrictions on Russian Black Sea commerce through the Straits, and demonstrate through a *série de faits*, a series of practical deeds, that he would and could pacify Greece on a just and humane basis. The tsar, like the British government, was ready to see what Ottoman efforts could produce in the way of an honourable settlement, acceptable to himself and to European opinion. Strangford had had a furious row with Nesselrode about Black Sea commerce, saying it vindicated the Ottoman complaint that, once the Four Points were won, Russia would think up some new claim.[83] It was the tsar's personal intervention, and his ability to convince Strangford that he had no personal ends to pursue in Greece, that induced the ambassador to take up the commercial matter when he got back to his post.

Strangford was back at his embassy in January 1823, and any doubts about his reception were quickly dissolved. For a start, there had been a very helpful change of personnel in his absence. Lutzov, his Austrian colleague, had been withdrawn, probably for an 'amour impropre', as Strangford called it, with a dragoman's wife; in his place was Baron Ottenfels, a bright, capable man whom Strangford knew already. There was a new French minister, Latour-Maubourg, 'a fine fellow but a confounded Liberal', who might be helpful. Above all, the fanatics were gone from the Porte. Halet had been executed, and Strangford's friend, Hamid Bey, was back. Strangford went to work at once, and the new ministry not only assented to a final liquidation of all outstanding matters, but expressed readiness to deal with the Black Sea commercial issue also, which Strangford thought might give him great trouble. So affable was the Sultan that the intended responses to Russia were sent to the British embassy in draft form to be modified by Strangford, before being posted off to St Petersburg. In a very real sense, Strangford was the author of the language in which the Ottomans came to terms with their great opponent. Everything went so well that his dispatches to London became quite jocular. His influence and popularity only fell when Nesselrode, who no doubt enjoyed the situation, took so long – four months – before acknowledging the Ottoman concessions.[84] Canning himself tried to banish Strangford's fears, writing, 'it should be remembered that Russia has perhaps something to reproach to [sic] us for having hurried her into it [the treaty of Bucharest of 1812] on terms not corresponding with the advantage which had been obtained by Russia in the course of the [preceding] war'.[85] Even so, it was the foreign secretary who was now wondering if the tsar would really allow Strangford to liquidate his long-standing quarrel with the Ottomans. Bagot wrote from St Petersburg: 'I think, but I may be wrong, that both Prince Metternich and Strangford are too much persuaded that, since Verona, they have the Emperor of Russia completely in hand. Be assured that no man living has him in hand.' Canning agreed: 'Strangford has certainly been fancying that he had the game more in his hands than he really has.'[86]

Strangford had, indeed, secured virtually all that the tsar had asked for in the '*série de faits*'. Ottoman troops were at last out of the Principalities. New hospodars – no longer Greeks, but now local boyars – were nominated and awaiting Russian approval.[87] The new Greek patriarch of Constantinople enjoyed the most remarkable public testimonies of the Sultan's respect. The Russian Black Sea commerce was restored, on the sole condition that Greek-owned vessels did not conceal themselves under the Russian flag. Furthermore, Nesselrode finally admitted that the Ottomans had cleared away all obstacles to the return of a Russian minister, and both Great Britain and Austria were pressing him for the resumption of diplomatic relations. Yet Strangford could write, 'I feel my ground here daily sliding from under me'. He attributed his deteriorating position, not to Nesselrode nor the Ottomans, but to 'a complete change at home' over the Greek question. 'It is now expected', he told Robert Gordon, 'that I shall buckle to and construct a sort of Spanish constitution for the Greeks.' So, having brought the Ottomans to make every concession asked of them, there was something more to be asked, and for the Greeks this time. 'I am in a bloody ill-humour and don't care who knows it.' In fact, he did not think he could remain at Constantinople any more. 'If Government wants to establish trial by jury, liberty of the press, and mail coaches among the Greeks, it must look out for another Agent for its philanthropical plans. . . . It is clear that we are turned Greeks in Downing Street.'[88]

Strangford, we may suppose, would have been astonished and relieved to see how Canning was writing to Bagot at this time. 'I need hardly assure you that you are not to believe anything you hear of supposed encouragement from us to the Greeks – not one word . . . our neutrality in this quarrel is as strict and sincere as in that of Spain, and I have not uttered a wish for the Greeks because they, right or wrong, are the assailants.'[89] It would be truer to say that what made Strangford's position at Constantinople difficult now was not any public utterance by British ministers, but the behaviour of British philhellenes in Greece, and the near impossibility of the Ottomans being able to produce any longer a '*série de faits*' in Greece that could deflect the interest of the tsar from that country.[90] How, indeed, did one suppress a revolution with humanity as well as success? It has never been done.

In July 1823, the Ottoman authorities told Strangford not to dare to raise the subject of Greece with them. He responded spiritedly by saying that if they would not listen to *him*, the European powers would sooner or later partition the whole of the Sultan's inheritance. 'It is true that in venturing upon this ground I risked much', he wrote, but there was no very visible impact at first.[91] The Ottomans now knew of the establishment in London of the Greek Committee, set up to raise funds for the insurgents. In a great scene with Strangford the *reis effendi* asked how the British government would react should the Sultan send money to subsidize Ottoman rebels against the authorities in the Ionian Islands. From Greece came tales – largely true – of insurgent leaders being entertained by the Royal Navy, of salutes being fired in Zante to celebrate

Ottoman defeats, of Ottoman merchant ships plucked out of Ionian harbours by Greek privateers. The last straw was when the Levant Company merchants, following the example of the British government, recognized the fact of Greek belligerency: in a public notice, the merchants had the gall to ask the Greeks to treat the bay of Syrna as a neutral area.[92] The Sultan was so furious that he refused a Levant Company subscription for the victims of the vast Aleppo earthquake of 1822. Strangford dared not interfere when Ionians in Constantinople were seized, and condemned to death, for running arms and volunteers to Greece. Quietly, he bought their release.[93]

Strangford and Canning did not come to an actual disagreement. To the end, Canning paid sincere tribute to Strangford's 'singular ability', and although he said otherwise to his friends, Strangford *was* ready to buckle down and mediate between the Ottomans and the Greeks. In fact, he was readier to act than the foreign secretary, who told him only to recommend 'an arrangement between the Turks and their Christian Subjects'. When he wrote 'His Majesty's Government must no longer be amused by unmeaning Promises', Canning was really warning the Sultan to produce the long-awaited '*série de faits*' while there was time left.[94] This was exactly the advice Prussia was giving through Miltitz and Austria through Ottenfels. At one point, Strangford leapt ahead of his instructions and consulted about the Greeks with Sir Thomas Maitland, the governor of the Ionian Islands, only to be admonished by Canning, who wrote that 'it would by no means suit the Policy of His Majesty's Government under any circumstances to take upon itself a positive Guarantee for the fulfilment of any arrangements entered into between the Turks and Greeks'.[95] Strangford now saw that Canning intended to play a waiting game, and that his Greek policy was implicit in the statement with which Wellington at Verona had terminated Great Britain's role in any more congresses. Great Britain would not, *come what may*, the duke had said, interfere by force in the affairs of Spain.[96] The same was evidently true with regard to the affairs of Greece. Just how truly Wellington spoke for Canning was made evident when Bagot was as ill advised as to attend an informal conference on Greece at St Petersburg in the summer of 1824. Canning had advised Bagot not to attend until a Russian ambassador was actually back on the Bosporus.[97] It was due to Strangford's tireless exertions that the tsar had agreed to send one back. When Bagot indiscreetly attended the tsar's conference, Canning recalled him, and offered the Russian embassy, the highest post in the diplomatic service, to Strangford. Within the year, Strangford was at his new appointment.

The Ottoman government was thoroughly frightened by the news of Strangford's imminent departure, for no other ambassador tried as much as he to pick his way between what he considered the legitimate and improper claims of Russia.[98] He served Russian interests fairly, and the tsar was delighted with his appointment to St Petersburg. The Ottomans would, in all probability, have entrusted a mediation with the Greeks to him, but by 1824 they were too late, and Strangford's final achievement was to prepare the way for the return of a Russian minister, by eliminating almost every cause of Russian irritation. Almost every cause, but not quite. To the end Strangford agreed that Russia had a general right, conferred by the treaty of 1774, to intercede on behalf of the Sultan's Christian subjects. She could intercede specifically for the Principalities by Article 7 of that treaty, and specifically for the Serbians by Article 8 of the treaty of 1812.[99] In the Greek case, he tried to resist a process by which the Russians and his own country too, facilitated a national movement which the Ottoman Empire was powerless to check.

It rarely falls to the lot of an ambassador to see an issue through to the end. He usually inherits problems, advances them so far, and hands them on to a successor. Consequently, it is difficult to draw any very satisfactory conclusions about Strangford at Constantinople. One sees, perhaps, the extraordinarily leisurely rate of early nineteenth-century diplomacy, and the immense labour of individual men carrying the whole weight of national interests. The smallest achievement took weeks to accomplish, and then might, because of slow communications, turn out to be inconvenient, redundant, or seriously at odds with the changing wishes of home governments. In Strangford's case, we see the impossible situation of ministers abroad who find themselves between hosts demanding action and home governments which have not made up their minds. One may notice further, the physically contracted life he led, in touch with Ottoman names rather than Ottomans, and obliged to suppose that the mass of papers which filled his daily routine actually referred to wider, human realities.

While it is clear that Canning did not dismiss Strangford, it is easy to believe the two men were near the parting of the ways. Strangford's request to come home made it tactically useful and administratively easy to switch him to St Petersburg. Canning irritated Strangford with his deference to public opinion, and in his turn saw the ambassador as a 'Holy Alliance' diplomat. It is true that Strangford was out of touch with some of the deepest sentiments of the age, but Canning chose to ignore many of them also. As foreign secretary, he had to live and work within a generally conservative context, and to accept its limitations. It was not an entirely repugnant situation for a progressive conservative, as both Sir Robert Peel and Benjamin Disraeli were to discover after him. Strangford, while much more conservative in his convictions, had some of Wellington's ability to turn about-face, hardly seeming to notice he had done so. The envoy who deplored the Greek cause in philosophical terms was turning sharply to the idea of dealing with it by 1824.

What Canning wanted for the Greeks in 1824, is, however, obscure and Strangford had an exaggerated idea of Canning's clarity of purpose. Both were ready to respond to 'facts'. They simply disagreed about what the 'facts' were. It is easy to disparage Strangford and the 'facts' he believed in when we know how the world went after 1824. We may also assume that Canning proved his ability to sense the future more accurately. This would be difficult to demonstrate before 1826, if at all. It is not unreasonable to suggest that the very documents upon which we presently construe Canning's great contribution to the cause of Greek independence can sustain a quite different interpretation. It is, for instance, possible to argue that, at those critical moments when the wheel of Greek fortune seemed finally bogged down, it was a Russian impetus which kept it in motion. This was what Strangford had suspected from the beginning, and he felt that Great Britain as well as the Ottoman Empire would eventually foot the bill.

NOTES

1. Letter to Strangford from Thomas Hughes, an American colleague at Stockholm, quoted in E. Barrington De Fonblanque, *Lives of the Lords Strangford* (London, 1877), p. 160.
2. Sir Charles Webster wrote of Strangford that he 'was violently pro-Turk, and his sympathies led him to action, which violated the neutrality prescribed to

him by his government': Charles K. Webster, *The Foreign Policy of Castlereagh, 1815–1822* (London, 1931), p. 354.
3. Strangford to Bagot, 4 Feb. 1821, *George Canning and His Friends*, ed. Josceline F. Bagot (London, 1909), ii. 330.
4. Canning wrote to Strangford's predecessor at St Petersburg, Sir Charles Bagot, that Strangford 'is a singularly clever fellow. He has done a great service; and I mean to reward him substantially. He has earned the succession to you at St. Petersburgh; and I destine him for it.' Bagot replied that the choice would be 'a most happy hit'. Canning to Bagot, 29 July 1824, Bagot to Canning, Aug. 1824, ibid., ii. 265, 268.
5. Strangford to Castlereagh, 25 April 1822, FO 78/107.
6. Castlereagh to Strangford, 14 Oct. 1820, FO 78/97.
7. Webster, *Castlereagh*, pp. 47–59 and ch. II, *passim*.
8. Castlereagh to Liston, 20 Nov. 1815, FO 78/84; Castlereagh to Frere, 29 Jan. 1816, FO 78/86.
9. Castlereagh to Strangford, 14 Oct. 1820, FO 78/97.
10. Webster, *Castlereagh*, pp. 96, 347.
11. Ibid., p. 88.
12. H.W.V. Temperley and Lillian M. Penson, *The Foundations of British Foreign Policy from Pitt to Salisbury* (London, 1938), pp. 48–63; Webster, *Castlereagh*, pp. 234–46; H.W.V. Temperley, *The Foreign Policy of Canning* (London, 1925), pp. 13–17.
13. *Parliamentary Debates*, new series, v (1821), 'Debate on the Declaration of the Allied Sovereigns at Laybach', 21 Jan. 1821, pp. 1254–60. Castlereagh's reaction to the 'Protocole Preliminaire' signed at Troppau is well covered in Webster, *Castlereagh*, pp. 298–306; Castlereagh's circular dispatch of 19 January 1821 concerning the right of intervention is reproduced in full in *European Diplomatic History, 1815–1914: Documents and Interpretations*, ed. H.N. Weill (New York, 1972), pp. 28–30.
14. Strangford to Castlereagh, 24 March 1821, FO 78/98.
15. Castlereagh to Strangford, 14 Oct. 1820, FO 78/97. While on the way to Constantinople, Strangford spoke to the British high commissioner to the Ionian Islands, the flamboyant Sir Thomas Maitland, concerning the status of the islanders. Both agreed that, while the Ottomans must be made to recognize that the islanders came under British protection, to extend British citizenship to them would certainly risk Ottoman displeasure. Strangford to Castlereagh, 26 Feb. 1821, FO 78/98. C.W. Crawley, *The Question of Greek Independence: A Study of British Policy in the Near East, 1821–1833* (Cambridge, 1930), pp. 20–2; Douglas Dakin, *The Greek Struggle for Independence* (London, 1973), pp. 36–40.
16. Strangford to Castlereagh, 24 March 1821, FO 78/98; 18 Aug. 1821, FO 78/100.
17. Castlereagh to Liston, 20 Nov. 1815, FO 78/84.
18. Strangford to Castlereagh, 10 March, 21 April 1821, FO 78/98. The dispatch mentions the tsar's letter disavowing any connection with the Ipsilantis uprising. Strangford's opinion of the letter was that it was neither explicit nor completely convincing. The controversy surrounding Russia's part is covered in C.M. Woodhouse, *Capodistria, The Founder of Greek Independence* (London, 1973), chs. 10 and 11, *passim*.
19. Dakin, *Greek Struggle*, pp. 41–9.
20. Strangford to Castlereagh, 25 April 1821, FO 78/98; 12 June 1821, FO 78/99.
21. Strangford to Castlereagh, 10 May 1821, FO 78/98.
22. Strangford to Castlereagh, 23 July 1821, FO 78/99.

Lord Strangford and the Greek Revolt

23. Strangford to Castlereagh, 26 July 1821, FO 78/99.
24. Castlereagh to Strangford, 13 July 1821, FO 78/97.
25. Strangford to Castlereagh, 23 July 1821, FO 78/99. Castlereagh to Strangford, 3 Aug. 1821, FO 78/97. On 6 August, Strangford, perhaps expecting to hear of complaints from Stroganov, wrote to Castlereagh stating that never in his 18 years in the diplomatic service had he been so humiliated as he was at that moment by Stroganov's suggestion that he had not been co-operating with the Russian minister. Of particular concern was Stroganov's allegation that Strangford's refusal to sign the collective note, presented by the various ministers to the Porte, was a cause of existing Russo-Ottoman friction, and that Strangford was therefore guilty of duplicity. Strangford observed that Stroganov 'was prepared to consider a . . . difference of opinion as a signal of personal hostility'. Strangford further defended himself by saying that if the Ottomans had heard of any Anglo-Russian differences, it was Stroganov's fault for not being friendly and open with him. Strangford to Castlereagh, 6 Aug. 1821, FO 78/100. Upon the receipt of Castlereagh's dispatch of 3 August, Strangford suggested that Baron Nicolai should also examine the correspondence from the ministers of the other powers for comparison. Strangford to Castlereagh, 10 Sept. 1821, FO 78/101.
26. Woodhouse, *Capodistria*, pp. 218–36.
27. Strangford to Castlereagh, 12 June 1821, FO 78/98; 26 June, 10 July 1821, FO 78/99.
28. Strangford to Castlereagh, 12 and 26 June, 26 July 1821, FO 78/99.
29. Strangford to Castlereagh, 12 June, 2 July 1821, FO 78/99.
30. Strangford to Castlereagh, 10 July 1821, FO 78/99.
31. Strangford to Castlereagh, 23 July 1821, FO 78/99. Woodhouse, *Capodistria*, pp. 263–4; Crawley, *Greek Independence*, p. 17. Both Woodhouse and Crawley state that Kapodistrias, and not Nesselrode, was the author of the Russian reply to the Ottoman letter.
32. Strangford to Castlereagh, 30 July 1821, FO 78/99; 5 Aug. 1821, FO 78/100.
33. Planta to Stratford Canning, 8 Aug. 1821, Webster, *Castlereagh*, Appendix G, pp. 582–4.
34. Castlereagh to A'Court, 1 Jan. 1816, FO 70/74.
35. Castlereagh to Rose, 28 Dec. 1815, *Correspondence, Despatches, and Other Papers of Viscount Castlereagh*, ed. marquis of Londonderry (London, 1851), xi. 104–7.
36. Castlereagh to Frere, 29 Jan. 1816, FO 78/86.
37. Castlereagh to Cathcart, 1 Jan., 11 Feb. 1816, FO 65/102.
38. Pozzo di Borgo to Wellington, 11 Aug. 1817, *Supplementary Despatches, Correspondence, and Memoranda of Field Marshal, Arthur, Duke of Wellington, K.G.*, ed. duke of Wellington (London, 1858–72), xii. 30.
39. Strangford to Castlereagh, 10 and 26 July 1821, FO 78/99.
40. Mindful of the need to preserve the *status quo* in Europe, Castlereagh foresaw trouble between Russia and the Ottoman Empire should the Ottomans continue their campaign of repression against the Greeks. He therefore instructed Strangford to push for some form of conciliation between the Sultan and his Greek subjects. Castlereagh to Strangford, 5 Aug. 1821, FO 78/97. Webster, *Castlereagh*, pp. 361–2.
41. Metternich to Francis I, 29 Oct. 1821, *Memoirs of Prince Metternich, 1815–1829*, ed. Prince Richard Metternich (translated by Mrs Alexander Napier) (London, 1881), iii. 557.

42. Webster, *Castlereagh*, p. 326. According to Webster it was Prince Esterhazy, the Austrian minister at London, who made this statement about Castlereagh.
43. Metternich to Francis I, 29 Oct. 1821, *Memoirs of Metternich*, iii. 557. In the same letter Metternich went on to claim that his influence with Castlereagh had had a decided effect in the instructions sent to Bagot and Strangford. 'That gives me the advantage', he triumphantly told the Emperor, 'of being able to prove to Russia how far one can go with England when one understands her language.' The fact that Castlereagh made a point of inviting the Countess Dorothea Lieven to Hanover may also have distracted Metternich, or at least put him in a more congenial frame of mind. Irby C. Nichols, Jr., *The European Pentarchy and the Congress of Verona, 1822* (The Hague, 1971), p. 9.
44. Webster, *Castlereagh*, pp. 374–5.
45. Castlereagh to Sidmouth, 9 Oct. 1821, FO 92/45; Bagot to Castlereagh, 5–17 Sept. 1821, *Correspondence of Castlereagh*, xii. 429–32.
46. Castlereagh to Alexander I, 28 Oct. 1821, FO 65/126; Castlereagh to Bagot, 28 Oct. 1821, FO 92/47; Webster, *Castlereagh*, pp. 373–9. Metternich's letter to the tsar was sent on 31 October. See Nichols, *European Pentarchy*, p. 10; H.A. Kissinger, *A World Restored: Metternich, Castlereagh, and the Problems of Peace, 1812–1822* (Boston, 1957), pp. 300–1.
47. Dakin, *Greek Struggle*, pp. 33–4.
48. Lord Byron, in the *Age of Bronze*, wrote
    These these shall tell the tale, and Greece can show
    The false friend worse than the infuriate foe
    But this is well: Greeks only should free Greece,
    Not the barbarian, with his mask of peace.
    How should the autocrat of bondage be
    The king of serfs, and set the nations free?
    Better still serve the haughty Mussulman,
    Than swell the Cossaque's prowling caravan:
    Better still toil for masters, than await,
    The slave of slaves, before a Russian gate. . .
49. Bagot to Castlereagh, 20 Oct., 29 Nov. 1821; Bagot to Planta, 29 Nov. 1821: FO 65/129; Webster, *Castlereagh*, pp. 382–9.
50. Planta to Bagot, 20 Jan. 1822, *Canning and His Friends*, ii. 123.
51. Webster, *Castlereagh*, pp. 379–80; Dakin, *Greek Struggle*, p. 143.
52. Strangford to Castlereagh, 10 May 1821, FO 78/98; 23 July 1821, FO 78/99.
53. Strangford to Castlereagh, 26 July 1821, FO 78/99; 18 Aug. 1821, FO 78/100.
54. Strangford to Castlereagh, 6 Aug. 1821, FO 78/100.
55. At first Strangford upheld the inviolability of the British flag. He soon, however, agreed to allow ships bearing the British flag to be searched. Strangford to Castlereagh, 31 March, 10 April 1821, FO 78/98.
56. Strangford to Castlereagh, 1 and 10 May 1821, FO 78/98.
57. Strangford to Castlereagh, 5 Aug. 1821, FO 78/102. Nesselrode's answer to the Porte's letters of 15 June and 18 July did not reach Constantinople until November, or at least Strangford says he did not see it until then. Strangford to Castlereagh, 10 Nov. 1821, FO 78/102.
58. Strangford to Castlereagh, 25 April 1821, FO 78/98; 12 June 1821, FO 78/99.
59. Strangford to Castlereagh, 17 Sept. 1821, FO 78/101. As can be seen from the date, this statement was made by Strangford in September 1821, not spring 1822 as the text suggests.
60. Strangford to Castlereagh, 23 Feb. 1822, FO 78/106.

61. Metternich to Strangford, 31 July 1822, *Memoirs of Metternich*, iii. 639.
62. Strangford to Castlereagh, 26 Nov. 1821, FO 78/102.
63. Castlereagh to Strangford, 29 April, 29 July 1822, FO 78/105.
64. Strangford to Castlereagh, 10 Nov. 1821, FO 78/102. Strangford reported in some disbelief that Hamid Bey was officially dismissed because he was 'addicted to the use of spiritous liquors'.
65. Strangford to Castlereagh, 25 Sept. 1821, FO 78/101.
66. Strangford to Castlereagh, 10 Nov. 1821, FO 78/102.
67. Strangford to Castlereagh, 5 March, 25 April 1822, FO 78/107; 25 May 1822, FO 78/108.
68. Strangford to Castlereagh, 10 May 1822, FO 78/108.
69. Castlereagh to Strangford, 9 July 1822, FO 78/105.
70. Woodhouse, *Capodistria*, p. 267.
71. Dakin, *Greek Struggle*, pp. 91–9.
72. Ibid., pp. 87–9; Douglas Dakin, *The Unification of Greece, 1770–1923* (London, 1972), p. 47.
73. Dakin, *Greek Struggle*, p. 78 and ch. III, *passim*.
74. Temperley, *Canning*, pp. 329–30.
75. Castlereagh's 'Instructions for the Duke of Wellington', *Despatches, Correspondence, and Memoranda of Arthur, Duke of Wellington (New Series) 1819–1832*, ed. duke of Wellington (London, 1867–1880), i. 284–8. That part of Castlereagh's instructions most often cited is his cautious statement of the need to anticipate that changing circumstances in Greece may force Great Britain's hand:

> It may be difficult for this country, if a *de facto* government shall actually be established in the Morea and the western provinces of Turkey, to refuse to it the ordinary privileges of a belligerent; but it must be done with caution and without ostentation, lest it should render the Turks wholly inaccessible to our remonstrances.

76. Strangford to Castlereagh, 15 April 1822, FO 78/107.
77. Strangford to Castlereagh, 25 June 1822, FO 78/108. Author's italics.
78. Hamilton to Gordon, private, 25 May 1822, Add. MSS 43213, fo. 175; Strangford to Castlereagh, 26 Aug. 1822, FO 78/109.
79. Strangford to Castlereagh, 5 Oct. 1822, FO 78/110; Temperley, *Canning*, pp. 324–5; Nichols, *European Pentarchy*, pp. 51–2. In a letter to Metternich, Strangford gave vent to his anger at Nesselrode's memo:

> A victim was necessary for offended Russian pride, and they wanted to offer me up as the holocaust. But the sacrifice shall not be killed without resistance, and the calf, while struggling, shall shake the temple. They have thrown down the gauntlet! Well I shall take it up, and since they have made me the champion of the Turks, I shall play the role.

Nichols, *European Pentarchy*, p. 52. Wellington's own reaction to the Nesselrode memo is included in Wellington to Nesselrode, 2 Oct. 1822, *Despatches of Wellington*, i. 337. The marquis of Londonderry (formerly Sir Charles Stewart), the British ambassador at Vienna and Castlereagh's half-brother and heir, wrote to Bagot in November that 'Strangford is still here, grumbling and out of heart; he has not been used well, and I can't say how matters will end'. Londonderry to Bagot, 15 Nov. 1822, *Canning and His Friends*, ii. 139.

80. Strangford to Gordon, private, 5 and 23 March, 17 Sept. 1822, Add. MSS 43213, fos. 49, 56, 94.
81. Canning to Strangford, 12 Oct. 1822, *Despatches of Wellington*, i. 530. Canning's supplementary instructions to Wellington are included in Canning to Wellington, 27 Sept. 1823, ibid., i. 301–8; Nichols, *European Pentarchy*, pp. 68–72.
82. Strangford to Canning, 26 Nov. 1822, FO 78/110; Wellington to Canning, 28 Nov. 1822, *Despatches of Wellington*, i. 598.
83. Strangford to Canning, 5 Oct. 1822, FO 78/110. Strangford's dispatch of 5 October, concerning the Black Sea commerce issue, touched off a minor dispute between himself, Wellington, and Canning. Wellington to Canning, 28 Oct., 5, 12, and 18 Nov. 1822, *Despatches of Wellington*, i. 454, 490, 523, 539; Strangford to Wellington, 29 Oct. 1822, ibid., i. 469; Canning to Strangford, 15 Nov. 1822, FO 78/105; Nichols, *European Pentarchy*, pp. 246–50.
84. Strangford to Canning, 25 Jan., 28 Feb. 1823, FO 78/114; 25 June, 10 July 1823, FO 78/115.
85. Canning to Strangford, 9 May 1823, FO 78/113.
86. Bagot to Canning, 14 June 1823, Canning to Bagot, 14 July 1823, *Canning and His Friends*, ii. 184, 178.
87. Strangford to Canning, 28 Feb. 1823, FO 78/114; Strangford to Metternich, 28 Feb. 1823. Paul W. Schroeder, *Metternich's Diplomacy at Its Zenith, 1820–1823* (Austin, 1962), pp. 191–2.
88. Strangford to Gordon, private, 25 April 1823, Add. MSS 43213, fo. 127.
89. Canning to Bagot, 14 July 1823, *Canning and His Friends*, ii. 181.
90. Strangford to Canning, 16 July 1823, FO 78/115.
91. Strangford to Canning, 7 Sept. 1823, FO 78/116.
92. Strangford to Canning, 2 Feb. 1824, FO 78/121; 10 and 17 April 1824, FO 78/122.
93. Strangford to Canning, 25 Feb. 1824, FO 78/121.
94. Canning to Strangford, 14 Feb. 1823, FO 78/113.
95. Canning to Strangford, 9 May 1823, FO 78/113. This was in response to Strangford's dispatch of 10 Feb. 1823 in which the foreign secretary was informed of Strangford's consultations with Maitland. Strangford to Canning, 10 Feb. 1823, FO 78/114. Prior to this Strangford had written to Maitland expressing his view that a party within the divan might be ready to talk of a settlement with the Greeks along the lines granted to the Serbs. Maitland was to make use of this information with the Greek leaders. Strangford to Maitland, 1 Feb. 1823, in Maitland to Bathurst, 26 March 1823, CO 136/1090. See also Crawley, *Greek Independence*, pp. 28–9.
96. Canning to Wellington, 27 Sept. 1823, *Despatches of Wellington*, i. 305; Temperley, *Canning* pp. 63–5; Nichols, *European Pentarchy*, pp. 94–7.
97. Canning to Bagot, 15 Jan., 24 April 1824, *Canning and His Friends*, ii. 211, 238.
98. Strangford to Canning, 26 July 1824, FO 78/123; 15 Sept. 1824, FO 78/124.
99. Strangford to Canning, 26 July 1824, FO 78/123.

CHAPTER VII

The Philhellenes, George Canning and Greek Independence

In the eighteenth century, a young gentleman embarking on the Grand Tour of Europe as the culminating experience of his formal education normally expected his tutor to devise an itinerary which would take them both through places of cultural and historical importance in France, the Rhineland, Switzerland, Northern Italy, and, less often, Iberia. In the process of discovering that his command of living languages rarely equalled his grounding in the classics, a gentleman's tour also helped to fix, for better or worse, opinions about foreign people and places which might well last unchanged for the rest of his life, a point of some importance when one remembers how often Grand Tourists became British legislators. Towards the end of the century, when the Revolutionary and Napoleonic wars closed off large sectors of the European continent for years at a stretch, those taking the Grand Tour were necessarily deflected from familiar to less-frequented regions, and more particularly to the lands fringing the Mediterranean which remained accessible through courtesy of British naval supremacy. The remoter lands of the Levant – the Ottoman Empire, Egypt, the Holy Land, and beyond – continued to attract a trickle of the hardiest travellers, as they always had done. It was in the Balkans, however, and most notably in Greece, that the number of visitors increased most sharply after 1809, a year of restored Anglo-Ottoman relations, if we may judge by such criteria as the number of books issued on classical travel, and the references such works contain to those other travellers their authors encountered in the course of their journeys.

One may doubt if the situation ever produced the swarm of philhellene locusts which Chateaubriand recollects in one of the very best books of this genre, a book in which he asserted that there was no road in the Peloponnese, however remote, on which one could for long escape the dusty Englishman, armed with a bagful of classical texts. On the other hand, the travellers came in sufficient numbers, and wrote enough books, to clear away much earlier ignorance of Balkan topography and society. A review of John Cam Hobhouse's *Travels in Albania*, for instance, employed a typical reviewing gambit by drawing attention to the accurate information Hobhouse had collected regarding a country which the illustrious Gibbon, only a few years before, had believed 'as little known to the civilised world as the wilds of North America'. What might fairly be described as the rediscovery of Greece is, therefore, commonly believed to have come at a particularly favourable moment, as the Greek War for Independence came a mere six years after the establishment of the universal peace of 1815.[1] Thus Terence Spencer thinks the Balkan version of the Grand Tour inspired 'the notion that there existed an earnest moral obligation for Europe to restore liberty to Greece as a kind of payment for the civilisation which Hellas had once given the world'.[2]

The periodical literature of the period certainly testifies to the growth of knowledge about and interest in Greece,[3] and in the *Quarterly*, the *Edinburgh*, *Blackwood's Magazine*, the *Eclectic Review*, and one or two other journals of lesser fame and circulation, such as the *Literary Panorama*, reviewers gave increasing attention to works on Balkan and oriental travel. In the *Eclectic* alone, long reviews of 46 books of eastern travel appeared between 1805 and 1825, with the reviews of particularly celebrated books, like Richard Chandler's *Travels in Asia Minor* and *Travels in Greece*, running through as many as five consecutive issues. By the end of the Napoleonic era, a reviewer of William Leake's *Researches in Greece* could declare:

> The exclusion of Englishmen from those parts of the continent which were formerly the chief objects of enquiry to the curious has of late years induced many of our travellers to direct their attention to a country highly interesting for the wrecks it contains of ancient grandeurs, and from the contrast between *its former state of glory and its present degradation* (my italics).

Napoleon, then, however indirectly, is to be seen as one of the founders of the modern Greek state, though this was no more his intention than it was Hitler's, by his bestiality to Jews, to promote the cause of Israel. Besides deflecting travellers to the Balkans, Napoleon was himself very interested in the prospects of oriental empire, as he showed by his occupation of Egypt and the Ionian Islands, by his correspondence with Ali Pasha of Janina, and by his resourceful diplomacy at Constantinople and beyond. He stirred the simmering, international altercation known as the Eastern Question, which was formerly and predominantly a Russian preoccupation, abetted by Austria and, intermittently, resisted by France. In the years immediately after 1815 there was some hope in England that the Eastern Question might go away; the foreign minister, Viscount Castlereagh, experimented with a 'complying policy' which was deferential to the prior interest of Russia in the fate of the Ottoman Empire. Progressively, this Walpolean style had to be given up, and the debate about the eventual fate of the Sultan's territories began to tinge the political speculations of Balkan travellers: 'the present circumstances of the Turkish dominions in general, but particularly of European Turkey', an *Eclectic* reviewer observed in 1806, 'have long excited in an uncommon degree, the attention and expectation of the public'. This was something of an exaggeration, and remained so long after the impact on the public of the portentous conspiracy of Napoleon and the tsar of Russia at Tilsit in 1807. The travellers, and their readers, were not yet ready to respond to the appeals of a David Urquhart, who would invite his countrymen within another generation to recognize in the mountaineers of remote Transcaucasia, 'the defenders of your Indian Empire . . . the doorkeepers of Asia . . . the champions of Europe'. But that day would come, and would be accelerated by Russia's intervention in the Greek question of the 1820s, most of all by the fright she was to give Great Britain in 1829 by her military campaigns against the Sultan and the peace she would force him to accept.

The statistics of opinion are notoriously hard to collect and harder to interpret, and Graecophilism (meaning here a sympathy for the Greek national movement) was no necessary consequence of the cultural philhellenism of British travellers, a circumstance which still seems to surprise and irritate modern Graecophiles. In the first quarter of the nineteenth century, British philhellenes were disposed mainly to enjoy themselves, to indulge their classical enthusiasms without intertwining into the books they wrote any long digressions on the encroachments of Russia or the interests of Great Britain in the East. They were largely content to ignore Russian designs, and as for the Greek national movement, few travellers indeed were astute enough to recognize the occasional glimpses afforded them of what was largely, until the outbreak of 1821, a subterranean current. Indeed, one sometimes begins to feel that the literature of Balkan travel was the vehicle of the new snobbery rather than of any new political enlightenment. Three years after the Greek revolt had begun, a reviewer sighs grandly:

> How times are altered since the tour of Europe, the grand tour, was the *ne plus ultra* of gentlemen travellers! No one can now pretend to have seen the world who has not made one of a party of pleasure up the Nile or taken a ride on camel back across the Syrian desert. As for France, and Flanders, and Switzerland . . . to have seen these countries is no longer worth speaking of.

This too was exaggeration. Camel rides over the Syrian desert were still rare and dangerous. Beyond the Bosporus or the Levant coasts, the visitor was penetrating a heathen, barbaric realm, linguistically and racially alien.

By comparison, Greece was familiar terrain, even hallowed terrain, at least for many classically educated men, whose proto-Baedekers were the classics themselves, from which they could often quote at length and verbatim. In the contracted circle of Greek travel, the snobbery became ever more intense:

> No man is now accounted a traveller who has not bathed in the Eurotas and tasted the olives of Attica; while, on the other hand, it is an introduction to the best company, and a passport to literary distinction, to be a member of the Athenian Club, and to have scratched one's name upon a fragment of the Parthenon.[4]

If one had a name too long to scratch, like the earl of Elgin, one could of course try to take parts of the Parthenon home, a practice indulged by many and opposed by few. On the Acropolis, Hobhouse was taken aback by a fresh inscription near the space in the Erechtheion from which Elgin had removed one of the Caryatid women who support the entablature on their heads. 'Quod non fecerunt Goti hoc fecerunt Scoti', the inscription ran: 'What the

Goths failed to do here, the Scots managed.' At Sunion, the scratchings of Hobhouse's travelling companion, Lord Byron, are still to be seen.[5]

Philhellenism was a craze, a game, a sentimental journey, a profoundly moving act of homage, a state of mind, a fad, an affectation. It was for the educated and the affluent. With the appropriate classical texts, and possibly compass, measuring staffs, and notebooks,[6] one travelled in Greece and the islands, identifying, verifying, and measuring sites and ruins, in general marvelling at the accuracy of the classical record, or finding gratifying points of detail where it went wrong. Without becoming more enmeshed in the enthusiasms and prejudices of these people and their activities than is necessary for present purposes, the journeyings of Dr Walsh, chaplain to the British embassy at Constantinople, may be touched upon as typical.[7]

Being well-read, Walsh knew before he descended into the caverns on the island of Poros that they had been described by Pliny, Pausanias, and Strabo. Being a romantic, his prose was overwhelmed at times by his exalted state of mind, so that, instead of merely recording that he strolled back to his lodging near the supposed site of Troy at sunset, he writes: 'I set out to return . . . about the time that Priam left the city to proceed to the Grecian camp to beg the body of Hector.'[8] Being gullible, and landing in Corfu 'to gratify my classical recollections . . . I enquired for the gardens of Alcinous': he was escorted to them promptly. Being late in the exploration game, he knew the bitterness of not being first; finding an altar in the bowels of the earth, his discovery turned out to be covered in initials, some going back to 1672.[9] Being gregarious, he spoke to all the tourists he encountered, amongst whom was Lord Charles Murray, son of the duke of Atholl, travelling with a tutor who turned out to be the son of Arthur Young, the economist.[10]

The Reverend Doctor Walsh had one unusual experience given to few travellers. His guide to the antiquities of Athens

> made an oration over his fallen countrymen . . . he surprised me by sentiments which I thought it impossible he could entertain. He said that the time was near at hand when his countrymen would no longer be cowed under the dominion of the Turks, no more than his ancestors under that of the Persians, and their object was to establish

a free constitution, similar to that of the Ionian Islands, and if possible, under the protection of England. . . . At this time the most distant rumour of such an event had not transpired; I supposed what he said was the chimera of a heated imagination, excited by the place in which we stood, and I little thought that a few weeks would realise it.[11]

In fact, Walsh was to be in the Ottoman capital when the news of the Morean revolt became known there, and he has left us one of the most graphic accounts of the Ottoman reception of the information.[12] The hint given him while he was still in Athens of the shape of things to come was a rare moment.[13]

C.M. Woodhouse claims, in a rather ill-tempered beginning to an interesting book on the philhellenes, that travellers before Byron were enchanted with classical ruins, but hardly noticed the living Greeks at all. The travellers were, he claims, 'oblivious of anything that had happened there since the 4th century B.C.', and only began to mend their ways when the greatest romantic poet of the age – even the greatest Englishman of the century – set a better example. Byron, we are told, loved the Mediterranean people despite their faults and foibles, and refused to be upset because Greek peasants and village school masters no longer construed Greek as English university men thought they should.[14] This is not quite the message of the travel literature of the period. Numerous writers, *before* Byron as well as after him, were fascinated by the living Greeks, and went to absurd lengths to find resemblances, of character as well as physiognomy, between them and their ancient ancestors. Byron himself, as a young man, was a typical traveller, filching skulls from sarcophagi, carving his initials on columns, and saying of Greek men, 'all are beautiful, very much resembling the busts of Alcibiades'. As for the living Greeks, Byron was again typical of his generation of Englishmen, in that he had strong reservations about their character, and seems at times to have preferred Ottomans. He told his mother categorically that 'the principal Greeks . . . though inferior to the Turks . . . are better than the Spaniards, who, in their turn, excel the Portuguese'.[15] Others were yet more forcible. John Morritt, for instance, says: 'I assure you the Turks are so much more an a honourable race that I believe if ever this country was in the hands of the Greeks and Russians, it would be hardly livable.'[16] Naturally, this was a minority view in an age in which the Ottomans held a position resembling that of the Devil in Christian morality: if they had not existed, it would have been necessary to invent them. But the opinions that the Greeks were honourable, admirable, sensitive to their great past, and deserving of independence were held by a small minority also, and to ascribe adverse opinions of the living Greeks wholly to condescension and superficiality ignores the eagerness with which many philhellenes looked for, and were disappointed not to find, noble and ancestral qualities of mind surviving after 25 centuries in a rural and generally impoverished population. Such expectations were naïve, no doubt, but it was surely a tribute to the Greeks that men who would not have thought of the possibility of finding in the Spaniards or the Dutch the elements of character which once made them resourceful imperialists, should have been ready to accept the possibility of surviving Greek instincts for freedom and democracy. And however critical of the living Greeks many travellers may have felt, the large outpouring of books at least familiarized many readers with the debate about the differences between the ancient Greeks and their descendants. This was preferable to oblivion, as the Serbs, who fought earlier and longer for their independence largely unheeded by Europe, could have told the Greeks.

To conclude, numerous authors saw – were determined to see – 'all that symmetry of features and brilliancy of complexion which inspired the poets and heroes of old, still flourishing in a delightful degree'.[17] There is no question but that this search for visible similarities sometimes ran to absurdity, as when Walsh, becalmed at Mykonos, told some of the local people that Pliny had written that the natives of the island were all bald. A Greek 'repelled the charge with great indignation; and when he mentioned it to the crowd, they all took off their caps, and exhibited a bush of hair floating in the breeze'.[18] But this nostalgic searching surely carried a profound implication for the future. Even grudging minds acknowledged the distant possibility, and in enthusiastic minds there was the conviction, that the seeming degradation of the Greeks was accidental and temporary, whereas their true nature, their capacity for greatness, was permanent. In short, philhellenes often *wanted* to believe that a hereditary nobility of mind and feature persisted stubbornly among the Greeks in their polluted, Ottoman environment. In a country like England, there was a strong feeling that the condition of political independence itself would rekindle the ancient virtues. This may have been a romantic opinion, but it was held by Benthamites, too, who thought of themselves as pragmatic folk. The removal of the Ottomans, followed by the emancipation of the Greeks from their distressing condition of ignorance, would produce a renaissance of democracy and prosperity in the immortal land. It was strongly implied that the world just needed light, as if ignorance only, and not vested interests also, resisted change.

* * *

The conversion of the cultural enthusiasm of well-to-do philhellenes into active support for the cause of Greek political independence became a practical issue with the outbreak of the Morean revolution in the spring of 1821. It is suggested by Virginia Penn that the latter arose 'naturally' out of the former, 'out of . . . the particular favour in which Greece itself was held by many persons',[19] but this is not what actually happened, and it would have been surprising indeed if the generality of Grand Tourists, considering their social origins, turned out also to be supporters of bloody revolution, even against Ottomans. In fact, British support for the Greeks was hard to mobilize, slow to appear, and difficult to sustain. By the end of 1822, only 12 of the 489 European volunteers who have been identified as fighting in Greece were British.[20] Consequently, there is no British name among the Poles, Italians, French, Germans, and Swiss who were liquidated in the great disaster at Peta on 16 July 1822, though there is a Dutchman, a Hungarian, and a Mameluke.[21] In the same period, the vessels carrying European volunteers to Greece sailed mostly from Marseilles, and were financed by German and Swiss Greek committees. An analysis of pro-Greek pamphlets appearing in French, German, and English – admittedly a pointer rather than proof – shows 31 in French, 37 in German, and only 12 in English during the first two years of the revolt.[22] As to Greek committees themselves, the first appeared in, of all places, reactionary Madrid, and others sprang up in Paris, Marseilles, Genoa, Munich, Stuttgart, Zurich, Berne, and Darmstadt before a London Greek Committee appeared in the spring of 1823. Even then, it was brought into existence by two determined men, John Bowring and Edward Blaquière, rather than by a wave of public demand.[23] The

London Greek Committee was active for just over a year. Attendance at meetings was falling by the summer of 1824, and the committee withered away gradually after that, having, in the opinion of many, 'wrecked itself through folly rather than through knavery'.[24] There was actually a good bit of knavery, too, and no individual could ever have been proud to have been a member of the London Greek Committee. The most imaginative thing the committee did was to appoint Byron as one of its commissioners in Greece, where he was intended to disburse the money raised for the Greeks in Great Britain. In practice, he disbursed no money to the Greeks but his own. None from London reached him.

The London Greek Committee had 85 members, including 37 Members of Parliament, of whom only one was Tory. Only a very few committee members – Byron, Leicester Stanhope, Henry Gally Knight, Hobhouse, Thomas Gordon – knew Greece personally and, strange though it may seem, it is probable that most members were not particularly Graecophile. Virtually all, on the other hand, had records or intentions as reformers of one kind or another, and many had done battle for parliamentary reform, economical reform, administrative reform, slavery abolition, overhaul of the criminal code, and other such causes. This may help to explain the committee's limited success on behalf of Greece. It was all very well for Blaquière to say, 'I ventured to assure the Greeks that they might safely calculate on the success of an Association formed without any regard to party distinction'.[25] The parliamentary members of the committee were Whigs, radicals, Benthamites, and therefore seen by the majority party as men who would forever find causes, if for no other reason than to harass the government with them. They included Henry Brougham, who defended Queen Caroline against George IV's intention to divorce her; Sir Francis Burdett, who had fought many a tumultuous debate and been in the Tower for contempt of Parliament; 'Radical Jack' Lambton who, as earl of Durham, would advance Canada towards independence; Lord John Russell, a future prime minister who would push the first measure of parliamentary reform in 1832; Joseph Hume, the watchdog of government expenditure; Sir James Mackintosh, the law reformer; Lord Erskine, a former lord chancellor; Byron's friend, Hobhouse, who hated the current foreign secretary, George Canning, and wrote anonymous pamphlets attacking him;

Christopher Hely-Hutchinson, an Irish member opposed to the Act of Union of 1800. The figure-head of the committee was the celebrated Jeremy Bentham, who was remarkably erudite yet without the least awareness of what humanity is really like. He and his associates seemed to the Tory rank and file in Parliament, and their followers outside, to be too clever and doctrinaire to be trusted, particularly with money. Additional suspicion grew out of the circumstance that many on the committee were Scots or Irish. Byron himself was ironically amused by the committee's 'enthusymusy', and irritated by its inclination to see Greece as potentially a laboratory for social and political experiments instead of a distracted land experiencing terrible distress. Nevertheless, he entered the committee's service, and was flattered and pleased when first invited to do so.

Before turning to Byron, we may notice the extent of the committee's achievement. It could not easily invite general support for a revolution. The chairman, in his opening address, guardedly said Greece had become 'highly interesting to the friends of humanity, civilisation and religion'. The public would be asked to subscribe funds for a land 'associated with many sacred and sublime recollections'.[26] There was nothing unusual in the committee's money-raising style. Through circular letters, pamphlets,[27] and public meetings it sought to inform and to enlist a broad response to its appeal for funds. Disappointed in its solicitation of gifts, it turned to loans. Prominent in all its activities were Bowring, the committee secretary, who had a most undeserved reputation for understanding money, and that 'radical international busybody',[28] Blaquière, who wrote a wildly optimistic book, *The Greek Revolution*, packed with falsehood, which purported to show that it was elementary common sense for Great Britain to support the creation of a strong Greek state in the Levant at the expense of the 'crazy and unnatural edifice', the Ottoman Empire.[29] The frontispiece map to Blaquière's volume shows a Greek state stretching north to the Drina, and east to the Vardar, though excluding Salonika. In the text, Blaquière struck out freely against the calumniators of Greece, namely the 'European merchants' in the East – meaning chiefly the merchants of the Levant Company – and 'the whole tribe of Jews', to say nothing of Sir William Gell and his 'miserable verbiage'. He also reserved a rather wheedling style for his middle-class readers, and besides mentioning 'industry, sobriety and abstemiousness' as the dominant characteristics of Greek manhood, he told English womanhood that 'those of Greece are more like themselves in all that constitutes female excellence, than any other women I could name'.[30]

Blaquière was also very agitated by the attention revolutions in South America seemed to be receiving in government circles to the neglect of Greece. This may account for such observations as 'Greece will be found to possess a far greater portion of really learned and well educated men than the whole of the South American republics put together', and 'I should have no hesitation whatever in estimating the physical strength of regenerated Greece to be fully equal to that of the whole South American continent'.[31] As for the safety of any British money put into Greece, 'a land flowing with milk and honey', Blaquière said the first loan to be floated in London, for £800,000, was 'a sum which the smallest island in the Archipelago would be justified in borrowing, and fully able to repay'.[32] It is difficult to establish Blaquière's success as a public lecturer as he spoke in industrial cities like Birmingham, Manchester, and Liverpool and the county towns like Bath, Salisbury, and Winchester. Probably it was unwise of him to say the favourite authors of thoughtful Greeks were Vattel, Montesquieu, and Bentham, with a preference for the last's 'sublime and benevolent labours' in the fields of jurisprudence and moral philosophy.[33] For, contrary to what is often said about the Greeks enjoying a sympathetic press in Great Britain in these years, an actual examination of the newspapers shows an erratic graph of popularity, with an ominous boredom setting in by 1824, a year in which the Greeks fell into civil war. But for the Ottoman massacre at Chios, in 1822, there might have been no London Greek Committee at all. Up to that event, there was a growing tendency for British observers to think the Greeks little, if any, better than the Ottomans in their methods of waging war. Volunteers going out to Greece met other volunteers returning, sickened and disillusioned by their experience.

By the end of 1824, the committee had raised something over £11,000 in outright gifts, a small proportion of the total of £90,000 raised throughout the Christian world. As Hobhouse explained to Byron: 'We have dispatched more than 2,000 letters, which bring in a few driblets, but there is no important result, no congregated mass of efficient sympathy.' The trouble was that, although the committee's appeals were politically non-partisan, the response was not. The Established Church, most members of the ruling Tory party, and the English universities kept their distance. Ironically, after enlisting Byron as a servant of the committee, the poet's name often had to be kept in the background during direct appeals to those 'respectable classes' which had been riddled with the grapeshot of his sarcasm and offended by his rather public private life. Apart from the 'Athenian' earl of Aberdeen (another name-carver and collector of antiques) and a few others, the fashionable circles in which Byron traditionally moved provided disappointing sums, and probably less in total than the £1,000 given by the city of London or the subscription of the Liverpool merchant community. Individuals abroad, such as the king of Bavaria, and the Swiss banker, Jean Gabriel Eynard, raised more in gifts than the committee managed to collect in the world's richest city. So did the Society of Friends, which began operations earlier than the committee, raised more, and spent what it raised more honestly and wisely. Simultaneously with its solicitation of gifts, the committee tried to raise a loan on the London Exchange where, predictably, it met with a better response. The first loan, for £800,000, was soon all taken up, partly because £100 worth of shares could be purchased for £59, partly because the interest offered was a solid five per cent. This was a higher return than any British government bonds offered at that date. As things turned out, the shareholders received no return on their money for 50 years, in spite of Blaquière's golden promises.

The Greeks did poorly also. There were formidable deductions from the £800,000; £64,000 commission to Messrs Ricardo, the bankers; two years' interest was held back; a sinking fund was started with some of the money; after other deductions, the amount actually sent to Zante amounted to £298,700. When we add the payment of other outstanding Greek bills, and the value of arms and ammunition sent out, the committee disbursed £454,700 to and for the Greeks. Two years later, in the spring of 1825, a second Greek loan, for the much greater sum of £2 million, was floated at 55½, and this time the value of specie, armaments, and stores sent directly to Greece reached a mere £291,000. The committee, fast fading out of existence, said it had nothing to do with sponsoring this second loan, and the newspapers carried acrimonious correspondence for several months in which contractors, Greek deputies, bankers, and committee members were attacked by name. An American shipbuilder was paid £155,000 but provided no ship in return; £20,000 were spent on cannon which never left England. The redoubtable Admiral Cochrane, invited to put himself at the head of the Greek navy, demanded a lump sum of £57,000, a retaining fee of £4,000 a year, a guaranteed pension of £2,000 a year, and his Brazilian debts paid. 'The persons principally responsible for this waste of money', wrote Finlay in his *History*, 'were Mr. Hobhouse, now Lord Broughton; Mr. Edward Ellice; Sir Francis Burdett; Mr. Hume; Sir John Bowring . . . and Messrs. Ricardo.'[34] He could have thrown in the resident Greek representatives in London, Ioannis Orlandos and Ioannis Louriotis, who embezzled £40,000, though admitting to only a third of that. When it became known in London in 1826 that a third Greek loan was in contemplation, but to be raised in Switzerland, the *Morning Post* remarked that: 'the reputation of the Greek Committee cannot have reached Geneva. So gross has been the mismanagement of the two former loans that not one shilling more could be raised in England as long as any of its members are known to have a part.'[35]

American and Swiss philhellenes who visited England in 1826 were amazed at the chilliness of popular feeling with regard to Greece, and the positive hostility of many former and active British philhellenes. When one turns to diplomacy, therefore, it is to discover that the British foreign secretary, George Canning, was under negligible pressure to assist the Greeks at the time he recognized their struggle officially in 1823, and not much swayed by popular feeling in 1827, one way or the other, when he initiated active intervention in the Ottoman–Greek struggle. The romance had gone stale by then.[36] But Canning had by then found other, larger reasons for action, as we shall see.

★ ★ ★

The most famous of all Grand Tourists, and the most illustrious and controversial member of the London Greek Committee was, of course, Lord Byron, who first visited the Balkans and the Levant soon after the Anglo-Ottoman peace treaty of 1809.[37] Other British travellers in the area at that same time included J.H. Fazakerly, Frederick North (later earl of Guilford), Henry Gally Knight, John Galt, Captain Leake, F.S.N. Douglas, Richard Church, and C.R. Cockerell, most of whom were to support the Greek revolution in some way or another 12 years later. It is usual, however, to set Byron's achievement far above that of any other British philhellene, and typical opinions inform us that he 'lifted the [Greek] cause from the muddied byways of party politics, and rendered it at once an enterprise, a novelty, an excitement and a very emotional romance';[38] that Byron was, and remains, for the Greeks 'a poet, a hero, and a god';[39] that 'the little nations' of Europe, crushed under Prince Metternich's heel, 'turned to Byron', with Greece in particular sending him 'her signal of despair'.[40] Harold Nicolson believes 'Lord Byron accomplished nothing at Missolonghi except his own suicide; but by that single act of heroism he secured the liberation of Greece'.[41] Rhetorical as they may seem when assembled here, these large claims, restored to their proper contexts, read as the considered judgements of authors who have written at length about the poet. They are also, one may suppose, common beliefs among Byron's admirers, but they will bear some re-examination for all that.

The first opinion, for example, speaks of Byron lifting the revolutionary cause from the byways of party politics. Now if this means British politics then the real difficulty was to insinuate Greek affairs into parliamentary discussion at all, a task which Byron, as an outsider to British political circles, was bound to leave to others, and with which those others – the London Greek Committee members – had slight success. If Greek politics is meant, Byron failed here, too, and he became extremely bitter in his condemnation of the revolutionary leaders who were unable to take his advice and close ranks, and who seemed to want British money as a means of purchasing political visibility in Greece rather than as a means of financing campaigns against Ottomans. 'Whoever goes to Greece at present', Byron declared soon after landing there again in 1823, 'should do it as Mrs. Fry went into Newgate – not in the expectation of meeting any especial indication of existing probity, but in the hope that time and better treatment will reclaim the present burglarious and larcenous tendencies which now followed this General Gaol Delivery [the revolution]. . . . The worst of it is that . . . they are such damned liars.'[42]

Sentiments of this kind, coupled to Byron's tendency to admonish the Greek leaders firmly yet without heat, therefore lead one to suspect that the second opinion offered above, which sees him as hero and god, is very much a matter of dates. It is true that his death on 19 April 1824 was a major event. In the moving letter to Hobhouse announcing Byron's death, the faithful Pietro Gamba wrote: 'Your friend the light of this country, the boast of your country, the saviour of Greece, is dead. . . . I cannot tell you the inconsolable grief of his friends – and of the whole of Greece.'[43] It is also true that the Greek provisional government proclaimed special funeral honours which included, besides the firing of 37 cannons for 20 days, the virtual suspension of the Easter celebrations. The martyrdom of Byron was in the making. If one may judge from the surviving diaries and letters of the Greek leaders, however, they knew neither how to use the living Byron nor how to listen to him. When he baulked at joining the divided provisional government – 'I did not come here to join a faction, but a nation' – it was even put about that he was a Turk in disguise, and Hobhouse was probably right in thinking that, had he lived, Byron would have grown no bigger among the Greeks in reputation or achievement.[44] Adamantios Koraïs, the leading intellectual of the age who thought the whole revolution was premature anyhow, was quite clear in his own mind: 'the death of Byron is not all that great a loss for Greece.'[45] Quite right. Byron's death was a gain, a remarkable piece of luck, for, contrary to the third in the quartet of opinions expressed above, no one in Greece sent Byron any 'signal of despair'. It was the London Greek Committee which asked him to go. As to the fourth opinion, he accomplished both more and less than Nicolson supposes, more than 'his own suicide' but considerably less than 'the liberation of Greece'. How much less?

When Blaquière visited Byron at Genoa in the summer of 1823, bringing him an invitation to join a committee which in actuality hardly yet existed, the latter's imagination was fired, and his life given a new and final direction. It was only later that Byron discovered that he had been tricked by Blaquière, whose bland assertion that 'the [Greek] cause is in a flourishing state' was untrue.[46] But by then there was no going back, for Bowring was using Byron's name in England to rally support for the revolutionaries. Until Blaquière's visit, Byron had not really paid much attention to the Greek revolution. After penning some of his most resonant lines on Greece in *Don Juan* in 1819, he followed events there with what André Maurois accurately calls 'an intermittent, melancholy interest'.[47] As he was the first to admit himself, Byron had a way of taking up causes zealously only to lose interest in them sharply, and after that 'I cannot for my life *échauffer* my imagination again'.

In 1823, the Byron met by Blaquière at the Casa Saluzzo near Genoa was bored with his mistress, Teresa Guiccioli, and depressed with himself, very sensitive about his age, his figure, and his achievements. He was also ill, dieting and purging himself against obesity, measuring his wrists anxiously each morning, writing lots of letters but verse hardly at all. In 1817, he had given his life another ten years to run; in 1823, the expectation was sharply narrowed down.[48] The zest with which, in the past, he had declared that he would settle in the Americas, visit Persia and Egypt, or buy the island of Ithaca, now burned low. He was homesick for England, and thought often of the wife from whom he was estranged and the child he would see no more. He grieved about dead friends like Shelley, 'about whom the world was ill-naturedly, and ignorantly, and brutally mistaken'. Tom Moore was right in thinking Byron remained very sensitive to the excommunicating voice of English society. Greece suddenly offered a chance of redemption. How else explain a remark like the following? 'If I live ten years longer you will see that it is not over with me. I don't mean in literature for that is nothing. . . . But you will see that I shall do something that will puzzle the philosophers of all ages.'

Notice that he wished to *do* something, not *write* something, and as he was afraid his new venture would seem another frivolity, and perhaps damage the Greek cause, the official status offered him by the London Greek Committee freed him 'from fear of censure at home and [gave] him a satisfactory status in Greece'. 'I hate antiquarian twaddle. Do people think I have no lucid intervals, that I would revisit Greece to scribble more nonsense? I will show them that I can do something better.' And so he determined to go again to 'the only place I ever was contented in'. The committee, by its use of his name in its publicity, made it impossible for him to retreat to Italy,[49] though he was to consider it often.

About the tasks ahead, Byron was restrained and modest and serious, leaving it to that professional liar and swashbuckler, Edward Trelawny, who sailed with him, to boast of 'buckling on the sword of liberty' and joining 'the glorious banner unfurled in Greece'. Trelawny, in fact, deserted the Greeks soon after buckling on his sword. Byron wrote simply, 'They all say I can be of use. . . . I do not know how, nor do they. But at all events, let's go.'[50] One Greek who watched the poet sail wrote ahead to his friends: 'Do what you can to see that he is pleased, not so much because he can provide funds . . . but rather, because if he is displeased he will do more harm than you can imagine . . . good references and good testimony from him are of essential importance.'[51]

Byron sailed for Greece in the *Hercules* brig, with five horses, 50,000 Spanish dollars, medical supplies, his dogs, his Venetian gondolier (later taken over by Benjamin Disraeli), and a small retinue of philhellene friends and doctors. Leaving Genoa in July, he reached Argostoli in Kefalonia in September, crossed to mainland Greece in January 1824, and was dead by mid-April.

In Kefalonia, where he passed half his 'campaign', the poet was surprised and delighted at his reception by the British authorities, but instantly wary of the competing claims made upon him and his money by the leading political factions of mainland Greece, by Petros Mavromichalis (Petrobey) in Mani, Theodoros Kolokotronis in Corinth, and the island interest in Hydra. He was very disappointed with the abundant signs of Greek disunity and admonished the leaders in Nafplion that it 'refroidera l'enthusiasme et arrêtera les efforts des Européens et mes compatriotes'.[52] At first, he advised the London Greek Committee to send out more 'pecuniary succours',[53] advice he presently reversed but which the committee ignored. The large sums eventually sent out after his death were embezzled as freely as the amounts kept back in London to pay to various military and naval contractors. Pietro Gamba says correspondence, of all kinds, took up about two hours a day of an otherwise leisurely existence, and the letters to and from the mainland greatly depressed Byron, and explain the long list of very unflattering remarks about the Greek leadership to be found in his letters to England and Italy. Not the Greeks alone but the few Graecophiles in Greece, too, wanted him to come across to the mainland, Frank Abney Hastings[54] believing he would heal the political divisions, while Leicester Stanhope, drawing upon comparisons no one else would have ever used, advised Byron he was awaited as 'a Messiah' and a 'sort of Wilberforce, a Saint, whom all parties are endeavouring to seduce'!

Byron took his time, and was enormously influenced against crossing over to the mainland prematurely by a letter from Ioannis Theotokis, as we shall see. George Finlay, the future historian of Greece, who met Byron at this time, later recalled his 'sagacious and satirical comments on the *chiaroscuro*' of begging letters from Nafplion, and when Trelawny suggested going to Greece, Byron replied crossly, 'What Greece?'. Byron had had difficulty leaving Teresa: now he wrote to her, 'I was a fool to come here', and he promised to rejoin her in Italy in the spring of 1824.[55] He discontinued his diary, telling Dr Muir,[56] 'I found I could not help abusing the Greeks in it, so I thought it was well to give it up'. To others he said he felt forced to change his mind about Greeks in general, particularly when he found out the scale of atrocity in which they, as much as the Ottomans, engaged. 'They are such barbarians that if I had the government of them, I would pave the roads with them.'[57]

These sentiments amazed his entourage in Kefalonia, and when Trelawny went ahead to the mainland, he wrote belittlingly of 'the *Child*'[58] he had left behind at Argostoli. Yet Byron was undoubtedly right not to add his voice to the babel of discord at Nafplion, which is not to say he was right again when he decided instead to join Prince Alexandros Mavrokordatos, the first president of the provisional government, but by now virtually a refugee from its quarrels, in Missolonghi. Certainly Stanhope, like Trelawny, was disgusted with Byron's decision, and thought he became simply Mavrokordatos's 'puppet'.[59] It is extremely difficult, on the other hand, to suggest any more effective course Byron might have followed. The committee in London hoped he would go to the Greek provisional government's seat, Nafplion. Only a few Greek leaders, like Mavrokordatos and Spiridhon Trikoupis, doubted that he should. It may, nevertheless, be as well that Byron was not, as Stanhope regretted he was not, 'divisible'. The Greek cause was disunited enough.

Some Greeks still mattered to Byron, and they were the ordinary, anonymous peasants, caught up in the tragicomedy of the war in western Greece, far removed from the bickerings of Nafplion and the Ottoman dominated area north-east of Athens. The nearer Byron came to these people, and the squelching miseries of the lagoon of Missolonghi, the more his heart was moved, and the closer he came to the combination of spirit and action through which he sought personal salvation. Trelawny was, of course, in one respect right: 'The instinct that enables the vulture to detect carrion from afar is surpassed by the marvellous acuteness of the Greeks in scenting money. The morning after our arrival [in Argostoli] a flock of ravenous Zuliote refugees alighted on our decks, attracted by Byron's dollars . . . night and day they clung to his heels like a pack of jackals.'[60]

But harassing as they were, Byron could laugh at the Suliots, and inwardly weep for them. We expect him to cover his deepest emotions with a self-protecting sarcasm, as when he says that, should he survive the war, 'I shall write two poems on the subject – one an epic, and the other a burlesque'. But the emotions were there, and his diatribes against the political leadership are a measure of his concern for the ordinary men, forgotten by history, who underwrite all large and violent causes with their blood. In January 1824, he finally crossed to join Mavrokordatos in Missolonghi, where he was received, in a borrowed uniform, like 'a delivering angel'.[61] His practical influence was just beginning to make a mark when he died, his death hastened by fatigue, frustration, and murderously incompetent doctors.

The decision to join Mavrokordatos was inspired by three men and a memory. The men were Charles James Napier, the British resident in command in Kefalonia, the Corfiot Theotokis, and Mavrokordatos himself. After 30 years of the military life, Napier could say, 'I never saw men better formed for soldiers' than the Greeks. The revolutionaries also, he thought, had a great incentive for fighting on regardless of the odds: they could not go back. 'If they do not fight hard the Turks will chop them into kabobs', a reasonable prediction. It was the Greek leaders Napier could not tolerate and, like Byron, he felt the best way to spend the London Greek Committee's money would be to maintain a regular Greek army with most of it, and relieve Greek refugees with the rest. If this army could set out against the Ottomans, with incidental orders 'to plunder all [Greek] chiefs but not to injure a single poor person',[62] so much the better. As Napier had been indulgent to volunteers passing through Kefalonia, and even facilitated their travel, Byron thought the resident would be an ideal commander for the new Greek army. He advised the London Greek Committee to send out an artillery unit also, manned by experienced gunners.

Theotokis sent Byron advice in a letter[63] from Tripolizza in September, addressed to Count Delladecima. The following passages are the critical ones:

> Greece has never been in greater danger since the Revolution. How can the few inhabitants maintain so unequal a struggle? The Peloponnese has been deaf to appeals for help, not realising that if the mainland is lost, it also will fall, and the name of Greece will be forever extinguished. The Peloponnese is the theatre of two rival factions, each of which aims at self-aggrandisement and at seizing and misapplying the public revenues. The establishment of a General Assembly . . . has proved a failure, the public revenues have been squandered. The leaders have so completely betrayed the nation that this year's revenues have amounted to under 2½ million piastres, when they should have been 12 million, and even these revenues have been forcibly misapplied by the monstrous Government. As a result a heavier burden has fallen on the people than under the Ottoman rule. Much discontent has resulted. . . . The arrival of Lord Byron at Cephalonia with a sufficient sum of money caused both factions to try to secure his person and his funds. . . . They should have advised Lord Byron to make his way to Western Greece, where his arrival would have secured the relief and provisioning of Missolonghi and would have inspired with fresh courage the population of that part. His funds would provide for the payment of 8 or 10 armed ships. . . . Three thousand armed troops in the Morea would soon rally around him, if they were sure they would not find themselves abandoned. . . . If Milord lands in the Morea, as he has been pressed to do, he will accomplish little for Greece. . . . Patriotic and liberal sentiments are unknown there. . . . I long with all my heart that Greece should be saved by the good counsels and benefits of a Patriot. Greece possesses all the materials necessary to constitute a state, brave soldiers, fearless sailors, talents, territorial wealth, sufficient friends, a quiet and moderate people. She only needs a motive force behind these material resources.

Mavrokordatos, a Fanariot Greek and first president of the assembly, had had to fly from the wrath of Kolokotronis, and had nearly been lynched before making his way to western Greece to carry on the war. Articulate, multilingual, patriotic, and shrewd,

Mavrokordatos had a mixture of practical abilities and political finesse which impressed Byron. He also handled Byron with skill, writing that his appearance in Missolonghi would 'electrify' the rebels. Byron was gratified and hoped the prediction might come true. Inevitably, it came to be argued that Mavrokordatos duped Byron, but who was not anxious to dupe Byron? Byron decided to join Mavrokordatos because, as he explained to London, 'as I pay a considerable portion of the clans I may as well see what they are likely to do for their money – besides, I am tired of hearing nothing but talk, constitutions, or Sunday Schools, and what not'.[64]

A memory of distant days also beckoned Byron. It was 14 years since the memorable nine-day journey made with his friend Hobhouse from Preveza to 'Tepaleen' and the court of Ali Pasha, and now the same cloud-filled mountains rose before him, the mountains of Albania which, 'indeed, I have seen more of than any Englishman (except a Mr. Leake)'.[65] He landed at Missolonghi in uniform, a soldier rather than a negotiator by intention, and within a short time his house 'was filled with soldiers; his receiving room resembled an arsenal of war. . . . Its walls were decorated with swords, pistols, Ottoman sabres, dirks, rifles, guns, blunderbusses, bayonets, helmets and trumpets, fantastically suspended.'[66]

Byron was unable to realize his ambition to see active service, although he worked hard to retrieve something from the misunderstanding by which the Greek provisional government supposed he represented a wealthy and politically influential London Greek Committee, much as he himself originally was led by Blaquière to suppose that the Greek leaders exercised general control over a roughly unified national territory. A 'corps of one hundred Germans' which Napier told him were in Missolonghi turned out to be 26 strong, though others trickled into the poet's headquarters to enjoy, in St Clair's apt phrase, 'the hitherto unknown sensation of being paid'. The Byron Brigade, as it came to be called, had mustered about 50 European volunteers in all, few of them British, at the time its leader and paymaster died. To the end he had hopes of achieving something with it: 'For three hundred pounds I can maintain at more than the *fullest pay* of the Provisional Government, rations included, one hundred armed men for *three months.*'[67] He also paid out his own money for Stanhope's artillery train, to Greek sea-captains, and to Greek and

Ottoman refugees. He was instrumental in starting a dispensary, and he exhorted William Parry and his artificers, without much success, to establish a gun foundry and ammunition plant with equipment brought out from Woolwich arsenal. He financed the journal called *Ellenika Kronika*,[68] one of several, mostly short-lived, newspapers: the *Ellenika* had around 40 subscribers, mostly in London and Europe. At the time of his death, when he was paying large amounts of money each week from his own pocket,[69] Byron was intending to lead an attack on Lepanto, which the Ottomans held. All these wearying tasks, which involved much altercation and slow progress, Hobhouse called 'the most glorious undertaken by man'.[70] Byron merely hoped such activities might have 'at least *temporary* utility'. Temporary is the right word. The Byron Brigade broke up soon after the poet's death. Some of the volunteers met their death in Greece. Some went home. Some joined the Ottomans.[71] It has been proposed, nevertheless, that the importance of Byron lies in the fact that he was 'the only possible link between . . . the radical reformers at home and the romantic crusaders in the field'.[72] In fact, the 'radical reformers' in England had no links with the later volunteers who were inspired by Byron's death and poetry and who were, for the greater part, Bonapartists, disappointed professional revolutionaries, and mostly Europeans. And, as is often overlooked, the second, bigger loan raised in England for the Greeks was not the work of the London Greek Committee at all.

Like most of the Graecophile volunteers in the war of independence, Byron was not well understood while alive nor greatly appreciated in the immediate aftermath of his death. After the noble funeral oration delivered by Trikoupis, his body was returned to England, less the lungs[73] (*not* the heart), and the generality of Greeks had to take it on trust that a great poet had been among them. Byron's Missolonghi house was destroyed by the Greeks in defending the town in 1826.[74] *The Bride of Abydos* seems to have been the first Byron poem translated into Greek, in 1837, and in Ottoman Smyrna at that.[75] In 1861, the European colony in Athens was requested by the Greek government to select names for special commemoration along with the Greeks who fell in the war of independence, and they chose the Swiss Meyer, the Frenchman Fabvier, and Byron. In 1881, Byron's statue was raised in the Zappeion garden. In Great Britain, the Byron controversy grew after his death, but his contribution to the Greek cause was a negligible part of the controversy. With his private memoirs destroyed in John Murray's office by the misplaced scruples of his friends, Byron's enemies were free to speculate endlessly and at his expense about his treatment of his 'princess of parallelograms', Lady Byron, and his widow was able in her turn to gratify them, and to enlarge her case against his memory, cherishing every scabrous detail, gathering and pressing fantasies with pious care, like a collection of rare plants.

★ ★ ★

On 15 May 1824, an obituary notice in *The Times* declared that 'the whole of Lord Byron's latter days' had been given to 'the noblest of enterprises, the deliverance of Greece'. This was a warmer view of the deceased and the cause he served than was customary with the British press, including *The Times* itself, by 1824. It became generally believed, nevertheless, that the poet had died, if not exactly a hero,[76] at least as a man of action and, in the following years, the most popular portrait of Byron was undoubtedly the one painted by Thomas Phillips, which shows him in Albanian garb and which today hangs in the British embassy in Athens.

The circumstances of his death did little to mitigate Byron's lurid reputation at home in England. The corpse which lay in state in Great George Street attracted a long file of the curious, but few people from the circles in which the poet had once moved. If the poet and critic, Allan Cunningham, reported accurately that news of the death struck London 'like an earthquake',[77] then the best people in society composed themselves again extraordinarily quickly. Of the 47 carriages draped in black for the funeral procession, only three had occupants, a tribute, as has been observed, to the social status of the deceased rather than to the man himself. In the corridors of political power, the death meant very little. Hobhouse was right. There was no 'congregated mass of effective support' for the Greeks in Great Britain to which officials in government departments or honourable members of the House need respond. In far-off Greece, the Byron Brigade was breaking up fast,[78] leaving behind an ephemeral British reputation which would be revived 'by Lord Guilford and Tricoupes, and organised into a party by the Zante Committee of Rama, Stephanou and Dragona'.[79] It would never be much of a party, nor enjoy wide support among Greeks. The offer of the Greek crown, dangled in order to obtain firmer British support, would be fastidiously refused by London.

According to Count Kapodistrias,[80] Alexander I's erstwhile adviser on foreign affairs, a grudging attitude towards the Greek cause was only to be expected of the British. As he reminded Leicester Stanhope, who called on Kapodistrias in his Genevan seclusion, struggling republics could hardly expect kindly support from kings.[81] Also, Great Britain had ambitions and plans of her own in the eastern Mediterranean which ran counter to Greek interests. Had she not, for instance, seized part of the rightful patrimony of the Greeks by her occupation of Corfu, Kapodistrias' birthplace, as well as other Ionian Islands? Furthermore, had she not cynically sold off Parga, the great mainland fortress on the coast of Epirus, to the Albanian adventurer, Ali Pasha of Janina, in order to isolate her new possessions in the lower Adriatic from contact with peninsular Greece?

Kapodistrias had a case. Sir Thomas Maitland ruled the Ionian Islands as if they were a crown colony. He dismissed his private secretary for expressing Graecophile sympathies too candidly. In London, Lord Castlereagh, the foreign secretary, who disliked Kapodistrias and called him 'the mongrel minister' of Russia, blunted Ottoman hopes of obtaining the islands, and while he got as far as clarifying, at least to his own satisfaction, that Ionian Greeks could not be regarded as Ottoman subjects, he never explained to anybody whose subjects they actually were. During a visit to London in 1819, Kapodistrias had one or two glacial interviews with the foreign secretary,[82] and obviously drew small comfort from the Castlereagh formula that the Greeks must await the workings of 'Time and of Providence'. It was when the tsar spoke in a similar vein in 1822 that Kapodistrias felt constrained to resign from Russian service, feeling he could no longer serve Greece and Russia simultaneously, as he had once hoped. In his *Memoirs*, the famous Corfiot complained that the British were far too ready to see him as an instrument 'for establishing sooner or later the absolute dominion of Russia in the Orient'.[83] This exaggerates British vigilance at that time, and ignores Castlereagh's declared readiness.

as we find it in his instructions to his ambassador at Constantinople, to follow a policy of deference to Russian leadership in the Levant. Russia certainly justified the foreign secretary's hope that the Greek revolt should not be permitted to weaken the system of collective security organized by the conservative courts of Europe at the peace settlement of 1815.[84] Through his coolness for the enthusiasms of Kapodistrias, Castlereagh upset poets as well as liberals, and Shelley wrote of him, 'I met murder on the way, he had a face like Castlereagh'. And yet, was George Canning, Castlereagh's successor at the Foreign Office, notably more disposed to assist the Greek rebels? And if so, when?

Originally, Castlereagh hoped the revolution in Greece would die of neglect. When it survived into a second year, he came round to the possibility of recognizing the belligerents, declaring 'it will be difficult, if a *de facto* government be established in the Morea, to refuse [it] the ordinary privileges of a belligerent'. At the time of his death, in August 1822, Castlereagh was busy drawing up instructions for his own guidance at the forthcoming congress of Verona, and in them he proposed the possibility of recognition of the Greek revolt 'with caution and without ostentation, lest it should render the Turks wholly inaccessible' to British advice. With the consent of his cabinet colleagues, Castlereagh believed he would be able at Verona to obtain an amnesty for the Greeks at the very least, and just possibly 'the creation of a qualified Greek government'. He meant something like the autonomy of the Danubian principalities of Moldavia and Wallachia. Succeeding Castlereagh, Canning found no reason to alter the Verona instructions for Great Britain's new envoy, the duke of Wellington, simply adding the observation that 'the Turks now seem to have the upper hand', thus making it inadvisable for Great Britain to 'interfere between Russia and the Porte or between the Porte and the Greeks'.[85] It was the 'complying policy' all over again, though with quite a different motive behind it now. Castlereagh was wary of any issue that might weaken the solidarity of the main courts of Europe; Canning was an isolationist by instinct, chary of collective action on anything, and most of all on behalf of a losing cause.

The distance in political outlook between the two foreign secretaries must not, therefore, be exaggerated. As practising statesmen, they differed in diplomatic style and tactical method, with Castlereagh preferring the collective action which Canning abjured. The difference was as much temperamental as ideological, and it is a simplification to treat Castlereagh as the cold reactionary, opposed and eventually succeeded by Canning, the generous liberal who subverted the ultra-conservative congress system, and presently became the 'liberator' of South America as well as Greece.

This too-favourable view of Canning grew originally out of the enthusiastic reminiscences of his loyal secretary, A.G. Stapleton, as well as from Canning's own flair for devising popular justifications for his diplomatic decisions. On the other hand, Stapleton's rhetoric has had a formidable momentum, and his eulogisms are to be found here and there in the writings of later historians whose own researches actually invalidate, or at the least moderate, the faithful secretary's conclusions. H.W.V. Temperley, for instance, who was Canning's first systematic biographer and who recognized Stapleton's inflationary influence on Canning's reputation, still felt it possible to epitomize his subject's Greek achievement in an Ottoman proverb: 'The two Cannings gave freedom to Greece.'[86] There is no such Ottoman proverb; did it exist, it would be inaccurate even for a proverb. A more recent biographer is close to the truth where he suggests that there is actually very little evidence to support the idea that Canning was ever disposed to sentimentality in diplomacy.[87] Indeed, Canning often took the trouble to abjure such an idea for himself, and in the case of Greece said more than once that nothing could be done 'for the sake of Epaminondas and St. Paul', that is, for the sort of motives inspiring cultural philhellenism.

The remark could be read as one of Canning's little flippancies, but in fact, he meant it very seriously. Presumably this is why so many liberal people felt disappointed in him when he was alive. He had no correspondence with Byron, who felt he could not approach him.[88] Hobhouse detested him as 'a sophist, a rhetorician, and a political adventurer'.[89] John Bowring, also of the London Greek Committee, was disgusted when Canning asked him what language Great Britain could possibly hold out to Russia in support of Greece. Blaquière grieved in 1824 that some acts of 'conciliation and atonement' were seriously overdue, and that neglect of Greece, which was 'among the most palpable errors of a late minister [Castlereagh]', still seemed official policy.[90] His particular dis-

The Philhellenes and Greek Independence

appointment was that there had been no sequel to the recognition of the Greeks as belligerents, foreshadowed by Castlereagh but actually carried out in 1823 by Canning.

Canning was one of the best classical scholars of his generation. His verses on the abject state of the modern Greeks were poignant enough and known enough to be quoted by Kapodistrias over a Paris dinner table.[91] As foreign secretary, Canning attended the Guildhall dinner for Orlandos and Louriotis in the spring of 1823, when the two deputies came to sign the contract for the first Greek loan. There is, as a result, some excuse for the Greeks, though less for historians, in thinking that the recognition of Greek belligerency was the thin edge of a wedge, the first public expression by the new foreign secretary of sympathy for a rebel cause which he intended should triumph.[92] Recognition was certainly of practical value to the improvised Greek fleet, which could henceforth interdict quite legally the trade of neutrals with the Ottoman enemy. Canning, however, told the London officials of the Levant Company that the recognition had been provided at their insistence and for the benefit of their Eastern trade: it was supposed that if the Greek ships swarming in the sea-lanes of the Aegean were treated as belligerents then they might behave less like pirates. The Ionian Islands administration had already recognized the Greeks purely in order to protect Ionian shipping, and merchants in the Levant ports, like merchants in Liverpool – Canning's parliamentary constituency – were familiar with the devastation of Austrian shipping which resulted from Metternich's obstinate refusal to recognize Greek belligerency.[93] Recognition, therefore, was a measure proposed by many people who had little reason to like the Greeks. It was, for example, badly wanted by the generally pro-Ottoman British residents in the Levant. Canning said it was required by 'the facts' of the situation in 1823.[94]

Beyond this, he was quite unsure of what to do next. Like most incumbents of the Foreign Office, he shared the bureaucratic instinct of British officials to hammer policies out of materials supplied by other countries and foreign statesmen. This, as is generally acknowledged, he did with extraordinary skill, but it was not enough for pro-Greeks, who lost confidence in him and, from 1824, in the chances of Greek survival. Up to this point, the difference between Canning and his predecessor over Greece appears to be that Castlereagh would have been pleased, but Canning probably concerned and sad, if the Ottomans had managed to prevail. Like his countrymen in general, Canning was slow to respond to the Greek cause, inconstant in the attention he gave it, frequently chagrined by the behaviour of the revolutionaries themselves, and only led forward on their behalf when larger interests than those of the Greeks alone seemed to be involved.

Another explanation sometimes adduced to explain Canning's tardiness over Greece is to the effect that he thought time was on the side of the rebels. This, presumably, has to be argued by observers who baulk at the idea that Canning would ever have allowed the Greeks to go under. Temperley, for instance, writes of Canning's playing 'a lone hand in the Eastern Question, going farther than any Power in his recognition of the Greeks', and R.W. Seton-Watson refers to the foreign minister's 'skilful steering'. Douglas Dakin speaks of Canning paying lip-service to the European concert until 'he was ready for some master stroke'.[95] Where does the evidence actually point? Originally, the possibility of Greek victory seemed strong. But by 1824 Byron was dead, the Foreign Office was receiving doom-laden reports about civil war among the Greeks, the Sultan's formidable viceroy of Egypt, Muhammad Ali, had seized Crete, and in the spring of 1825 Ibrahim Pasha disembarked the first troops of the best army in the East on the western shores of the Morea. The British flag, it should be noted, floated above 25 of Egypt's chartered transport ships, the Austrian flag above 35.

By this time, Canning had been at the Foreign Office for almost three years, and had received various pleas from the Greeks to which, we are told, he was privately sympathetic. This may well be so, but in his official capacity he was very cautious, even grudging.[96] In 1823, Petrobey appealed to Canning for aid and protection for the Morea, but got no reply. In 1824, the foreign secretary refused an international conference on Greece, a refusal which advanced his plan to end diplomacy-by-congress, but left the Greeks in a very vulnerable situation. Also in 1824, Canning withdrew his close friend, Sir Charles Bagot, from the embassy at St Petersburg for discussing Greece without authorization from London.[97] Viscount Strangford, the British ambassador at Constantinople, was admonished for discussing Greek prospects with Sir Thomas Maitland, the British high commissioner in the Ionian Islands. The

Greek deputies in London had difficulty in obtaining interviews at the Foreign Office. In October 1824, the Foreign Enlistment Act was promulgated once more, and this time some volunteers in Greece were struck off the army and navy lists. The War Office recalled Leicester Stanhope. It is not clear that Canning was in any position to screen the volunteers from official censure, or that he wished he was. When Trelawny's relative, Sir Christopher Hawkins, called at the Foreign Office to solicit help in getting Trelawny out of trouble and out of Greece, Canning would not do anything in case his actions 'endangered the lives and the property of other British Subjects in the Turkish Empire'.[98] Canning also notified the Greek deputies that there was a likelihood that government action against volunteers abroad would get stronger yet. When the Greeks again tried to put themselves under British protection, this time by the formal Act of Submission in 1825, they were once more refused. Some Greeks thought any further appeal to London naïve. Others, according to Dakin, thought such an approach 'lacking in finesse', an unwise narrowing of options. Help might still come from other capitals than London. Presently, it did.

Had Canning been moving by 'skilful steering' towards a constructive, pro-Greek policy, something of it would surely have peeped out somewhere in his correspondence with Strangford. The correspondence in question is decidedly meagre, yet almost completely approving in its tone. Furthermore, Canning, who was not afraid to demote, proposed that Strangford should be promoted to St Petersburg, now the highest post in the British diplomatic service.[99] The appointment would please the tsar. But as Strangford was entitled to some months of leave first, Canning sent his own cousin, Stratford Canning, ahead of Strangford, to sound out Russian views on Greece. 'I think of putting the Greek question into his [Stratford's] hands and sending him on a special mission to St Petersburg to treat it there,' he explained to Bagot in mid-1824. Stratford only set out at the very end of the year, a leisurely tempo if diplomatic action was supposed to save the Greeks promptly. And yet it was not before time that Canning should now have decided to 'talk Greek' with the tsar of Russia.

Canning's leisurely style had worried Bagot for a long time. Bagot believed Russia would not be restrained forever from interference in the Greek crisis, and found evidence of this in the proposal, made by the tsar in the spring of 1823, to establish three self-governing Greek principalities in the South Balkans. The proposal caused uproar and indignation among the Greek leaders at the time, and has been belittled by historians ever since, but the main point was, as Bagot saw, that Russia had at last given notice, after a long silence on the subject, that she would not allow Greek fortunes to fall below a certain level, and certainly not as far as the annihilation which Metternich ardently desired, and which Canning would not, it seems, have resisted had the Ottomans been competent enough (they were strong enough) to present him with a *fait accompli*. It was the tsar who would accept no such *fait accompli*, and Bagot was anxious that Canning should not fall into the same trap as Metternich in thinking he might; 'be assured that no man living has him [the tsar] in hand'. Canning was not easily moved. 'I cannot conceal from myself that we as well as France have something to explain and extenuate with the Porte,' he declared, thinking of Graecophile volunteers who had gone to Greece.[100] As over Latin America, so over Greece, the prime minister, the earl of Liverpool, did more than support Canning. He pushed him at times. He pushed him now. In the summer of 1824, Canning had 'snubbed and snouched' Bagot for talking Greece with the tsar without authorization from London. The foreign secretary's argument was that Russia must resume first the diplomatic relations broken off with the Ottoman Empire in 1821, before there could be any international conferences on the subject of Greece. By the end of the same year, urged on by Liverpool and Bagot, he sent Stratford Canning to St Petersburg because he was finally converted to recognition of the dangers in his own waiting game. Once he had thought the Greeks would win their war with only informal foreign aid. He now came to see that it was their near collapse that might save them and that if Great Britain stood aside forever, Russia would not. 'Every success of the Turkish army renders the Greeks more and more objects of sympathy and compassion, and every failure contributes to place Turkey in the light of a more tempting and easy prey.' He therefore decided to ask 'with how much less than complete separation and independence Greece would be satisfied'. He addressed the question not to the Greeks themselves, but to the tsar.

Canning simply would not coerce the Sultan. 'To preserve the peace of the world is the leading policy of England,' he wrote. Most striking in the instructions to Stratford Canning is the foreign secretary's readiness to consider anything between 'unconditional submission' and 'unconditional independence'. One presumes he intended to exclude each of these extremes from consideration but it is hardly warrantable to claim that in these instructions Canning is seeking the means of 'giving freedom to Greece'. Rather, he was looking for a Russian initiative to which he might respond. The most conclusive proof of this lies in his instruction to his cousin that, should a formula for solving the Greek question be found in St Petersburg, he should press on to Constantinople to urge that formula on the Sultan. Stratford Canning, in fact, came home, and it was after his return, with news of the growing estrangement of Metternich from Alexander I, that Canning began to see the opportunity to subvert the Holy Alliance through the Greek issue. For the first time, he glimpsed that the Greeks might yet do unexpectedly well, and he began to speak of 'adjusting the balance of neutrality'. Yet when the Greek deputies approached him in 1825 for a British protectorate, he refused them again. He would not move faster than the tsar. To the Greek deputies, he explained that acceding to their request would be seen as 'territorial aggrandisement' by the other powers and would 'break up the present system of treaties'.[101] It therefore seems reasonable to conclude that, when the wheel of Greek fortune became stuck in the mud, it was Alexander I who got it turning again, by throwing off Metternich's restraints ostentatiously, and by making it plain to Stratford Canning during his visit to Russia that he was ready to work with Great Britain. The initiative Canning sought to give to the Russians was returned to him, and only then did he decide to find out what the Ottomans would accept by way of a compromise on Greece. Total independence hardly figured in his expectations or, more significantly, his wishes.

A multiplicity of other duties, so burdensome that they pulled down Canning's health relentlessly, are as important as his personal uncertainties in explaining the tardiness of his Greek policy. Until the end of 1824, when he could only discuss Greece with Stratford Canning in the intervals of a crowded parliamentary schedule, he was heavily involved, with the prime minister's aid, in winning a grudging Cabinet over to the recognition of the South American republics. The problems of Latin America, which he described as 'out of all proportion greater' than those of the Near East, helped, nevertheless, to clarify his thinking when he had more time to give to the latter area. For one thing, Latin America taught him to believe that a country which is powerless to retain its colonies (in this case, Spain) can hardly expect to have a serious voice in their disposal. For another, the promulgation of the Monroe Doctrine was a reminder of the dangers of falling behind in the diplomatic game. That doctrine showed Washington's interest in cutting away European toe-holds in the Americas, but also the credit to be reaped in Latin America from an anti-colonial stance. In the Near Eastern context, the Sultan's pretension to dispose of Greece in his own way sounded as empty as the promulgations of Madrid; the tsar was as likely to move on Greece as the United States had done in her hemisphere; there was even a hint in President Monroe's most famous speech that *his* countrymen might move to the aid of the Greeks while Great Britain hesitated.[102] To the lessons from the United States may be added some hints from Paris where the Société Philanthropique had just been established, with more grandiose schemes than those of the London Greek Committee: the Société believed that a French prince should rule a free Greece.

With the recognition of the new republics of the New World behind him, Canning was able to liquidate his long-standing quarrel with George IV – partly by terrifying the king with the intimation that he might retire from politics, but only after exposing the king's conspiracy with Metternich and the Russian ambassador, Prince Lieven, and his formidable wife, to be rid of his foreign secretary – to annihilate the remnant of Metternich's influence over the conduct of British diplomacy, and to discipline the Lievens, who were also ordered from St Petersburg to cultivate Canning with the same assiduity they had formerly given to subverting his position.[103] By 1825, therefore, Canning had come a very long way since the day, two years previously, when George IV told the Austrian envoy, Prince Esterhazy, that he detested Canning but could see no easy way to be rid of him.[104] Within months of the resolution of their estrangement, George IV became a champion of his foreign secretary, and society was amused to see Dorothea Lieven exerting her considerable charms, and successfully, over George Canning.

None of this brought immediate results for the Greeks. Stratford Canning returned from Russia in the spring of 1825, loitering in London for months before setting out for Constantinople with a new wife. Strangford, returned from Constantinople, was also dilatory in setting out for St Petersburg. Once there, he fell into Bagot's old trap, and discussed Greece without permission. For his rashness, he was silenced by Canning with a dispatch which has since become known as the 'padlock'.[105] The intention was that Stratford Canning should act the part of broker between Greeks and Ottomans and that Strangford should merely relay the eventual result to his hosts. It was too much for the new Baron Penshurst, who resigned his embassy in protest against his treatment. There was, nevertheless, one man in England who could not be snubbed, 'snouched', or padlocked, and that was the duke of Wellington. Sent to St Petersburg to congratulate the new tsar, Nicholas I, on his accession in 1826, the duke was drawn into signing the notorious protocol of St Petersburg, a document which set a term to Ottoman, *but finally to Canning's*, prevarications. The wheel of Greek fortune was turning again, and the issue rested no longer on Stratford Canning's brokerage. It rested on the menacing advocacy of Russia who now sent an ultimatum to the Sultan. Lord Holland was not far wrong in writing to Lord John Russell: 'We have somehow or another exasperated the two great Powers on the Continent – the Cabinet of St. Petersburg and the public opinion of France, and we have done so without serving ourselves, or our pretended Allies. . . . Neither Turks nor Greeks have to thank us.'[106]

The protocol of St Petersburg is the first diplomatic document to refer to Greece as a prospective political entity. Without proposing any frontiers, the protocol committed its signatories to the onerous task of persuading the Sultan to create a vassal state of Greece. The Greeks would pay an annual subsidy in return for complete control over their own political, religious, and economic life. Obviously, this was the longest forward step taken on behalf of the Greeks after five years of revolution, and when the details were leaked to *The Times*, it became an irreversible step, committing Canning more deeply than he had ever intended.[107] The foreign secretary had, of course, wanted a measure of collaboration with Russia, and most notably after Stratford Canning, writing from Constantinople, assured him that 'the Turkish government is dead to any consideration but that of force'. Furthermore, Canning had warned the Ottomans in return that their obduracy might yet end Great Britain's neutrality and oblige her to stop the fighting in Greece by means of a naval intervention. But his chief hope in sending Wellington to Russia, as he explained to Earl Granville, his ambassador at Paris, had been to restrain the Russians while keeping pressure on the Ottomans – 'to save the Greeks through the agency of the Russian name upon the fears of Turkey *without a war*' (my italics).[108] Unfortunately, an ultimatum was sent to the Ottoman Empire while Wellington was still in Russia, thus fulfilling Bagot's erstwhile warnings that the tsar would not be restrained forever, and while Great Britain herself was not a party to that ultimatum, the protocol came so closely on its heels that Ottoman ministers believed, not unreasonably, that they saw Great Britain aligned behind Russia. Looking back through the foreign secretary's memoranda and dispatches, one sees how earnestly he had tried to avoid giving this impression, how much he had wanted an exactly opposite situation to obtain, one in which Russian power stood restrained behind Great Britain's diplomacy. His instructions to Bagot had played up the idea that, if the tsar lost patience and proceeded against the Sultan, he would do so alone, abandoned by conservatives like Metternich, but abandoned too by Great Britain, a country which 'would not see the Turkish power destroyed'. To Stratford Canning, he had explained that the Ottomans should give their particular trust to the British since 'we are at present free from all arrangements with other Powers', and as late as October 1825 he was still insisting that 'things are not yet ripe for our interference'. The Greek situation was transformed then, not by the protocol alone, but by the protocol seen, as the world saw it, in conjunction with the Russian ultimatum to the Sultan.[109]

The Russian ultimatum[110] made no reference whatever to Greece, a subject the tsar left, as we have seen, to the implementation of the protocol. By the ultimatum, the Sultan was given six weeks in which to withdraw the Ottoman troops which had loitered in the Principalities since suppressing the first Greek uprising, led by Alexandros Ipsilantis, in 1821. The Russians took the trouble to recapitulate in great detail the rights and privileges of the peoples of the Principalities and of Serbia, and delivered these on the point of a sword. News of the protocol, superadded to the ultimatum, persuaded Mahmud II to give way, and his delegates negotiated his surrender in the convention of Akerman, signed in October. By then, the British foreign secretary was in Paris, discussing the possibility of expanding the protocol into a treaty to which the French foreign minister, the count of Villèle, was anxious that France should be a party.

The timing is of great interest. A few months before, the foreign secretary had notified the prime minister that 'the time approaches when something must be done' to resolve the impasse in the Near East, but he refused to budge until 'Austria as well as France has put into our hands the dealing – first with Russia and then with the parties to the war'.[111] The minister who visited Paris in the summer of 1826, to lay the ground for the eventual treaty of London, was highly excited about Austria's imminent isolation and humiliation. Canning wrote to Stratford Canning as if the Austro-Russian rift produced by the protocol was somehow due to him and his policy: 'I have resolved them [the Holy Alliance powers of Austria, Russia and Prussia] into individuality, and having done so, employ the *disjecta membra* each in its own respective place . . . without scruple or hesitation.'[112] On 6 July 1827, the momentous treaty was finally signed in London, which had now become the negotiating centre of the Greek crisis. The treaty put teeth into the protocol of the year before. The three signatory powers, Great Britain, Russia and France, agreed to put 'a term to the sanguinary struggle which', while producing anarchy in Greece, 'brings each day fresh obstacles to the commerce of the European nations'. The decision to stop the fighting had been taken.[113] A month later on 8 August, Canning died, and so never lived to hear of the battle of Navarino.

Like Prince Bismarck after him, Canning has been credited with greater initiatives than were actually at his disposal. Like the great German again, his narrow power base led him to work hard for royal support. Canning's ambitious nature, and his acute awareness of his personal vulnerability within the Tory party, turned him into an orchestrator of public opinion, seeking from an extra-parliamentary audience the support which Cabinet and party colleagues were ever on the brink of withholding. Had he lived to hear of Navarino, the odds are that he would have interpreted the 'untoward event' as a triumph for his Greek policy, and the world might have forgotten how shuffling and improvised that policy really was. Indeed, the world *did* forget, for over a century.

It was left to three of the European powers to resolve the long crisis, and rescue the Greeks, with an inadvertent show of irresistible force at Navarino on 20 October 1827. It has been common, at least in British writing, to treat Navarino and the consequent creation of Greece as a posthumous triumph for George Canning's diplomatic persistence and liberal intent, and the reader may feel there is still something to that claim. If, however, notice is taken of the new state as actually set up, it will be apparent that the mutual distrust and shuffling manoeuvres of the leading international personalities, *which feelings Canning exhibited as much as any*, persisted to the end, and had been there from the beginning. The new state was an impoverished peninsula with well under a million people. There was considerable debate over whether or not it should contain Athens. Taken from the heathen ruler of Constantinople it was placed under a German princeling at least as alien, who had no Greek and would not give up his Roman Catholic faith to gratify his new subjects. Nineteenth-century Greece became a byword for poverty, corruption, and petty despotism, a sorry piece of international handiwork. Its politics were anything but democratic and the first king had eventually to be turned out. Most important perhaps, there was a change of management but no social revolution. Few, except urban, Greeks were better off than before and the new Greece was much as Byron and Canning would have forecast.

His low estimate of the prospects for a new Greek state had much to do with Canning's hesitancy in trying to produce one. The man was almost untouched by romantic liberalism and regarded himself as an enlightened Tory; as such he believed, as we would expect of an opponent of parliamentary reform, that popular government does not guarantee good government. On the other hand, his Irish background was of a kind which made him sympathetic to the removal of Catholic disabilities, and he can have had no quarrel with the idea of reducing the area of operation of the religious obscurantism of the Ottomans. Disposed by education and tastes towards philhellenism, Canning was nevertheless only a very reluctant Graecophile, a common enough combination for one of his time and social standing. As a realist, he saw increasing awkwardness in making a stand on behalf of revolutionaries who seemed barely able to sustain their position as belligerents. Also as a realist, he doubted that the democratic instinct burned in every Greek heart, or that it should be expected to do so in a poor society marked by much feudal subservience and political illiteracy. He always spoke, upon the basis of what evidence it would be instructive to know, as if the case for South American independence were far better founded in social and political realities.

At the level of action, therefore, Canning was without a preconsidered Greek 'policy', and what now passes under that title suggests that Canning was far more interested in proceeding according to certain principles of diplomatic action than in achieving a definable Greek goal. The best he expected for the Greeks was some degree of autonomy consistent with continuing Ottoman suzerainty, an idea which could have come from the analogous case of the Danubian Principalities, or even from his Indian experience at the board of control. He did not exploit every passing opportunity to advance the Greek cause; there were some opportunities between 1822 and 1827 which he could not exploit, but also some he did not choose to exploit. This caused disappointment and agony in Greece as the revolutionary power base narrowed and crumbled. What were the underlying principles which guided, but also sometimes restrained, George Canning? They include an anxious fear of becoming enmeshed in and immobilized by congress diplomacy; a preference for dealing with foreign courts in turn rather than simultaneously; a not quite forgivable vanity in wanting to reap as much personal credit as possible; above all, a great fear of defeat, born, no doubt, of his personal vulnerability in British politics. Over Greece and other causes, he at times moved more slowly than other statesmen would have done, and mainly because, as John Wilson Croker so accurately said of him, Canning often kept a sharper eye on the problems on his flanks than the main ones in front of him. Canning defended his own slowness, sometimes by pretending he had a master-plan, sometimes by producing some variation of his motto that 'procrastination is akin to sleep'. Now procrastination is nothing of the kind, and there were, fortunately, men like Bagot and Liverpool to remind him that breaking the barometer does not hold up the weather. In such moments, Canning is telling us that he was often in the position of wishing to exercise none of the options open to him, while lacking the means to produce the one he did want: it is a confession of powerlessness dressed up in the language of the waiting game. His constructive action over Greece belongs to the last 18 months of his life, and to the task of converting the protocol of St Petersburg into an international instrument for mediating the Ottoman–Greek struggle. Using Croker's imagery again, we can reasonably conclude that Canning's Greek policy was protracted by his determination to resolve some of those side-issues as he went along, most particularly the isolation of Austria, the humiliation of Prince Metternich, and the dissolution of congress diplomacy. But nothing, as he said himself, 'for Epaminondas and St. Paul', except as residual legatees.

NOTES

1. W.E. Meade, *The Grand Tour in the Eighteenth Century* (New York, 1914); W.G. Rice, 'Early English Travellers in Greece and the Levant', *Essays and Studies in English and Comparative Literature* (1933), pp. 205–60; B.H. Stern, *Rise of Romantic Hellenism in English Literature, 1732–86* (Menasha, 1940); T. Spencer, *Fair Greece, Sad Relic* (London, 1954).
2. Spencer, *Fair Greece*, p. viii.
3. W.C. Browne, 'The Popularity of English Travel Books about the Near East, 1775–1825', *Philological Quarterly*, xv (1936), 70–80; xvi (1937), 249–71; same, 'Byron and English Interest in the Near East', *Studies in Philology*, xxxiv (1937), 55–64.
4. A reviewer in the *Quarterly Review*, xi. 458, quoted in Spencer, *Fair Greece*, p. 229.
5. Hobhouse was not always shocked by initials. He thought it 'agreeable' to find those of Lord Aberdeen on a column at Delphi; see Lord Broughton (i.e. Hobhouse), *Travels in Albania in 1809 and 1810* (London, 1858), i. 247.
6. From such notebooks, travellers wrote their volumes for publication. Hobhouse, anxious to record everything, took two gallons of ink and vast quantities of paper on his travels. No one could speak as an expert on the basis of classical knowledge alone: one had to know the writings of other travellers. Byron drew heavily on travel books, and quoted them in his footnotes, to show the authenticity of his poetical settings. For *The Giaour, The Bride of Abydos, Childe Harold*, etc., he drew on E.D. Clarke, W.G. Browne, Sir William Gell, J.L. Burckhardt, Henry Holland, and numerous others. In its turn, his verse became a guidebook of sorts, so that Holland, visiting the court of Ali Pasha, remarked that Byron had 'admirably characterised this scene, as he saw it in the Seraglio of the Vizier at Tepelini. His pictures are as minutely accurate in their descriptive details as they are splendid and imposing in the poetry'. Byron, in his first Eastern journey, met Ali Pasha at Tepelini. See Peter Quennell, *Byron: A Self Portrait: Letters and Diaries* (London, 1950), i. 58.

7. Rev. Robert Walsh, *A Residence at Constantinople, during . . . the Commencement, Progress, and Termination of the Greek and Turkish Revolutions* (London, 1836).
8. Ibid., i. 208.
9. Ibid., pp. 149–63.
10. Ibid., p. 172.
11. Ibid., p. 134.
12. Ibid., pp. 299–322.
13. Walsh was sympathetic without being sanguine, and detected the same chronic lack of purpose among the Greeks which was to confound so many of the European volunteers who fought in Greece after 1821. After a night in a leaky hut on Antiparos, he wrote (*A Residence*, i. 165): 'All their winters are equally severe, yet they take no precaution to guard against them, as if, like the grasshopper, they thought it would always be summer . . . there is not a roof that will keep out rain, I believe, in all the Cyclades.'
14. C.M. Woodhouse, *The Philhellenes* (Rutherford, 1971), p. 24 *et seq*.
15. To his mother, 28 May 1809, in Quennell, *Byron*, i. 58.
16. *Letters of John B.S. Morritt of Rokeby, Descriptive of Journeys in Europe and Asia Minor in the Years 1794–1796*, ed. C.E. Marindin (London, 1914), quoted in Spencer, *Fair Greece*, p. 232.
17. One of the most-read books of this kind, by S.N. Douglas, was specifically called *An Essay on Certain Points of Resemblance between the Ancient and Modern Greeks* (London, 1813).
18. Walsh, *A Residence*, i. 167.
19. Virginia Penn, 'Philhellenism in England – Part I', *Slavonic Review*, xiv (1936), 364; for Part II, see pp. 647–60.
20. W. St Clair, *That Greece Might Still Be Free* (London, 1972), p. 356.
21. Ibid., p. 101.
22. Ibid., p. 372.
23. For a complete membership list, see Woodhouse, *Philhellenes*, appendix II. Blaquière is often called a committee member, but he was not one, although he was the committee's most indefatigable servant, and made its greatest catch, Byron, for which see below. See also E.S. de Beer and W. Seton, 'Byroniana: The Archives of the London Greek Committee', *Nineteenth Century*, c (1926), 396–412; Penn, 'Philhellenism', Part II.
24. De Beer, 'Byroniana', p. 397.
25. E. Blaquière, *The Greek Revolution* (London, 1824), p. 352.
26. St Clair, *That Greece Might Still Be Free*, p. 143.
27. T.S. Hughes, *An Address to the People of England in the Cause of the Greeks, Occasioned by the Late Inhuman Massacres in the Isle of Scio* (London, 1822), and *Considerations upon the Greek Revolution* (London, 1823); Rev. R. Chatfield, *An Appeal to the British Public in the Cause of the Persecuted Greeks* (London, 1822), and *A Further Appeal* (London, 1823); Lord Erskine, *An Appeal to the People of Great Britain on the Subject of Confederated Greece* (London, 1824).
28. D. Dakin, *The Greek Struggle for Independence, 1821–1833* (Berkeley, 1973), p. 109.
29. Blaquière, *Greek Revolution*, p. 317.
30. Ibid., pp. 286, 352.
31. Ibid., p. 305.
32. Ibid., p. 303 n. The book was actually rushed into print to counteract the poor publicity the Greeks were receiving for their barbarous fighting methods, but

even more because the value of the first Greek bonds slipped badly in 1824. Bowring was in a great panic, and showed up badly, forcing the Greeks to buy back the bonds he had originally purchased, but insisting on repurchasing them when the price rose again. For details, see St Clair, *That Greece Might Still Be Free*, pp. 205–23.
33. Blaquière, *Greek Revolution*, p. 309.
34. G. Finlay, *History of Greece*, ed. H.R. Tozer (Oxford, 1877), vi. 434 *et seq.*, says Hume and Bowring were 'deeply embedded in the pastry which Cobbett called the Greek pie', that Burdett floated 'on the cream of Radicalism', with Hobhouse 'supporting himself above the thin milk of Whiggery by holding vigorously at the baronet's [i.e. Burdett's] coat-tails'. For the details, see Penn, 'Philhellenism', Part II.
35. Ibid., p. 655.
36. In its first phase, the Greek struggle was sustained by German and Swiss money and volunteers; the British and 'Byronic' phase ran from spring 1823 to the end of 1824; the most effective foreign volunteer intervention came after that, when the centre of European Graecophilism moved to Paris.
37. His travelling companion, Hobhouse, wrote up their adventures in *Travels in Albania*. Byron's own diary of the journey was destroyed at Hobhouse's request, seemingly because of the candour with which it revealed the poet's homosexual experiences.
38. Harold Nicolson, *Byron: The Last Journey* (London, 1924), p. 69.
39. Woodhouse, *Philhellenes*, p. 92.
40. H. Spender, *Byron and Greece* (London, 1924), p. 15.
41. De Beer, 'Byroniana', p. 399.
42. L.A. Marchand, *Byron: A Biography* (New York, 1957), iii. 1,116.
43. Pietro Gamba to Hobhouse, 20 April 1824, quoted in the prologue to Doris L. Moore's superb volume, *The Late Lord Byron* (Philadelphia, 1961).
44. 'Had he lived I am not sure that he could not one day or the other have had cause to regret that he had not fallen by the fevers of Messolonghi, just as Pompey grieved that he had not died in Campania', quoted in Marchand, *Byron*, iii. 1239.
45. G. Valetas, *Korais* (Athens, 1965), ii. 438.
46. St Clair, *That Greece Might Still Be Free*, p. 152.
47. A. Maurois, *Byron* (New York, 1930), p. 491.
48. Byron's premonitions of imminent death were reinforced by recollections of a fortune-teller's prediction, when he was still a boy, that his 37th year would be his last; see Maurois, ibid., pp. 47, 356. In 1823 and 1824, we find him saying, 'I should prefer a grey Greek stone . . . to Westminster Abbey', Woodhouse, *Philhellenes*, p. 99. To Goethe, he promised to visit Weimar and do personal homage 'if ever I come back'; *The Works of Lord Byron: Letters and Journals*, ed. R. E. Prothero (London, 1898–1901), vi. 237. To Medwin, he declared, 'I mean to return to Greece and shall in all probability die there', Maurois, *Byron*, p. 379. He had a great fear of ending his days like Swift, 'a grinning idiot', Marchand, *Byron*, iii. 1,187. To Trelawny, he said, 'If I live another year you will see this scene [of Stromboli at night] in a 5th Canto of *Childe Harold*', Marchand, ibid., p. 1,095.
49. After Byron's death, Leicester Stanhope informed Hobhouse, 'Byron was sorry now and again that he ever came to Greece. He expressed anger at the Greek Committee for publishing his letter from Genoa in which he talked of going, so that when his intention was made known, he thought himself bound

to act up to it'; in Lord Broughton, *Recollections of a Long Life* (London, 1865), iii. 160.
50. To Trelawny, *Works of Byron*, vi. 224.
51. Metropolitan Ignatios to Mavrokordatos, July 1823, quoted in R. Fletcher, 'Byron in Nineteenth-Century Greek Literature', *The Struggle for Greek Independence*, ed. R. Clogg (London, 1973), p. 229.
52. Byron to Mavrokordatos, 7 Sept. 1823, in de Beer, 'Byroniana', p. 405.
53. Ibid., p. 406.
54. Ibid., p. 409.
55. Finlay, *History of Greece*, vi. 325; Marchand, *Byron*, iii. 1,123. 'I shall fulfil the object of my mission for the committee – and then (probably) return into Italy for it does not seem likely that as an individual I can be of use to them.'
56. *Works of Byron*, vi. 430.
57. J. Kennedy, *Conversations on Religion with Lord Byron* (London, 1830), p. 299. Gamba said candidly that Byron 'had imbibed a greater personal esteem for the character of the Turks than for their slaves'; see Marchand, *Byron*, iii. 1,115. His doctor, Julius Millingen, asked Byron why he had come to Greece at all when his sentiments were so strongly anti-Greek. 'Heartily weary of the monotonous life I had led in Italy . . . sickened with pleasure, more tired of scribbling than the public [was of reading it] I felt the urgent necessity of giving a completely new direction to the course of my idea; and the active, dangerous yet glorious scenes of the military career struck my fancy.' See Julius Millingen, *Memoirs of the Affairs of Greece* (London, 1831), p. 6.
58. Trelawny to Mary Shelley, 24 Oct. 1823, in Marchand, *Byron*, iii. 1,131.
59. Moore, *Late Lord Byron*, pp. 173–5.
60. E.J. Trelawny, *Recollections of the Last Days of Shelley and Byron* (London, 1858), p. 202.
61. Marchand, *Byron*, iii. 1,159. Uniforms fascinated Byron; an inventory of those he took from Genoa is in ibid., iii. 1,098 n. For the 'very magnifiques' Albanian clothes he could not resist buying in earlier years, see Byron to his mother, 12 Nov. 1809, in Quennell, *Byron*, i. 58.
62. Sir W. Napier, *Life and Opinions of General Sir Charles Napier* (London, 1857), i. 336.
63. Theotokis to Delladecima, 27 Sept. 1823, in de Beer, 'Byroniana', p. 408.
64. Ibid., p. 407.
65. Byron to H. Drury, 3 May 1810, in Quennell, *Byron*, i. 64.
66. Millingen, *Memoirs*, p. 90.
67. Byron to Douglas Kinnaird, 23 Dec. 1823, *Works of Byron*, vi. 287–9.
68. Marchand, *Byron*, iii. 1,157.
69. W. Parry, *The Last Days of Lord Byron* (London, 1825), p. 40.
70. Hobhouse to Byron, 23 Feb. 1824, *Lord Byron's Correspondence*, ed. J. Murray New York, 1922), ii. 294.
71. De Beer, 'Byroniana', p. 411, claims that 'Meyer alone of the men at Missolonghi died in action . . . and that . . . all the others deserted Greece'. Not quite true, but true enough. For a more detailed analysis, see St Clair, *That Greece Might Still Be Free*, ch. 19.
72. Woodhouse, *Philhellenes*, p. 71.
73. The lungs were deposited in the church of St Spiridion, and their fate is not known. The town of Missolonghi was almost destroyed when the Ottomans recaptured it in 1826.
74. Spiridion Tricoupi, *Histoire de la Révolution Grecque* (1862), iii. 341.

75. Fletcher, 'Byron', p. 241.
76. Hobouse said there was 'not the slightest necessity even in appearance for his [Byron's] going abroad', but as others have pointed out, this was Hobhouse 'shutting off remembrance' of such occasions as the famous entertainment at Lady Jersey's where the guests all walked out as Byron walked in with his half-sister, Augusta, on his arm. See Moore, *Late Lord Byron*, p. 295.
77. *London Magazine*, x (1824), 114.
78. St Clair, *That Greece Might Still Be Free*, p. 228 *et seq.*
79. *British Intelligence of Events in Greece, 1824–1827: A Documentary Collection*, ed. David Dakin (Athens, 1959), p. 14 *et seq.*
80. C.M. Woodhouse, *Capodistrias*, (London, 1973), pp. 199, 299.
81. L. Stanhope, *Greece in 1823 and 1824* (London, 1827), pp. 12–15; C.W. Crawley, 'John Capodistrias and the Greeks before 1821', *Cambridge Historical Journal*, xiii (1957), 162–82.
82. C.M. Woodhouse, *Capodistrias*, pp. 209–14; *Correspondence of Castlereagh*, xii. 140–6, 162–4.
83. Woodhouse, *Capodistrias*, p. 298.
84. Castlereagh to Strangford, 20 Jan., 29 April, 9 and 29 July 1822, FO 78/105.
85. *Despatches, Correspondence, and Memoranda of Field Marshal Arthur, Duke of Wellington, K.G.*, ed. duke of Wellington (London, 1867–80), i. 284; H.W.V. Temperly, *The Foreign Policy of Canning, 1822–1827* (London, 1925), pp. 13–17, 165–8; Dakin, *Greek Struggle*, p. 148.
86. H.W.V. Temperley, 'Joan Canning on Her Husband's Policy and Ideas', *English Historical Review*, xiv (1930), 409–26; A.G. Stapleton, *Political Life of George Canning* (London, 1837) and *George Canning and His Times* (London, 1859); H.W.V. Temperley, *England and the Near East: The Crimea* (London, 1936), p. 52.
87. P.J.V. Rolo, *George Canning* (London, 1965), p. 263.
88. Temperley, *Canning*, says (p. 329) 'Canning had known Byron well', but the poet told John Murray that the only prominent minister known to him was Robert Peel. See Marchand, *Byron*, i. 480.
89. Woodhouse, *Philhellenes*, p. 86.
90. Blaquière, *Greek Revolution*, pp. 322–3.
91. Woodhouse, *Capodistrias*, p. 309.
92. Dakin, *Greek Struggle*, p. 150.
93. V.J. Puryear, 'Odessa, Its Rise and International Importance, 1815–50', *Pacific Historical Review*, iii (1934), 192–215; M.S. Anderson, *The Eastern Question* (New York, 1966), p. 60.
94. Byron remarked (de Beer, 'Byroniana', p. 206): 'The Greeks are acting in my opinion neither wisely nor well in permitting for a moment the predatory detention of Ionian vessels – if they choose to commence privateering – be it so – but let it be without pretensions to any better excuse than that of necessity.'
95. Temperley, *Canning*, p. 344 *et seq.*; R.W. Seton-Watson, *Britain in Europe* (Cambridge, 1938), p. 102; Dakin, *Greek Struggle*, p. 152.
96. To Granville, 3 Jan. 1825, he explains that 'doing nothing is often a measure, and full as important a one, as the most diligent activity': Stapleton, *Canning*, p. 609. To Bagot, 22 Jan. 1824, he explains that 'blessed is he who invented procrastination, for it is akin to sleep'; *George Canning and His Friends*, ed. J. Bagot (London, 1909), ii. 214.
97. Canning's pre-condition for talking about the Greeks with Alexander I was the resumption of Russo-Ottoman relations, broken off in 1821. Bagot took

The Philhellenes and Greek Independence

the *appointment* of a new ambassador, Ribeaupierre, as sufficient warrant for him to attend discussions on the Greeks. Canning did not. He wanted Ribeaupierre in Constantinople first. Bagot claimed the Russians duped him. See Canning to Bagot, 29 July 1824, and Bagot to Canning, August 1824, *Canning and His Friends*, pp. 242, 257, 265, 269.

98. Moore, *Late Lord Byron*, p. 205.
99. For Strangford, see above ch. V.
100. Seton-Watson, *Britain in Europe*, p. 101; Wellington, *Despatches*, ii. 535.
101. Dakin, *Greek Struggle*, pp. 152, 154, 175.
102. Temperley, *Canning*, pp. 121–31, 145–51; for the interraction of American and Greek affairs in Canning's thinking, see Canning to Bagot, 22 Jan. 1824, *Canning and His Friends*, ii. 214.
103. Temperley, *Canning*, pp. 240–58.
104. Ibid., p. 147.
105. The 'padlock' is in Canning to Strangford, 31 Dec. 1825, FO 65/181; Strangford described its effect to Bagot, 4 Feb. 1826 (in *Canning and His Friends*, ii. 329) as follows, 'I have served my country with tolerable success for four-and-twenty years abroad. It is hard to be treated . . . as if I were a troublesome child, with a thump on the back, and a peevish, "Be quiet!".'
106. *Early Correspondence of Lord John Russell, 1805–40*, ed. Rollo Russell (London, 1913), i. 296.
107. Text of the Protocol is in *Recueil d'actes internationaux de l'Empire Ottoman*, ed. G. Noradounghian (Paris, 1900), ii. 114; Theodor Schiemann, *Geschichte Russlands unter Kaiser Nikolaus I* (Berlin, 1904–19), ii. 139; Wellington, *Despatches*, ii. 470.
108. Canning to Granville, 13 Jan. 1826, in Stapleton, *Canning*, p. 470.
109. Seton-Watson, *Britain in Europe*, p. 110; Temperley, *Canning*, p. 343; Canning to Granville, 31 Oct. 1825, in Stapleton, *Canning*, p. 446.
110. *Recueil d'actes internationaux*, ii. 116.
111. Canning to Liverpool, 25 Oct. 1825, in Stapleton, *Canning*, p. 468.
112. S. Lane-Poole, *Life of Stratford Canning* (London, 1888), i. 431.
113. *Recueil d'actes internationaux*, ii. 130.

CHAPTER VIII

Stratford Canning, Mahmud II, and Greece

Stratford's instructions from the Foreign Office in October 1825 for his second mission to Constantinople were quite straightforward: Greece was to be his sole preoccupation.[1] It was not his duty to get a Russian ambassador back to Constantinople: 'His Majesty's government does not intend that your Excellency should take up the burden which Lord Strangford has laid down.' Very little was to be said about the past, except to assure the Ottomans that the long absence of any British ambassador bore no relation to the reasons for which Russia withheld hers. There was no 'diminished interest' in London in the cause of Ottoman integrity, and the Sultan's ministers must draw a clear line between the philhellene activities of private British subjects and the British government. Pro-Greek propaganda and organizations, organized by the Lord Mayor of London or other public men, were entirely without government backing and beyond government control. If the old complaint was raised against recognition of the Greeks in 1823 as belligerents, Stratford was to stress that 'a certain degree of force and consistency, acquired by any mass of population engaged in war, entitles that population to be treated as a belligerent'. The Ottoman government had not quashed, and could not quash, the revolt, and the Greek captains ruled the seas. It was unrealistic to treat as pirates a maritime fighting force which 'covers the sea with its cruisers', and the Sultan would be wise to face facts now. 'Most earnestly do we wish that the Ottoman Porte . . . incline its ear to the advice of its friends, and set about the pacification of Greece while the contest is as yet unentangled with foreign aid and alliance.'

So far, Canning appeared to be arguing impartially from the facts of the real situation, but further passages in the instructions admitted, perhaps as a result of Stratford's pressure, that no Christian power would side with the Ottomans, while more than one might side with the Greeks: 'There is not a nation in Europe that would side with the Porte against the Greeks' and to suppose 'that Greece can ever be brought back to what she was in relation to the Porte is vain'. There was even a danger of transatlantic interference as 'all the inhabitants of both Americas, to a man, are in their hearts, favourers of the Greek cause; and might, at no distant period, become active co-operators in it'.

In thus invoking the New World to justify redressing the balance of the Old, Canning was stretching truth to suit his own ends – he would have been the first to object to American intervention. It was also decidedly inaccurate to imply that neither Austria nor Prussia would approve a restoration of Ottoman power in Greece. Nevertheless, Canning invited the Sultan to entrust a mediation to the one power which was still uncommitted. And what would Britain do if her offer of help was accepted? As the Greeks had approached her ministers in October 1825 with an Act of Submission, a route of communication with the rebels now existed. Britain could find out what the Greeks wanted, and submit these terms to the consideration of the Sultan.

Scarlet fever, which devastated Stratford's party at Corfu and detained him there for some weeks, gave him an opportunity to anticipate his instructions by finding out in advance the terms the Greeks wanted. His idea was simply to save time, but the fact of his having been in conclave with Greek representatives first did not help the Ottoman government to recognize him as an honest broker when he eventually reached Constantinople. Nearness to the seat of war undoubtedly raised Stratford's Greek sympathies, and in Corfu, whence he was able to look across to the rough mountains of the immortal land, he heard tales of butchery and reprisal which filled him with horror and dismay. Missolonghi was under an Ottoman siege, the Peloponnese virtually Egyptian. On 8 January 1826, his transport lay through the night within the steep encircling harbour at Cerigo. The village lights shone out boldly, although Ibrahim's headquarters were only at Modon, and the Ottoman kaptan pasha at Patras had 80 warships to carry out his patrols. Gazing on some impudently small privateering craft, Stratford found his thoughts dwelling on 'those most noble and redeeming features of the Greek character which ages of ruthless oppression have not been able to efface'.²

Through Captain Hamilton, the most active of British captains on the Ionian station and the best known to the Greek provisional government, Stratford enquired if the authorities at Napoli di Romania wished to make any use of his good offices at the Porte. The reply was a personal visit, when Stratford reached Hydra, from Konstantine Zographos and Alexander Mavrocordates of the Greek provisional government. 'I could only receive them privately,' Stratford says in his memoirs, 'with such reserves as my official character and due respect for a friendly power [the Ottoman Empire] imposed', but the qualification must have been lost on his guests who saw his whole mission as Canning's response to the Act of Submission. On the other hand, they remembered that Canning had answered the demand of their deputies in London – a demand for independence as the only alternative to a fight to the finish – with an offer to do his best, when the moment came, to obtain a 'fair and safe compromise', and Mavrocordates took a less intransigent and fatalistic line with Stratford.³

The military plight of the Greeks also made it necessary for the provisional government to lower its terms, and Stratford was glad to hear that semi-independent status was now acceptable to it. Tribute would be offered the Sultan, and compensation for Turks who elected to leave the new principality. Desperate though their predicament was, the two visitors said the Greek provisional government must stand firm on one matter: no region which had been in revolt could be surrendered to the Ottomans again. Stratford did not have to ask why. In reply, he said he thought something could be done on this basis, and that the frontiers of a new Greek principality would present the greatest problem of all. This proved to be only too true. During these conversations, which took place on 9 January, a small vessel brought news from Hydra to the effect that Alexander I had died on 1 December. Stratford could not see Constantine, the tyrant of Poland, dallying over Greece as his predecessor had done, and decided to get to Constantinople as quickly as possible. In London, Canning heard the 'lamentable and astounding' news on 3 January, and wrote to Stratford: 'I am not one jot abated of my preference for separate intervention.'⁴

Stratford was speeded on his way by a visit from Andreas

Miaulis, the famous Greek admiral. 'Nothing could be more desponding than the language of this intrepid man,' who said that if the Egyptians could take Missolonghi in the next four weeks, then the war for independence would collapse.[5] Ibrahim, Miaulis told him, had cleverly avoided landing at Athens, which would have involved him in a bitter struggle at the isthmus of Corinth, and made a master-stroke by putting his troops ashore in the western Morea, and from thence biting deeply into the neighbouring territory, north as far as Patras, east to Tripolizza. Ibrahim had 12,000 regulars alone, and a swarm of irregulars: by contrast, the effective Greek fighting force was about 1,500, and had to be reinforced for any especially ambitious operation. Against the large Ottoman naval force at Patras, Miaulis went on, he could muster 30 vessels at most. As an islander, Miaulis blamed the mainland Greeks for this desperate situation, and he said that unless the provisional government gave up entirely its grandiose ideas of a large, autonomous territory, the exhausted and ravaged islands would have to make a separate deal with the Sultan. The political leaders were all squabbling, no one ever got paid, no authority commanded universal respect. Miaulis dreamed of salvation from abroad, more particularly from Britain. Lord Cochrane had been engaged by the Greek Committee in London to come and command the Greek effort by sea. One day soon perhaps, financed by Britain, with crews inspired by the love of freedom, the Greeks would demolish Turkish and Egyptian sea power, and Greece would be reborn. Stratford sighed for such a solution: it was the only easy one he could envisage.

A day or two later, he put in at Ipsara, with its neat terrace of houses running along the sunlit quay.

> The admiral's steward went ashore with the full expectation of finding a market well stocked with all the objects he required. Imagine his surprise when the truth broke upon him. A deathly silence indoors as well as without, not a voice, not a footstep, not an inhabitant; the town a mere shell, plausible to the eye, but utterly void of life.

That afternoon, Stratford went ashore for some shooting and came across a heap of dead women and children at the bottom of a cliff, with two tattered ghouls combing through the human debris: 'Heavens, how I longed to be the instrument of repairing such calamities by carrying my mission of peace and deliverance to a successful issue.'⁶ On 4 February, Stratford reached the Dardanelles, and as he and his suite transferred to a sloop for the last leg of their long journey to Constantinople, the ship's band played the Greek national anthem. Stratford, quite overcome, wept, not for the Greeks alone, but for the whole human tragedy. For a month more, his transport was held up by contrary winds, but Stratford could not wait. He took horse at Canakkale and, leaving wife, suite, baggage, and papers to follow when they could, rode to Lapsaki, crossed to Rodosto (Tekirdag), and reached Constantinople after a three nights' journey.

> The latter part of our road stretched along the walls of old Stamboul, and just as I turned round the last tower to get into the town at the head of its harbour, a large horned owl, enlivened by the dusk, hooted from the ivy in which it was nestled. So close was the sound to my ear, and so dismal was its tone, that it seemed to follow up our previous vexations, and to indicate a fresh series of mischances on shore.⁷

Canning had warned Stratford that the British palace in Pera would be in a 'dilapidated and dangerous' condition, but Stratford was astonished that the changeable Bosporus climate could ravage so intemperately, and in little over a dozen years, a building on which Robert Adair had spent thousands of pounds. Once more, the palace was a wreck, and Stratford took up residence in the summer house at Tarabya, built of wood in the traditional style, with wide eaves and long shuttered windows, hot in summer, cold in winter, exposed to the blasts of the violent wind which blew from the Black Sea, yet retrieved from all these disadvantages by standing upon one of the most exquisite sites in the world. Repairs to the palace were put in hand once more, and Mrs Canning was allowed to cultivate her domestic talents on a grand scale, selecting curtains, furniture, lights, and carpets with little regard for expense – after all, it was George Canning who passed the bills. Life was easier in another respect which gratified Stratford very much. There was no longer a Levant Company to deal with. Its consuls and other servants, including the dragomans, now came under the undivided control of the embassy, and Stratford had power to make vice-consuls at discretion, and pay them £33 a year. It was his power to unmake, nevertheless, which made the staff rather anxious as it lined up before him for the first time, and he was determined that the dragomans in particular should feel the lash of discipline as they had never felt it before. It galled him to have to distribute £2,200 as bounty on Strangford's recommendation among men whose loyalties seemed so dubious, who spoke English with an exotic accent when they knew it at all, and whose cronies were the equally unreliable dragomans of other embassies.[8] William Turner, the official sent out from home to wind up the affairs of the Levant Company, seemed to justify all his suspicions of these Levantine servants by disclosing that the first dragoman, Francis Chabert, was divulging embassy information to the Prussians and the Austrians, and exchanging coded letters with his former chief, the pro-Metternichian Strangford, now ensconced in St Petersburg. For the moment, Stratford chose to conduct diplomatic relations at the Porte through the nominal third dragoman, Frederick Pisani, resolving to take up the whole question of interpreters with his cousin when he had an opportunity to do so.[9]

The immemorial courtesies were gone through once more before serious business could begin. Gorgeously dressed messengers brought Stratford 40 trays of flowers on 5 March, and on the 22nd, the grand vizier escorted him to Topkapi. He witnessed again the spectacle, half-ceremony, half-riot, of the janizaries being paid and fed. Then in once more through the Orta Kapi (middle gate) to the throne room, and the debasing ritual of presentation to the Sultan with his arms pinned to his sides. The experience was laughable in 1810, but now that he was 39, an experienced minister, a privy councillor, and a full ambassador, he was furious, and drew malicious pleasure from the sensation when the master of ceremonies found out later that the British ambassador had not been dispossessed of his sword before presentation. Mahmud II, like Stratford, was older and wiser, though neither age nor emotion touched his long, sardonic face. Mahmud did not register recognition, nor exercise his discretion to speak, but Stratford was soon to know more about his fierce will and sensational, deep-laid plans.

One of the greatest events in the domestic history of the Ottoman Empire, the destruction of the janizaries, was to take place in June, but as the plan existed only in the resolute heart of the

Sultan as yet, Stratford is to be forgiven for feeling that the Ottoman government seemed weaker than ever. Wherever he looked, there was more corruption and less talent. Men who passed as ministers would not have been entrusted with a sweet-shop in England: men of ability were in minor or distant appointments. 'Fanatical as well as despotic,' Stratford commented with concern, 'he [Mahmud II] has no idea but that of governing through the superstitious prejudices of his people.'[10] The traditional means of diplomatic access to the royal personage, official and secret, were withdrawn, and the *reis effendi* was the sole channel of communication left. Other ambassadors had given up trying to make any impression: the Russian chargé d'affaires, Minciaki, told Stratford he had had no dealings with Ottoman officialdom for over six months, while the Austrian Internuncio was sitting tight and giving no trouble. The French ambassador went on leave a few days before Stratford arrived. And now the *reis effendi* told the French dragoman that the British ambassador must accept this situation. He would get no answer to his enquiries. This proved only too true, and after only a couple of skirmishes with the *reis effendi*, which left him limp with exhaustion, Stratford wrote home the warning that 'the Turkish government is dead to any consideration but that of force . . . they are become by habit callous to all admonition not accompanied with evident proofs of a determination to act'.[11]

The rebuffs Stratford experienced were not totally undeserved. In his anxiety to anticipate Russian intervention, he had pressed for an interview with the *reis effendi* even before his credentials were submitted, had been received, and had promptly lost his temper. He expounded his instructions at length, but spoilt the effect of his offer of mediation by declaring that he would not be 'trifled with' over the depopulation rumour. He wanted an explicit promise that Ibrahim would not be allowed to carry out his threat. Now the *reis effendi* could do nothing to humour his visitor, for Mahmud II's violent refusal to make any arrangement with the Greeks paralysed his ministers with fear. Furthermore, the depopulation rumour was denied by the *Shaykh ul-Islam* in a dignified proclamation, bearing every sign of truth, and the *reis effendi* dared not, under such circumstances, go to the divan and say the British embassy wanted a further denial for the government in London. Pisani, at Stratford's elbow, softened the asperity of his master's words, but details of the scene reached Mahmud II, who replied with a lofty refusal of British offers of help. This refusal was intended for Ottoman officials only: Pisani got a copy, and Stratford returned to the attack with a complaint against a document he was not supposed to have seen. The *reis effendi* enjoyed the chance to be rude, said a denial of the depopulation rumour would not be supplied, and, to the argument that the Russians could not be provoked *ad infinitum*, 'replied in a tone of sarcastic irony that the Porte was of course on the point of acceding to all the demands of Russia, and turning round to two of his colleagues in office, who happened to be present – Is that not so, gentlemen, said he, we mean without a moment's hesitation to do everything that is required of us?'[12] Stratford blamed the Prussians and the Austrians for this firmness: in fact, someone much bigger was responsible. Mahmud II did not trust Britain any more than Russia, nor would he talk Greece with anyone. This puzzled Stratford, for 'he fears to employ, and cannot get rid of, the janizaries'.[13] Who else could suppress the Greeks? The Sultan had an answer to this, too, and saw no reason why he should not hold off the tsar while he dealt with the Greeks. It was five years since Russia took her ambassador away, but nothing had happened since. As usual, Europe could not agree, so Stratford's haste was not very convincing. Stratford gave up ideas of further, direct diplomacy and resorted once more to the conventional technique of sitting in his residence, and sending his dragomen to do battle at the Porte. But not for long.

Meanwhile, in London, Canning was staking much on his cousin's success at the Porte. 'I hope,' he informed Granville, 'to save Greece through the agency of the Russian name upon the fears of Turkey, without a war,'[14] and he augmented Stratford's instructions with a supplement of explosive force when, in October, he was told of the depopulation rumour by the Russian ambassador: 'Great Britain will not permit the execution of a system of depopulation which exceeds the permitted violence of war, and transgresses the conventional restraints upon civilization.'[15] He added that Britain was ready to act alone on this subject. His ideal, nevertheless, was that the Ottomans should give way peaceably, and in his instructions for Strangford, who left for Russia at the same time Stratford set out for the Porte, he stressed that he would not intervene in the eastern crisis by force.[16] But such complete reticence no longer represented his true feelings, as the pro-Ottomans in the cabinet well knew, and the duke of Wellington candidly expressed his fears over the prospect of a Greek state. If the Greeks could win independence for themselves, it would still be 'no small subject for consideration' in Britain, but as even this seemed a remote chance now, he hoped Canning would align with Austria and France to prevent Russia from setting up a puppet state.[17]

On 8 January, Canning speculated on the sterner qualities of the new tsar, Nicholas I, in a letter to Stratford. He said it appeared that Alexander I was on the point of declaring war at the moment of his death, and that no one could predict what Nicholas I might do, so Stratford must do all in his power to bring the Sultan to reason. On the 12th, Canning sent for the Russian ambassador, and disclosed his intention to send the duke of Wellington on a complimentary visit to the tsar. The king's letter of congratulation to Nicholas I was drawn up on 7 February, and Wellington's orders on the 10th. Copies of these were likewise sent to Stratford, with a warning to return them and not lodge them in the embassy archives. They said that the British government must await the result of Stratford's exertions, but that if they failed, the duke would 'express the willingness of the British government' to work with Russia in securing an arrangement between Greeks and Ottomans. If Stratford failed in his mission, and even if a subsequent joint Anglo-Russian offer of mediation was refused, Britain would not treat Ottoman recalcitrance as a *casus belli*; on the other hand, the Ottomans could not expect Britain to restrain Russia. The London government could not hope 'to interpose, with the consent of the country, any effectual resistance to whatever enterprise Russia might undertake at the impulse, and under the pretext of so enormous a moral as well as political provocation'.[18] Canning hoped, nevertheless, that Russia and Britain would find it possible to proceed in step as 'in the union of the two powers the best chance of success was to be found'. Stratford was told to supplement Wellington's efforts by returning to the charge at Constantinople:

> Whatever the reception of your first overtures may have been, you will ask an audience of the *reis effendi* immediately upon the receipt of

this dispatch and urge upon him in the most strenuous manner to obtain from the divan an instant declaration of their readiness to treat for an accommodation with the Greeks (upon any reasonable basis which the Ottoman government may suggest) as being the single and indispensable condition by which war with Russia may be averted.

Stratford was also instructed to press again with the depopulation problem. It was to be made quite clear that the Christian powers would not permit 'a new Barbary state' to grow up on the European side of the Mediterranean, and if the Sultan did not restrain Ibrahim, Britain would, and alone if necessary. If the Ottomans gave way to Stratford's pleadings, Wellington was to be informed directly in St Petersburg.[19]

Because Stratford took four months to reach his post, these instructions were drawn up in London about the time Stratford rode into Constantinople. Furthermore, Wellington left St Petersburg on his homeward journey without hearing from Stratford and the little Stratford received from Wellington he did not like at all. In this sense, therefore, Stratford's mission failed in its main purpose, namely, to anticipate Russian intervention with a *fait accompli*. Wellington was received at St Petersburg, as Strangford crossly put it, like 'a Divinity', on 2 March, which only encouraged his pathological vanity and his habit of thinking that a little soldierly common sense could disperse the difficulties in which politicians and kings became so tiresomely enmeshed.[20] He came, as he said before leaving home, 'to induce the emperor of Russia to put himself in our hands', yet, distrusting Canning and his ideas in the way he did, he ended by putting himself in Russian hands. Small wonder that Canning was mystified by Wellington's first dispatches from Russia, for Wellington was patently more concerned to avert a near-eastern war than worry himself about 'saving Greece'.

Two documents of major importance were drawn up during Wellington's brief Russian visit. The first was a Russian ultimatum of six weeks' duration, sent to the Sultan, of which the pro-Ottoman Wellington thoroughly approved. Wellington was, in fact, enormously relieved that this ultimatum, reflecting faithfully his first conversations with Nesselrode and the tsar, made no reference to Greece, but concentrated instead upon the Ottomans' failure to honour existing treaties between themselves and Russia, and he thought the Sultan could have no motive for refusing it. Haggling between the Ottomans and Russians over the disputed clauses of the treaty of Bucharest of 1812 had been going on since the European peace settlement in 1815, and the Ottoman attitude seemed, to Wellington, so frivolous and irresponsible, that the new tsar was within his rights in refusing any further 'negative or illusory answer' to his reasonable claims. With this point of view, it would be hard to disagree, and the Ottoman government had been unwise in its refusal to answer notes on the subject of Russian claims. What is more surprising is Wellington's clear conviction that, if the Ottomans honoured their existing obligations, the Greek business would be dropped permanently. In a positively exultant private letter to Stratford, dated 27 March, he wrote: 'The Porte may rely upon it that the present emperor will never interfere in the cause of the Greeks excepting as our own government would in the form of a friend. . . . I am quite certain that the desire here is to finish all little questions with the Porte and to remain at peace.' If the Ottomans acted sensibly and promptly, 'relations between this government and the Porte will become more cordial than they have ever been', and a sort of moratorium would descend on the old Eastern Question. The only close parallel with such complacency is that of another warrior-politician in 1841, when Commodore Napier apologized to the Foreign Office for having solved the Eastern Question single-handed.[21] The Russian ultimatum of 1826 was presented at the Porte on 5 April, and demanded the complete withdrawal of Ottoman forces from the Principalities and the release of the Serbian delegates treacherously imprisoned by the Sultan's orders when they came to Constantinople to negotiate a clarification of their people's rights under the 1812 treaty. The Russians did not solicit Stratford's support, nor would Stratford have been free to give it, though he took his meagre opportunities to remind the *reis effendi* informally that Ottoman bad faith was madness. Wellington's letter only reached Stratford after the presentation of the Russian ultimatum.

Within a week of penning his letter to Stratford, begging him to support the Russian ultimatum so that the Greek question could be dropped, Wellington signed the famous protocol of St Petersburg; signed on 4 April, it was revealed to Canning by Wellington personally on the 27th, and leaked to *The Times* on 8 May. Stratford, however, only heard of the protocol in late May, which was unfortunate as he was pleading ignorance of it weeks after its existence had been revealed to the *reis effendi* by the Internuncio. Even worse, Canning attached to his official disclosure of the protocol an injunction that Stratford must not discuss it with the Porte until so authorized, and the authorization did not come before September. Thus, in the period before hearing of the protocol, Stratford was despondent at Wellington's news that Russia was giving up the Greek question, and after hearing of it, was further frustrated by being restrained from threatening the Ottoman government with its possible consequences. But then the protocol changed the pre-existing situation in respects which were not quickly measured, and Canning only began to elucidate its practical consequences in exchanges with the Russian ambassador in late August.

It is usually said that Wellington was the dupe of Nesselrode and Count Lieven, recalled to Russia specially to assist in the deception.[22] How else does one explain his signature on a document which took up the subject of Greece a mere week after that subject had, according to Wellington, been interred? Madame Lieven wrote:

> By us the question was presented to the Duke in a new light. It was not the revolution that we patronized; we wished to stop the insurrection, to control the movement; we wished to establish in Greece the conservation of order; for it was proved that the Turks were powerless, that we desired a regular state of things, a hierarchical discipline, all of which sounded well in the ears of the duke of Wellington. He entered under full sail into this order of ideas.[23]

All this suggests some outcome more dramatic than the protocol actually was. The protocol laid down that, in the event of Stratford's mediation proving unsuccessful, Russia and Britain would attempt a joint mediation. The use of force was not mentioned as an ultimate resource. Rejecting any special advantages for themselves, the two great powers would work towards the establishment of a Greek principality, which would remain a tributary and dependency of the Porte, but otherwise manage its own affairs, enjoying freedom of conscience and an independent economy. The boundaries of the Greek principality were a matter for further negotiation, and the other great powers would be invited to accede to the protocol, and perhaps guarantee its ultimate handiwork. There was nothing very dramatic in all this. The Russians had managed to commit the British, but conversely the British now had a chain on the Russians. Canning, after his first surprise, admitted that Wellington had not gone further '*in support of the Greeks* [emphasis added] than the British government thought proper'.[24] The protocol only committed the two countries to a policy for action which each had long regarded as the one likely to prevail in the end. Both were pleased with it.

Stratford Canning neither liked nor trusted the duke of Wellington, and would not be budged by the optimistic letter of 27 March, which seemed to shelve the Greek question for the sake of Russo-Ottoman reconciliation. The truth is that a menacing and unpredictable Russia was extremely convenient to Stratford in his dealings with the Porte, and a friendly tsar, such as Wellington promised, would make Stratford himself appear as a fool and a liar. The Internuncio would see to that. For the present, therefore, he decided against advancing Wellington's arguments, which seemed detrimental to his own success, until he heard from London: 'I fear His Grace will feel disappointed at the barbarous manner in which I have kept his light under a bushel.' The thought, nevertheless, wormed its way into Stratford's mind that his cousin was being overborne by the reactionaries of the Cabinet, and he dreaded the prospect of having to drop the cause of the Greeks. From Vienna, Henry Wellesley wrote to him that this had virtually been decided on. Stratford could only plead with Canning to adhere to the tough line as long as he was foreign secretary: 'I had really hoped the time was come when, using a warlike language for the sake of avoiding war, but prepared for the worst, you would have enabled me to force the Sultan's hands.'[25] The protocol, when he heard of it, seemed the answer to his prayer, but he was unable to use it as a lever of negotiation until September, and in the interim the Internuncio convinced the divan, not unreasonably, that Britain would not dash into action nor allow Russia to do so. And as the months passed, the Greek cause wilted further, in the field as in the council chamber.

On 6 April, two days after Wellington signed the protocol of St Petersburg, the third Greek National Assembly met at Epidavros, a nervous, disunited, and quarrelsome body which made Stratford 'tremble for the safety of the Greek people and the basis of their political existence'.[26] On 28 April, he was rowed back up the Bosporus after an excursion to Topkapi to see baskets of human ears, allegedly cut from the slain at Missolonghi. Miaulis had said the Greeks could not survive the fall of that place, and Stratford now wrote, 'without a miracle, the insurrection cannot be much longer maintained'.[27] Missolonghi had, indeed, fallen, and before it did so, the Epidauros assembly hastened to new measures, setting up a committee of 13 to rule for six months, petitioning London again, and sending Stratford full powers to do all he could for the floundering cause. An appeal was sent forth to 'all ye who have Greek blood in your veins, to prepare your sinewy arms against the barbarous enemy of Christendom', but the full powers to Stratford showed how far the old pretension to full independence had shrunk. Signed by 110 Greek leaders on 14 April, the letter to Stratford deplored 'la guerre de déstruction . . . directement contraire aux véritables interèts des deux parties belligérantes . . . scandale pour le monde chrétien'. Running through its more practical suggestions, Stratford was able to tell his cousin that the Greeks 'offer tribute, and acknowledgment of the suzerainty of the Porte; they require in other respects total separation from Turkey; they require an armistice during the negotiation [the sure sign of a losing side] and expect the guarantee of His Majesty's government to any act of pacification'.[28] He was, nevertheless, extremely cautious in replying, writing to the Greek leaders that he could do nothing for the moment, but hoped fresh instructions from London would enable him 'plaider la cause de la paix et de l'humanité'. He did not speak of independence except to say that he was glad the Greeks no longer expected it – 'la rêve d'indépendence' he called it – and were concentrating on 'la correction des griefs essentiels' instead. He would not allow the Greeks to concentrate refugees in Poros and Milos under British naval protection, though his heart ached for the homeless and he and his young wife knelt in prayer for them nightly.[29]

The long delays in the receipt of instructions from London, the silence of Wellington in St Petersburg, and the unexpected upward turn in Ottoman military fortunes, lowered Stratford's hopes for the Greeks, so that by mid-1826, and at a time when his sympathy for the victims of the war was undiminished, perhaps even more deeply felt than ever before, he was disillusioned by the weakness of the Greek resistance and confused by the changing policies of his own country. His anger with the Ottomans was unconcealed and fierce, as the tale of suffering lengthened, and in June, after a further visit to Topkapi where 5,498 human ears had now been gathered, his grief and rage boiled over, and he was the only European minister who refused to congratulate the Sultan on the taking of Missolonghi. As he tartly said, the Egyptians took it, and by treachery anyway.[30] There was an element of purely personal feeling in his attitude also, since it was almost impossible for his wife to visit Stamboul in case she saw the nameless and dreadful human trophies on show there. She became virtually a prisoner restricted to Tarabya and Buyukdere by land, and sails up the Bosporus by water. She was pregnant, and had a miscarriage towards the end of the year. Yet, in spite of his repugnance at the conduct of the Ottoman forces in Greece, Stratford was changing his mind about the Greeks. In 1823, his cousin recognized Greek 'belligerency' as a 'fact': in mid-1826, Stratford decided sadly that this 'fact' was all but gone. With the Ottomans marching on Athens, the people of Spezia being evacuated to Hydra, and the large lump of Newcastle coal at Napoli (collected there for Cochrane's steamers) in danger of capture by the Egyptians, the Greek leadership was showing its worst instead of its best characteristics and, as Stratford now believed, its unfitness for political responsibility. Greek peasants could still die for their valley or their village, but no one, he felt, had any capacity for the more pedestrian and difficult duty of living and working for a free Greece. This was a terrible blow to a man who wanted to believe that the spirit of democracy smouldered inextinguishably in every Greek heart, but he accepted the conclusion, none the less, that the Greeks were, after all,

> unfit for a state of complete independence, and even if there were no resistance on the part of the Turks, the powers of Europe would dread the establishment in their immediate vicinity of a new state so utterly unprepared for the arduous duties of self-government. The general assembly of Greece has therefore judged wisely in giving up

Stratford Canning, Mahmud II, and Greece

the original scheme of independence. . . . The time may come when other and better habits than these of the last four centuries may so far strengthen and improve the national mind in Greece as to make it fit for exercising the highest powers of government.[31]

In Stratford's view, all the talk about French or British candidates for a Greek throne was therefore misplaced – there was not going to be a Greek kingdom for anyone to rule. By the end of July, he hardly bothered to leave the Bosporus to conduct business at the Porte, leaving the field to the Internuncio, whom he passed frequently at the leafy waterfront at Bebek. They exchanged nods only. The Austrian, and his Prussian colleague, maintained for Ottoman comfort the argument that the protocol had no teeth, and it was beginning to look as though they were right. Minciaki, the Russian chargé, whom Stratford liked, said he had no orders about Greece. In this sullen calm, the Sultan himself suddenly went into action.

For some weeks, excitement in the Ottoman capital had been running high. Stratford noticed, on 28 May, that something important seemed at hand. The officials at the Porte were seeing no one from the embassies. Then there came a rumour that Sultan Selim III's project of a new model army was being taken up again, although 'the fatal name of Nizam i-Jedid was studiously avoided'.[32] The rumour was soon confirmed. A *hatti serif*, reorganizing the Ottoman army, was promulgated on the 28th. In all, 196 new regiments were to be raised, recruited in part from the existing janizary *ortas*, thus providing an overall force of 30,000 men. It was said that the leading janizary officers were in on the secret, and that the ulema had given a rather grudging consent. At first, Stratford predicted 'serious disturbances, and perhaps the destruction of the Sultan himself',[33] but as June opened, all seemed quiet, and Mahmud II was said to have worn the cap of the new army units in full divan. A few janizaries, egged on to protest against these westernizing antics, were 'privately strangled' in the fortress at Rumeli Hisar.[34] Strongly backed by his grand vizier, the Sultan appeared to have leapt his ditches safely. Then, on 15 June, as Stratford was clearing up some papers at the residence of his consul-general in Pera, he heard the sound of gunfire in the afternoon. Mahmud II's 'whiff of grapeshot' was making history. The embassy gatekeeper, just back from Constantinople, burst in with the news.

On the previous evening, a mob of angry janizaries had stoned the office of their aga, and proceeded to loot the residence of the grand vizier. Sunrise on the 15th showed that this was no isolated incident, and 15,000 janizaries assembled in the great arena, the Hippodrome of Byzantine days, in front of the mosque of Sultan Ahmet. The mufti and the ulema met in anxious conclave in the ruins of the grand vizier's house, but Mahmud II himself took up an exposed position, which some of his unhappy ministers were obliged to share, on the porch of the mosque. Negotiations with the rebels were protracted through a hot and noisy midday, the dust growing with the tumult. The janizaries demanded the dissolution of the new army units, and the heads of the grand vizier, their own aga, and the reformist pasha of the Bosporus. Messengers crossed and recrossed between the Sultan and the Hippodrome without useful result, and Mahmud II prolonged them deliberately so that by the time the janizaries kicked over their cooking kettles, and by that symbolic act of defiance spurned their master's food and pay, his plans were complete. Artillery quietly appeared beneath the trees of Hagia Sofia, and along the promenade outside the outer gate of the royal palace. The green flag of the Prophet was unfurled at Topkapi, and criers ran through the streets calling the people to the defence of the Sultan. When Stratford looked up from his papers at the sound of the artillery, the Sultan had taken the decision for which he had waited 20 years: the 'whiff of grapeshot' accounted for 1,200 almost at once, and the janizary barracks were fired. Many more janizaries came over to the Sultan's side as soon as the Prophet's flag was waved before them. The populace hunted down those who tried to flee from the Hippodrome, and the grand vizier, setting up court in the middle of all the carnage, tried summarily all who were brought before him. To a bold rebel who tried to argue with him, he replied simply that 'he was entirely dependent for rank and life on the breath of the Caliph'. Forgiveness was out of the question: the rebel was bowstringed and thrown on the mounting pile of corpses. Taken altogether, Stratford's information adds little that is new to a well-authenticated episode, but his interpretation of it is interesting. He did not, for instance, connect the destruction of the janizaries with the need for an improved performance on the part of the Ottoman army in the field and, on the contrary, he thought the fashion in which Mahmud II could turn his back on a major crisis in foreign affairs, snubbing all the embassies in the process, proved the Sultan's overriding interest in his personal weakness *vis-à-vis* his subjects and his army. Certainly, if the Greek war had commanded a higher priority in Mahmud II's thinking, he would have reformed the navy before the army.[35]

By the end of June, Stratford estimated the number of the executed, over and above those who fell in the Hippodrome, at 6,000.[36] A committee sitting at Topkapi sentenced men to death with the remorseless regularity of a French Revolution tribunal. The scope of the persecution widened daily so that old, retired public servants and obscure petty officials found themselves under interrogation for the indiscreet remarks and criticisms of their youth. No one who had spoken out for the janizaries, or ever been one, or who had opposed Selim III, had a hope of survival, and even boatmen, firemen, and gardeners, retired many years from active service, were scrutinized again. Many were banished, too, for adhering too uncompromisingly to old attitudes or for experimenting too boldly with new ideas, for, as Stratford learned from his dragomans, 'Mahometanism, as well as Christianity, has its free thinkers, men of expatiating minds, not over fond of moral restraints, and devoted to the gentlemanly engagements of lettered ease and polite conversation'. A former Ottoman minister in London, Ismail Effendi, was rusticated, along with several of the ulema, to Bursa. But, above all, Mahmud II was concerned to suppress the Bektasi dervishes, the fanatical confederates of the janizaries, and by July they were being executed in growing numbers.[37]

The continuing slaughter became indiscriminate and senseless, as though the Sultan knew not where to stop. The 'whole tribe of capitalists' became intensely worried when a very rich Jew, with claims on the state worth 16 million piastres, was executed in his elegant Bosporus home, and his fortune of 4 million piastres confiscated.[38] On 14 August, Stratford reported to London the virtual collapse of the whole apparatus of Christian privilege in the Ottoman Empire: European merchants were being bustled into gaol on the least pretext, the entire Ionian community of Galata was herded out of its houses by order of the governor, and de Kletzl, the senior Austrian dragoman, was bastinadoed to death. Stratford, fearful for his wife and the safety of the British community, advised everyone under his official care to keep out of sight and out of trouble, and there is no question that he was a very frightened man. There was no question either of lodging protests at the Porte at a time when, in his own words, 'the entrance to the Seraglio, the shore under the Sultan's windows, and the sea itself are crowded with dead bodies, many of them torn and in part devoured by the dogs'.[39] For once, the Sultan was absolute master of his own capital, and none dared stand in his way. Or, almost none. A body of women protested first against the reign of terror – 'a strange occurrence in this country' – by marching to the Saray, and on the last day of August, Mahmud II was given a sterner warning when Constantinople was ravaged by an immense fire which reduced the offices of the Sublime Porte to ashes. The homeless dragged their carts through the smoking streets, the waterfront and bazaars were silent: public order existed only because public life had ceased. On so distracted a city, the Sultan's capitulation to the Russians at Akerman made no impression whatsoever.[40]

Sultan Mahmud's revolution – for he was the innovator, and the reactionaries were swept out – seemed likely, for a time, to bring him down also, but by October, his survival was assured and the incident of 15 June passed into history. At Smyrna, Salonika, and Edirne, janizary units gave in unconditionally, and accepted the abolition of their order. The most serious protests were the most hopeless, coming from isolated garrisons in Aleppo and Erzerum. Reported janizary riots in Bosnia and Konya turned out to be rumours only, and a commission was unmolested in its work of demolishing all the Bektasi *tekkes* in Rumelia. But, as Stratford knew, this was not enough. Mahmud II had made his state more vulnerable than before, and must complete the reconstruction of his new army very quickly. He must win back the confidence of his people, and show them that he was no enemy of religion. He needed also to revive languishing trade conditions. But was Mahmud II aiming at anything more than the modernization of his armed forces? 'To effect such changes,' Stratford wrote,

> *knowledge, money,* and *time* are wanting, in addition to an unprejudiced as well as a most resolute and persevering mind in the

sovereign. But *knowledge* must flow into this country from Christendom, which it is now a marked feature of the Sultan's policy to keep aloof. *Money*, as the days of the conquest are over, must be raised by encouraging trade and production. . . . With respect to *time*, a declining and enfeebled empire is perilously dependent on the forbearance of its neighbours.

To Stratford, the Sultan was a man with the right instincts but without the necessary knowledge: only westerners could teach him how to westernize. What they would teach must go beyond merely technological expertise: 'It is most probable that at no very distant period the Ottoman government will be constrained by the fear of worse to come to renounce a large portion of its fanatical prejudices, and be content to receive the elements of *political instruction* [emphasis added] from one or more of the Christian powers.'[41] Stratford became excited by the possibility that the Sultan might prove susceptible to European guidance and that, under bold leadership, the antiquated, theocratic empire would be led in the direction of a capitalistic economy, a decent and honest public administration and, more remotely, some form of ecumenical government resting on the most educated class. As each of these phenomena had reached its highest development in Britain, it was logical, Stratford believed, that the Ottomans should take Britain as their teacher. The ambassador was in no doubt that the theocratic foundations of the Ottoman state must disappear: all modern states were secular, and necessarily so. The modernization of an Islamic Ottoman Empire presented no greater difficulties than, say, the regeneration of Roman Catholic Spain. It was a very English point of view, bold, confident, and over-simplified.

Gradually, the rigours associated with the 'auspicious incident' passed away. The units of the new army, significantly called the Victorious Soldiers of Muhammad, drilled publicly in their new European uniforms, carrying pistols at their belts in place of *yatagans*. They came now under a new official, the serasker, or commander-in-chief, and the old office of janizary aga disappeared. Stratford put new recruits at 7,000 as early as August; by the completion of the military reforms, there were 12,000 in Constantinople alone, and the entire new Ottoman army was estimated at 96,000 men by 1828. Mahmud II played a prominent part in the introduction of the reforms, and was infatuated with military manuals, whose contents he had read to him. There was a Galata story to the effect that when a royal chaplain began to declaim in the mosque with his back to Mecca, Mahmud called out, 'Right about, face'.[42] The financing of the army was expected to prove costly, and Mahmud II did not leave his anxious subjects in doubt for very long. After effecting his own private economy, which consisted of dismissing over a hundred cooks, he placed a new tax on shopkeepers and began an exhaustive examination of everyone who enjoyed inherited janizary pensions and privileges: most of those had to be repurchased. The reconstruction of the Sublime Porte was simply charged to the account of wealthy private individuals. The elevation of the master of the mint to a seat in the divan suggested that a currency revaluation, among other fiscal measures, was at hand.

If Mahmud II had forgotten the Greeks for the moment, Stratford had not, and from 15 June until the end of September, when he was ordered into action again by his cousin, he maintained a steady harassing fire at the Porte, sending in much free advice which cannot have endeared him to the Sultan. To raise the Greek question, after the fall of Missolonghi, as though it were still a live issue, proved to the Ottoman ministers that Britain was far from the neutrality she professed.[43] Stratford, in fact, was in a very subdued mood, and had lost a good deal of faith in the cause he was pleading. Nothing shows his loss of confidence more clearly than his change of tactics, to which he may have been persuaded by the kaptan pasha and the rising star of the divan, Nejib Pasha. The former officer told Stratford candidly but civilly that he could hardly expect to have much reputation with the Sultan when it was so generally believed in Constantinople, by Europeans as well as Ottomans, that Britain was behind the remnant of Greek resistance – why, otherwise, was Cochrane coming? – and might even have stirred the janizaries: Nejib, a successful conciliator of the Turkish and Egyptian commanders in Greece, advised the British minister not to antagonize a Sultan engrossed with a delicate and dangerous situation.

As a result, Stratford changed his methods without letting his instructions languish entirely, and began to promote his official business by sending in unsigned memoranda for the eyes of the Sultan. The supposition was that such papers would be passed through hands of ascending dignity as though they were petitions from Ottoman subjects, and Stratford thought he had a special talent for concocting them: one example will suffice to show the reliance he placed on flattery. On 18 June, three days after the janizaries were suppressed, he put in a plea for the Greeks in the most obsequious terms.[44] It began with the remark that, in 1821, 'the Greeks were not more oppressed than usual' but that they were 'to a certain extent excusable in longing for a change'. Their misfortune was that they lived so far from the Porte: *rayas* living near the seat of Ottoman government never thought of revolt. Somehow, Stratford went on, the revolt had prospered, though everyone knew that Turks were braver than Greeks. There followed some heavy play on the majesty of Ottoman sovereignty, and a strong hint, which probably represented Stratford's genuine belief, that the best arrangement now would be one in which the Sultan guaranteed the Greeks a measure of local autonomy and personal rights. In this way, Russian intervention would be kept at bay, and the Greeks would be grateful for ever. Only the Sultan could take the necessary decision which would secure him the approval of posterity and enthrone him near the Prophet in the afterlife – 'the happiness and prosperity of *millions* from the wisdom and magnanimity of *one*'.

For the moment, flattery got Stratford nowhere, though it was a method to which he was often to have recourse, always in a disagreeably clumsy way, in his dealings with Mahmud II's successor, Abdulmejid. On 5 August, he was again refused a formal denial of the depopulation rumour; on the 18th, he was refused information about the Akerman negotiations. On 1 September, a more direct and unflattering approach, in which he tactlessly spoke of the Ottomans' 'inability to reduce maritime Greece', was turned away. On the 30th, he received the sort of instructions for which he had chafed all summer, and which permitted him to revert to the more congenial diplomacy of menace. They were the outcome of his cousin's recent discussions in London with the returned Russian ambassador, Prince Lieven.[45] Even then, his embassy was one long frustration, until the protocol of April 1826 became the treaty of London of July 1827.

Meanwhile, the Greek cause slumped further, thus strengthening Stratford's conviction that independence was out of the question, and could not, in fairness to the Ottomans, be the aim of any European intervention that might emerge from the protocol of April. His news was drawn from many sources, and his picture of the fall of Missolonghi on 22 April, for instance, was assembled from letters from Georgios Karaiskos, the Greek leader, from a report from the Austrian consul at Patras, from a young Ottoman soldier, and from conversation with 'an intelligent traveller' who had spoken with refugees from the doomed town.[46] Through these and many other correspondents, Stratford was enabled to conclude that while Missolonghi itself provided evidence of a depopulation in miniature, Ibrahim's bigger scheme for repeopling the Morea with Egyptians was only rumour. Ibrahim himself was not doing much beyond squabbling with his father's ancient rival, the kaptan pasha, who was extremely reluctant to risk his fine ships against the Greek fireships. Even so, there was enough suffering in Greece to attract Stratford's concern, and when Consul Meyer at Prevesa notified him that 3,500 of the Missolonghi survivors had been shipped to Egypt, he followed their fate with some care, and was delighted when he heard that most were redeemed by European merchants, and even 'Turkish Grandees'.[47]

The land war had run down: that at sea went on as before, a confused struggle in which the Greeks took all foreign shipping as their prey, and hardly pretended to discriminate between honest neutral merchantmen and carriers of Turkish or Egyptian goods. The conduct of the privateers strengthened the argument of Austria, whose shipping suffered most, that independence for such people was sheer extortion without any foundation in right. Ranging as far west as Matapan, the pirates struck at British ships constantly, six being taken in June alone in the Silona passage, the happy-hunting ground of the Andros privateers. The captures were stripped, as if by locusts, of cargo, ropes, and sails, and the boys 'shockingly abused'.[48] Another British vessel, the *Skylark*, landed munitions for the Greeks at Napoli, to be apprehended by pirates as soon as it quit the harbour. In Rhodes, a further vessel was taken from its moorings: the British crew, idly sipping *raki* on the waterfront, watched it sailing past. In September, Stratford was infuriated when he heard that another merchantman had been boarded, and the captain's wife and niece raped.

The Greek provisional government was in no position to placate his wrath. Over-fastidious observance of the laws of the sea would have encouraged the privateers to avoid the Napoli prize-court altogether and, as the government received 15 per cent of all prize-money, it could not afford to be too impartial. Stratford invoked the help of the Mediterranean commander, Sir Harry Neale, and ordered consuls to warn British merchant captains to take particular care in observing the laws of neutrality: carriers of Ottoman cargoes, or cargo for Ottoman consignees, could not expect redress through him if attacked by the privateers. The warning was unpopular for, as Captain Hamilton told Stratford, the British consuls at Smyrna, Alexandria, and Beirut irresponsibly urged British merchants to trade with both belligerents, and were probably themselves speculating in various commodities, particularly British cottons. Old established firms, like Briggs and Company in Egypt – 'notorious for its enmity to the Greek cause' – whose prosperity rested frankly on transactions with Egyptian and Turkish importers and retailers, had huge sums committed to the trade, and in one instance a Briggs cargo, worth 'considerably above one hundred thousand dollars' was run into Napoli. The resultant case lasted 25 days, and only the stoutest defence by 'the Clerk and Schoolmaster' of a navy frigate got the illiterate captain off.[49]

By and large, relations between Stratford and the navy were good, while those with the merchants were bad. The navy captains, like the ambassador, were furious with the governor of Malta, who released captured privateers the moment they were turned over to him on the grounds that he had no jurisdiction over them, while the merchants, who were usually resident in one of the Ottoman ports and were pro-Ottoman in their politics, wanted all Greek shipping, whether bearing the papers of authorization of the Napoli government or not, to be swept off the seas. The British navy obliged them, often in very striking actions, as when Captain Hamilton surprised the notorious pirate, Vasso, with a flotilla of 19 ships, and burned the lot, but in Constantinople and Smyrna the feeling among the merchants was that this was not enough. The navy was tainted with Grecism.

Under these circumstances, it is not surprising that the merchants feared the advent of Cochrane, whose leisurely approach to the East produced feverish speculation. What would befall the merchants if Cochrane, with the steamers reputedly being built in the Thames for the Greek service, bombarded an Ottoman port? In August, Stratford received a petition in which they pleaded that the famous admiral and hero of Chile, 'who vends his services to the highest bidder and reflects no honour on his native country', should be detained in England by order of the government.[50] The Ottoman government was just as worried as the expatriate merchants, and the *reis effendi* asked Stratford how a private individual could violate the relations of friendship existing between his country and the Ottoman Empire, to which Stratford could only offer the reply that the English law officers had been consulted, and had ordained that private individuals, or officers of the active list who were ready to risk the loss of their commissions under the terms of the Foreign Enlistment Act, were free agents. For the moment, Stratford thought the question unimportant. So far as he knew, only three Englishmen remained in Greek service. But he admitted, rather grudgingly, that Cochrane could create great difficulties, and he advised Consul Werry to tell the merchants of Smyrna that, if Cochrane bombarded the port, he thought it very improbable that the Royal Navy would be ordered to attack him or to defend Smyrna. Cochrane, the object of all this speculation, was still 'arriving' in Greece at the end of 1826, as he had been for most of the year.[51] When he did arrive, he kept clear of the Ottoman mainland, and the only important blow struck there was the audacious sack of Alexandretta by Greek pirates.

On 30 September, Stratford received his cousin's direction to communicate formally to the Porte the existence of the protocol of 4 April, and he enjoyed employing his treacherous first dragoman, Chabert, whom he believed all along to be encouraging the Ottoman government to stand firm against him, as his intermediary on this occasion. 'I informed the *reis effendi* by means of my first interpreter that His Majesty's government and the court of Russia had determined to proceed to the execution of the agreement settled at St. Petersburg last spring.' Here was Mahmud II's last chance to be sensible, his last chance to do business civilly with the British embassy before being forced to accept Anglo-Russian demands submitted at sword point. Almost immediately, the *reis effendi* sent his master's refusal to consider any European proposals which suggested a modification of the Sultan's power in Greece:

it would be 'contrary to the religion and political rights of the Turkish Empire'.[52] In his usual way, Stratford attributed to blind perversity an attitude of resistance which drew strength from several quarters. Long familiarity with the protocol, communicated to them months before by the Internuncio, had given the divan some contempt for it. Senior Ottoman officials were not convinced that France would act against them, and were sure that Austria and Prussia would not. More than this, Mahmud II himself believed the protocol was just a Russian technique for getting him to give way quickly at Akerman, where his representatives were told by their Russian counterparts that, if only Mahmud II would honour his treaties, evacuate the Principalities entirely, and settle the disputed frontier in Transcaucasia, the Greek question would simply die of neglect. In this expectation, the Sultan authorized his delegates to accept the Russian terms, and sign a convention on 7 October, thus conceding the points the Russians had worked for since 1816.

★ ★ ★

At the end of 1826, Stratford could only look back on a year of frustrations, rebuffed by the Ottomans, unable to advance the Greek business, and neglected by his cousin more than he had expected. With nothing achieved, his thoughts turned homeward again, to a parliamentary career. To his old foreign office friend, Planta, he wrote: 'I shall think myself not only the most fortunate but also the most miraculous of diplomats if I am destined to be the mediator of the bases of pacification between Turks and Greeks', and he referred to his worsening health – 'a good deal shaken' – and his firm intention to make the end of 1827 'the extreme term of my residence here' unless British policy acquired urgency, direction, and determination.[53]

George Canning could not spare the time to inform his relative in the East of all the difficulties he was experiencing at home in the way of turning the protocol into an instrument for action. As soon as the Russian ambassador, Prince Lieven, returned to London in August, the foreign secretary was faced with the task of restraining Russia from action until he could persuade his ministerial colleagues to contemplate its eventual use, should all pacific methods fail to move the Sultan. He aptly described his role between the Russian government and the British ministry when he wrote: 'I have to accommodate my pace to both, like a man walking between two companions, lame of opposite legs.'[54] Not that he was in favour of force if there was any hope of avoiding it; he pointedly told Lieven that Stratford had been unable to produce clear proof that the depopulation of the Morea was seriously intended by the Egyptians and that, in these circumstances, the one instance in which Britain was in unqualified favour of the use of force had been removed. In his own mind, he was thinking of declaring Greece independent as a means of preventing a Russian resort to force also, but it was extremely difficult to raise such a solution with his colleagues.

In Princess Lieven's view, Canning was 'as anti-Turk as it is possible to be', but she was mistaken. Canning was still anxious to conserve as much as he could of the Ottoman Empire, provided her rulers behaved decently towards their Christian subjects. Princess Lieven was, on the other hand, absolutely right in thinking Canning 'the only member of the English Cabinet, who is well disposed, entirely well disposed, towards Russia', and anxious to work with her in order to solve the Eastern difficulty. His colleagues were suspicious, and Earl Bathurst complained that 'it has long been a great object with the Foreign Office to take a part for the Greeks as being a very popular cause among a large description of well-meaning people'.[55] Wellington wanted Cochrane arrested. The main difference between Canning and his colleagues lay, not in their opinions on Greece or the Ottoman Empire, but in their respective attitudes towards Russia. Even here, Canning agreed that Russia ought to be denied a free hand in the Levant and shared to the full even Lord Ellenborough's suspicions. But his idea was to work out a solution with Russia which would permit the Ottoman Empire to survive substantially as before, which would do something for the Greeks, and check that isolated action by Russia which everyone feared, but which his colleagues did not know how to prevent and which, by their failure after his death to maintain the obligations of the treaty of London, they allowed to come to pass in 1829, when Russia attacked the Ottomans alone. It may be noticed in passing, as further evidence of ministerial confusion, that the very men who made it so difficult for Canning to negotiate with Lieven were the same ones who turned down a French proposal to guarantee the integrity of the Ottoman Empire when France was brought into the negotiation for turning the protocol into a plan of action.

Russia was obliged to wait while Canning, visiting Paris, tried to bring the Bourbons into a triple alliance: the French were more than ready, while making it clear that they would not merely adhere to the protocol argued by Russia and Britain. In February 1827, Nicholas I informed London that any *projet* which the British and French governments might propose to Russia must include a time limit beyond which, all diplomacy having failed, the three powers would send a joint naval force into the zone of war in order to prevent 'all aid of men, arms, or ships, whether Egyptian or Turkish, from reaching Greece or the Archipelago'.[56] Thus, finally, Canning had to face up to a problem from which, for a long time, personal inclination as well as Cabinet difficulties had kept him in retreat. The protocol had avoided the specification of an ultimate resort to force: a new treaty could not. Lieven was very helpful to Canning, but was also firm and loyal to his master's mood: Russia would not be held back if Britain remained inactive. On 22 and 23 March, with Lieven telling Canning, 'I have exhausted all the latitude the instructions of my court reserved for me', the two men thrashed out the details of the treaty of London, which then only awaited ratification and the agreement of France.[57] And on 12 April, George Canning became prime minister of England. Only a man with his high parliamentary influence and power could have persisted for so long in the face of so many discouragements, and now that he was not to be denied, Peel, Eldon, Wellington, Westmoreland, Bathurst, and Melville walked out of the ministry. Until the formal signature of the treaty, on 6 July, France worked to bring in Prussia and Austria, and these two to delay the production of a final and formal arrangement. A proposal to withdraw the European ambassadors from Constantinople met with French resistance, caused delay, and was finally dropped. Canning himself hoped Austria would join, and to the end was anxious to avoid hostilities if the threat of a blockade of the Greek coasts should bring the Ottomans to treat. But there was much else to do, constructing a new ministry, breaking in a new foreign secretary, explaining his progress to the king: William Huskisson said his own labours were 'as dust in the balance' compared with Canning's, and as the new prime minister was already much weakened by an illness he had at the beginning of the year, his new responsibilities sapped his remaining powers in under four months. On 8 August, a copy of the treaty of London reached Stratford, and on the same day, George Canning died at Chiswick.[58]

* * *

Stratford was an outsider, allowed only occasional glimpses of diplomatic activities in Europe. Guilleminot, who returned to his post as French ambassador in September 1826, brought some information concerning Canning's imminent visit to Paris, but Ribeaupierre, who could have told him far more, did not arrive as Russian minister until February 1827, and when he did turn up, played an unfriendly role, boasting to his colleagues that he was 'l'organe de la force', but letting the *reis effendi* believe that it was Stratford who still forced the pace with regard to Greece.[59] The news of Canning's serious illness in January, which the Lievens feared might kill him, and of the earl of Liverpool's stroke in February, a further cause of confusion and delay, reached Constantinople only belatedly, thus heightening Stratford's feelings of isolation and neglect. Above all, however, he was cross to notice Ribeaupierre's ascendancy, though one of his biggest complaints in 1826 had been the absence of the Russian and French ambassadors. 'I was little prepared,' he grumbled in March, 'for discovering that England and Russia had changed places in the estimate of the Porte', and he heard that the *reis effendi* had called him 'little better than a Greek'.[60] In April, he and Ribeaupierre made a joint approach to the Porte, inviting the Sultan to act while there was still time, but the Internuncio, and possibly Ribeaupierre, who was thirsting for action of the military kind, brought it to naught. The interpreters who carried the appeal to the *reis effendi* were escorted from his office before they could say a word: in short, Stratford said, the Ottoman attitude breathed 'the stern, relentless spirit of a fanatic despotism'.[61]

From Canning's appointment to the premiership on 12 April until June, Foreign Office silence was almost complete, except for some solemn discussion about repairs to the embassy which drove Stratford mad. He first learned of Canning's negotiations with Lieven over the final form of a treaty, from his Russian counterpart. A private letter from Planta, which reached him only on 21 May, told him of his cousin's elevation and of 'the voluntary retirement of embarrassing colleagues', but left Stratford wondering who would be the new foreign secretary and, even more, why Planta's letter was not accompanied by firm instructions.[62] 'I verily believe that they have forgotten at the office that I exist', he told Wellesley, his taciturn colleague at Vienna, and on the last day of May he wrote as follows to his cousin:

> For myself, I am only anxious to know whether anything more is to be done and what. There are moments when I say that things cannot be left where they are; three great powers will never allow themselves to be laughed at, as alas they now are by these impracticable Turks. At others, my heart fails; I think of your fear of embroiling Europe, and the impossibility of carrying the seraglio by measures just short of war, and looking as if they might at any day terminate in that expedient. I take courage again when I consider where you now are, and that the Sultan however obstinate, and however angry and fanatic, is too essentially weak to resist by war such measures as you might decide on taking to check Ibrahim Pasha's injuries and to reconcile his Highness to our proposals of mediation. At all events, I trust that you will come to a decision without reference to the progress of the campaign, which may be one of triumph to the Turk, and bring the Greeks not so much nearer to submission but to extermination.
>
> The situation of the embassy is really distressing, and humiliating, not to say critical. If the Turks persist in their obstinacy, I wish that you would think seriously of changing the ambassador, not into a minister plenipo., but into the lowest kind of chargé d'affaires with orders, known also to the Porte, to communicate constantly with the admiral of the squadron cruising in the Archipelago. I am really inclined to think that our business would gain by the arrangement.[63]

Stratford's affection for his cousin was undiminished, as he presently proved by putting the embassy into mourning on the death of the premier's mother (an arrangement he never observed, it may be noticed in passing, when members of the royal family died, though protocol invariably required it), but his patience and pride were being tested to the utmost. Notification of Lord Dudley's appointment to the Foreign Office reached him in June, but 'alas, not a line, not a word beyond'. To Planta, he expressed again the sentiments already addressed to Canning, demanding that Britain either give up all idea of mediating or resort to the threat of sterner measures. He repeated the suggestion of replacing the ambassador with a chargé d'affaires.[64] While it is beyond question that Stratford was horrified by the consequences of an Ottoman recovery in Greece, because of the hideous persecution which would follow in its train, it is also apparent that the prospect of personal defeat galled him exceedingly. Was the Internuncio to have the last laugh, along with the Ottomans? Would Chabert, his half-obsequious, half-contemptuous dragoman, yet have the pleasure of writing to Strangford, for the enjoyment of the whole Metternichian gang, that the Holy Alliance and its principle of immovability had once again triumphed? 'It will not do for us to *sneak* out of the business. That were too good a triumph for our numerous enemies. . . . I do entreat you by our friendship and the honour of our country to lose no time . . . to come to a decision in some sense and to inform me of it without delay.'[65] The treaty of London was signed on 6 July, and disclosed in *The Times* a week later. Only then was a copy sent off to Constantinople, hardly a brisk rate of business, and in a caustic letter to Dudley on 30 July, Stratford referred to a treaty 'concluded as I presume, under Your Lordship's auspices, and as I conjecture, about the middle of May'.[66] By the time the treaty reached him, Stratford knew all about it from other quarters: Ribeaupierre told him when it was signed, Guilleminot told him the contents, and he believed that Ibrahim Pasha, Captain Hamilton, and the Greek provisional government all knew about it before him. In any case, he did not expect the Sultan to listen to the demands which he and his Russian and French colleagues were now enabled to lay before the Sublime Porte. Only military intervention would bring the Sultan face to face with reality.

Stratford's guess proved right. After Akerman, Mahmud II was absolutely opposed to further concession, and there is every sign that it was a personal rather than a collective decision, the Sultan's and not the divan's. In truth, Mahmud II could not afford to give way, even had he chosen to do so. Though he had his way in military affairs, his people were reserving their opinion on him, until they saw what he might do next. Sympathy for the janizaries showed itself briefly but dramatically in the town of Kara Hisar, which was burned to the ground during demonstrations against the new army units. Even in the new units themselves, there was an unexpected revolt of officers, suppressed with executions in 'appalling' number, according to Stratford. The civilian population was both curious and suspicious of the new troops, and much fun was made of the fact that the recruits, young and raw, were taking as much as 12 days to march from Adrianople to Philipopolis; the best janizary units, urged along by their wild music, used to do the journey in 32 hours, and practically without a pause. Nevertheless, for Mahmud II there could be no going back on his plans; he garrisoned every important town in his realm with the new units, except Bursa which was entirely loyal to him, and beyond that sent all available units to Greece. His greatest problem was to find money. Despite a new export tax of 12 per cent on silk, and a rather novel stamp duty of 2½ per cent on imported manufactures, army pay soon fell into arrears, and stayed there, perhaps as a matter of policy. But small wonder that Mahmud II turned his eyes greedily to the religious foundations, the mosques and the schools, whose total incomes were believed to exceed fifty million piastres a year. For the moment, however, the new army had to do its best, short of pay and medical arrangements, and with its cavalry regiments only mounted by forced 'gifts' of horses from pashas and agas.

What is more, the army's best seemed more than sufficient to cope with the last struggles of the Greeks by land. In January 1827, Athens fell to the Ottomans, and Karaiskos' attempt to relieve the Acropolis was defeated in May, Karaiskos himself being among the slain. George Wood, one of the British dragomans acting as an observer in Greece, wrote that Ibrahim, after a long period of inactivity in which many detected a wish to return home, had suddenly gone into action again in the Morea, commencing a programme of systematic village-burning and terrorism by firing Gastouni, a small township, and cutting off the ears of the entire population.[67] The Greeks replied in kind, but a massacre of Ottoman prisoners at St Spiridion in the Piraeus only led to the resignation from the Greek cause of the volunteer commander-in-chief, General Sir Richard Church, who wrote to the provisional government at Napoli, 'the cause of Greece has been to me until this moment dearer than anything in the world: it shall not be dearer to me than my honour'.[68] Then, letters from Mavrocordates brought Stratford the most dramatic news of all: the Acropolis fell to the Ottomans on 5 June, its garrison escaping through the Ottoman lines to Aegina. The success of the Greeks at sea – in May, Cochrane's associate, Captain Hastings, destroyed four Ottoman transports in the gulf of Volo with Congreve rockets – did not counterbalance the land situation and even, Stratford thought, prolonged the agony of the Greek people. He feared Cochrane, not for any damage that sailor might do the Ottoman fleet, but in case the Greeks mistakenly decided to take Cochrane's advice and fight on for complete independence. This could only help the Ottomans, leaving Stratford and his colleagues to 'mediate for a shadow'.[69] This was just what Mahmud II wanted, for time was on the side of his new army, and he pressed on. Even as the terms of the treaty of London were conveyed to the Porte, new regiments were mobilizing, British and German cloth was providing their uniforms, Egypt their drill sergeants, Brescia their muskets. Mahmud II, according to a French rumour, was immersed in the *Code Napoléon*, but Stratford was nearer the mark in predicting that the Sultan was 'not so much actuated by comprehensive views of national improvement as by motives of self-preservation, and the love of absolute dominion'. And it was 'love of absolute dominion' which led Mahmud II to refuse to discuss Greece. Meanwhile, Mavrocordates wrote to Stratford, 'il ne nous reste que l'espérance de ce que l'Angleterre fera'.[70]

Small wonder that, in Greece, when the treaty of London became known, 'men went mad with joy'; that bells rang out in Corfu; and 'Christians gave thanks to God'.[71] The treaty was theoretically an impartial intervention, but with the Greek cause virtually lost, any intervention favoured the Greeks. The signatories of the treaty proposed an immediate armistice and acceptance by the Ottomans of mediation within a month: the clauses of their agreement were addressed to both belligerents, but the plan for action rested upon the possibility of an Ottoman refusal, the Greeks having invited European mediation long before. Should it be necessary, the contracting powers would intervene in the struggle to impose the armistice, 'without, however, taking any part in the hostilities between the two contending parties', a phrase intended to mean that they would simply prevent further supplies from Egypt or Turkey reaching the peninsula of Greece.[72] With peace established, the allies would negotiate the frontiers of the new Greece with both the contending parties, and not the Ottomans alone. Greece was to remain an Ottoman sovereign territory, paying annual tribute, but her internal administration would be Greek.

The treaty was presented at the Sublime Porte on 16 August by the British, French, and Russian chief dragomans, but several days before that, Stratford and Guilleminot had written to Admiral Codrington and Admiral de Rigny, their countries' naval chiefs in the Mediterranean, recommending them 'to invite the commanders of the belligerent forces to abstain from committing themselves to any further offensive operation'.[73] Ribeaupierre had no Russian naval commander with whom to communicate as yet but gave his adherence, 'pleine et entière', to the wording his colleagues gave to their instructions.[74] Stratford's letter advised Codrington to act immediately, saying that he expected separating the combatants would prove easier than getting the Sultan to accept the mediation. The Sultan, in fact, anticipated the ambassador's approach with a broadside aimed particularly at the British. Though pretending not to be a rejoinder to Stratford's long pressure for a mediation, it obviously was so, and quoted against him Strangford's opinion that Greece was an internal Ottoman problem, as well as making the point that the Greeks had received quite illegal assistance from 'une certaine puissance amie'.[75] The proclamation, in which the Sultan made plain his determination to keep Greece, which he had received from 'le maître de l'univers', was sent to all the embassies in Constantinople, and its contents were seemingly known outside the legations too on the afternoon when Frederick Pisani, Desgranges of the French embassy, and one of the Franchini brothers, representing Russia, filed into the office of the *reis effendi* with the terms of the treaty of London.

In light, perhaps, of the Sultan's stubbornness, the ambassadors had shortened the period within which the mediation must be accepted from four to two weeks. Desgranges presented the document without comment, and the *reis effendi* laughed nervously, and tried to refuse it. What was it? he asked. They did not know. He tried to give it back. It was laid on his sofa, and the dragomans withdrew. When the *reis effendi* opened the letter, he discovered that it contained an ultimatum:

> un nouveau refus, une réponse évasive ou insuffisante, ou bien même un silence complet de sa part mettrait les Cabinets Alliés dans la

> nécessité d'avoir recours aux mesures qu'elles jugeront les plus efficaces pour faire cesser un état de choses devenu incompatibles avec les véritables intérêts de la Porte, avec la sûreté du commerce en général et la parfaite tranquillité de l'Europe.[76]

Never before had the Sultan been confronted with such unanimity; even Prussia instructed her ambassador to send a supporting letter. The Internuncio, also ordered to associate himself with his colleagues, would not do so, and was reprimanded for his refusal. On 1 September, the same dragomans recrossed the Golden Horn for the official Ottoman reply. As Stratford expected, the *reis effendi* answered with a negative, 'positive, absolue, définitive, invariable, éternelle'.[77] The resources of diplomacy were exhausted, and Stratford, writing home to say so, asked for his release, and for someone else to superintend the future of Greece.

Stratford was worried. Already, he expected the orders to the admirals to produce 'some decisive intelligence of a gunpowder description'.[78] It was difficult to see how it could be otherwise, for while the allies had as yet shown no intention of interfering in the land fighting in Greece, their intention to impose an armistice through the agency of warships was fraught with danger. The admirals were instructed 'to prevent the measures which you shall adopt against the Ottoman marine from degenerating into hostilities'[79] but, after Canning's death, no one was very clear how this could be done. The problem was entrusted to Huskisson and Sir George Cockburn, at the Admiralty, the former proposing, not very intelligently, that neutral shipping should not be stopped or searched, 'provided they were *bonafide* and *innocent* neutrals', while the latter felt only armed escorts should be 'detained'. Codrington, a pro-Greek but obedient officer, sought the clear-cut orders which politicians so often deny to men of action, and wrote of his 'uncomfortable uncertainty as to what he was to do' to Stratford.

> Neither I nor the French admiral can make out how far we are by force to prevent the Turks, if obstinate, from pursuing any line of conduct which we are instructed to oppose, without committing hostility. Surely it must be like a blockade; if an attempt be made to force it, by force only can that attempt be resisted.[80]

Stratford replied after consulting his Russian and French colleagues:

> On the subject of *collision*, for instance, we agree that, although the measures to be executed by you are not adopted in a hostile spirit, and although it is clearly the intention of the allied governments to avoid, if possible, anything that may bring on war, yet the prevention of supplies, as stated in your instructions, is ultimately to be enforced, if necessary, and when all other means are exhausted, by cannon shot.[81]

Codrington embodied the sense of Stratford's reply in a general order to his captains. In later times, when Navarino had passed into history, Stratford conceded that had he known more of Codrington's 'fiery and enterprising spirit', he would have spoken only of 'coercion or forcible means' rather than 'cannon shot', but the end result would hardly have been any different.[82] The *Morning Chronicle* and other critics naturally fastened on Stratford's elucidation, but whatever was said against him, he had not added anything to Codrington's instructions. He made explicit what the Admiralty, whether from confusion, cowardice, or incompetence, left implicit in its orders.

Stratford, like all the other Europeans resident in the Ottoman dominions, prayed that hostilities would be avoided, and was told by the *reis effendi* that, in a fit of rage, the Sultan cried out that the streets of Constantinople would run with Christian blood if the European powers committed any warlike act. The British minister had a strong personal reason for his disquiet, telling Planta: 'Eliza shows signs of being in a situation which makes it my duty not to expose her to any unnecessary risk.'[83] Writing to the consuls throughout the Levant, he instructed them to send him immediate news of any collision, and from Codrington he obtained a vessel which lay off the Dardanelles 'to receive the female portion of my family', that is, the wives of the consuls and dragomans as well as Mrs Canning. The Russians, similarly, had two ships, 'seemingly merchantmen', lying off Buyukdere, to whisk Ribeaupierre away.[84] On 2 September, the Greek provisional government, now at Aegina, accepted the intervention of the powers, and on the 4th, Stratford received news of his cousin's death. It was an immense blow, the greatest he ever sustained in his public career, and it led the Ottomans to half-expect some sensational reversal of the plans they now associated with the name Canning. Stratford once again reveals himself in his correspondence as a man of rather brittle morale, and the grim pleasure with which he sent in the ultimatum on 16 August slipped within the month to cautious anxiety. It was left to Ribeaupierre to tell the Porte in unambiguous terms that if any embassy was touched, Russia would take the Principalities at once. Stratford meanwhile thought the French might desert the alliance and hatch a counter-alliance with Austria, Prussia, Muhammad Ali, and the Sultan. On 2 October, he heard that a large Egyptian expedition, consisting of four sail, 15 frigates, 17 corvettes, and 24 transports bearing 5,000 Egyptian troops had got past Codrington and slipped into the harbour at Navarino, and blamed the event on the collusion of de Rigny and the French officers in the Egyptian fleet.

A little-regarded piece of the history of modern Greece also occurred in Constantinople about this time, and served to depress Stratford's spirits further: the Greek patriarch went in procession to the Porte to receive pardon and amnesty for those regions of Greece which had sent in notices of submission. Believing they could only be forgeries, or have been extorted by the Ottomans, he sent Pisani to try and inspect them. The dragoman returned, saying petitions, seemingly genuine, had come in from Janina, Negropont, Neopatria, Loidoviki, Carponisi, and the general areas of Arta, Livadia, Thebes, and Athens. Stratford even began to persuade himself that Codrington should be called off, since to curb the Greeks by sea where they had been supreme while doing nothing to check the Ottomans by land 'would surely be no less absurd than unjust in as much as it would have the effect of paralysing the exertions of that party which has accepted our offers with gratitude and of favouring the Turks who have rejected the same proposals with disdain'.[85] He wrote a very stern letter to Colonel Cradock, the man his late cousin had sent to Egypt to win the pasha from the side of Mahmud II, censoring that officer for having misled everyone into thinking that Muhammad Ali was by now virtually a neutral.[86]

The fortnight of grace allowed the Turks and Egyptians expired on 7 September, the Egyptian fleet joined the Turkish in Navarino on the 9th, and Codrington arrived off the same harbour on the 11th. It was now his task, under his orders from the admiralty and the terms of the treaty of London, to 'impede further hostilities'. On the 19th, he notified the Turkish admiral of the treaty, and his intention to enforce it, and when some Turkish warships tried to leave the harbour two days later, he herded them back in. On the 25th, both Codrington and de Rigny went ashore to speak to Ibrahim, the pair of them sitting side by side on a sofa otherwise covered by the recumbent Egyptian princeling. Ibrahim tried to play for time, but they put aside the gold coffee cups and requested a firm promise that Ibrahim would suspend all hostilities for twenty days. Hand on heart, Ibrahim promised, and declared his promise sacred. The following day, he sought to be released from it, having heard that the Greeks were attacking Patras. Codrington refused. On 1 October, a very large naval force – seven frigates, 28 corvettes and brigs – tried to sail for Patras, and a Turkish admiral came aboard Codrington's flagship to explain that they had sailed with his, Codrington's, permission. Codrington rectified this erroneous opinion with a single shot across the bows of the leading Turkish ship, and again the Turks retired. A number of them slipped out of Navarino under cover of darkness and worsening weather, but on the 5th, Codrington rounded them up and brought them back again. So, up to this point, Codrington was the soul of discretion, and had used even cannon shot without producing hostilities. Ibrahim had been shown that Codrington meant business, and when hostilities finally came it was not the result of Codrington interpreting his orders one way or another, but a retaliation to Turkish cannon shot. Codrington, after all, had delighted Howe on the Glorious First of June, and Nelson at Trafalgar, with his expertise as a gunner.

On 14 October, the allied squadrons of Codrington, de Rigny, and the Russian admiral, Heiden, assembled off Navarino and Ibrahim, thwarted in his hopes of getting ships to Patras, began the destruction of the land area visible from the sea; after three days of watching villages going up in flames, the allied commanders were sent ashore to remind Ibrahim of his promise of 25 September. On the 18th, a demand for an interview produced the reply that Ibrahim's whereabouts were unknown, and the admirals decided that, since they could not prevent the devastation from their present position, they would enter the harbour 'in order to renew to Ibrahim propositions which entering into the spirit of the treaty were evidently to the advantage of the Porte itself'. Codrington later explained that his main 'proposition' would have been for the Egyptian ships to go home, yet there are signs that his tolerance was wearing thin. Heiden said Russia and the Ottoman Empire were at war and urged him on; de Rigny, caught like many Frenchmen between Egyptian loyalties and some pro-Greek feelings, also supported Codrington without reserve. Codrington gave out final orders on the 19th, and they contained the suggestive phrase, 'No shot must be fired before a given signal, so that it may be the Turks who open fire'.[87] Writing to his wife the same day, he said – and it was, under the circumstances now imminent, a decidedly ambiguous metaphor – 'My own squadron will think it a pity if it all ends in smoke. Such however is my own expectation.'[88] On the 20th, the allied force sailed in, in double line rather than battle formation, but with the tompions out of the gun mouths. The latter point impressed the Turks. They hardly knew what a battle formation was. Codrington refused a Turkish request to keep his ships outside the harbour, entered without incident, and dropped anchor. But a ship's boat sent to move a fireship was fired upon, despite its flag of truce: its parent ship, *Dartmouth*, returned the musket fire. The French flagship joined in, and was fired on by an Egyptian neighbour with cannon. The battle became general, between 24 allied and 89 Turkish and Egyptian ships.

> One Sunday afternoon some days later I was on the point of going to our daily meeting at the French embassy, when a shabby bit of paper, like a note picked up in the street, was put into my hands. I opened it hastily and found that it contained intelligence of the deepest interest. Captain Cotton, in command of a cutter or small sloop, reported that he had been becalmed at a distance of several miles from the island of Cerigo, and in that position had heard a violent and protracted cannonade attended from time to time with loud explosions. He had subsequently reached Smyrna, and the intelligence was forwarded to me forthwith. It could not be doubted that a general action had taken place, and that several ships on one side or the other had been blown up. I thrust it into my pocket, and went on to the conference. Dispatches from the squadrons were read over, and some ordinary business was transacted. The reports were quite satisfactory and M. Ribeaupierre was about to retire with me, in compliment to M. Guilleminot's dinner hour, when I begged a moment's pause in order to communicate a few lines which might prove of interest to all of us. So saying I drew the explosive note from my pocket and placed it quietly in the general's hands. As he read, the colour forsook his face, and presently turning to me, he said, 'Trois têtes dans un bonnet – n'est ce pas?' I could have added, 'et dans un panin, peut-être' but I confined myself to a word of assent.[89]

The ambassadors agreed to send in an explanation, but not an apology, to the Porte, and also a request to be informed if the Ottoman Empire intended to declare war. The *reis effendi* already knew of the battle, having heard from the pasha of Smyrna by the same messenger who brought Stratford's 'shabby bit of paper'. Consul Werry, an insubordinate pro-Ottoman was the pasha's informant, and Stratford asked the Foreign Office to dismiss him for his indiscretions.[90] The *reis effendi* controlled himself only by a very great effort, and said relations with the embassies would be maintained for the present. A few days later, with every embassy prepared for war with the Ottoman Empire, and anti-European demonstrations in Constantinople, the dragomans were told to collect the Sultan's reply to the ambassadors. Stratford sent for Chabert, who

> came with evident symptoms of fear, pale and trembling, like a conscience-stricken culprit. There was no mistaking his state of mind. I looked at him, probably with some corresponding expression of countenance, and said, 'I perceive, sir, that you are unequal to this occasion; sit down, and I will send another interpreter to the Porte'.[91]

The substitute chosen brought back a stern reply to the effect that the *ambassadors* had violated the law of nations. Wisely, the ambassadors did not seek to reply, and Stratford, half-expecting some violence, began to burn embassy papers which, as he said, 'might have been misinterpreted by angry examiners'.[92]

A few days later, Codrington's own account of the battle of Navarino arrived. It was written only hours after the destruction of the Turkish and Egyptian fleet. 'A great many have blown up, and several have been sunk, and the harbour is so covered with wrecks, that I imagine such a scene has scarcely ever been witnessed.' Codrington made no attempt to throw any of the responsibility on to Stratford, and it was no contradiction of his earlier attitude that Stratford should now feel Codrington had gone too far. Stratford's recommendation to use cannon shot as an ultimate resource in the interdiction of war supplies sent to the Morea did not give Codrington any warrant to use cannon shot to stop 'this brutal war of extermination', and while the ambassador recognized that the sailor had cut a very difficult knot for the diplomatists, he did not condone the entry of the allied force into Navarino harbour. It was, he thought, 'a flagrant breach of courtesy' and a decision unsupported by the letter or spirit of the Admiralty's instructions.[93]

The ambassadors found themselves in a sort of quarantine, with Ottoman guards patrolling outside their residences at night, and Stratford swore a thousand times that once he got away from the country, he would be careful never to be trapped into a return. Only a few years before, he knew, he and his colleagues would have been thrown into the grim dungeon of the Seven Towers, and Mahmud II showed no sensitivity to European feelings. By contrast, dispatches from Egypt said Muhammad Ali had accepted the loss of his fleet with quiet resignation, and Stratford took an early opportunity to recommend the withdrawal of Ibrahim from Greece.[94]

A dispatch from Dudley, dated 16 October, gave Stratford the opportunity he wanted; although it made no suggestion of breaking off relations, Stratford adroitly used it to that end. The dispatch actually was intended to be a final warning to the Sultan, and stressed that Britain still sought 'the integrity of the Ottoman Empire'. But once Russia turned 'from armed mediation to downright hostility, the Porte would be exposed to a powerful and exasperated enemy whose aggression would be justified in the sight of mankind by the infatuated obstinacy which has misguided her counsels'.[95] Determined to leave Constantinople, and afraid that everything might yet be brought to a standstill, Stratford meanwhile urged the Foreign Office that 'the allied powers must either resort to stronger measures or be content to be baffled by the inflexibility and inert force of the Turkish government'.[96] He suggested to his colleagues, and they needed little persuasion, to ask for their passports, on the ground that the Ottoman Empire was refusing to disclose her intentions towards Greece or Britain, France, and Russia. The *reis effendi* received Stratford privately on 15 November, and was fully aware that this was his country's last chance to settle peacefully, but could do nothing since the extremists in the divan were holding out for a change of heart in the new government in London. Stratford himself expected some such change, and also believed in a plot in London to have him withdrawn. Consequently, he pressed the *reis effendi* as hard as he could for a concession over Greece, being determined to leave if he did not get one. Private interest abetted his haste at every turn: he was very disturbed by a letter from Addington, his old Washington associate, which ran, 'England is no country for a poor, and unconnected man. Society shuts its door in his face. . . . England is the most ferociously aristocratic and exclusive country, in point of society, in the world.' Young men went abroad to seek their fortunes. Hiley Addington hinted pretty strongly that Stratford must come home to find his.[97]

The divan, cruder in its perceptions than the patriotic *reis effendi*, saw Dudley's dispatch and Stratford's pleadings as a chance to separate Britain from the alliance, and on 20 November, only four weeks after Navarino, the dragoman of the Porte brought Stratford a remarkable proposition. 'If His Majesty's government would abstain from pressing the Greek question, the Porte was ready to enter into engagements most advantageous to Great Britain and the Sultan would in that case even go to the length of according a kind of constitution to his people.' The *reis effendi* was instructed by Mahmud II to negotiate with the British ambassador at home, and even to give way, in the last resort, over Greece. At midnight, and after several hours talking, the *reis effendi* came round cautiously to the point. Almost carelessly, he asked how much territory the Ottoman Empire stood to lose if she consented to a mediation, conducted solely by Stratford. He was told it was now too late to exclude Russia and France but not too late to trust Britain to restrain Russia. Rebuffed, the *reis effendi* concluded the meeting with a long diatribe against the Greeks, calling them 'a houseful of scorpions whose owner was unjustly prevented from clearing the tenement of its obnoxious inhabitants'.[98] Stratford invited him to keep his patience and consider the Greek question 'like a statesman'. But it was, of course, singularly abhorrent for an Ottoman to think in terms of surrendering Islamic territories to the control of infidels.

Stratford went home to Buyukdere and advised his wife to begin her packing. His secretaries sorted the correspondence for a few days, and handed most of it into the custody of the Dutch embassy. British merchant ships had the greatest difficulty in getting permission to sail out through the Dardanelles, and of 120 ships which arrived at Constantinople in the last five weeks of Stratford's residence, only 25 got away before him. There was, in fact, great loss through confiscation of cargoes after he left, and British merchants suffered heavily. The Ottomans argued that the three ambassadors had no authority from their courts to leave their posts. Refused their passports, the ambassadors agreed to leave without them. Stratford and Guilleminot left on the same day, Ribeaupierre ten days later. They agreed to meet in Corfu.

On the evening of 8 December, with heavy sheets of rain sweeping along the Bosporus shore, the 'family' of the British ambassador assembled at the residence of the consul-general in Pera, attachés, consuls, dragomans, and their wives. Descending through the squelching and deserted lanes – Mahmud II had ordained that all good Muslims must be indoors by 8:30 p.m. – they joined a small merchant ship and, after running aground at one place, reached the Dardanelles, and the custom-house at Kilid Bar, in broad daylight. Knowing they could not escape identification, the ship was inspected. Stratford went ashore personally to wait on the pasha, who did not know him and thought he was simply a traveller. 'The windows of his Excellency's apartment looked out upon the water, and when I saw that our vessel had cleared the line of his guns, I told him who I was, and explained the circumstances under which I had left Constantinople. He took my communication with Turkish gravity, and good humour.'[99] A British frigate at Smyrna conveyed the party to Corfu. There Eliza Canning had her twenty-first birthday, as she had formerly had her eighteenth. In theory, her husband should have awaited his colleagues and his government's instructions there, but instead he pushed on to London at speed, leaving her to follow at the more leisurely pace her health now required. In Smyrna and Constantinople, the British consuls took down their flags on 15 January 1828. Kapodistrias, as first president, was just arriving in Greece.

NOTES

1. Canning to Stratford (various dispatches), 12 Oct. 1825, FO 78/133. Stratford's instructions were drawn up by Strangford. The latter wrote to Bagot, 'I am directed by Canning major to prepare not only my own instructions, but those of Canning minor – a pretty job – for the purpose of executing which I am now *planted* in London'. Strangford to Bagot, 30 Aug. 1825, *George Canning and His Friends*, ed. Josceline Bagot (New York, 1909), i. 292.
2. Stratford to Canning, 16 Dec. 1825, FO 78/133.
3. Memoirs, in Lane-Poole, *Life*, i. 398 ff. The shrewd Fanariot, Mavrocordates, preferred compromise to death or glory, particularly in the existing situation, and he knew that small embryonic societies cannot deliver ultimatums to great

states. The Principalities, under Greek Fanariot leadership, had extricated themselves from Ottoman domination by putting the prosaic comforts of autonomy under Russian patronage ahead of heroic dreams of immediate independence. If in Greece, as in the Principalities, the Ottoman population could be edged out, and administration was centred in experienced Fanariot hands, then life could be made more bearable and taxation cut down sharply. Men like Canning could help to bring this situation about. Mavrocordates was therefore candid enough about the seriousness of the military position and conceded to Stratford that the defiant fatalism of the provisional government might not be the most effective way of helping Europe to help Greece. The only sentiment that Mavrocordates concealed was his excitement at the death of Alexander I, and the possibility that Russia might, under new royal leadership, take up the Greek cause with resolution. Otherwise, he talked about the form autonomy under continued Ottoman suzerainty might take.

4. Stratford to Canning, 10 Jan. 1826, FO 78/141; memoirs, in Lane-Poole, *Life*, i. 388; Canning to Stratford, 6 and 9 Jan. 1826, FO 78/140; Canning to Stratford, 9 Jan. 1826, FO 352/13A/1.
5. Stratford to Canning, 10 Jan. 1826, FO 78/141. It was Miaulis' son who had carried the Act of Submission to London. Miaulis himself might well have frustrated the Egyptian landings in Greece had his quarrelling countrymen followed his resolute example and put external enemies first. In fact Missolonghi held out until 22 April.
6. Memoirs, in Lane-Poole, *Life*, i. 389–90.
7. Ibid., p. 391.
8. Bartholomew Pisani, the incomparable first dragoman of earlier days, was ill and died on 8 Sept. 1826. He was, wrote Stratford, 'skilled beyond any of his professors' in Ottoman Turkish. See Stratford to Canning, 8 Sept. 1826, FO 78/144.
9. See A.B. Cunningham, *Eastern Questions in the Nineteenth Century: Collected Essays*, ed. E. Ingram (London, 1992), pp. 1–22. See also memo by Cartwright, 10 Oct. 1825, FO 78/135.
10. Stratford to Canning, 19, 20, and 27 April 1826, FO 78/141; Lane-Poole, *Life*, i. 400 *et seq*.
11. Stratford to Canning, 19 April 1826, FO 78/141. The next day Stratford reported the Ottoman losses at Missolonghi as numbering 5,000, yet he still felt, after what he had seen and heard in Greece, that 'without a miracle the Greek insurrection cannot be much longer maintained'. See Stratford to Canning, 28 April 1826, FO 78/141.
12. Stratford to Canning, 7 April 1826, FO 78/141. This bitter reaction stunned Stratford who wrote home asking for fresh instructions in the belief that, as things now stood, any further pressure on his part would be 'attended with more prejudice to our interests than benefit to Greece'. Stratford to Canning, 28 April 1826, FO 78/141.
13. Stratford to Canning, 19 April 1826, FO 78/141.
14. Canning to Granville, 13 Jan. 1826, A.G. Stapleton, *George Canning and His Times* (London, 1859), pp. 471–2.
15. Canning to Stratford, 10 Feb. 1826, FO 78/140; Canning to Stratford, 9 Jan. 1826, FO 352/13A/1. The Russian ambassador, Prince Lieven, provided the information about the depopulation project. In late October Lieven told Canning that Russia had information that before Ibrahim Pasha's army was put in motion, an agreement was made between Mahmud II and Muhammad

Ali whereby Ibrahim Pasha was to retain whatever part of Greece he conquered and 'that his plan for disposing of his conquest is . . . to remove the whole Greek population, carrying them off into slavery in Egypt . . . and to repeople the country with Egyptians and others of the Mohammedan religion'. 'Memorandum on the conference 25 Oct. [1825]', *Despatches, Correspondence, and Memoranda of Field Marshal Arthur Duke of Wellington*, ed. duke of Wellington (London, 1867–80), ii. 547.
16. Canning to Strangford, 14 Oct. 1825, FO 65/149.
17. Wellington to Canning, 22 Nov. 1825, *Despatches of Wellington*, ii. 568–70.
18. Canning to Wellington, 10 Feb. 1826, *Desptaches of Wellington*, iii. 85–93. A copy of these instructions was sent to Stratford, who was told to read them and return them to London. See Canning to Stratford, secret and confidential, 14 Feb. 1826, FO 78/140.
19. Canning to Stratford, 10 Feb. 1826, FO 78/140.
20. Strangford to Bagot, 7 March 1826, *Canning and His Friends*, ii. 335.
21. Wellington to Stratford, private, 27 March 1826, in Stratford to FO, 28 April 1826, FO 78/142. In 1841 Napier wrote:

> I do not know whether I have done right or not in settling the Eastern Question. . . . The French are in a rage. . . . You have seen me as a lord high admiral, a commodore, and a general, I have now turned a negotiator, and have made peace with Mehemet Ali. . . . I shall either be hung by the government or made a bishop.

Temperley, *Crimea*, p. 133.
22. See Charles W. Crawley, *The Question of Greek Independence: A Study of British Policy in the Near East, 1821–1833* (London, 1930), p. 58; H. W. V. Temperley, *The Foreign Policy of Canning, 1822–1827* (London, 1925), pp. 354–5.
23. Quoted in Temperley, *Canning*, p. 355. See also H. W. V. Temperley, 'Princess Lieven and the Protocol of 4 April 1826', *English Historical Review*, xxxix (1924), 55–77. In the first Temperley argues that Canning was prepared to act with Russia and framed Wellington's instructions accordingly; in the second, he suggests that Canning was taken by surprise by the protocol. Madame Lieven certainly agreed on the latter score, and wrote *à propos* of Canning's acceptance of the news: 'He showed to me naïvely enough his hesitation and even his regret.' What disturbed Canning? Unquestionably, his main concern was for the obscurities of the international situation; this 'diplomatic revolution', which brought about an alignment with Russia that was difficult to accommodate within 'liberal' politics. But surely too, there was the failure of Stratford's unilateral effort to bring the Ottomans to reason, for that failure, followed by the protocol, committed Britain to action without allowing her the sole direction of even her own policy over the Eastern Question. In signing the protocol, Wellington obviously thought that the Ottomans must find Britain and Russia militarily irresistible. In accepting the protocol, Canning must have wondered if the Sultan would listen to Britain *as a friend* now that an Anglo-Russian alignment existed. A tributary Greece, as opposed to a totally free state, would also lean far more on Russia, so Britain seemed committed to the 'hospodarization' of Greece, and further qualifying Ottoman authority. Finally, the protocol did not restrain Russia from unilateral intervention if the Sultan rejected the joint mediation.
24. Temperley, *Canning*, p. 391. For the full text of the St Petersburg protocol, 4 April 1826, see ibid., appendix vii, pp. 586–94.

25. Stratford to Canning, 29 April 1826, Lane-Poole, *Life*, i. 406.
26. 'Memo on Greek affairs', n.d., in Stratford to Hamilton, 27 May 1826, FO 78/142.
27. Stratford to Canning, 28 April 1826, FO 78/141.
28. Stratford to Canning, 17 May 1826, FO 78/142.
29. Stratford to Hamilton, 25 May 1826, in Stratford to Canning, 27 May 1826, FO 78/142. News of the St Petersburg protocol, arriving at the embassy from London in late May, only seemed to justify Stratford's caution further, for the protocol spoke of a tributary, but not of an independent Greece. 'It is needless to dwell on the surprise and embarrassment which I experienced on learning the course of policy adopted by the Russian cabinet' and the duke of Wellington, Stratford explained to his cousin. He had arrived at Constantinople threatening Russian vengeance unless the Sultan made concessions to the Greeks. Then within weeks, the Russian ultimatum came, making no reference whatever to Greece, and so silencing him. And finally the protocol, taking up Greece after all, but only the cause of a semi-independent Greece. How could he explain these sudden changes to the Porte? The 'pacific policy of Great Britain forbids indeed my looking at any interference of a real and decisive nature.' See Stratford to Canning, 27 May 1826, FO 78/142.
30. Stratford to Canning, 4 May 1826, FO 78/142.
31. 'Memo on Greek affairs', n.d., in Stratford to Hamilton, 27 May 1826, FO 78/142.
32. Stratford to Canning, 16 June 1826, FO 78/143.
33. Stratford to Canning, 29 May 1826, FO 78/142.
34. Stratford to Canning, 17 June 1826, FO 78/143. 'It falls to my lot,' Stratford began his dispatch, 'to record one of the most remarkable events which has occurred in the history of the . . . Empire.'
35. Stratford to Canning, 16, 17, and 18 June 1826, FO 78/143; see also Lane-Poole, *Life*, i. 417–26.
36. Stratford to Canning, 22, 28, and 30 June 1826, FO 78/143. Stratford put the total number of janizaries at 150,000; the true number was probably close to 35,000.
37. Stratford to Canning, 12 Aug. 1826, FO 78/144.
38. Ibid.
39. Stratford to Canning, 20 June 1826, FO 78/143; see also Lane-Poole, *Life*, i. 422.
40. Stratford to Canning, 31 Aug., 8 Sept. 1826, FO 78/144.
41. Stratford to Canning, 30 Sept. 1826, FO 78/145.
42. Stratford to Canning, 8 Sept. 1826, FO 78/144.
43. To raise the Greek question three days after the destruction of the janizaries was not the best timing. As Stratford found out months later, the slaughter of the remaining garrison and civilians at Missolonghi by the Ottomans was provoked by the Greeks hanging captive Egyptians from the ramparts and burning wounded Ottomans on pyres. See Meyer to Rudsdell, 7 June 1826, FO 78/145.
44. Stratford to Canning, 18 June 1826, FO 78/143.
45. Stratford to Canning, 1 Sept. 1826, FO 78/144. For Stratford's new instructions, see Canning to Stratford, 15 Aug. 1826, FO 78/140; Canning to Stratford, private, 5 Sept. 1826, FO 352/13A/1.
46. Stratford to Canning, 30 May 1826, FO 78/142.
47. Meyer to Stratford [several reports], in Stratford to Canning, 30 June, 22 and

23 Aug., 7 Sept. 1826, FO 78/143.
48. Stratford to Canning, 10 June 1826, FO 78/142.
49. Stratford to Canning, 12 June 1826, FO 78/143. See also Hamilton to Neale, 29 March 1826, in Stratford to Canning, 28 April 1826, FO 78/142.
50. Stratford to Canning, 30 June, 22 Aug. 1826, FO 78/143; Stratford to Hamilton, 18 Aug. 1826, FO 352/15A/3.
51. Stratford to Canning, 20 Oct., 10 Dec. 1826, FO 78/145.
52. Stratford to Canning, 30 Sept. 1826, FO 78/145.
53. Stratford to Planta, 25 Feb. 1827, FO 352/17/3.
54. Quoted in Temperley, *Canning*, p. 394.
55. Bathurst to Wellington, 5 Sept. 1826, *Despatches of Wellington*, ii. 402; Wellington to Stratford, 2 Aug. 1826, ibid., p. 355; Canning to Stratford, private, 3 July 1826, FO 352/13A/1.
56. Temperley, *Canning*, p. 398.
57. Lieven to Canning, 23 March 1826, quoted in Temperley, *Canning*, p. 399.
58. FO to Stratford, 14 July 1827, FO 78/151. In this dispatch Canning discusses the treaty of London as a 'treaty for the pacification of the Levant'. Soon afterwards, the time allowed the Porte for the acceptance of the treaty was cut from four to two weeks. See Dudley to Stratford, 26 July 1827, FO 78/151.
59. See Crawley, *Greek Independence*, p. 74.
60. Stratford to Canning, 16 and 19 March 1827, FO 78/153.
61. Stratford to Canning, 24 April 1827, FO 78/153.
62. Planta to Stratford, 13 April 1827, Stratford to Planta, 21 May 1827, FO 352/17/3.
63. Stratford to Wellesley, 9 July 1827, FO 352/17/3; Stratford to Canning, private, 30 May 1827, FO 78/154.
64. Stratford to Planta, 11 June 1827, FO 352/17/3; Stratford to Dudley, 3 July 1827, FO 78/155.
65. Stratford to Planta, 11 June 1827, FO 352/17/3. In late May Stratford wrote to Canning asking him to get rid of Chabert, saying 'he has already been too long here'. Stratford to Canning, private, 30 May 1827, FO 78/154.
66. Stratford to Dudley, 30 July 1827, FO 78/155.
67. Encl. by Wood in Stratford to Canning, 29 May 1827, FO 78/154.
68. Encl. by Church in Stratford to Canning, 29 May 1827, FO 78/154.
69. Stratford to Canning, 25 Jan., 26 Feb., 19 March, 28 April 1827, FO 78/152, 153.
70. Stratford to Canning, 30 May 1827, FO 78/154; encl. by Mavrocordates in Stratford to Dudley, 12 June 1827, FO 8/155.
71. Quoted in Crawley, *Greek Independence*, p. 79; Stratford to Dudley, 30 July 1827, FO 78/155.
72. The period of acceptance was cut back to two weeks following *The Times* disclosure of the treaty. This news was relayed to Stratford in a blunt letter in which Dudley, after commenting on the Austrian and Prussian refusal to be party to the treaty and of the dispatch of an agent to Egypt to warn off Muhammad Ali, concluded that Britain might have to proceed with 'a very different kind of (intervention/interference)' if necessary. Dudley to Stratford, 13 and 14 July 1827, FO 352/19A/1.
73. Stratford to Codrington, 6, 7, and 13 Aug., 29 Sept. 1827, FO 352/17/7; Stratford to Dudley, 9 Aug. 1827, FO 78/155.
74. Ribeaupierre to Stratford, 7 Aug. 1827, FO 352/18/2, see also Stratford to Dudley, 9 Aug. 1827, FO 78/155.

Stratford Canning, Mahmud II, and Greece

75. See Stratford to Dudley, 12 June 1827, FO 78/155.
76. Stratford to Dudley, 19 Aug. 1827, FO 78/155.
77. Stratford thought that Muhammad Ali's decision to allow his fleet to sail after all tipped the scales towards the Sultan's final refusal of the ultimatum and war. Stratford to Dudley, 21 Aug. 1827, FO 78/155.
78. Stratford to Planta, 1 Oct. 1827, quoted in Lane-Poole, *Life*, i. 449.
79. This phrase is repeated in Stratford's dispatch to British consuls, 8 Sept. 1827, in Stratford to Dudley, 15 Sept. 1827, FO 78/156.
80. Codrington to Stratford, 12 Aug. 1827, Adm. 1/467.
81. Stratford to Codrington, 1 Sept. 1827, quoted in Lane-Poole, *Life*, i. 449.
82. Memoirs, in ibid.
83. Stratford to Planta, 1 Oct. 1827, FO 352/17/3.
84. Stratford to Dudley, 16 Sept., 1 Oct. 1827, FO 78/156.
85. Stratford to Dudley, 2 Oct. 1827, FO 78/157.
86. Encl. to Cradock, 28 Sept. 1827, in Stratford to Dudley, 2 Oct. 1827, FO 78/157.
87. Quoted in C.M. Woodhouse, *The Battle of Navarino* (London, 1965), pp. 106–7.
88. Quoted in ibid., p. 108.
89. Memoirs, in Lane-Poole, *Life*, i. 451.
90. Stratford to Dudley, 14 April 1828, FO 78/165.
91. Memoirs, in Lane-Poole, *Life*, i. 453.
92. Ibid., pp. 453–4.
93. Codrington to Stratford, 16 and 20 Oct. 1827, in Stratford to Dudley, 6 Nov. 1827, FO 78/157; memoirs, in Lane-Poole, *Life*, i. 453.
94. Stratford to Dudley, private, 28 Jan., 10 Feb. 1828, FO 78/165.
95. Dudley to Stratford, 16 Oct. 1827, FO 78/151.
96. Stratford to Dudley, secret and confidential, 20 Nov. 1827, FO 78/158.
97. Addington to Stratford, 25 June 1827, FO 352/19B/7.
98. Stratford to Dudley, 20 Nov. 1827, FO 78/158; Wood to Stratford, 18, 19, 21, and 22 Nov. 1827, FO 352/17/5.
99. Memoirs, in Lane-Poole, *Life*, i. 456.

Bibliography

I. DOCUMENTS AND CORRESPONDENCE

ABERDEEN, GEORGE GORDON, EARL OF, *The Correspondence of Lord Aberdeen and Princess Lieven, 1832–54*, ed. E. Jones Parry (London, 1939).
ADAIR, ROBERT, *A Reply to the Charges of Robert Adair Esq. against the Bishop of Winchester, in Consequence of a Passage Contained in His Lordship's Memoirs of the Right Hon. W. Pitt* (London, 1821).
—, *Negotiations for the Peace of the Dardanelles in 1808–09, with Despatches and Official Documents* (2 vols., London, 1845).
—, *Two Letters . . . to the Bishop of Winchester, in Answer to the Charge of a Treasonable Misdemeanour Brought by His Lordship against Mr. Fox and Himself in His Life of . . . William Pitt* (London, 1821).
AUCKLAND, WILLIAM EDEN, BARON, *The Journals and Correspondence of William, Lord Auckland*, ed. G. Hogge (4 vols., London, 1860–62).
British Documents on the Origins of the War, eds G.P. Gooch and H.W.V. Temperley (11 vols., London, 1927).
British Intelligence of Events in Greece, 1824–1827: A Documentary Collection, ed. David Dakin (Athens, 1959).
BURGES, JAMES BLAND, *Selections from the Letters and Correspondence of James Bland Burges*, ed. J. Hutton (London, 1885).
BURKE, EDMUND, *A Letter . . . to His Grace the Duke of Portland, on the Conduct of the Minority in Parliament Containing Fifty-Four Articles of Impeachment against the Rt. Hon. C.J. Fox. From the Original Copy, in the Possession of the Notable Duke* (London, 1797).
—, *Correspondence of Edmund Burke*, ed. T.W. Copeland *et al.* (10 vols., Cambridge and Chicago, 1958–78).
—, *Works of the Right Hon. Edmund Burke* (8 vols., London, 1854–89).
BYRON, GEORGE GORDON, BARON, *Byron: A Self Portrait. Letters and Diaries, 1798–1824*, ed. Peter Quennell (2 vols., London, 1950).
—, *Lord Byron: Selected Letters and Journals*, ed. Leslie A. Marchand (Cambridge, Mass., 1982).
—, *Lord Byron's Correspondence, Chiefly with Lady Melbourne, Mr. Hobhouse, the Hon. Douglas Kinnaird, and P.B. Shelley*, ed. John Murray (2 vols., London, 1922).

—, *The Works of Lord Byron: Letters and Journals*, ed. R.E. Prothero (6 vols., London, 1898–1901).
CANNING, GEORGE, *Some Official Correspondence of George Canning*, ed. E.J. Stapleton (2 vols., London, 1887).
—, *George Canning and His Friends*, ed. Josceline Bagot (2 vols., New York, 1909).
CASTLEREAGH, VISCOUNT, *Memoranda and Correspondence of Robert Stewart, Viscount Castlereagh*, ed. marquis of Londonderry (12 vols., London, 1848–54).
CHATHAM, WILLIAM PITT, EARL OF, *Correspondence of William Pitt, Earl of Chatham*, eds W.S. Taylor and J.H. Pringle (4 vols., London, 1838–40).
COLLINGWOOD, CUTHBERT, BARON, *The Private Correspondence of Admiral Lord Collingwood*, ed. E. Hughes (London, 1957).
Corps de Droit Ottoman, ed. G. Young (7 vols., Oxford, 1905–6).
Diplomacy in the Near and Middle East: A Documentary Record, ed. J.C. Hurewitz (2 vols., Princeton, 1956).
ELLENBOROUGH, EDWARD LAW, EARL OF, *A Political Diary, 1828–1830*, ed. Lord Colchester (2 vols., London, 1881).
European Diplomatic History, 1815–1914: Documents and Interpretations, ed. H.N. Weill (New York, 1972).
FOX, CHARLES JAMES, *Memorials and Correspondence of Charles James Fox*, ed. Lord John Russell (4 vols., London, 1853–57).
GENTZ, FRIEDRICH VON, *Briefe von und an F. von Gentz*, ed. C. Wittichen (3 vols., Berlin, 1909).
—, *Zur Geschichte der Orientalischen Frage, 1823–1829* (Vienna, 1877).
GEORGE III, *The Later Correspondence of George III*, ed. A. Aspinall (5 vols., Cambridge, 1963–70).
Geschichte des Abfalls der Greichen vom Turkischen Reiche, ed. Baron A.F. Prokesch von Osten (6 vols., Vienna, 1867).
GLADSTONE, WILLIAM EWART, *The Gladstone Diaries*, ed. M.R.D. Foot and H.C.C. Matthew (9 vols., Oxford, 1968–).
GRANVILLE, GRANVILLE LEVESON-GOWER, EARL, *Lord Granville Leveson-Gower: Private Correspondence, 1781–1821*, ed. Castalia, Countess Granville (2 vols., London, 1916).
GREVILLE, CHARLES, *The Charles Greville Diary*, ed. Philip W. Wilson (2 vols., London, 1927).
HISTORICAL MANUSCRIPTS COMMISSION: *Manuscripts of J.B. Fortescue Esq., Preserved at Dropmore* (10 vols., London, 1892–1927).
LEEDS, FRANCIS GODOLPHIN OSBORNE, DUKE OF, Royal Historical Society: *Political Memoirs of Francis, 5th Duke of Leeds* (London, 1884).
MALMESBURY, JAMES HARRIS, EARL OF, *Diaries and Correspondence of James Harris, First Earl of Malmesbury*, ed. earl of Malmesbury (4 vols., London, 1844).
MILES, WILLIAM AUGUSTUS, *Authentic Correspondence with M. Le Brun, the French Minister and Others, to Feb. 1793* (London, 1796).
MORRITT, JOHN B.S., *Letters of John B.S. Morritt of Rokeby, Descriptive of*

Journeys in Europe and Asia Minor in the Years 1794–1796, ed. C.E. Marindin (London, 1914).

MURRAY KEITH, SIR ROBERT, *Memoirs and Correspondence (Official and Familiar) of Sir Robert Murray Keith, K.B. Envoy Extraordinary and Minister Plenipotentiary at the Court of Dresden, Copenhagen and Vienna, From 1769 to 1792*, ed. Amelia Gillespie Smith (2 vols., London, 1849).

Parliamentary History of England from the Earliest Period, ed. W. Cobbett (36 vols., London, 1820).

Recueil d'actes internationaux de l'empire Ottoman, ed. Gabriel Noradounghian (4 vols., Paris, 1897–1903).

Recueil des Traités et Conventions conclus par la Russie avec les puissances étrangères, ed. Fedor F. de Martens (15 vols., St Petersburg, 1874–1909).

ROYAL HISTORICAL SOCIETY: *Despatches from Paris, 1784–1790*, ed. O. Browning (2 vols., London, 1909–10).

RUSSELL, LORD JOHN, *Early Correspondence of Lord John Russell, 1805–40* ed. Rollo Russell (2 vols., London, 1913).

—, *The Later Correspondence of Lord John Russell, 1840–1878*, ed. G.P. Gooch (2 vols., London, 1925).

SPENCER, GEORGE, EARL, Navy Records Society: *Private Papers of George, Second Earl Spencer, First Lord of the Admiralty 1794–1801*, eds J. Corbett and H.W. Richmond (4 vols., London, 1913–24).

STANHOPE, LEICESTER FITZGERALD CHARLES, EARL, *Greece in 1823 and 1824; Being a Series of Letters and Other Documents on the Greek Revolution, Written during a Visit to That Country. To Which Is Added the Life of Mustapha Ali* (London, 1824).

—, *Greece in 1823 and 1824 . . . A New Edition, Containing Numerous Supplementary Papers, Illustrative of the State of Greece in 1825 . . . To which Are Added Reminiscences of Lord Byron* (London, 1825).

STANLEY, EDWARD, DEAN, *The Letters of Dean Stanley*, eds R.E. Prothero and E.G. Bailey (2 vols., London, 1893).

SUTTON, ROBERT, *The Despatches of Robert Sutton*, ed. Adkes Nimet Kurat (London, 1957).

THOUVENEL, EDOUARD, BARON, *Nicholas Ier et Napoléon III: les préliminaires de la guerre de Crimée (1852–1854) d'àpres les papiers inédites de M. Thouvenel*, ed. Louis Thouvenel (Paris, 1891).

VICTORIA, *The Letters of Queen Victoria, 1837–61*, first series, eds A.C. Benson and Viscount Esher (3 vols., London, 1907).

Vostochnaya Voyna 1853–56 q v Sviazi s Souremennoi ei Poiltscheskoi Obstanovkoi, ed. A.M. Zaionchkovski (2 vols., St Petersburg, 1908–13).

WELLESLEY, RICHARD, MARQUIS, *The Wellesley Papers*, ed. L.S. Benjamin (2 vols., London, 1914).

WELLINGTON, ARTHUR WELLESLEY, DUKE OF, *Despatches, Correspondence, and Memoranda of Field Marshal Arthur, Duke of Wellington*, ed. duke of Wellington (8 vols., London, 1867–78).

—, *Supplementary Despatches and Memoranda of Field-Marshal Arthur Duke of Wellington*, ed. duke of Wellington (15 vols., London, 1858–72).

Wood, Richard, Royal Historical Society: *Early Correspondence of Richard Wood*, ed. Allan Cunningham (London, 1966).

II. MEMOIRS, TRAVELLERS' TALES, AND CONTEMPORARY WORKS

Argyll, George Douglas, Duke of, *George Douglas, Eighth Duke of Argyll, Autobiography and Memoirs*, ed. duchess of Argyll (2 vols., London, 1906).
Baldwin, George, *Political Recollections Relative to Egypt* (London, 1801).
Barker, John, *Syria and Egypt under the Last Five Sultans of Turkey: Being Experiences during Fifty Years of Mr. Consul-General Barker*, ed. E.B.B. Barker (London, 1876).
Beaujour, Louis Auguste Félix de, *A View of the Commerce of Greece, Formed after an Annual Average, from 1787–1797*, trans. Thomas Hartwell Horne (London, 1800).
Bessières, J., *Mémoire sur la vie et la puissance d'Ali Pacha* (Paris, 1820).
Blackstone, Sir William, *Commentaries on the Laws of England* (4 vols., London, 1783).
Blaquière, Edward, *The Greek Revolution; Its Origin and Progess: together with Some Remarks on the Religion, National Character, &c. in Greece* (London, 1824).
Broughton, John Cam Hobhouse, First Baron, *A Journey through Armenia and . . . Turkey in Europe and Asia to Constantinople during the Years 1809 and 1810* (2 vols., London, 1813).
—, *Recollections of a Long Life*, ed. Lady Dorchester (6 vols., London, 1909–11).
Bulard, Arsene François, *De la peste orientale d'après les matériaux recueillis à Alexandrie, au Cairo, à Smyrne et à Constantinople, pendant les années 1833, 1834, 1835, 1836, 1837 et 1838* (Paris, 1839).
Burnaby, Frederick Gustavus, *On Horseback through Asia Minor* (2 vols., London, 1877).
Busbecq, Augierius Ghislain de, *A.G. Busbequii . . . Legationis Turcicae Epistolae quatuor. Quarum priores duae . . . in lucem prodierunt sub nomine Itinerum Constantinopolitani et Amasiani. Adjectae sunt duae alterae. Ejusdem de re militari contra Turcam instituenda consilium* (Paris, 1589).
—, *Life and Letters of Ogier Ghislain de Busbecq*, eds. C.T. Forster and F.H. Blackburne Daniell (English trans., 2 vols., London, 1881).
Chalcondylas, Laonicus, *Laonici Chalcondylae . . . De Origine et rebus gestis Turcorum libri decem, nuper è Graeco in Latinum conuersi: Conrado Clausero . . . interprete . . . Adiecimus Theodori Gazae, & aliorum . . . eiusdem argumenti, de rebus Turcorum aduersus Christianos, & Christianorum contra illos . . . gestis di uersa opuscula, etc.* ed. J. Heroldt (Basel, 1556).
—, *L'Histoire de la décadence de l'Empire grec, et établissement de celuy des Turcs* (French trans., Paris, 1584).
Chateaubriand, François René de, Viscount, *Travels in Greece,*

Palestine, Egypt, and Barbary, during the Years 1806 and 1807, trans. Frederic Shoberl (2 vols., London, 1811).
CHATFIELD, ROBERT, *An Appeal to the British Public, in the Cause of the Persecuted Greeks, etc.* (London, 1822).
—, *A Further Appeal to the British Public, in the Cause of the Persecuted Greeks* (London, 1823).
CHAUMETTE DES FOSSÉS, JEAN BAPTISTE GABRIEL AMEDÉE, *Voyage en Bosnie dans les années 1807 et 1808* (Berlin, 1812).
CLARKE, EDWARD DANIEL, *Travels in Various Countries of Europe, Asia, and Africa* (6 vols., London, 1810–1816).
COCKBURN, HENRY, *Memorials of His Time* (Edinburgh, 1856).
COLSON, FÉLIX, *De l'état présent et de l'avenir des principautés de Moldavie et de Valachie; suivi des traités de la Turquie avec les Puissances européennes, et d'une carte des Pays Roumains* (Paris, 1839).
CURZON, ROBERT, *Visits to Monasteries in the Levant* (5th ed., London, 1865).
DE KAY, JAMES ELLSWORTH, *Sketches of Turkey in 1831 and 1832* (New York, 1833).
DEMIAN, J.A., *Statistiche Beschreibung der Militär-Grenze* (Vienna, 1806).
DRAGASANU, I.C., *Peregrinual Transilvan* (Bucharest, 1842).
ELLIOT, SIR HENRY GEORGE, *Some Revolutions and Other Diplomatic Experiences* (London, 1922).
ERSKINE, THOMAS, LORD, *An Appeal to the People of Great Britain on the Subject of Confederated Greece* (London, 1824).
ETON, WILLIAM, *A Survey of the Turkish Empire* (London, 1799).
FRASER, JAMES BAILLIE, *A Winter's Journey from Constantinople to Teheran, with Travels through Various Parts of Persia* (2 vols., London, 1838).
GALT, JOHN, *Letters from the Levant* (London, 1813).
GARDANE, PAUL ANGE LOUIS DE, *Journal d'un voyage dans la Turquie d'Asie et la Perse, fait en 1807 et 1808* (Paris, 1809).
GREEN, P.J., *Sketches of the War in Greece* (London, 1826).
GREY, EDWARD, FIRST VISCOUNT GREY OF FALLODEN, *Twenty Five Years* (New York, 1925).
HAMMER-PURGSTALL, JOSEPH VON, BARON, *Geschichte des Osmanischen Reiches* (10 vols., Pest [Vienna], 1827–35).
HERTSLET, EDWARD, *Recollections of the Old Foreign Office* (London, 1901).
HOGARTH, DAVID GEORGE, *A Wandering Scholar in the Levant* (London, 1896).
HOLLAND, HENRY, *Travels in the Ionian Islands, Albania . . . during the years 1812 and 1813* (London, 1815).
HUGHES, THOMAS SMART, *An Address to the People of England in the Cause of the Greeks, Occasioned by the Late Inhuman Massacres in the Isle of Scio* (London, 1822).
—, *Considerations upon the Greek Revolution with a Vindication of the Author's 'Address to the People of England', from the Attacks of Mr. C.B. Sheridan* (London, 1823).

Bibliography

ISMAIL KEMAL BEY, *Memoirs of Ismail Kemal Bey*, ed. S. Story (London, 1920).
KENNEDY, JAMES, *Conversations on Religion, with Lord Byron and Others, Held in Cephalonia, a Short Time Previous to His Lordship's Death* (London, 1830).
KINGLAKE, ALEXANDER WILLIAM, *Eothen*, ed. H. Gorvett-Smith (London and Toronto, 1927).
KNOLLES, RICHARD, *The Generall Historie of the Turkes, from the First Beginning of That Nation to the Rising of the Otheman Familie . . . Together with the Lives and Conquests of the Otheman Kings and Emperours unto the Yeare 1610* (2nd ed., London, 1610); revised by Paul Rycaut (6th ed., 2 vols., London, 1687–1700).
LAYARD, AUSTEN HENRY, *Early Adventures in Persia, Susiana, and Babylonia, Including a Residence among the Bakhtiyari and Other Wild Tribes before the Discovery of Nineveh* (2 vols., London, 1887).
LEAKE, WILLIAM MARTIN, *Travels in the Morea* (3 vols., London, 1830).
LEYBLICK, BADIA Y, *Travels of Ali Bey* (London, 1816).
MACFARLANE, CHARLES, *Constantinople in 1828: A Residence of Sixteen Months in the Turkish Capital and Provinces, with an Account of the Present State of the Naval and Military Power, and of the Resources of the Ottoman Empire* (London, 1829).
—, *Turkey and Its Destiny: The Result of Journeys Made in 1847 and 1848 to Examine into the State of That Country* (2 vols., London, 1850).
MALMESBURY, JAMES HARRIS, EARL OF, *Memoirs of an ex-Minister: An Autobiography* (2 vols., London, 1884).
MCCULLOCH, JOHN RAMSAY, *A Dictionary, Practical, Theoretical and Historical of Commerce and Commercial Navigation* (London, 1832–39).
METTERNICH, CLEMENS WENZEL VON METTERNICH-WINNENBERG, PRINCE, *Memoirs of Prince Metternich, 1815–1829*, ed. Prince Richard Metternich, trans. Mrs. Alexander Napier (8 vols., London, 1881).
MILES, WILLIAM AUGUSTUS, *The Conduct of France towards Great Britain Examined* (London, 1793).
MILLINGEN, JULIUS, *Memoirs of the Affairs of Greece, . . . with . . . Anecdotes Relating to Lord Byron, and an Account of His Last Illness and Death* (London, 1831).
MONRO, V., *Summer Ramble in Syria, with a Tartar Trip from Aleppo to Stamboul* (2 vols., London, 1835).
MOURADJA D'OHSSON, IGNACE DE, *Tableau géneral de l'Empire Othoman, divisé en deux parties, dont l'une comprend la Législation Mohométane, l'autre l'histoire de l'Empire Othoman* (7 vols., Paris, 1788–1824).
OLIVIER, GUILLAUME ANTOINE, *Voyage dans l'empire Othomane, l'Egypt, et la Perse* (3 vols., Paris, 1801–7).
PARRY, WILLIAM, *The Last Days of Lord Byron; with His Lordship's Opinions on Various Subjects, Particularly on the State and Prospects of Greece* (London, 1825).
PEARS, SIR EDWIN, *Forty Years in Constantinople: The Recollections of Sir*

Edwin Pears, 1873–1915 (London, 1916).
PERTUSIER, CHARLES, La Bosnie considérée dans ses rapports avec l'Empire Ottoman (Paris, 1822).
PITTON DE TOURNEFORT, JOSEPH, Rélation d'un Voyage du Levant . . . contenant l'histoire ancienne et moderne de plusieurs îsles de l'Archipel, de Constantinople, des côtes de la Mer Noire, de l'Arménie, de la Georgie, des frontières de Perse et de l'Asie mineure, etc. (2 vols., Paris, 1717).
POUJADE, EUGENE, Chrétiens et Turcs.: Scènes et Souvenirs de la vie politique, militaire et religieuse en Orient (Paris, 1859).
POUQUEVILLE, FRANÇOIS CHARLES HUGHES LAURENT, Voyage en Morée à Constantinople, en Albanie, et dans plusiers autres parties de l'Empire Othoman, pendant les années 1798–1801, enrichi d'un précis historique et geographique sur l'ancienne Empire, et de cartes dressées par M. Barbié de Bocage, etc. (3 vols., Paris, 1805).
REDCLIFFE, STRATFORD CANNING, VISCOUNT STRATFORD DE, The Eastern Question (London, 1881).
RYCAUT, SIR PAUL, The History of the Turkish Empire, from the Year 1623, to the Year 1677, Containing the Reigns of the Three Last Emperors . . . (London, 1687).
SLADE, ADOLPHUS, Records of Travels in Turkey, Greece &c., and of a Cruise in the Black Sea, with the Captain Pasha, in the Years 1829, 1830 and 1831 (2 vols., London, 1833).
STAPLETON, AUGUSTUS GRANVILLE, The Political Life of the Right Honourable G. Canning . . . from Sept 1822, to His Death . . . Together with a Review of Foreign Affairs Subsequently to That Event (3 vols., London, 1831).
THORNTON, THOMAS, The Present State of Turkey (2nd ed., 2 vols., London, 1809).
TIRPITZ, ALFRED PETER FRIEDRICH VON, My Memoirs (2 vols., London, 1919).
TOMLINE, G., Memoirs of the Life of William Pitt (2 vols., London, 1821).
TOTT, FRANÇOIS, BARON DE, Mémoires sur les Turcs (3 vols., Amsterdam, n.d.).
—, Memoirs of Baron de Tott. Containing the State of the Turkish Empire and the Crimea, during the Late War with Russia. Trans. from the French (London, 1785).
TOWNSHEND, ARTHUR FITZHENRY, A Military Consul in Turkey: The Experiences and Impressions of a British Representative in Asia Minor (London, 1910).
TRELAWNY, EDWARD JOHN, Recollections of the Last Days of Shelley and Byron (London, 1858).
UBICINI, ABDOLONYME, Letters on Turkey, trans. by Lady Easthope (2 vols., London, 1856).
URQUHART, DAVID, The Spirit of the East, Illustrated in a Journal of Travels through Roumelia during an Eventful Period (2 vols., London, 1838).
—, Turkey and Its Resources (London, 1833).

Bibliography

VILLÈLE, JEAN BAPTISTE, DE, COUNT, *Mémoires* (5 vols., Paris, 1880).
VITZTHUM VON ECKSTAEDT, CARL FRIEDRICH, *St. Petersburgh and London, the Reminiscences of Count Charles Vitzthum*, ed. Henry Reeves (London, 1887).
VOLNEY, CONSTANTIN FRANÇOIS DE, COUNT, *Travels through Syria and Egypt in 1783, 1784 and 1785 . . . Trans. from the French* (2 vols., London, 1787).
WALSH, ROBERT, *A Residence at Constantinople, during . . . the Commencement, Progress, and Termination of the Greek and Turkish Revolutions* (2 vols., London, 1836).
WILKINSON, JOHN GARDNER, *Dalmatia and Montenegro: With a Journey to Mostar in Herzegovina, and Remarks on the Slavonic Nations: The History of Dalmatia and Ragusa, the Uscocs, etc.* (2 vols., London, 1848).
WILKINSON, WILLIAM, *An Account of the Principalities of Wallachia and Moldavia: with . . . Political Observations Relating to Them* (London, 1820).
WITTMAN, WILLIAM, *Travels in Turkey, Asia-Minor, Syria and . . . into Egypt during the Years 1799, 1800, and 1801* (London, 1803).
WRAXELL, SIR N.W., *The Historical and Posthumous Memoirs of Sir Nathaniel William Wraxall, 1772–1784*, ed. H.B. Wheatley (5 vols., London, 1884).

III. MONOGRAPHS AND GENERAL WORKS

ANDERSON, M.S., *Britain's Discovery of Russia, 1553–1815* (London, 1958).
—, *The Eastern Question, 1774–1923: A Study in International Relations* (London, 1966).
ANTLASMASI, EDIRNE, *Dilve Tarih-Cografiva Fakultesi Dergisi*: IX (Ankara, 1951).
ASHLEY, EVELYN, *The Life of Henry John Temple, Viscount Palmerston* (2 vols., London, 1876).
BALFOUR, LADY BETTY, *Life of George, Fourth Earl of Aberdeen* (London, 1922).
BEESLEY, E.S., 'The Turkish Revolution', *The Positivist Review*, xvi (1908).
BERKES, NIYAZI, *The Development of Secularism in Turkey* (Montreal, 1964).
BLAISDELL, D.C., *European Financial Control in the Ottoman Empire: A Study of the Establishment, Activities, and Significance of the Administration of the Ottoman Public Debt* (New York, 1929).
BOLSOVER, G.H., 'David Urquhart and the Eastern Question in 1833–1837', *Journal of Modern History*, viii (1936).
—, 'Lord Ponsonby and the Eastern Question (1833–1839)', *Slavonic Review*, xiii (1934–35).
BOPPE, A., *L'Albanie et Napoléon, 1797–1814* (Paris, 1914).
—, *La Mission de l'Adjutant-commandant Mériage à Vidin* (Paris, 1886).

BROWN, W.C., 'Byron and English Interest in the Near East', *Studies in Philology*, xxxiv (1937).
—, 'The Popularity of English Travel Books about the Near East, 1775–1828', *Philological Quarterly*, xv (1936); xvi (1937).
BUCKLE, HENRY THOMAS, *The History of Civilization in England* (2 vols., London, 1857).
BUXTON, CHARLES R., *Turkey in Revolution . . . With 33 illustrations and a Map* (London, 1909).
Cambridge History of British Foreign Policy, 1783–1919, The, eds A.W. Ward and G.P. Gooch (3 vols, New York, 1922–23).
Cambridge Modern History, The, eds A.W. Ward, G.W. Prothero, and Stanley Leathes (14 vols., London, 1902–12).
CIRCOURT, A., COUNT, *Histoire de l'Action commune de la France et de l'Amérique pour l'indépendance des Etats-Unis . . . traduit et annoté par le comte A. de Circourt* (3 vols., Paris, 1876).
CLARKE, EDWARD C., 'The Ottoman Industrial Revolution', *International Journal of Middle East Studies*, i (1974).
CLOGG, RICHARD, ed., *The Struggle for Greek Independence: Essays to Mark the 150th Anniversary of the Greek War of Independence* (London, 1973).
COCKBURN, HENRY, *Life of Lord Jeffrey* (2 vols., London, 1852).
CONAN, L., *From Granpa's Tea Chest* (London, 1951).
CRAWLEY, C.W., 'John Capodistrias and the Greeks before 1821', *Cambridge Historical Journal*, xiii (1957).
—, *The Question of Greek Independence: A Study of British Policy in the Near East, 1821–1833* (Cambridge, 1930).
CUNNINGHAM, ALLAN, 'The Levant Trade in 1912: The Journal of Christophe Aubin', *Archivum Ottomanicum*, viii (1988).
DAKIN, DOUGLAS, *British and American Philhellenes during the War of Greek Independence, 1821–1833* (Thessalonika, 1955).
—, *The Greek Struggle for Independence, 1821–1833* (London, 1973).
DANIEL, N., *Islam, Europe, and Empire* (Edinburgh, 1966).
DE BEER, E.S., AND WALTER SETON, 'Byroniana: The Archives of the London Greek Committee', *Nineteenth Century*, c (1926).
DILLON, E.J., 'The Unforeseen Happens as Usual', *Contemporary Review*, xciv (1908).
DOUIN, GEORGES, *Navarin* (Cairo, 1927).
EARLE, E.M., *Turkey, the Great Powers, and the Baghdad Railway: A Study in Imperialism* (London, 1923).
ELLIOT, HENRY GEORGE, 'The Death of Abdul Aziz and of Turkish Reform', *Nineteenth Century*, xxiii (1888).
EMBREE, A.T., *Charles Grant and British Rule in India* (New York, 1962).
EMIN, AHMED, *The Development of Modern Turkey as Measured by its Press* (New York, 1968).
FILITTI, J.C., 'Notice sur les Vogoridi', *Revue histoire du Sud-Est Europe*, vi (1927).
FINLAY, G., *A History of Greece from Its Conquest by the Romans to the Present*

Bibliography 333

Time, B.C. 146 to A.D. 1864, ed. H.R. Tozer (7 vols., Oxford, 1877–1971).
FONBLANQUE, E. BARRINGTON DE, *Lives of the Lords Strangford* (London, 1877).
GERCEK, S.N., *Turk Gazeteciligi, 1831–1931* (Istanbul, 1931).
GIBB, HAMILTON ALEXANDER AND HAROLD BOWEN, *Islamic Society and the West: A Study of the Impact of Western Civilization on Moslem Culture in the Near East* (London, 1950).
GOULD, A.G., 'Lords or Bandits? The Derebeys of Cilicia', *International Journal of Middle East Studies*, vi (1976).
HALPERN, JOEL MARTIN, *A Serbian Village* (New York, 1958).
HELMREICH, E.C., *The Diplomacy of the Balkan Wars, 1912–1913* (Cambridge, Mass., 1938).
HENDERSON, GAVIN B., *Crimean War Diplomacy and Other Historical Essays* (Glasgow, 1947).
HOBSBAWM, ERIC J., *Primitive Rebels: Studies in Archaic Forms of Social Movement in the 19th and 20th Centuries* (Manchester, 1959).
HORN, D.B., 'The Diplomatic Experience of the Secretaries of State, 1660–1852', *History*, xli (1956).
HOSKINS, H.L., *British Routes to India* (London, 1928).
HOWARD, H.E., *The Partition of Turkey: A Diplomatic History, 1913–1923* (Norman, 1931).
—, 'Brunnov's Reports on Aberdeen, 1842', *Cambridge Historical Journal*, iv (1932–34).
HUREWITZ, J.C., 'Ottoman Diplomacy and the European State System', *Middle East Journal*, xv (1961).
ISSAWI, CHARLES P., *Economic History of the Middle East, 1800–1914: A Book of Readings* (Chicago, 1966).
ITZKOWITZ, NORMAN, *Ottoman Empire and Islamic Tradition* (New York, 1972).
JÄCKH, E., *The Rising Crescent* (New York, 1944).
JONES-PARRY, E., 'Under-Secretaries of State for Foreign Affairs, 1782–1855', *English Historical Review*, xlix (1934).
KALDIS, WILLIAM P., *John Capodistrias and the Modern Greek State* (Madison, Wisc., 1963).
KARAL, ENVER ZIAYA, 'Ebu Bekir Ratib Efendi'nin "Nizam-i Cedit" Islahatinda Rolu', *Turk Tarih Kongresi, Ankara 12–17 Nisan 1956: Kongreye sunulan tebligler* (Ankara, 1960).
—, *Halet Efendinin Paris Büyük Elciligi* (Constantinople, 1940).
—, *Osmanli Interatorlugunda ilk nufus sayimi* (Ankara, 1943).
KARPAT, KEMAL, ed., *The Ottoman State and Its Place in World History* (Leiden, 1974).
KERNER, R.J., 'Russia's New Policy in the Near East after the Peace of Adrianople', *Cambridge History Journal*, v (1937).
KINGLAKE, ALEXANDER W., *The Invasion of the Crimea: Its Origin and Account of its Progress down to the Death of Lord Raglan* (8 vols., London,

1863).
KISSINGER, HENRY A., *A World Restored: Metternich, Castlereagh, and the Problems of Peace, 1812–1822* (Boston, 1957).
KNIGHT, GEORGE WILSON, *Lord Byron's Marriage: The Evidence of Asterisks* (London, 1957).
LAGARDE, L., 'Note sur les journaux français de Constantinople à l'époque révolutionnaire', *Journal Asiatique*, ccxxxvi (1948).
LANE-POOLE, STANLEY, *Life of the Right Honourable Stratford Canning, Viscount Stratford de Redcliffe* (2 vols., London, 1888).
LECKY, WILLIAM EDWARD HARTPOLE, *A History of England in the Eighteenth Century* (8 vols., London, 1878–90).
LEON, G.B., *Greek Merchant Marine* (Athens, 1972).
LEWIS, BERNARD, *The Emergence of Modern Turkey* (London, 1961).
—, 'The Impact of the French Revolution on Turkey', in *The New Asia: Readings in the History of Mankind*, eds G.S. Métraux and F. Crouzet (London, 1965).
LUKE, HARRY CHARLES, *The Making of Modern Turkey: The Old Turkey and the New: From Byzantium to Ankara* (London, 1955).
LYBYER, ALBERT HOWE, *The Government of the Ottoman Empire in the Time of Suleiman the Magnificent* (Cambridge, Mass., 1913).
MARCHAND, L.A., *Byron: A Biography* (London, 1957).
MARRIOTT, JOHN ARTHUR RANSOME, *The Eastern Question: An Historical Study in European Diplomacy* (4th ed., Oxford, 1940).
MARTIN, KINGSLEY, *The Triumph of Lord Palmerston: A Study in Political Opinion in England before the Crimean War* (London, 1924).
MARTIN, THEODORE, *The Life of His Royal Highness the Prince Consort* (5 vols., London, 1875–80).
MATHESON, CYRIL, *The Life of Henry Dundas, First Viscount Melville, 1742–1811* (London, 1933).
MAUROIS, ANDRÉ, *Byron* (2 vols., Paris, 1930).
MAXWELL, HERBERT E., *The Life and Letters of George William Frederick, Fourth Earl of Clarendon* (2 vols., London, 1913).
MCCULLAGH, FRANÇOIS, *The Fall of Abd-ul-Hamid* (London, 1910).
MEADE, WILLIAM EDWARD, *The Grand Tour in the Eighteenth Century* (New York, 1914).
MEARS, E.G., *Modern Turkey: A Politico-Economic Interpretation, 1908–1923* (New York, 1924).
MEDLICOTT, W.N., 'Gladstone and the Turks', *History*, xiii (1928).
—, 'Lord Salisbury and Turkey', *History*, xii (1927).
MERRIMAN, ROGER BIGELOW, *Suleiman the Magnificent, 1520–1566* (Cambridge, Mass., 1944).
MOORE, DORIS L., *The Late Lord Byron: Posthumous Dramas* (Philadelphia, 1961).
MOORE, W.E., *The Impact of Industry* (Englewood Cliffs, N.J., 1965).
NAFF, THOMAS, 'Ottoman Diplomatic Relations with Europe in the Eighteenth Century: Patterns and Trends', in *Studies in Eighteenth Cen-*

tury Islamic History, ed. Thomas Naff and Roger Owen (Carbondale, 1977).
—, 'Reform and the Conduct of Ottoman Diplomacy in the Reign of Selim III, 1789-1807', *Journal of the American Oriental Society*, lxxxiii (1963).
NAPIER, WILLIAM FRANCIS PATRICK, *The Life and Opinions of General Sir J. Napier* (4 vols., London, 1857).
NELSON, RICHARD R., 'A Theory of the Low Level Equilibrium Trap in Underdeveloped Economies', *American Economic Review*, xlvi (1956).
NICHOLS, IRBY C., JR. *The European Pentarchy and the Congress of Verona, 1822* (The Hague, 1971).
NICOLSON, HAROLD, *Byron: The Last Journey, April 1823–April 1824* (London, 1924).
NURI, MUSTAFA, *Netaie ul-Vukuat* (4 vols., Istanbul, 1877-79, 1909-18).
PAPST, EDMOND, *Les Origines de la guerre de Crimée: La France et la Russie de 1848 à 1854* (Paris, 1912).
PARKER, CHARLES STUART, *Life and Letters of Sir James Graham, second baronet, of Netherby, P.C., G.C.B., 1792-1861* (2 vols., London, 1907).
PATON, ANDREW ARCHIBALD, *Researches on the Danube and the Adriatic; Or, Contributions to the Modern History of Hungary and Transylvania, Dalmatia and Croatia, Servia and Bulgaria* (2 vols., Leipzig, 1861).
PEARS, SIR EDWIN, *Life of Abdul Hamid* (London, 1917).
PENN, VIRGINIA, 'Philhellenism in England, 1821-27', *Slavonic Review*, xiv (1936).
PENZER, NORMAN MOSLEY, *The Harem: An Account of the Institution as It Existed in the Palace of the Turkish Sultans with a History of the Grand Seraglio from Its Foundation to the Present Time* (London, 1936).
PHILLIPSON, COLEMAN AND NOEL BUXTON, *The Question of the Bosphorus and Dardanelles* (London, 1917).
PISANI, P., *La Dalmatie de 1797 à 1815: Episode des conquêtes napoléoniennes* (Paris, 1893).
PURYEAR, V.J., *England, Russia and the Straits Question, 1844-1856* (Berkeley/Los Angeles, 1931).
—, *France and the Levant (from the Bourbon Restoration to the Peace of Kutayah)* (Berkeley/Los Angeles, 1941).
—, *Napoleon and the Dardanelles* (Berkeley/Los Angeles, 1951).
RAMSAUR, ERNEST EDMONDSON, *The Young Turks: Prelude to the Revolution of 1908* (Princeton, 1957).
REGLA, PAUL, *Les Secrets d'Yildiz* (Paris, 1897).
RICE, W.G., 'Early English Travellers in Greece and the Levant', *Essays and Studies in English and Comparative Literature* (London, 1933).
ROBERTS, M., *The Whig Party* (London, 1939).
ROBINSON, GERTRUDE, *David Urquhart: Some Chapters in the Life of a Victorian Knight-Errant of Justice and Liberty* (Oxford, 1920).
RODKEY, F.S., 'Lord Palmerston and the Rejuvenation of Turkey, 1830-1841', *Journal of Modern History*, i (1929); ii (1920).

—, 'The Attempts of Briggs and Co. to Guide British Policy in the Levant in the Interest of Mahomet Ali', *Journal of Modern History*, v (1933).
ROLO, PAUL JACQUES VICTOR, *George Canning: Three Biographical Studies* (London, 1965).
ROSE, JOHN HOLLAND, *William Pitt and National Revival* (London, 1911).
ROSEN, G., *Geschichte der Türkei* (Leipzig, 1866).
ROSTOVSKY, ANDREI LOBANOV, *Russia and Europe, 1789–1925* (Durham, N.C., 1947).
ROY, GILLES, *Abdul Hamid, le sultan rouge* (Paris, 1936).
RYAN, ANDREW, *The Last of the Dragomans* (London, 1951).
SAINT DENYS, A. DE JUCHEREAU, *Révolutions de Constantinople en 1807 et 1808* (2 vols., Paris, 1918).
SCHIEMANN, THEODOR, *Geschichte Russlands unter Kaiser Nikolaus* (4 vols., Berlin, 1904–19).
SCHLECHTA-WSSEHRD, OTTOKAR M. VON, *Die Revolutionen in Constantinopel in den Jahren 1807 und 1808* (Vienna, 1882).
SCHROEDER, PAUL W., *Metternich's Diplomacy at Its Zenith, 1820–1823* (Austin, Tex., 1962).
SETON-WATSON, R. W., *Britain in Europe, 1789–1914: A Survey of Foreign Policy* (Cambridge, 1937).
SHAW, STANFORD J., *Between Old and New: The Ottoman Empire under Selim III, 1789–1807* (Cambridge, Mass., 1971).
—, 'The Nineteenth-Century Ottoman Tax Reforms and Revenue System', *International Journal of Middle East Studies*, vi (1975).
—, *History of the Ottoman Empire and Modern Turkey* (2 vols., Cambridge, Mass., 1976).
SIMPSON, F.A., *Louis Napoleon and the Recovery of France, 1848–1856* (London, 1923).
SKOK, P., 'Le mouvement illyrien et les Français', *Le Monde slave*, xii (1935).
SOLOVEYTCHIK, GEORGE, *Potemkin: A Picture of Catherine's Russia* (London, 1949).
SOREL, ALBERT, *The Eastern Question in the Eighteenth Century: The Partition of Poland and the Treaty of Kainardji* (London, 1898).
SOUTHGATE, DONALD, *The Most English Minister: The Policies and Politics of Palmerston* (London, 1966).
SOUTSOS, NICHOLAS, *Notions Statistiques sur la Moldavie* (Jassy, 1849).
SPENCER, TERENCE JOHN, *Fair Greece, Sad Relic: Literary Philhellenism from Shakespeare to Byron* (London, 1954).
SPENDER, EDWARD HAROLD, *Byron and Greece* (London, 1924).
ST CLAIR, WILLIAM, *That Greece Might Still Be Free: The Philhellenes in the War of Independence* (London, 1972).
STANMORE, SIR ARTHUR GORDON, LORD, *The Earl of Aberdeen* (New York, 1893).
STAPLETON, AUGUSTUS GRANVILLE, *George Canning and His Times* (London, 1859).

Bibliography

STAVRIANOS, L.S., *The Balkans since 1453* (New York, 1965).
—, 'The Balkan Committee', *Queen's Quarterly*, xlviii (1941).
STERN, BERNARD HERBERT, *The Rise of Romantic Hellenism in English Literature, 1732–1786* (Menasha, 1940).
STOIANOVICH, TRAIAN, 'The Conquering Balkan Orthodox Merchant', *Journal of Economic History*, xx (1960).
STOWE, HARRIET BEECHER, *Lady Byron Vindicated: A History of the Byron Controversy, from Its Beginning in 1816 to the Present Time* (Boston, 1870).
SVORONOS, N., *Le Commerce de Salonique au XVIIIe siècle* (Paris, 1956).
TANPINAR, A.H., *XIX Asir Türk Edebiyati Tarihi* (Constantinople, 1956).
TEMPERLEY, H.W.V., *England and the Near East: The Crimea* (London, 1936).
—, *The Foreign Policy of Canning, 1822–1827* (London, 1925).
—, 'Princess Lieven and the Protocol of 4 April 1826', *English Historical Review*, xxxix (1924).
—, 'Stratford de Redcliffe and the Origins of the Crimean War', Parts I and II, *English Historical Review*, xlviii, (1933); xlix (1934).
—, 'Joan Canning on Her Husband's Policy and Ideas', *English Historical Review*, xlv (1930).
—, AND LILLIAN M. PENSON, *The Foundations of British Foreign Policy from Pitt to Salisbury* (London, 1938).
THOMAS, M.A., *The Secretaries of State, 1681–1782* (Oxford, 1932).
TRICOUPI, SPIRIDION, *Histoire de la Révolution Grecque* (Paris, 1862).
UZUNÇARSILI, ISMAIL HAKKI, *Meshur Rumeli Ayanindan Tirsinikli Ismail, Yilik Oglu Süleyman Agalar ve Alemdar Mustafa Pasa [The Famous Rumelia Notables: Tirsinikli Ismail and Yilik Oglu Süleyman Agas and Alemdar Mustafa Pasa]* (Istanbul, 1942).
VALETAS, G., *Korais* (Athens, 1965).
VAMBÉRY, A., 'Europe and the Turkish Constitution: An Independent View', *Nineteenth Century*, lxiv (1908).
—, 'Personal Recollections of Abdul Hamid and His Court', *Nineteenth Century*, lxvi (1909).
VERETÉ, M., 'Palmerston and the Levant Crisis, 1832', *Journal of Modern History*, xxiv (1952).
VUCINICH, W., *The Ottoman Empire: Its Record and Legacy* (Princeton, 1965).
WALKER, FRANKLIN A., 'The Rejection of Stratford Canning by Nicholas I', *Bulletin of the Institute of Historical Research*, xl (1967).
WALPOLE, SPENCER, *The Life of Lord John Russell* (2 vols., London, 1889).
WARRINER, DOREEN, ed., *Contrasts in Emerging Societies: Readings in the Social and Economic History of South-Eastern Europe in the Nineteenth Century* (London, 1965).
WATERFIELD, GORDON, *Layard of Nineveh* (London, 1963).
WAUGH, T., *Turkey, Yesterday, Today and Tomorrow* (London, 1930).
WEBB, PAUL C., 'The Royal Navy in the Ochakov Affair of 1791', *International History Review*, ii (1980).

WEBER, SHIRLEY HOWARD, *Voyages and Travels Made in the Near East during the XIX century. Being part of a larger catalogue of works on geography, cartography, voyages and travels, in the Gennadius Library in Athens* (Princeton, N.J., 1952).

WEBSTER, CHARLES K., *The Foreign Policy of Castlereagh, 1815–1822* (2 vols., London, 1925–31).

—, *The Foreign Policy of Palmerston 1830–41* (2 vols., London, 1951).

—, 'Urquhart, Ponsonby and Palmerston', *English Historical Review*, lxii (1947).

WELCH, C.E., ed., *Political Modernization: A Reader in Comparative Political Change* (Belmont, Cal., 1967).

WITTLIN, ALMA STEPHANIE, *Abdul Hamid, the Shadow of God* (London, 1940).

WOOD, ALFRED C., *A History of the Levant Company* (London, 1935).

—, 'The English Embassy at Constantinople, 1660–1762', *English Historical Review*, xl (1925).

WOODHOUSE, C.M., *The Battle of Navarino* (London, 1965).

—, *Capodistria, the Founder of Greek Independence* (London, 1973).

—, *The Philhellenes* (London, 1969).

YASA, IBRAHIM, *Studies in Turkish Local Government* (Ankara, 1955).

ZALLONY, M.P., *Essai sur les Fanariotes; suivi de quelques reflexions sur l'état actuel de la Grèce* (Marseilles, 1924).

ZIMMERMAN, CARLE C. AND RICHARD E. DU WORS, eds, *Sociology of Underdevelopment* (Calgary, 1970).

Index

(Arrangement of material within entries is predominantly chronological though some material of a topical nature is alphabetically ordered.)

Abbott, Edward 74, 84–5
Abdulhamid I, Sultan 2, 6, 10, 39, 58, 60
Abdulmejid I, Sultan 297
Aberdeen, 4th earl of (George Hamilton Gordon) 146, 244
A'Court, William, *see* Heytesbury 207
Adair, Sir Robert
    mission to Russia (1791) 32–50, 106; events of mission 39–46; Fox's alleged connection 32–3, 34–9, 46–8
    embassy to Ottoman Empire 103–43; instructions 105, 107–8; journey to Turkey 108–12; negotiates treaty of Dardanelles 112–13, 115–17, 135; policies towards other powers 121–4, 130–1; hopes to negotiate European coalition in Vienna 106, 118, 123–4, 131, 132; exploits Franco-Russian rift 107, 118, 121–2; at Constantinople embassy (1809–10) 124–38, 148, 280; and French ambassador 130–1, 132, 134, 136, 137–8; suggests Anglo-Ottoman naval co-operation 132; attempts to negotiate Russo-Ottoman peace 122, 123, 124, 133–8; colonial compensation plan 138, 151, 182; procures Austrian plan for attack on Ottomans 179; and Ali Pasha 158; and British naval blockade 165; lack of Foreign Office support 108, 136; departure 168
    and Stadion 106, 122, 133–4; Whig sympathies 32, 106, 107
Addington, Hiley 317
Adriatic Sea; British naval blockade 148, 159; *see also* Ionian Islands
Ahmet Effendi 61
Ainslie, Sir Robert 5; difficulties in 2nd Russo-Ottoman War 5–6, 7, 9, 10; relationship with Ottomans 5, 58, 59, 78; and Foreign Office 5, 58, 59, 68; Catherine II demands dismissal 6, 60; and Baldwin 87, 88; sale of *barats* 90;

on French grain-carriers 93; retirement 51, 52, 58, 59, 68
Akerman, convention of 267, 294, 297, 301
Aleppo: *baratlıs* 89; earthquake 225; janizaries suppressed 294; Levant Company 74, 75, 84–5; trade 71, 163
Alexander I, tsar: and Napoleon 132, 170; and congress diplomacy 192, 194; and Transcaucasian border 198; and Ipsilantis' invasion of Moldavia 199, 208; horror of revolution 202, 203; and Greek Revolt 195, 204–5, 209, 212, 213, 218, 219–20; at congress of Verona 222; Strangford acts for 222, 223, 225, 226; and Kapodistrias' resignation 256; estrangement from Metternich 263; death 278
Alexandria 74, 148
Ali Pasha of Janina 156, 173, 201, 235; and Britain 105, 108, 116–17, 157–61, 195, 253, 256; defeat and execution 216
America, South; revolutions 243, 263–4, 269
Arakcheiev, Count Aleksei 172
Arbuthnot, Charles 108, 124, 125, 215
Athens 290, 307–8, 312
Auckland, 1st baron (William Eden): and 2nd Russo-Ottoman war 5, 16–17, 18, 19, 20, 24; and French wars 62; resignation 96
Aust, George 57, 65
Austria: in 2nd Russo-Ottoman War 2, 7–9, 10–11, 13–14, 16, 20; congress of Sistovo with Ottomans 15–16, 61; rift with France (1808–9) 118, 121–2, 123; contacts with Russia 121–2; alliance with Britain 123; war against France 123, 125, 129, 130; peace of Schönbrunn 132–3; *rapprochement* with France 137, 138; and treaty of Bucharest 173–4; and alliances of 1812 178–9; and Ottoman integrity 104, 179; suppresses revolutions in Italy 195; rift with Russia 263, 267; and Greek question

195, 216, 267, 269, 282, 288, 291, 298, 304, 306; and treaty of London 303, 310; territorial interests, (Danubian Principalities) 2, 8, 11, 14, 15, 39, 122, 138, 173, (Galicia) 8, 10, 13, 15, 132, 134, 178, (Serbia) 2, 15, 66, 173, 178; *see also* Vienna

Bagot, Sir Charles: on tsar 209, 212, 220, 223; withdrawn from St Petersburg 190, 225–6, 260, 262; concern over Canning's inactivity over Greece 261–2, 269
Baldwin, George 74, 85–8
Baltic Sea 168–9
barats 66, 75, 83–5, 88–91, 113, 118–19, 223
Basra 83–4
Bathurst, Benjamin 123
Bathurst, 3rd earl (Henry Bathurst) 133, 211, 302, 303, 305
Bentham, Jeremy 242, 243
Benwell, Mary 43–4, 47
Berthold (dragoman) 108, 110
Bessarabia: and 2nd Russo-Ottoman war 8, 11, 13, 16, 39, 40, 138; Russia gains in treaty of Bucharest 172, 180, 197; *see also* Ochakov
Bessborough, countess of 32, 33
Bidwell, John 108, 161
Black Sea: access *see* Dardanelles; British merchants and 4–5, 26–7, 86, 182, 118, 182; Greek merchants under Russian flag 119, 126, 223; Polish trade 18, 21; Russia and trade 61, 90, 126, 222, 223; in treaty of Dardanelles 118
Blaquière, Edward 240, 241, 242, 244, 247, 258–9
Boscawen, Admiral Edward 94
Bowring, Sir John 240, 242, 245, 247, 258
Braxfield, Lord (Robert Macqueen) 54
Briggs and Company (cotton merchants) 299
Britain *see individual events, institutions and personalities; for details of relations with other countries, see under individual countries*
Brougham, Henry Peter (baron Brougham and Vaux) 189, 241
Bucharest, treaty of: negotiations 133–8, 150–1, 168–83; ambiguities 181, 196, 197–9, 203; Ottoman reception 180–1, 197, 215, 223; Stratford Canning's contribution 150, 172, 175–8, 179–81, 182, 183, 197; significance 182–3
Bulgakov, Yakov 2, 6
Bulgaria: banditry 69, 93; grain supplies 93, 154; plague 68, 127
Burdett, Sir Francis 241, 245

Burges, James Bland 17, 39, 46
Burke, Edmund 22, 60, 62; and Adair 33–4, 36, 38, 39, 46; defection to Pitt 33, 52–3
Byron, Lord (George Gordon) 245–55; early travels in Greece 237, 253; London Greek Committee appoint commissioner 241, 247–8; in Kefalonia 249–50; at Missolonghi 250, 251–4; death 246, 247, 254–5, 260
  and Canning 258; philhellenism 212, 238, 245–55; private life 71, 248, 250, 255; on Russo-Ottoman war 127; and Strangford 188
Byron Brigade 253, 254, 255

Callimachi, Charles 79, 83
Callimachi family 96
Camden, 1st earl (Charles Pratt) 23
Canning, George: employed at Foreign Office (1795) 57; abandons Fox for Pitt 57; deference to Russian interests (1807) 105; and Adair 32, 105–6, 106–7, 107–8, 128; abandons Egypt 110; duel with Castlereagh 129, 144; fall 129, 133, 144; and George IV 190, 264
  and Greek Revolt 257–70; and Strangford 189–90, 191, 223, 225, 226–7, 261; and treaty of Bucharest 197; philhellenism 258–9; initial waiting policy towards Greece 111, 221, 224, 225–6, 227, 245, 257, 259–62; change to active policy (1825) 191–2, 196, 262–4, 276–7, 278; and protocol of St Petersburg 265–7, 270; policies, 1826–27 245, 265–70, 283, 284–8, 301–4; policy assessed 267–70
  and South American republics 263–4, 269; and isolation of Austria 269; and Stratford Canning 301, 305; and treaty of London 303; as prime minister 303, 304–5; death 267, 304, 311; on Dutch diplomacy 136; Hobhouse and 241, 258
Canning, Eliza 280, 289, 290, 311, 318
Canning, Stratford (1st viscount Stratford de Redcliffe) 1; with Adair's embassy to Turkey 108, 111, 112, 115, 125, 136; as minister-plenipotentiary 124, 131–2, 138, 144–5; on corrupt state of Ottoman Empire 127–8; as minister at Constantinople 144–87; lack of Foreign Office support 146–7, 160, 161–2, 168, 173; diplomatic style 147–50, 161, 162, 164–5, 176; temper 147, 174; correspondence 148–9, 161, 171–2, 176, 177, 182, 304–5; rivalry with Latour-Maubourg 150, 162, 164, 165, 168, 174, 176; first diplomatic contacts with

Index

Ottomans 150–2; search for naval supplies 152–4; and grain trade 154–5, 176; and Egypt 154–7, 174; and Ali Pasha 157–61; and British merchant shipping 161–7; and piracy 149, 161–7, 169, 174, 176; Ottoman attitude to 167–8; and treaty of Bucharest 150, 172, 175–8, 179–81, 182, 183, 197; and dragomans 165, 174; and Ottoman request for aid (1810) 168–9; and Mahmud II 169, 177; distrust of Austrians 171; severs relations with *reis effendi* 173, 174; special mission to Russia 261, 262, 263, 265–6
 second mission to Constantinople 276–323; instructions 276–7; in Greece 277–80; Greek sympathies 277–8, 280, 289, 290; presentation to Sultan 281; and *reis effendi* 282–3, 286, 300–1, 304; attempt to mediate settlement in Greece 283, 284–8; Greeks give full powers to act 289; on needs of Ottoman modernization 294–5; approaches Mahmud II over Greece 296–7; and treaty of London 297, 306, 309, 310–11; and Foreign Office 300–1, 304–6; and Canning 301, 305, 311; advises admiral to impose armistice 309, 310–11; and battle of Navarino 314–15; breaks off relations with Ottomans 316–18; leaves Turkey 317–18; and Abdulmejid 297
Capitulations 87, 88–91, 293–4, 295; *see also* barats
Carmarthen, marquis of *see* Osborne, Francis Godolphin
Castlereagh, Viscount (Robert Stewart): and French war 110, 129; duel with Canning 129, 144; and Liston 182; and Strangford 189, 191, 192–3, 203, 213, 216–17, 221; and congress diplomacy 191, 192, 194, 206–7; and Ionians' citizenship 196; on Russo-Ottoman territorial claims 197, 198; and Greek Revolt 202, 203, 208–12, 216–17, 256–7, 257–8, 259; complying policy towards Russia 206–7, 208, 235, 256–7; and Quadruple Alliance 206–7; suicide 189, 218, 220
Cathcart, Earl (William Schaw) 211
Catherine II, tsarina: and 2nd Russo-Ottoman War 2, 4, 5, 6, 13, 16, 39, 40; and Adair's mission 41, 42, 47; and Ainslie 6, 60; order to Selim III on trade tariffs 82
Caulincourt, Armand de 112
Cerigo 163, 277
Chabert, Francis 176, 281, 300, 306, 315

Chandler, Richard 234
Chassaud, Peter 74
Chateaubriand, François-René, vicomte de 233–4
Chatham, 1st earl of (William Pitt) 3–4, 23, 129
Chenier, André 80
Chios 107, 109; massacre 218, 220, 243
Choiseul, Duke of 5, 6–7, 9, 76, 98
Church, General Sir Richard 211, 246, 307
Clarke, Edward Daniel 153
Cochrane, Admiral Sir Thomas 245, 279, 296, 299–300, 302, 308
Cockburn, Sir George 310
Cockerell, C.R. 246
Codrington, Admiral Sir Edward 309, 310–11, 312–14, 316–17
Collingwood, Admiral Cuthbert 109–10, 128
colonies, British: British extension 162, 163; foreign trade with 115, 118, 170; treaty compensation suggestion 138, 151, 172–3, 182
congress diplomacy: Alexander I and 192, 194; Canning and 269; Castlereagh and 191, 192, 194, 206–7; Ottoman dislike of 189, 198, 220; and suppression of revolution 194–5; and small states 207–8
Constantine Pavlovich, Grand Duke 278
Constantinople: Ionian population 196, 215, 225, 293; janizaries suppressed 291–4; palace revolutions 79–80, 110–11, 113–14, 128; Patriarch 223, 312 (*see also* Grigorios); printing reintroduced 80; Russian demands for restoration of Greek churches 202, 212, 213–14
Constantinople embassy, British: ambassadors *see* Adair; Ainslie; Canning, Stratford; Liston; chaplains *see* Dallaway, Walsh; staff 70–1, 280–1 (*see also* dragomans); interregnum after Liston 90; condition of building 124–5, 148, 195, 280, 304; Tarabya summer residence 280, 290; *see also* Levant Company
Corfu: Levant Company agent 75; French occupation 109, 130, 156, 157, 158–9, 173, 174; piracy 163; Walsh on 237; British occupation 130, 256; Stratford Canning at 277–8; reception of treaty of London 308
Cotton, Admiral Sir Charles 109
Cotton, Sir Dodmore 165
cotton trade 71, 72, 73–4, 125, 163, 299
Cradock, Colonel John Hobart 312
Crete 107, 109, 260
Crimea 8, 10, 11, 61, 103; *see also* Sebastopol

Croker, John Wilson 188, 269
Cumberland, duke of (Ernest Augustus) 188
Cunningham, Allan (1784–1842) 255
Cyprus 75, 163

Dainese (Stroganov's banker) 215
Dallaway, Revd (embassy chaplain) 67
Damat Mehmed 59
Dandrino (Ionian spokesman) 130
Dané, Antonio 70
Danube: Russo-Ottoman war (1806–12) 151, 168; question of frontier 196, 197–8, 199, 203
Danubian Principalities: Russian occupation 7, 16, 66; Austria's interest 2, 8, 11, 14, 15, 39, 122, 138, 173; British policy 122, 123, 124; Russo-Ottoman negotiations (1810) 137–8; Bucharest negotiations 172, 173–4; Napoleon and 137, 178; Ipsilantis' invasion 199–200; Ottoman army remains 199–200; Russian demands for Ottoman withdrawal 202, 203, 204, 205, 212, 213, 217, 220, 222, 226, 285–6; evacuated by convention of Akerman 301; Russia threatens, if Constantinople embassies harmed 312; *see also individual principalities and* Ochakov
Danzig 8, 10, 11, 13, 15, 16, 25, 40
Dardanelles: Ottoman policing 85; French blockade 91, 93; Duckworth's violation 106, 107, 109, 112, 119–20, 167; closure to warships by treaty of Dardanelles 116, 119–20, 121, 126, 127, 134
Dardanelles, treaty of: negotiations 112–13, 115–17; signed 117; terms 117–21; secret clauses 120–1, 167; subsidy promised to Ottomans 115, 116, 120, 138, 146–7, 151–2, 168
Denmark 3, 8, 14, 20, 125
Descorches (formerly marquis de Sainte Croix) 66, 76, 93, 95
Desgranges (dragoman) 309
Devonshire, 5th duke of (William Cavendish) 11
Dietz, Heinrich 9, 10–11, 12–13
diplomacy: commerce 65, 70, 71–4, 83, 126; communications 5, 86–7, 111, 113, 116–17, 122, 226; Foreign Office structure 55–8; monitoring of diplomatic bag 42–3; as profession 55–8; Vienna as centre 106
Disraeli, Benjamin (1st earl of Beaconsfield) 69, 227, 249
Douglas, F.S.N. 246
dragomans: British 6, 67, 70, 118, 119, 125, 147, 165, 176, 280–1; delegation to 76–7, 147, 165; foreign 76–7; *see also individual*

names and families
Dramali Pasha 219
Drovetti, Bernardin 156, 157
du Bayet, Albert 97
Duckworth, Admiral Sir John Thomas 106, 107, 109, 112, 119–20, 167
Dudley, 1st earl of (John William Ward) 305, 316
Dundas, Henry (1st viscount Melville): and Baldwin 88; and consul-generalship of Alexandria 86; and Foreign Office 52; and French wars 62; and Jacobinism 76; and Ochakov ultimatum 17; Pitt's friendship 52; pro-Russian policy 64, 105; and routes to India 21; and Scotland 53–4
Dundas, Robert Saunders (2nd viscount Melville) 105

East India Company 56, 157
Ebubekir Effendi 78, 79, 96
Eden, William *see* Auckland, 1st baron
Edirne 10, 294
Egypt: Mamelukes 60, 87–8, 155, 174; Ottoman recovery 60, 87; and Red Sea trade 86–8; French invasion 55, 88, 92, 105, 235; under Muhammad Ali 110, 154–7, 174, 260, 316; British invasion fails (1807) 106, 155; grain trade 154, 155, 157; France plans expedition 156, 171; and Greek Revolt 219, 277, 312–17; *see also* Muhammad Ali
Eldon, 1st earl of (John Scott) 189, 303, 305
Elgin, 7th earl of (Thomas Bruce): insight into Eastern Question 2, 25–6; in Ochakov debate 25–6; in Berlin 63; in Constantinople 2, 71, 84, 108–9; and Parthenon 236–7
Ellenborough, 1st earl of (Edward Law) 302
Ellice, Edward, the elder 245
Elliot, Sir Gilbert (1st earl of Minto) 52–3
Epidavros 219, 289
Erfurt conference 116, 122, 138
Erskine, Thomas (1st baron Erskine) 241
Eton, William 64–5, 72, 105
Ewart, Joseph: and Hertzberg's plan for alliance 8–9, 11–12, 17, 63; and Pitt's ultimatum 20, 24, 40; death 25
Eynard, Jean Gabriel 244

Fawkener, Robert: mission to Russia 36, 40, 41–2, 43; Adair's knowledge of 44, 45, 46, 47
Fazakerly, J.H. 246
Filiki Eteria 196, 200, 201, 203, 211, 212
Finlay, George 245, 250

Index 343

First Coalition 64, 93, 97
Fonton, Félix 76
Foreign Office 55–8; *see also* Planta; Adair; Ainslie; Canning, Stratford; Liston; Strangford
Foresti, George 75, 148, 158, 159
Fouché, Joseph 146
Fox, Charles James: pro-Russian policies 4, 59; and Prussian plans for alliance 11; in Ochakov debate 20, 21–2, 25; and Vorontzov 20, 40, 41; and Adair's mission to Russia 32, 33, 34, 35–6, 38–9, 41, 43, 45, 47; Burke and followers dissent with 33, 52–3, 57; Liston's friendship 52
France: and 2nd Russo-Ottoman War 2–3, 4, 5, 6–7; British rivalry 3–4, 5; Revolution 9–10, 14; Ochakov debate and 22, 23; outbreak of war with Britain 29, 46, 51, 52, 53; Anglo-Russian agreement against 59; Ottoman relations (1790s) 61, 62, 66, 70, 77, 79, 82, 95–8; Russian attitude 63, 95–6, 97–8; Prussian alliance 63, 96; navy in Mediterranean 67, 72, 73, 91–5; British Levant merchants support Revolution 75–6; commerce in Ottoman Empire 72, 86, 90, 93; invasion of Egypt 55, 88, 92, 105, 235; treaty of Tilsit *see separate entry*; Russo-British alignment against 104, 105, 106; abortive negotiations with Ottomans 112; occupies Ionian Islands 109, 130, 235; and Russia (1808–9) 107, 116, 118, 121–2, 132, 136, 138; war against Austria 118, 121–2, 123, 125, 129, 130, 132–3, 137, 138; relations with Ottomans 129, 130–1, 150–1; and Persia 134–5; provisioning of Corfu 156, 157, 158–9, 173, 174; rift with Russia (1810–11) 169–70, 170–1; annexes German coast 169, 170; plans eastern expedition (1811) 156, 170–1; and treaty of Bucharest 173, 177–8, 183; abandons eastern ambitions 104, 124; and alliances of 1812 178–9; invades Russia 178–9, 180, 183; and Greek revolt 209, 240, 264, 267, 282; and protocol of St Petersburg 302–3; and treaty of London 312; and battle of Navarino 312–17; *baratlis* 90, 118; privateers 162, 163–4
Franchini brothers (dragomans) 204–5, 309
Franklin, Benjamin 52
Fraser, General Alexander Mackenzie 106
Frederick I of Prussia (the Great) 2, 7
Frederick William II of Prussia 12, 13, 16, 20
Frere, John Hookham 124, 192, 207

Galatis, Nikolas 200
Galib Effendi: and Adair 111, 112; negotiating at Jassy 133, 135; asks Britain for aid 168; dismissed as *reis effendi* 174; and treaty of Bucharest 174, 175, 176, 180; in divan (1822) 217–18
Galicia 8, 10, 13, 15, 132, 134, 178
Galitzin, Prince Dmitri 41, 197
Galt, John 246
Gamba, Pietro 247, 249
Ganteaume, Admiral Honoré 95, 97
Gardane, General Claude Mathieu 129
Gell, Sir William 242
Gentz, Friedrich von 189, 221
George III of Great Britain 11, 51, 81, 117
George IV of Great Britain 190, 208, 217, 218, 264
Georgia 2; Russo-Persian war 134–5, 179
Gibbon, Edward 234
Giurgevo 175, 180
'Glorious First of June', battle of the 93, 313
Gobis, Dr (Sultan's physician) 6
Goltz, Baron Bernard von der 25, 46
Gordon, Thomas 241
Graecophilism 235
Grafton, 3rd duke of (Augustus Henry Fitzroy) 23
grain trade: Black Sea 85, 90, 93, 126, 154; Egypt 154, 155, 157; Levant Company and 154, 196
Grand Tour 233–4
Greece: rising of 1770 211; Britain contemplates support (1807–9) 105, 108, 146; Ipsilantis' expedition *see* Ipsilantis, Prince Alexander; rising in Morea 195, 200, 201, 209, 218, 238, 240; initial reactions in Europe 195, 200; Ionians' role 196; Ottomans hold Russians responsible 199, 200; tsar reluctant to go to war 195, 204–5, 209, 212, 213, 218, 219–20; Castlereagh and 202, 203, 208–12, 216–17, 256–7, 257–8, 259; France and 209, 240, 264, 267, 282; Russian Four Points 212–13, 216, 217, 218, 220; Ottoman campaigns in Morea (1822) 219; Canning's initial waiting policy 111, 221, 224, 225–6, 227, 245, 257, 259–62; Britain recognizes Greeks as belligerents 191, 225, 257, 259, 276; Russia demands practical deeds from Sultan 222, 223, 225, 226; civil war breaks out 260; Greek Act of Submission to Britain 261, 277, 278; Canning's move to active policy 191–2, 196, 262–4, 276–7, 278, 283, 284–8; Stratford Canning visits 277–80; progress of war (1826) 277, 279–80, 289–91,

297–300, 307–8; rumours of depopulation of Morea 282–3, 285, 297, 298, 302; Canning's policies (1826–27) 245, 265–70, 283, 284–8, 301–4; Mahmud II refuses to negotiate 282, 283; protocol of St Petersburg 265–7, 270, 286–8, 300–1; Russian ultimatum to Sultan 265, 266; treaty of London *see separate entry*; provisional government accepts intervention of powers 311; battle of Navarino 267, 268, 312–17; condition after independence 268
    atrocities in war 214, 243, 250, 279–80; internal factions 219, 249, 250, 260, 279, 289, 290; navy 253, 259, 276, 279; piracy 153, 162, 163, 225, 298–9, 300; Strangford views as internal Ottoman matter 189–90, 309; trade 153–4, 163, (Russian *baratlis*) 119, 126, 223; travel writers 233–4, 235–9; *see also* philhellenism
Greek Committees 240; *see also* London Greek Committee
Grenville, Thomas 24–5, 62
Grenville, William Wyndham (Baron Grenville): Speaker of Commons 53; and Ochakov debate 17, 18, 22–3, 25; becomes foreign secretary 25, 40, 46, 59; and Adair's mission 39, 41, 46; lack of Eastern policy 52, 57–8, 59–60, 62, 76, 92; Foreign Office under 55–8; and Low Countries 62–3; and Third Partition of Poland 63; pro-Russian policy 63–4, 105; and Liston's embassy 65–6; quashes consul-generalship in Alexandria 85–6
Grey, 2nd earl (Charles Grey) 24
Grigorios, Patriarch of Constantinople 189, 199, 201–2, 215–16
Guilford, earls of *see under* North
Guilleminot, Count Armand Charles 304, 306, 309, 310–11, 314–15, 318
Gustavus III of Sweden 10, 51
Gustavus IV of Sweden 51

Hailes, Daniel 17
Halet Effendi 222
Hamid Bey 204, 217, 222–3
Hamilton, Captain 278, 299, 306
Hamilton, Terrick 195, 220–1
Hamit Effendi 175
Hanseatic ports 169, 170
Hardenberg, Karl August von 171
Harris, Sir James 4, 17
Hasan Bey 87
Hastings, Frank Abney 249–50, 308
Hastings, Warren 53
Haugwitz, Count Christoph Augustus 63

Hawkins, Sir Christopher 261
Hayes, Anthony 74, 85
Heiden, Admiral 313, 314
Hely-Hutchinson, Christopher 242
Herbert, Baron d' 76
Hertslet, Edward 56
Hertzberg, Count Ewald von 7–13, 16, 39–40, 63
Hervey, Augustus John (Lord Hervey) 13
Heytesbury, 1st baron (William A'Court) 207
Hobhouse, John Cam: and Byron 247, 253, 254, 255; and Canning 241, 258; on Elgin Marbles 236–7; and London Greek Committee 241, 243–4, 245; *Travels in Albania* 234
Holland, 3rd baron (Henry Richard Vassall Fox) 19, 189, 265
Hood, Captain Samuel 92–5
Hoole, John 57
Hope, Admiral Sir Henry 166
hospodars 122, 199, 220, 223
Hubsch, Baron 125, 137
Hume, Joseph 241, 245
Humphrys, 'Citizen' (merchant) 75–6
Husayn Khan 134
Huskisson, William 57–8, 62, 303, 310
Hydra 163, 249, 278, 290

Ibrahim Aga (grand customer of Aleppo) 84
Ibrahim Bey 87
Ibrahim Effendi 79–80
Ibrahim Pasha 190, 260, 279, 282–3, 306, 307, 313
Impey, Sir Elijah 53
India: British expel French (1778) 86; Dundas' 'Scottishization' 54; Eastern Question and routes to 21, 86, 87, 105; Minto in 53; textiles 71; Wellesley in 109
Ionian Islands: Septinsular Republic 130, 159; French occupation 130, 235; British annexation 130, 182, 211, 256; Stratford Canning and 148, 154, 159–60; Royal Navy in 148, 152–4, 159, 161, 165–6, 224–5; and Greek Revolt 206, 224–5; Castlereagh and 256; *see also* Corfu
Ionians in Constantinople 196, 215, 225, 293
Ipsara 279–80
Ipsilantis, Prince Alexander: invades Moldavia 188, 199–200, 201, 203, 208; remnants of force 202, 215, 217; and *Filiki Eteria* 203, 212
Ipsilantis, Dimitrios 219
Ismail, Bessarabia 13, 16
Ismail Bey 217
Ismail Effendi 293

Index 345

Ismail Ferrukh 79
Italinski, Chevalier d' 169, 172, 174, 179, 180, 181
Italy 93, 195, 207
Izzet Mehmed Pasha 96

Jackson, Francis 17, 18, 19
Janina 312; *see also* Ali Pasha
janizaries 113, 114, 126, 128, 281; Mahmud II's suppression 281–2, 283, 291–4, 306
Jassy: Russian seizure 7; treaty of (1792) 20, 58–9, 61, 66, 181; Russo-Ottoman negotiations (1806–12) 126, 133, 135
Jervis, Admiral Sir John 95
Jezairli Hasan, Kaptan Pasha 60
Jones, Sir Harford 83, 84, 134, 135, 148
Jones, Sir William 57
Joseph II of Austria 2, 7, 12, 13, 39, 40
Jouannin, Joseph-Marie 134

Kamenski, Count Mikhail 151
Kapidagli, Konstantin 80
Kapodistrias, Count Ioannis: in Russian service 196, 218, 256; and Greek Revolt 210, 211; president of Greece 318; Castlereagh meets 256–7; and *Filiki Eteria* 203, 211; Galatis and 200
Karageorge 200, 201
Karaiskos, Georgios 298, 307
Katakazis, Gabriel 201
Kaunitz, Prince Anton von 2, 14
Keith, Sir Robert Murray 6, 13, 14, 68
Kelly, William 73–4
Kingsbergen, Jan Hendrick van 18, 19
Kletzl, de (Austrian dragoman) 293–4
Knight, Henry Gally 155, 241, 246
Kochubey, Count V.P. 59, 65–6, 96, 97, 133, 196
Kolettis, Ioannis 219
Kolokotronis, Theodoros 219, 249, 252
Konduriotis, Georgios 219
Koraïs, Adamantios 247
Kucuk Arif 174, 176, 179
Kucuk Huseyin 79, 95
Kutchuk-Kainardji, treaty of 214, 215, 226
Kutusov, Marshal Mikhail Larionovich 66, 70, 175, 179–80, 197

Laibach, congress of 208
Lambton, John George (1st earl of Durham) 241
Lansdowne, 1st marquis of *see* Petty, William
Latour-Maubourg, Florimond de 116; severs relations with Austria 125; and closing of Dardanelles 126; and Ionian Islands 130–1; rivalry with Adair 130–1, 132, 134, 136, 137–8; and Lady Hester Stanhope 149; rivalry with Stratford Canning 150, 162, 164, 165, 168, 174, 176; threatens invasion of Egypt 156; moves into Spanish embassy 173, 174; and Bucharest negotiations 177–8, 179; and Strangford 222
Lauriston, General 170
Laz Ahmet Pasha 174, 175, 180
Leake, William Martin 148, 157, 158, 234, 246
Leeds, duke of *see* Osborne, Francis Godolphin
Leopold II of Austria 13–14, 15, 16, 20
Lesseps, Comte Mathieu de 154–5
Levant Company: Adair and 125–6; and Black Sea trade 4–5, 26–7, 86, 118, 182; and Constantinople embassy 6, 56, 65, 83, 192, 280, (pays salaries) 5, 52, 67, 70, 91; decline 59, 65, 71–3, 74–5, (and revival) 75, 125, 162–3; grain speculation 154, 196; and Greek Revolt 191, 214–15, 225 242, 259; lack of patriotism 75–6, 111; Liston disciplines merchants 82–91; merchants expelled from Ottoman Empire 111, (return) 118; Stratford Canning and 161–7; and supply of Royal Navy 152, 153; abolition 196, 280
Lieven, Prince Christoph 264, 287, 297, 301, 303
Lieven, Princess (Dorothea von Benkendorff) 264, 287, 302
Lindsay, William 41, 42, 43, 46
Liston, Robert 51–102
  first embassy to Constantinople (1794–96) 53; and British community 74–6; and Foreign Office 59, 65–6; journey 67–8, 68–9, 79; and Levant Company merchants 71–4, 82–91; Ottoman contacts 78–9, 84; and Ottoman recognition of French Republic 66, 77, 95–8; and Royal Navy 91–5; salary 67, 88, 90, 91; and sale of protections 75, 88–91; and staff 67–8, 70–1
  Washington embassy 68, 90; second embassy to Constantinople (1812–21) 53, 68, 98, 150, 180, 182, 192
Liverpool, 2nd earl of (Robert Banks Jenkinson) 211, 262, 269, 304
London, treaty of (1827) 267, 303–4, 306; Britain fails to maintain obligations 302; Greek reaction 308; Ottoman reaction 309–10; Stratford Canning and 297; terms 308–9

London Greek Committee 224, 240–5, 246, 247–8, 252, 279
Loughborough, 1st baron (Alexander Wedderburn) 23
Louis, Sir John 120
Louriotis, Ioannis 245, 259
Ludolf, Count 172
Lutzov, Count 198, 203, 213, 215, 216, 217, 222

Mackintosh, Sir James 241
Mahmud II, Sultan: accession 114; and Adair 168; and Stratford Canning 169, 177, 281; and treaty of Bucharest 178, 181; and congress diplomacy 189; attitude to Britain 195–6; and Strangford 196; and Stratford Canning 281, 296–7; suppresses janizaries 281–2, 283, 291–4, 306; modernization 291, 294–5, 295–6, 306–7, 308; refuses to negotiate over Greece 282, 283, 296–7, 309; and treaty of London 306, 311
Mair (British commercial agent) 151
Maitland, Sir Thomas 211, 225, 256, 260
Malmesbury, 1st earl of (James Harris) 62, 106
Malta 110–11; British naval presence 157, 174; governor and privateers 299
Maltass, Stephen 155
Mamelukes 60, 87–8, 155, 174
Manesty, Samuel 83–4
Marie Antoinette, Queen of France 66, 96
Mavrokordatos (Mavrocordates), Alexandros 219, 250, 251, 252–3, 278, 307, 308
Mavromichalis, Petros 219, 249, 260
Medem, Count 77
Melbourne, Viscountess (Elizabeth Lamb) 33
Melek Mehmed Pasha 79, 96
Metternich, Prince: Napoleon's anger at approach to Russia 121–2; after Wagram 132; on France and Poland 136; Stratford Canning's distrust 171; alliance with France 178–9; on power politics 193; and Ipsilantis' invasion of Moldavia 199; last meeting with Castlereagh 208–9; and Strangford 189, 213, 216, 221; and Greek Revolt 195, 216, 218, 259, 262; at congress of Verona 222; estrangement from Alexander I 263; and Canning 264, 269; on East 55
Meyer (consul at Prevesa) 298
Miaulis, Andreas 278–9, 289
Miconi affair 94
Miles, William Augustus 33, 34, 46
Mill, James 57

Miltitz, Count 215, 217, 225
Minciaki (Russian diplomat) 282, 291
Missett, Ernest 154–5
Missolonghi: Byron at 250, 251–4; Ottoman siege 277, 279; capture 289, 290, 298
Moldavia 2, 93, 107; see also Ochakov and under Ipsilantis
Möllendorf, General Wichard von 19–20
Molo, Giuseppe 171–2
Montesquieu, baron de (Charles Louis de Secondat) 22
Moore, Thomas 248
Morea: Veli Pasha 156; revolt 195, 200, 201, 209, 218, 238, 240; Ibrahim Pasha in 190, 260, 279, 282, 307
Morier, David 111; and Adair 111–12, 123–4, 132; and Stratford Canning 145, 147, 153; on Mahmud II 169; Liston promotes 182; at congress of Vienna 111
Morier, Isaac 111, 149
Morritt, John 238
Mouradja d'Ohsson, Ignace de 76–7, 80, 96
Muhammad Ali 110, 154–7, 174, 260, 316
Mulgrave, 2nd baron (John Constantine Phipps) 25–6
Murad Bey 87
Murray, Lord Charles 237
Murray Keith, Sir Robert 6, 13, 14, 68
Murusi, Prince Constantin 130
Murusi family, Demetrius, George and Panagios 96–7, 134, 168, 180, 215
Muscovy Company 4–5, 21–2, 25, 40
Mustafa IV, Sultan 108, 114
Mustafa (Bayrakdar at Porte) 158
Mustafa Alemdar 114

Nafplion see Napoli di Romania
Napier, Sir Charles 286
Napier, Sir Charles James 188, 251–2, 253, 286
Napoleon I of France: and Ottoman Empire 2; anger at Metternich's approach to Russia 121–2; and Alexander I 132, 170–1; and Persia 134–5; and Danubian Principalities 138; plans eastern expedition (1812) 156; gives up eastern ambitions 104, 124; military successes 135, 234–5; *for details of military campaigns, see under* France
Napoleonic Wars 29; see also under France
Napoli di Romania (Nafplion) 163, 166, 250, 290, 298, 299
Nasif Effendi 6–7, 10
Navarino 163–4; battle of 267, 268, 312–17
Neale, Sir Harry 299
Nejib Pasha 296

Index 347

Nesselrode, Count Carl: and France 178; Ottoman approaches to 203, 204; on extradition of Ipsilantis' army 215, 217; and Strangford 221, 223; at congress of Verona 222; and protocol of St Petersburg 287
Netherlands: 2nd Russo-Ottoman War and 2, 3, 14, 19; and Triple Alliance 4, 7; Constantinople embassy 77; Walcheren expedition 128–9
Nicholas I, tsar 265, 284, 303
Nile, battle of the 86
Nizam-i-Cedid 79, 80–1
North, Frederick (2nd earl of Guilford, Lord North) 4
North, Frederick (5th earl of Guilford) 246, 255

Obrenovic, Milosh 198, 200
Ochakov: Russia captures 7; insists on retaining 16, 40; strategic unimportance 17, 18, 19, 25, 42
Ochakov debate 1–31; Prussian connection 1–2, 3, 21, 24–5, 26, 28, 40–1; Cabinet dissidents 18–19, 21, 23, 24, 40; parliamentary debate 20–6, 40; withdrawal of ultimatum 20, 36, 40, 41–2, 43; and trade 22, 26–7, 28; Pitt's personal assessment 27–9; Ottoman reaction 58–9
Odessa 18, 42, 134, 154, 201, 202
Oldenburg, duchy of 169, 170
Olifer (embassy *cancellier*) 70
Orlandos, Ioannis 245, 259
Osborne, Francis Godolphin (marquis of Carmarthen, 5th duke of Leeds): on outbreak of Russo-Ottoman war 5; and Prussian plan for alliance against Russia 8–9, 17; and Russian approach of early 1790 13; and Reichenbach conference 15; opposes Pitt's ultimatum policy 17, 18, 19, 40; and Ochakov debate 20, 23, 25; resigns 24, 40, 59
Ostermann, Count Ivan 15, 16
Ottenfels, Baron 222, 225
Ottoman Empire: loss of Crimea to Russia 61, 103; treaty with Russia (1774) 214, 215, 226; defeat of Mamelukes 60, 87; war with Russia and Austria (1788–92) *see* Russo-Ottoman War, Second; Prussia offers alliance 10–11, 11–12; treaty with Poland 12–13; reaction to Ochakov debate 58–9; Selim III's foreign policy 10, 61–2, 77–8, 82, 86, 95; internal government under Selim III 80–2; relations with France (1790s) 61, 62, 66, 70, 77, 79, 82, 95–8;

and British naval protection 67; relations with Russia (1790s) 66, 70, 82, 95–6, 97–8; treaty with Britain (1799) 105; Selim III deposed 79–80, 110–11, 114, 128; Mustafa IV deposed 114, 128; accession of Mahmud II 114; counter-coup of janizaries 113, 114, 128; war with Russia (1806–12) 126–7, 150, 151, 168, 177; hostilities with Britain (1807) 105–6; abortive negotiations with France 112; Adair's embassy *see under* Adair; treaty of Dardanelles with Britain *see separate entry*; relations with France 129, 130–1, 150–1; treaty of Bucharest *see under* Bucharest; attitude to Stratford Canning and Britain 167–8, 180–1, 195–6, 197; changes in government (1811) 174; quarrels with Russian ambassador 196–9, 200; severance of relations with Russia 202–5; repels Ipsilantis' invasion of Moldavia 199–200; reaction to Greek Revolt 199, 200, 238; campaigns in Greece *see under* Greece; and Russian Four Points 212–13, 216, 217, 218, 220; Russia demands freedom of Black Sea trade 222, 223; and practical deeds to pacify Greece 222, 223, 225, 226; re-establishment of relations with Russia 225, 226, 260, 262, 276; Russian ultimatum over Principalities and Serbia 265, 266–7, 285–6; Britain attempts to mediate over Greece 276–7, 283, 284–8; suppression of janizaries 281–2, 283, 291–4, 306; subsequent treatment of Europeans 293–4, 295, 296; convention of Akerman 267, 294, 297, 301; and treaty of London 309–10; battle of Navarino 312–17; Britain severs relations 316–18; Russian attack (1829) 235, 302
administration 81–2, 128, 282; European view as barbaric 22, 64–5, 238–9; military reforms, (Abdulhamid I) 60–1, 62, (Selim III) 78, 79, 80–1, 97, 114, (Mahmud II) 291, 294, 295–6, 306–7, 308; navy, (renovation) 60, 79, 80, (request for British ships) 129, 133, (and Greek Revolt) 279, 298–300, 312–17; 'Ottoman integrity' 103, 177, 179, 210–12, 276; *see also individual rulers, countries and topics*

Paget, Sir Arthur 104–5, 111, 115
Paget, Captain (of *Romney*) 94
Palmerston, 3rd viscount (Henry John Temple) 119
Parliament, British: Ochakov debate 20–6, 40; and Levant Company 72; Navigation Laws 115, 118; philhellenism 217;

Foreign Enlistment Act (1824) 261, 300
Parr, Dr 36
Parry, William 254
Pasvanoglu (pasha of Widin) 69, 93
Patriarch of Constantinople 223, 312; see also Grigorios
Peacock, Thomas Love 57
Peel, Sir Robert 227, 303, 305
Peninsular War 62, 109, 122, 128, 146, 154
Perceval, Spencer 129, 133, 146
Persia 129, 134–5, 177, 179, 195
Peta, battle of 240
Petrobey (Petros Mavromichalis) 219, 249, 260
Petty, William (1st marquis of Lansdowne, 2nd earl of Shelburne) 4, 23, 53
Peysonnel, Charles de 27
philhellenism: and barbarism of both sides in Greece 214, 243; Byron 212, 238, 245–55; Canning and 258–9; cultural 233–40, 258; and Graecophilism 235; and Ionian Islands 211; Levant Company 191; in Parliament 217; volunteers in Greek forces 223–4, 240, 243, 262, 276, 309; see also London Greek Committee
Phillips, Thomas 255
Photis, Archimandrite 202
piracy: Greek 153, 162, 163, 225, 298–9, 300; Stratford Canning and 149, 161–7, 169, 174, 176
Pisani, Bartholomew: and Liston 68–9, 70, 77, 79; and Adair's mission 112, 116, 117, 125; and Stratford Canning 165, 173, 174; on grain trade 93, 154
Pisani, Frederick 281, 282–3, 309, 312
Pitt, William: and Triple Alliance 7; reaction to outbreak of 2nd Russo-Ottoman War 3–6, 7, 39; rejects Hertzberg's plan for alliance 11–12, 39–40; mediator at Reichenbach 14–15; ultimatum to Russia 17–19, 21, (withdrawn) 36, 40, 41–2, 43; and Ochakov debate 1–2, 20–6, 58, (personal assessment) 27–9, (and Prussian interests) 1–2, 3, 21, 24–5, 26, 28, 40–1; has Adair's letters from St Petersburg 39, 43, 46; friendship with Dundas 52; and French wars 62; drinking 62; on risk of Russian or Austrian ascendancy 64
Planta, Joseph 144, 205–6, 208, 212, 213, 301, 304–5
Poland: reaction to outbreak of 2nd Russo-Ottoman War 3; Prussian plans 7–8, 10, 15, 16–17, 40; Ottoman treaty (1790) 12–13; and Reichenbach conference 15; Black Sea trade 18, 21; second partition 105; third partition 46, 63, 103; Russian-

French discussions 122, 136, 170; Napoleon's plans for, 1812 178; Elgin on Britain as protector 26; Ottoman expectation of same fate 103, 198; see also Danzig; Thorn
Porter, George Richard 162
Porter, Sir James 64, 80, 81–2
Portland, 3rd duke of (William Henry Cavendish Bentinck) 11, 52, 53
Potemkin, Prince Grigorii 2, 4, 42
Poti 176, 177, 181, 196, 198, 199
Pozzo di Borgo, Count 174, 207–8
Privy Council for Trade 26–7, 28, 86
Prosorowski, General A.A. 133
protections in Ottoman Empire, see barats
Prussia: and Triple Alliance 4; initiative in north while Austria at war with Ottomans 2; plans anti-Russian alliance 7–13, 16, 39–40, 63; ambitions in Poland 7–8, 10, 15, 16–17, 40; and Pitt's Ochakov ultimatum to Russia 1–2, 3, 21, 24–5, 26, 28, 40–1; approaches to Russia during Adair's mission 46; alliance with France 63, 96; abandons First Coalition 97; and alliances of 1812 178; and protocol of St Petersburg 291; and treaty of London 303, 310; Constantinople embassy 97, 146, 168

Quadruple Alliance 206–7

Ransome, Moreland and Hammersley (bankers) 43, 44–5, 47
Rashid Effendi 79, 94, 96
Red Sea 86–8, 157
Redern, Count Sigismund 18–19, 20
reforms, Ottoman military: Abdulhamid I 60–1, 62; Selim III 78, 79, 80–1, 97, 114; Mahmud II 291, 294, 295–6, 306–7, 308
Reichenbach, conference of 14–15, 16, 28, 38
Repnin, Prince Nikolai Vassilievich 13
Reshid Pasha, Celebi Mustafa 79
Ribeaupierre (Russian minister) 304, 306, 309, 312, 314–15, 318
Ricardo, Messrs (bankers) 244, 245
Richelieu, duke of (governor of Odessa) 134
Richmond, 3rd duke of (Charles Lennox) 17, 18, 20–1, 23
Rigny, Admiral Henri Gauthier de 309, 312, 313, 314
Royal Navy: Ochakov debate over deployment 1, 19–26, 40; Ottomans value as protector 67; ineffectual in Mediterranean (1790s) 73, 76; model for modernized Ottoman fleet 79; challenges French in Mediterranean 91–5; blockade

Index

of Turkey 113, 120; suggested cooperation with Ottomans 126, 127, 129, 132, 133, 134; Stratford Canning and 148, 152–4, 161; blockade in Adriatic and Mediterranean 148, 159, 165–6; Ottoman request for diversion in Baltic 168–9; in Malta 157, 174; and Greek Revolt 224–5, 289, 299, 312–17

Rumiantsev, Count Peter 2, 172

Russell, Lord John 241

Russia: conquest of Crimea 61, 103; treaty with Ottomans (1774) 214, 215, 226; and Britain (1780s) 3–4, 22; war with Ottomans (1788–92) see Russo-Ottoman War, Second; and French Revolution 63; diplomacy, 1789–90 11, 13, 15, 20; refuses negotiation unless guaranteed Bessarabia and Ochakov 16, 40; British ultimatum 17–19, 21, 36, 40, 41–2, 43, 58–9; Adair's mission 32–50; Prussian approach 46; defensive alliance with Britain (1795) 59, 97; and Third Partition of Poland 63; Britain proposes alliance 63–4; Ottoman relations (1790s) 66, 70, 82, 90, 91, 93, 95–6, 97–8; rivalry with France 95–6, 97–8; treaty of Tilsit, Erfurt conference *see separate entries*; Britain aligned with 104, 105, 106, (exploits Franco-Russian rift) 107, 118, 121–2; contacts with Austria 121–2; war against Ottomans (1806–12) 126–7, 150, 151, 168, 177; British attempts to mediate 121–4, 133–8; relations with French after Wagram 132, 136, 138; war against Persia in Georgia 134–5, 179; negotiations with Ottomans *see* Bucharest, treaty of; rift with France 169–70, 170–1; and Serbian rising 173; and alliances of 1812 178–9; French invasion 178–9, 180, 183; duel with Britain after 1815 193–4; diplomatic activity in Italy (1816) 207; and modification of treaty of Bucharest 196, 197–8, 199, 203; and Ipsilantis' invasion of Moldavia 199, 208; Ottomans suspect involvement in Greek Revolt 200; severance of relations with Ottomans 202–5; tsar's reluctance to intervene in Greece 195, 204–5, 209, 212, 213, 218, 219–20; British policy of compliance with 206–7, 208, 235, 256–7; Four Points to Ottomans 212–13, 216, 217, 218, 220; demands Ottoman abandonment of restrictions on Black Sea trade 222, 223; demands practical deeds from Sultan to pacify Greece 222, 223, 225, 226; and Strangford 215, 222, 223, 225, 226; return of minister to Constantinople 225, 226, 260, 262, 276; Stratford Canning's mission 261, 262, 263, 265–6; rift with Austria 263, 267; Wellington's special embassy 283, 284–8; protocol of St Petersburg 265–7, 270, 286–8, 300–1; ultimatum to Sultan over Principalities and Serbia 265, 266–7, 285–6; convention of Akerman 267, 294, 297, 301; treaty of London *see separate entry*; and battle of Navarino 312–17; attack on Ottomans (1829) 235, 302; *barats* 66, 90, 119, 126; Black Sea trade 61, 90, 126, 222, 223; *see also individual tsars and diplomats*

Russo-Ottoman War, Second (1788–92): outbreak 2, 39; reactions to outbreak 2–7, 39–40; campaigns (1788) 7, 40, (1789) 13, 16; Reichenbach conference 14–15, 16, 28, 38; congress of Sistovo 15–16, 61; Russia refuses mediation (late 1790) 16, 40; treaty of Jassy 20, 58–9, 61, 66, 181; *see also* Ochakov debate *and under* Bessarabia; Wallachia

Russo-Ottoman War (1806–12) 126–7, 150, 151, 168, 177

Said Ahmet 116–17, 158
Said Ali Effendi 79
St Julien, count of 134
Saint Marcel (French diplomat) 157
St Petersburg: British ambassadors *see* Bagot; Strangford; protocol of 265–7, 270, 286–8, 300–1
Salisbury, 3rd marquis of (R.A.T.G. Cecil) 104
Salonika 74, 154, 163, 294
Scharnhorst, Gerhard Johannes David von 178
Schönbrunn, peace of 132–3
Scotland 52, 53–4, 69
Scott, Walter 54
Sébastiani, General Horace 108, 119, 122
Sebastopol 2, 118, 126
Selim III, Sultan: accession, pursues war 10; deposed and murdered 79–80, 114; foreign relations under 10, 61–2, 77–8, 82, 86, 95; government under 80–2; and Levant Company 86; military reform 79, 80–1, 114; personality 80; sells privileges 91
Septinsular Republic 159, 211
Serbia: Austria and 2, 15, 66, 173, 178; Pitt's plans for 15; Russian patronage 138, 173, 177, 196, 197, 199, 226; and treaty of Bucharest 177, 181; Obrenovic elected hereditary prince 198; Russian ultimatum to Ottomans (1826) 266, 285–6

Serra Capriola, duke of 172, 176, 177
Shelburne, 2nd earl of *see* Petty, William
Shelley, Percy Bysshe 104, 257
Sheridan, Richard Brindsley 24, 33
Sibthorp, Dr (embassy physician) 67–8
Sicily 146, 156, 171, 172
Sistovo, congress of 15–16, 61
Smith, John Spencer 71, 76, 92, 95
Smith, Sir Sidney 67, 77, 79, 80, 91–2, 107
Smyrna: attack on European quarter (1797) 74; army recruits riot (1810) 169; janizaries suppressed (1826) 294; consuls 318 (*see also* Hayes; Werry); British merchants 118, 300; grain smuggling 154
Smythe, Percy Clinton *see* Strangford, 6th viscount
Société Philanthropique, Paris 264
Spain: embassy in Constantinople 70, 77, 173, 174; Ottomans recognize junta 129–30; Greek Committee 240; South American revolutions 264; *see also* Peninsular War
Spezia 163, 290
Stadion, Count 106, 122, 132, 133–4
Stafford, marquis of (Granville Leveson-Gower) 18, 23
Stanhope, Lady Hester 149–50
Stanhope, Leicester (5th earl of Harrington) 241, 250, 253, 256, 261
Stanley, Viscount 24
Stapleton, Augustus Granville 258
Stewart, Captain (of *Sea Horse*) 111
Stormont, Viscount 23, 25
Strachey, Edward 57
Strane, Nicholas 74, 75
Strangford, 6th Viscount (Percy Clinton Smythe) 188–232; and Levant Company 191, 214–15; instructions for Constantinople embassy 192–3; advises Ottomans to observe letter of existing treaties 197, 203, 208, 213, 214, 215; acts in Mahmud II's quarrel with Stroganov 193, 196, 202–3, 204, 205–6, 213–14, 215; and Four Points 213, 216–17; and Ionians in Constantinople 215, 225; and execution of Patriarch 189, 215–16; and Metternich 216, 221; meets Ghalib Effendi 217–18; at congress of Verona 220–2; acts for tsar in Constantinople 222, 223, 225, 226; made Baron Penshurst 189–90; embassy to St Petersburg 190, 226, 261, 265, 281, 283–4;
 and Castlereagh 189, 191, 192–3, 203, 213, 216–17, 221; and Canning 189–90, 223, 225, 226–7, 260, 261, 283–4;

character and views 188–91, 309; family 191, 195; Foreign Office and 191, 203, 205–6, 208, 213–16, 218–19, 221; Russian and Ottoman esteem 215, 226; Chabert's correspondence 281, 306; sees Greek Revolt as internal Ottoman matter 189–90, 309
Stratford de Redcliffe, 1st viscount *see* Canning, Stratford
Straton, Alexander 67
Stroganov, Count Grigory 193, 196–9, 200, 202–5, 213–14, 215
Stuart, Sir Charles 110
Sturmer, Count Barthelemy 125, 132, 171
Suez route 86, 87
Suleyman Pasha (Ali Pasha's agent) 158, 159, 161
Suleyman Pasha (of Baghdad) 83–4
Suvorov, Count Alexander 16, 95–6, 197
Sweden: and 2nd Russo-Ottoman War 3, 8, 10, 14, 15, 19; Gustavus III assassinated 51; Constantinople embassy 76–7, 96, 97, 146; and alliances of 1812 178
Syria 105, 156

taxation, Ottoman 77–8, 82, 83, 89, 296, 307
Theotokis, Ioannis 250, 251, 252
Thorn 8, 10, 11, 13, 16, 25, 40
Thornton (treasurer to Constantinople scale) 75
Thurlow, Edward (1st baron Thurlow) 18, 21, 23
Tilsit, treaty of 3, 29, 105, 107, 112, 235; and Principalities 122, 138
Tomasso (dragoman) 70
Tomline, George 35–7, 38
Tott, Baron François de 60, 80, 98
trade: with British colonies 115, 118, 170; British–Russian 4; and Ochakov debate 22, 26–7, 28; diplomacy and 65, 70, 71–4, 83, 126; Ottoman taxes 83; Red Sea 86–8, 157; *see also* cotton; grain; *and under* Black Sea; Greece; Levant Company
Transcaucasian frontier 176, 177, 181, 196, 198, 199, 301
Trelawny, Edward John 250, 251, 261
Trikoupis, Spiridion 250, 254, 255
Triple Alliance (1788) 4, 7, 39
Troppau, congress of 194–5
Troubridge, Admiral Sir Thomas 95
Turkey Merchants *see* Levant Company
Turner, William 74, 85, 281

Urquhart, David 235
United States of America 264, 277

Index

Vahid Effendi 112–13, 115–17, 126, 135
Veli Pasha 156
Verela, peace of 15
Vergennes, Charles Gravier, count of 3, 4
Verninac, Raymond 96, 97
Verona, congress of 217, 220–2, 225, 257
Vienna: Adair plans to negotiate European coalition in 106, 118, 123–4, 131, 132; congress of 112, 211; peace of Schönbrunn 132–3
Villèle, Count Jean Baptiste de 267
Vladimirescu, Teodoro 200
Volney, Count Constantin François de 60, 65, 98
Vondiziano (Levant Company agent) 75
Vorontzov, Count Simon 4, 11, 13, 15, 63; Whig connections 11, 20, 38, 40, 41

Wagram, battle of 129, 130, 131, 132
Wahabis 112, 155
Walcheren expedition 128–9
Wallachia 93, 107; in 2nd Russo-Ottoman War 2, 8, 11, 14, 15, 39
Walsh, Dr Robert 237–8, 239
Webster, Sir Charles 194
Wellesley, Arthur (1st duke of Wellington): in Peninsula 62, 128, 129; on treaty of Bucharest 182–3; at congress of Verona 220, 221, 225, 257; special embassy to Russia 284–8; and protocol of St Petersburg 265, 286–7; on Cochrane 302; resigns from ministry 303, 305
Wellesley, Henry 51–2, 288
Wellesley, Richard 145
Wellesley, Richard Colley (Marquis Wellesley): as foreign secretary 129, 133; and Adair 137; and Stratford Canning 144, 145–7, 151–2, 156, 168, 169, 172–3; and treaty of Bucharest 182–3; fails to form government (1812) 146; in India 109
Werry, Francis 110–11, 154
Werry, Samuel 218, 300, 315
Werther, Count (Prussian diplomat) 168
Whig Party: and Prussian plans for anti-Russian alliance 11; and Ochakov debate 21–2; Burke's secession 33, 52–3, 57; Adair's connections 32, 106, 107; Liston's connections 52; Russian connections 4, 11, 20, 38, 40, 41, 59; *see also* Fox, Charles James
Whitworth, Sir Charles 6, 16, 17; Adair and mission of 1791 25, 34, 41, 43, 46
Wilberforce, William 21
Wilkins, Charles 57
Windham, William 62
Wood, George 307
Wraxall, Nathaniel 41

Yeames, James 205
Yusuf Aga (of royal mint) 79
Yusuf Aga Effendi (ambassador) 57, 59–60, 61, 67
Yusuf Pasha (grand vizier): and 2nd Russo-Ottoman war 7, 9; and Ainslie 58, 59; disgraced 59; and Suez route 87
Yusuf Ziya Pasha (grand vizier): away at front (1808) 112, 135, 173; dismissed 174

Znaim, armistice of 132
Zographos, Konstantine 278

For Product Safety Concerns and Information please contact our EU representative GPSR@taylorandfrancis.com
Taylor & Francis Verlag GmbH, Kaufingerstraße 24, 80331 München, Germany

www.ingramcontent.com/pod-product-compliance
Lightning Source LLC
Chambersburg PA
CBHW052141300426
44115CB00011B/1469